Programming in
ADA

INTERNATIONAL COMPUTER SCIENCE SERIES

Consulting editors   **A D McGettrick**
University of Strathclyde

J van Leeuwen
University of Utrecht

Cover: A portrait of Ada, Countess of Lovelace, acknowledged to be the
world's first programmer. Adapted and reproduced by permission of John
Murray.

Programming in
ADA

second edition

J.G.P. Barnes (Alsys Ltd.)

ADDISON-WESLEY PUBLISHING COMPANY

London · Reading, Massachusetts · Menlo Park, California · Amsterdam
Don Mills, Ontario · Manila · Singapore · Sydney · Tokyo

Composition in Times and Univers on Linotron by
Book Economy Services, Burgess Hill, Sussex
Printed in the United States of America

British Library Cataloguing in Publication Data
Barnes, J.G.P.
  Programming in Ada 2nd ed. (International
  computer science series)
  1. Ada (Computer program language)
  I. Title   II. Series
  001.64'24   QA76.73.A35

  ISBN 0-201-13799-2

Library of Congress Cataloguing in Publication Data
Barnes, J.G.P. (John Gilbert Presslie)
  Programming in Ada.
  (International computer science series)
  Includes index
  1. Ada (Computer program language)
  I. Title.
II. Series.
QA76.73.A35B37 1984   001.64'24   83-3803

  ISBN 0-201-13799-2 (pbk.)

FGHIJK-DO-8987

To BARBARA

FOREWORD

In May 1979 came the eagerly awaited announcement by the United States High Order Language Working Group, that 'Green is Ada'.

We were all expecting it in our team and were thus not surprised, but the announcement was certainly an enormous pleasure for all of us. At that time we all considered the preliminary version of Ada to be perfect. It may sound strange, considering the amount of revision that was done in the next fifteen months leading to the July 1980 Ada definition. But there is an easy explanation. In order to design anything you must believe in what you design, you must be continually examining the interweaving of all the features. Certainly, many decisions are the result of compromises between conflicting goals, but after rehearsing time and time again the arguments leading to these compromises you end up by integrating them into the basic assumptions of your design. And so it is not surprising that the result should appear to be the perfect answer.

Clearly, further progress can only come by a reappraisal of implicit assumptions underlying certain compromises. Here is the major contradiction in any design work. On the one hand, one can only reach an harmonious integration of several features by immersing oneself into the logic of the existing parts; it is only in this way that one can achieve a perfect combination. On the other hand, this perception of perfection, and the implied acceptance of certain unconscious assumptions, will prevent further progress.

In the design of Ada, John Barnes has certainly shown a unique ability to switch appropriately between acceptance and reappraisal. In May 1979, John was as proud as anyone else in the design team about our achievement. But, even by the early days of June, John was already reflective, giving a sharp, even severe look to the Ada tasking model as if he had had nothing to do with its design. He authored the first Language study note, of a series of two hundred, called 'Problems with tasking'. The note outlined ten major problems perceived in the preliminary Ada tasking facilities. These problems occupied our team for several months in the Ada revision, and satisfactory solutions could then be given to these ten issues in the final Ada version. In my own case it undoubtedly took me much more time to become objective about preliminary Ada and I certainly was initially upset by John's sacrilege. But with time I have learned to value enormously this kind of interaction with John.

Programming in Ada is thus written by one of the key members of the Ada language design team, by someone who understands all facets of the design of the language, both in a constructive and in a critical manner. I am confident that — with humour as usual — John's enthusiasms and understanding of the spirit of the language will be passed on to readers of this book.

Versailles
May 1981

Jean D. Ichbiah

PREFACE

The second edition of this book has been prompted by the publication of the ANSI standard for Ada in January 1983.

Numerous changes occurred to Ada as a consequence of the ANSI standardisation process and I have thoroughly revised the text to conform to both the detail and the spirit of the new standard. The general purpose of the book remains unchanged but a little extra detail and a few more examples have been added in some areas.

I have also taken the opportunity to correct the various errors which crept into the first edition. I was greatly helped in this by numerous comments received from many readers and I would particularly like to thank Randall Barron, Theodore Chaplin, Donald Clarson, Edward Colbert, Ian Mearns, Angel Alvarez, Mike Tedd and Jo Whitfield for their comprehensive and constructive criticisms.

Reading
October 1983

J.G.P. Barnes

PREFACE TO THE FIRST EDITION

This book is about Ada, the new and powerful programming language originally developed on behalf of the US Department of Defense for use in embedded systems. Typical of such systems are those of process control, missile guidance or even the sequencing of a dishwasher. Historically these systems have been programmed in languages such as JOVIAL, CORAL 66 and RTL/2.

Based on Pascal, Ada is the first practical language to bring together important features such as data abstraction, multitasking, exception handling, encapsulation and generics. Although originally intended for embedded systems, it is a general purpose language and could, in time, supersede FORTRAN and even COBOL. The political and technical forces behind Ada suggest it will become an important language in the 1980's.

My purpose in writing this book is to present an overall description of Ada. Some knowledge of the principles of programming is assumed and an acquaintance with Pascal would be helpful but is not strictly necessary. The book is written in a tutorial style with numerous examples and exercises. I have also tried to explain the rationale behind many of the features of the language because this not only makes the discussion of more interest but also makes the facts easier to remember. Wherever possible I have tried to use examples which do not assume a particular application background; they are mostly drawn from parallels with normal human life or from mathematics which, after all, is the cornerstone of science and engineering. I hope the reader does not find the occasional attempt at humour misplaced; learning a programming language can be dull and any means of easing the burden seems worthwhile.

I would like to take this opportunity to thank those who directly or indirectly have helped me to write this book. First, I must acknowledge the US Department of Defense for permission to use material from the Ada Language Reference Manual. Then, I must acknowledge Jean Ichbiah and Robert Firth with whom I have had the pleasure of giving Ada courses in various parts of the world. These courses not only helped me to gain a useful perspective of the language as a whole but also provided the origins of some of the examples. Next, I must thank Andrew McGettrick for a great number of useful comments on the original draft and for spurring me on to completion with many helpful suggestions. I must also thank my colleagues on the UK Ada Study for their valued comments. Finally, I am deeply grateful to my wife for her untiring efforts in typing the manuscript; without her assistance the labour would have been much prolonged.

Reading
April 1981

J.G.P. Barnes

CONTENTS

Chapter 1 INTRODUCTION

Ada is a high level programming language originally sponsored by the US Department of Defense for use in the so-called embedded system application area. (An embedded system is one in which the computer is an integral part of a larger system such as a chemical plant, missile or dishwasher.) In this introductory chapter we briefly trace the development of Ada, its place in the overall language scene and the general structure of the remainder of this book.

1.1 History

The story of Ada goes back to about 1974 when the United States Department of Defense realised that it was spending far too much on software. It carried out a detailed analysis of how its costs were distributed over the various application areas and discovered that over half of them were directly attributed to embedded systems.

Further analysis was directed towards the programming languages in use in the various areas. It was discovered that COBOL was the universal standard for data processing and FORTRAN was a similar standard for scientific and engineering computation. Although these languages were not modern, the fact that they were uniformly applied in their respective areas meant that unnecessary and expensive duplication was avoided.

The situation with regard to embedded systems was however quite different. The number of languages in use was enormous. Not only did each of the three Armed Services have their own favourite high level languages, but they also used many assembly languages as well. Moreover, the high level languages had spawned variants. It seemed that successive contracts had encouraged the development of special versions aimed at different applications. The net result was that a lot of money was being spent on an unnecessary number of compilers. There were also all the additional costs of training and maintenance associated with a lack of standardisation.

It was therefore realised that standardisation had to be established in the embedded system area if the costs were to be contained. The ultimate goal was, of course, a single language. In the short term a list of interim approved languages was introduced. This consisted of CMS-2Y, CMS-2M, SPL/1, TACPOL, JOVIAL J3, JOVIAL J73 and of course COBOL and FORTRAN for the other areas.

The first step in moving towards the development of a single standard was the writing of a document outlining the requirements. The first version was known as Strawman and was published in early 1975. After receiving comments from various sources it was refined and became Woodenman. A further iteration produced Tinman in June 1976. This was quite a specific document and identified

1

the functionality required of the language.

At this stage many existing languages were evaluated against Tinman partly to see whether one of them could be used as the ultimate standard and partly to invoke detailed evaluation of the requirements themselves. As one might expect, none of the existing languages proved satisfactory; on the other hand the general impression was gained that a single language based on state-of-the-art concepts could be developed to meet the requirements.

The evaluation classified the existing languages into three categories which can be paraphrased as

'not appropriate'   These languages were obsolete or addressed the wrong area and were not to be considered further. This category included FORTRAN and CORAL 66.

'not inappropriate'   These languages were also unsatisfactory as they stood but had some interesting features which could be looked at for inspiration. This category included RTL/2 and LIS.

'recommended bases'   These were the three languages Pascal, PL/I and Algol 68 and were seen as possible starting points for the design of the final language.

At this point the requirements document was revised and reorganised to give Ironman. Proposals were then invited from contractors to design a new language starting from one of the recommended bases. Seventeen proposals were received and four were chosen to go ahead in parallel and in competition. The four contractors with their colour codings were CII Honeywell Bull (Green), Intermetrics (Red), Softech (Blue) and SRI International (Yellow). The colour codings were introduced so that the resulting initial designs could be compared anonymously and hopefully therefore without bias.

The initial designs were delivered in early 1978 and many groups all over the world considered their relative merit. The DoD judged that the Green and Red designs showed more promise than Blue and Yellow and so the latter were eliminated.

The development then entered its second phase and the two remaining contractors were given a further year in which to refine their designs. The requirements were also revised in the light of feedback from the initial designs and became the final document Steelman.[1]

The final choice of language was made on 2nd May 1979 when the Green language developed at CII Honeywell Bull by an international team led by Jean Ichbiah was declared the winner.

The DoD then announced that the new language would be known as Ada in honour of Augusta Ada Byron, Countess of Lovelace (1815-1852). Ada, the daughter of Lord Byron, was the assistant and patron of Charles Babbage and worked on his mechanical analytical engine. In a very real sense she was therefore the world's first programmer.

The development of Ada then entered a third phase. The purpose of this was to expose the language to a significant cross section of eventual users in order to allow them to comment on its suitability for their needs. Various courses were given in the USA and Europe and many teams then settled down to carry out their evaluations. Some 80 general reports were written and presented at a conference in Boston in October 1979. The general conclusion was that Ada was good but a few areas needed further refinement. In addition nearly a thousand shorter technical language issue reports were received. After considering all these reports the preliminary Ada design was revised and this resulted in the publication in July 1980 of the first definitive version of the language. It was then proposed to the American National Standards Institute (ANSI) as a standard.

The ANSI standardisation process occupied over two years and resulted in a certain number of changes to Ada. Most of these were small but often of subtle significance especially for the compiler writer. The ANSI standard Language Reference Manual (LRM) was finally published in January 1983 and it is this edition which forms the subject of this book.[2]

However, it should not be thought that Ada is just another programming language. It was also recognised that the language is just one component, although an important one, of the toolkit that every programmer should have available. It was therefore felt that additional benefit would be achieved if a uniform programming environment could also be established. And so, in parallel with the language design, a series of requirements documents for an Ada Programming Support Environment (APSE) were developed. These were entitled Sandman, Pebbleman and finally Stoneman.[3] These documents are less detailed than the corresponding language documents because the state-of-the-art in this area is still in its infancy. Nevertheless, it is hoped that the exercise will prevent unnecessary diversification and result in the development of one or more high quality APSEs. But that is another story outside the scope of this book.

1.2   Technical background

The evolution of programming languages has apparently occurred in a rather *ad hoc* fashion but with hindsight it is now possible to see three major advances. Each advance seems to be associated with the introduction of a level of abstraction which removes unnecessary and harmful detail from the program.

The first advance occurred in the early 1950s with high level languages such as FORTRAN and Autocode which introduced 'expression abstraction'. It thus became possible to write statements such as

```
X=A+B(I)
```

so that the use of the machine registers to evaluate the expression was completely hidden from the programmer. In these early languages the expression abstraction was not perfect since there were somewhat arbitrary constraints on the complexity of expressions; subscripts had to take a particularly simple form for instance. Later languages such as Algol 60 removed such constraints and completed the abstraction.

The second advance concerned 'control abstraction'. The prime example was Algol 60 which took a remarkable step forward; no language since then has made such an impact on later developments. The point about control abstraction is that the flow of control is structured and individual control points do not have to be named or numbered. Thus we write

```
if X=Y then P:=Q else A:=B
```

and the compiler generates the gotos and labels which would have to be explicitly used in languages such as FORTRAN. The imperfection of early expression abstraction was repeated with control abstraction. In this case the obvious flaw was the horrid Algol 60 switch which has now been replaced by the case statement of languages such as Pascal. (The earlier case clause of Algol 68 had its own problems.)

The third advance which is now occurring is 'data abstraction'. This means separating the details of the representation of data from the abstract operations defined upon the data.

Most existing languages take a very simple view of data types. In all cases the data is directly described in numerical terms. Thus if the data to be manipulated is not really numerical (it could be traffic light colours) then some mapping of the abstract type must be made by the programmer into a numerical type (usually integer). This mapping is purely in the mind of the programmer and does not appear in the written program except perhaps as a comment. It is probably a consequence of this fact that software libraries have not emerged except in numerical analysis. Numerical algorithms, such as those for finding eigenvalues of a matrix, are directly concerned with manipulating numbers and so these languages, whose data values are numbers, have proved appropriate. The point is that the languages provide the correct abstract values in this case only. In other cases, libraries are not successful because there is unlikely to be agreement on the required mappings. Indeed different situations may best be served by different mappings and these mappings pervade the whole program. A change in mapping usually requires a complete rewrite of the program.

Pascal introduced a certain amount of data abstraction as instanced by the enumeration type. Enumeration types allow us to talk about the traffic light colours in their own terms without our having to know how they are represented in the computer. Moreover, they prevent us from making an important class of programming errors – accidently mixing traffic lights with other abstract types such as the names of fish. When all such types are described in the program as numerical types, such errors can occur.

Another form of data abstraction concerns visibility. It has long been recognised that the traditional block structure of Algol 60 is not adequate. For example, it is not possible in Algol 60 to write two procedures to operate on some common data and make the procedures accessible without also making the data directly accessible. Many languages have provided control of visibility through separate compilation; this technique is adequate for medium sized systems but since the separate compilation facility usually depends upon some external system, total control of visibility is not gained. The module of Modula is an example of an appropriate construction.

Another language which made an important contribution to the development of data abstraction is Simula 67 with its concept of class. Many other experimental languages too numerous to mention have also made detailed contributions.

Ada seems to be the first practical language to bring together the various categories of data abstraction. We are probably too close to the current scene to achieve a proper perspective. There are no doubt several imperfections in Ada data abstraction just as FORTRAN expression abstraction and Algol 60 control abstraction were imperfect. However, Ada is an important advance and offers the possibility of writing significant reusable software libraries for areas other than numerical analysis. It should therefore encourage the creation of a software components industry.

1.3 Structure and objectives of this book

Learning a programming language is a bit like learning to drive a car. Certain key things have to be learnt before any real progress is possible. Although we need not know how to use the windscreen washer, nevertheless we must at least be able to start the engine, engage gears, steer and brake. So it is with programming languages. We do not need to know all about Ada before we can write useful programs but quite a lot must be learnt. Moreover many virtues of Ada become apparent only when writing large programs just as many virtues of a Rolls Royce are not apparent if we only use it to drive to the local shop.

This book is not an introduction to programming but an overall description of programming in Ada. It is assumed that the reader will have a significant knowledge of programming in some high level language. A knowledge of Pascal would be helpful but is not strictly necessary.

Chapter 2 gives a brief overview of some Ada concepts and is designed to give the reader a feel of the style and objectives of Ada. The rest of the book is in a tutorial style and introduces topics in a fairly straightforward sequence. By Chapter 7 we will have covered the traditional facilities of small languages such as Pascal. The remaining chapters cover modern and exciting material associated with data abstraction, programming in the large and parallel processing.

Most sections contain exercises. It is important that the reader does most, if not all, of these since they are an integral part of the discussion and later sections often use the results of earlier exercises. Solutions to all the exercises will be found at the end of the book; it is hoped that these are correct although at the time of writing they have not all been submitted to an Ada compiler.

Most chapters conclude with a short checklist of key points to be remembered. Although incomplete, these checklists should help to consolidate understanding. Furthermore the reader is encouraged to refer to the syntax in Appendix 4 which is organised to correspond to the order in which the topics are introduced.

This book covers all aspects of Ada but does not explore every pathological situation. Its purpose is to teach the reader the effect of and intended use of the features of Ada. In a few areas the discussion is incomplete; these are fixed point arithmetic, machine dependent programming and input-output. Fixed point arithmetic is a highly specialised topic and will not be necessary for most programmers. Machine dependent programming (as its name implies) is so dependent upon the particular implementation that only a brief overview seems appropriate. Input-output, although important, does not introduce new concepts but is rather a mass of detail; again a simple overview is presented. Further details of these areas can be found in the Language Reference Manual (LRM) which is referred to from time to time.

Various appendices are provided in order to make this book reasonably self-contained; they are mostly based upon material drawn from the Language Reference Manual. Access to the LRM, which is the official definition of Ada, is recommended but should not be absolutely essential.

1.4   References

1   *Department of Defense Requirements for High Order Computer Programming Languages* – "STEELMAN", Defense Advanced Research Projects Agency, Arlington, Virginia, June 1978.

2   *Reference Manual for the Ada Programming Language,* (ANSI/MIL-STD-1815A) United States Department of Defense, Washington D.C., January 1983.

3   *Department of Defense Requirements for Ada Programming Support Environments* – "STONEMAN", Defense Advanced Research Projects Agency, Arlington, Virginia, February 1980.

Chapter 2 ADA CONCEPTS

In this chapter we present a very brief overview of some of the goals, concepts and features of Ada.

2.1 Key goals

Ada is a large language since it addresses many important issues relevant to the programming of practical systems in the real world. It is, for instance, much larger than Pascal which, unless extended in some way, is really only suitable for training purposes (for which it was designed) and for small personal programs. Some of the key issues in Ada are

- Readability – it is recognised that professional programs are read much more often than they are written. It is important therefore to avoid an over terse notation such as in APL which although allowing a program to be written down quickly, makes it almost impossible to be read except perhaps by the original author soon after it was written.

- Strong typing – this ensures that each object has a clearly defined set of values and prevents confusion between logically distinct concepts. As a consequence many errors are detected by the compiler which in other languages would have led to an executable but incorrect program.

- Programming in the large – mechanisms for encapsulation, separate compilation and library management are necessary for the writing of portable and maintainable programs of any size.

- Exception handling – it is a fact of life that programs of consequence are rarely correct. It is necessary to provide a means whereby a program can be constructed in a layered and partitioned way so that the consequences of errors in one part can be contained.

- Data abstraction – as mentioned earlier, extra portability and maintainability can be obtained if the details of the representation of data can be kept separate from the specifications of the logical operations on the data.

- Tasking – for many applications it is important that the program be conceived as a series of parallel activities rather than just as a single sequence of actions. Building appropriate facilities into a language rather than adding them via calls to an operating system gives better portability and reliability.

- Generic units – in many cases the logic of part of a program is independent of the types of the values being manipulated. A mechanism is therefore necessary for the creation of related pieces of program from a single template. This is particularly useful for the creation of libraries.

7

2.2 Overview

One of the most important objectives of programming is to reuse existing pieces of program so that the effort of detailed new coding is kept to a minimum. The concept of a program library naturally emerges and an important aspect of a programming language is therefore its ability to express how to use the items in this library.

Ada recognizes this situation and introduces the concept of library units. A complete Ada program is conceived as a main program (itself a library unit) which calls upon the services of other library units. These library units can be thought of as forming the outermost lexical layer of the total program.

The main program takes the form of a procedure of an appropriate name. The service library units can be subprograms (procedures or functions) but they are more likely to be packages. A package is a group of related items which may be other entities as well as subprograms.

Suppose we wish to write a program to print out the square root of some number such as 2.5. We can expect various library units to be available to provide us with a means of computing square roots and producing output. Our job is merely to write a main program to use these services as we wish.

For the sake of argument we will suppose that the square root can be obtained by calling a function in our library whose name is SQRT. In addition we will suppose that our library includes a package called SIMPLE_IO containing various simple input-output facilities. These facilities might include procedures for reading numbers, printing numbers, printing strings of characters and so on.

Our program might look like

```
with SQRT, SIMPLE_IO;
procedure PRINT_ROOT is
    use SIMPLE_IO;
begin
    PUT(SQRT(2.5));
end PRINT_ROOT;
```

The program is written as a procedure called PRINT_ROOT preceded by a with clause giving the names of the library units which it wishes to use. The body of the procedure contains the single statement

```
PUT(SQRT(2.5));
```

which calls the procedure PUT in the package SIMPLE_IO with a parameter which in turn is the result of calling the function SQRT with the parameter 2.5.

Writing

```
use SIMPLE_IO;
```

gives us immediate access to the facilities in the package SIMPLE_IO. If we had omitted this use clause we would have had to write

```
SIMPLE_IO.PUT(SQRT(2.5));
```

in order to indicate where PUT was to be found.

We can make our program more useful by making it read in the number whose square root we require. It might then become

```
with SQRT, SIMPLE_IO;
procedure PRINT_ROOT is
    use SIMPLE_IO;
    X: FLOAT;
begin
    GET(X);
    PUT(SQRT(X));
end PRINT_ROOT;
```

The overall structure of the procedure is now clearer. Between **is** and **begin** we can write declarations and between **begin** and **end** we write statements. Broadly speaking declarations introduce the entities we wish to manipulate and statements indicate the sequential actions to be performed.

We have now introduced a variable X of type **FLOAT** which is a predefined language type. Values of this type are a set of certain floating point numbers and the declaration of X indicates that X can have values only from this set. In our example a value is assigned to X by calling the procedure GET which is also in our package SIMPLE_IO.

Some small scale details should be noted. The various statements and declarations all terminate with a semicolon; this is unlike some other languages such as Algol and Pascal where semicolons are separators rather than terminators. The program contains various identifiers such as **procedure**, PUT and X. These fall into two categories. A few (63 in fact) such as **procedure** and **is** are used to indicate the structure of the program; they are reserved and can be used for no other purpose. All others, such as PUT and X, can be used for whatever purpose we desire. Some of these, notably FLOAT in our example, have a predefined meaning but we can nevertheless reuse them if we so wish although it might be confusing to do so. For clarity in this book we use lower case bold letters for the reserved identifiers and upper case letters for the others. This is purely a notational convenience; the language rules do not distinguish the two cases except when we consider the manipulation of characters themselves. Note also how the underline character is used to break up long identifiers into meaningful parts.

Finally observe that the name of the procedure, PRINT_ROOT, is repeated between the final **end** and the terminating semicolon. This is optional but is recommended in order to clarify the overall structure although this is obvious in a small example such as this.

Our program is still very simple; it might be more useful to enable it to cater for a whole series of numbers and print out each answer on a separate line. We could stop the program somewhat arbitrarily by giving it a value of zero.

```
with SQRT, SIMPLE_IO;
procedure PRINT_ROOTS is
    use SIMPLE_IO;
    X: FLOAT;
begin
```

```
        PUT("Roots of various numbers");
        NEW_LINE(2);
        loop
            GET(X);
            exit when X = 0.0;
            PUT("Root of ");
            PUT(X);
            PUT(" is ");
            if X < 0.0 then
                PUT("not calculable");
            else
                PUT(SQRT(X));
            end if;
            NEW_LINE;
        end loop;
        NEW_LINE;
        PUT("Program finished");
        NEW_LINE;
    end PRINT_ROOTS;
```

The output has been enhanced by the calls of further procedures NEW_LINE and PUT in the package SIMPLE_IO. A call of NEW_LINE will output the number of new lines specified by the parameter; the procedure NEW_LINE has been written in such a way that if no parameter is supplied then a default value of one is assumed. There are also calls of PUT with a string as argument. This is in fact a different procedure from the one which prints the number X. The compiler knows which is which because of the different types of parameters. Having more than one procedure with the same name is known as overloading. Note also the form of the string; this is a situation where the case of the letters does matter.

Various new control structures are also introduced. The statements between **loop** and **end loop** are repeated until the condition X = 0.0 in the **exit** statement is found to be true; when this is so the loop is finished and we immediately carry on after **end loop**. We also check that X is not negative; if it is we output the message 'not calculable' rather than attempting to call SQRT. This is done by the if statement; if the condition between **if** and **then** is true, then the statements between **then** and **else** are executed, otherwise those between **else** and **end if** are executed.

The general bracketing structure should be observed; **loop** is matched by **end loop** and **if** by **end if**. All the control structures of Ada have this closed form rather than the open form of Pascal which can lead to poorly structured and incorrect programs.

We might well ask what would have happened if we had not tested for a negative value of X and consequently called SQRT with a negative argument. Assuming that SQRT has itself been written in an appropriate manner then it clearly cannot deliver a value to be used as the parameter of PUT. Instead an exception will be raised. The raising of an exception indicates that something unusual has happened and the normal sequence of execution is broken. In our case the exception might be NUMERIC_ERROR. If we did nothing to cope with this possibility then our program would be terminated and no doubt the Ada

Programming Support Environment (APSE) will give us a rude message saying that our program has failed and why. We can, however, look out for an exception and take remedial action if it occurs. In fact we could replace our conditional statement by

```
begin
    PUT(SQRT(X));
exception
    when NUMERIC_ERROR =>
        PUT("not calculable");
end;
```

We will now consider in outline the possible general form of the function SQRT and the package SIMPLE_IO that we have been using.

The function SQRT will have a structure similar to that of our main program; the major difference will be the existence of parameters

```
function SQRT(F: FLOAT) return FLOAT is
    R: FLOAT;
begin
    -- compute value of SQRT(F) in R
    return R;
end SQRT;
```

We see here the description of the formal parameters (in this case only one) and the type of the result. The details of the calculation are represented by the comment which starts with a double hyphen. The return statement is the means by which the result of the function is indicated. Note the distinction between a function which returns a result and is called as part of an expression and a procedure which does not have a result and is called as a single statement.

The package SIMPLE_IO will be in two parts, the specification which describes its interface to the outside world and the body which contains the details of how it is implemented. If it just contained the procedures that we have used, its specification might be

```
package SIMPLE_IO is
    procedure GET(F: out FLOAT);
    procedure PUT(F: in FLOAT);
    procedure PUT(S: in STRING);
    procedure NEW_LINE(N: in INTEGER:=1);
end SIMPLE_IO;
```

The parameter of GET is an **out** parameter because the effect of calling GET as in

```
GET(X);
```

is to transmit a value out from the procedure to the actual parameter X. The other parameters are all **in** parameters because the value goes in to the procedures.

Only part of the procedures occurs in the package specification; this part is known as the procedure specification and just gives enough information to enable the procedures to be called.

We see also the two overloaded specifications of PUT, one with a parameter of type FLOAT and the other with a parameter of type STRING. Finally, note how the default value of 1 for the parameter of NEW_LINE is indicated.

The package body for SIMPLE_IO will contain the full procedure bodies plus any other supporting material needed for their implementation and which is naturally hidden from the outside user. In vague outline it might look like

```
with INPUT_OUTPUT;
package body SIMPLE_IO is
    . . .
    procedure GET(F: out FLOAT) is
        . . .
    begin
        . . .
    end GET;
    - - other procedures similarly
end SIMPLE_IO;
```

The with clause shows that the implementation of the procedures in SIMPLE_IO uses the hypothetical more general package INPUT_OUTPUT. It should also be noticed how the full body of GET repeats the procedure specification which was given in the corresponding package specification. (The procedure specification is the bit up to but not including is.)

The example in this section has briefly revealed some of the overall structure and control statements of Ada. Details of data types will be discussed in due course. One purpose of this section has been to stress that the idea of packages is one of the most important concepts in Ada. A program should be conceived as a number of components which provide services to and receive services from each other. In the next few chapters we will of necessity be dealing with the small scale features of Ada but in doing so we should not lose sight of the overall structure which we will return to in Chapter 8.

Perhaps this is an appropriate point to mention the special package STANDARD. This is a package which exists in every implementation and contains the declarations of all the predefined identifiers such as FLOAT and NUMERIC_ERROR. We can assume access to STANDARD automatically and do not have to give its name in a with clause. It is discussed in detail in Appendix 2.

Exercise 2.2

1   In practice it is likely that the function SQRT will not be in the library on its own but in a package along with other mathematical functions. Suppose this package has the identifier SIMPLE_MATHS and other functions are LOG, EXP, SIN and COS. By analogy with the specification of SIMPLE_IO, write the specification of such a package. How would our program PRINT_ROOTS need to be changed?

2.3   Errors

An Ada program may be incorrect for various reasons. Four categories are recognised according to how they are detected.

Some errors will be detected by the compiler – these will include simple punctuation mistakes such as leaving out a semicolon or attempting to violate the type rules such as mixing up colours and fish. In these cases the program will not be executed.

Other errors are detected when the program is executed. An attempt to find the square root of a negative number or divide by zero are examples of such errors. In these cases an exception is raised as we saw in the last section and we have an opportunity to recover from the situation.

There are also certain situations where the program breaks the language rules but there is no simple way in which this violation can be detected. For example a program must not use a variable before a value is assigned to it. If it does then the behaviour is quite unpredictable and the program is said to be erroneous.

Finally there are situations where, for implementation reasons, the language does not prescribe the order in which things are to be done. For example the order in which the parameters of a procedure call are evaluated is not defined. If the behaviour of a program does depend on such an order then it is illegal and said to have an incorrect order dependency.

Care must be taken to avoid writing erroneous programs and those with incorrect order dependencies. In practice if we avoid clever tricks then all will usually be well.

2.4   Input-output

The Ada language is defined in such a way that all input and output is performed in terms of other language features. There are no special intrinsic features just for input and output. In fact input-output is just a service required by a program and so is provided by one or more Ada packages. This approach runs the attendant risk that different implementations will provide different packages and program portability will be compromised. In order to avoid this, the Language Reference Manual describes certain standard packages that can be expected to be available. Other, more elaborate, packages may be appropriate to special circumstances and the language does not prevent this. Indeed very simple packages such as our purely illustrative SIMPLE_IO may also be appropriate. Further consideration of input and output is deferred until Chapter 15 when we discuss interfaces between our program and the outside world in general.

2.5   Terminology

Every subject has its own terminology or jargon and Ada is no exception. (Indeed in Ada an exception is a kind of error as we have seen!) A glossary of terms will be found in Appendix 3.

Terminology will generally be introduced as required but before starting off with the detailed description of Ada it is convenient to mention a few concepts which will occur from time to time.

The term static refers to things that can be determined at compilation whereas dynamic refers to things determined during execution. Thus a static expression is one whose value can be determined by the compiler such as

$2 + 3$

and a static array is one whose bounds are known at compilation time.

Sometimes it is necessary to make a parenthetic remark to the compiler where the remark is not a part of the program as such but more a useful hint. This can be done by means of a construction known as a pragma. As an example we can indicate that only parts of our program are to be listed by writing

pragma LIST(ON);

and

pragma LIST(OFF);

at appropriate places. Generally a pragma can appear anywhere that a declaration or statement can appear, after any semicolon and in some other contexts also. Sometimes there may be restrictions on the position of a particular pragma. For fuller details see Appendix 1.

Chapter 3 LEXICAL STYLE

In the previous chapter, we introduced some concepts of Ada and illustrated the general appearance of Ada programs with some simple examples. However, we have so far only talked around the subject. In this chapter we get down to serious detail.

Regrettably it seems best to start with some rather unexciting but essential material – the detailed construction of things such as identifiers and numbers which make up the text of a program. However, it is no good learning a human language without getting the spelling sorted out. And as far as programming languages are concerned compilers are usually very unforgiving regarding such corresponding and apparently trivial matters.

We also take the opportunity to introduce the notation used to describe the syntax of Ada language constructs. In general we will avoid using this syntax notation to introduce concepts but, in some cases, it is the easiest way to be precise. Moreover, if the reader wishes to consult the LRM then knowledge of the syntax notation is necessary. For completeness and easy reference the full syntax is given in Appendix 4.

3.1 Syntax notation

The syntax of Ada is described using a modified version of Backus-Naur Form or BNF. In this, syntactic categories are represented by lower case names; some of these contain embedded underlines to increase readability. A category is defined in terms of other categories by a sort of equation known as a production. Some categories are atomic and cannot be decomposed further – these are known as terminal symbols. A production consists of the name being defined followed by the special symbol ::= and its defining sequence.

Other symbols used are

[ ]   square brackets enclose optional items,
{ }   braces enclose items which may be omitted, appear once or be repeated many times,
| a vertical bar separates alternatives.

In some cases the name of a category is prefixed by a word in italics. In such cases the prefix is intended to convey some semantic information and can be treated as a form of comment as far as the context free syntax is concerned. Sometimes a production is presented in a form that shows the recommended layout.

15

3.2   Lexical elements

An Ada program is written as a sequence of lines of text containing the following characters

- the alphabet A-Z

- the digits 0-9

- various other characters " # & ' ( ) * + , − . / : ; < = > _ |

- the space character

The lower case alphabet may be used instead of or in addition to the upper case alphabet, but the two are generally considered the same. (The only exception is where the letters stand for themselves in character strings and character literals.)

Some other special characters such as ! may also be used in strings and literals. Certain of them may be used as alternatives to |, # and " if these are not available. We will not bother with the alternatives and the extra rules associated with them but will stick to the normal characters in this book.

The LRM does not prescribe how one proceeds from one line of text to the next. This need not concern us. We can just imagine that we type our Ada program as a series of lines using whatever mechanism the keyboard provides for starting a new line.

A line of Ada text can be thought of as a sequence of groups of characters known as lexical elements. We have already met several forms of lexical elements in Chapter 2. Consider for example

```
AGE := 43;   -- John's age
```

This consists of five such elements

- the identifier AGE

- the compound symbol :=

- the number 43

- the single symbol ;

- the comment   -- John's age

Other classes of lexical element are strings and character literals; they are dealt with in Chapter 6.

Individual lexical elements may not be split by spaces but otherwise spaces may be inserted freely in order to improve the appearance of the program. A most important example of this is the use of indentation to reveal the overall structure. Naturally enough a lexical element must fit on one line.

Particular care should be taken that the following compound delimiters do not contain spaces

=>	used in aggregates, cases etc.
..	for ranges
**	exponentiation
:=	assignment

/=	not equals
>=	greater than or equals
<=	less than or equals
<<	label bracket
>>	the other label bracket
<>	the 'box' for arrays and generics

However, spaces may occur in strings and character literals where they stand for themselves and also in comments.

Note that adjacent identifiers and numbers must be separated from each other by spaces otherwise they would be confused. Thus we must write **end loop** rather than **endloop**.

3.3 Identifiers

We met identifiers in the simple examples in Chapter 2. As an example of the use of the syntax notation we now consider the following definition of an identifier.

    identifier ::= letter {[underline] letter_or_digit}
    letter_or_digit ::= letter I digit
    letter ::= upper_case_letter I lower_case_letter

This states that an identifier consists of a letter followed by zero, one or more instances of letter_or_digit optionally preceded by a single underline. A letter_or_digit is, as its name implies, either a letter or a digit. Finally a letter is either an upper_case_letter or a lower_case_letter. As far as this example is concerned the categories underline, digit, upper_case_letter and lower_case_letter are not decomposed further and so are considered to be terminal symbols.

In plain English this merely says that an identifier consists of a letter possibly followed by one or more letters or digits with embedded isolated underlines. Either case of letter can be used. What the syntax does not convey is that the meaning attributed to an identifier does not depend upon the case of the letters. In fact identifiers which differ only in the case of corresponding letters are considered to be the same. But, on the other hand, the underline characters are considered to be significant.

Ada does not impose any limit on the number of characters in an identifier. Moreover all are significant. There may however be a practical limit since an identifier must fit onto a single line and an implementation is likely to impose some maximum line length. Programmers are encouraged to use meaningful names such as TIME_OF_DAY rather than cryptic meaningless names such as T. Long names may seem tedious when first writing a program but in the course of its lifetime a program is read much more often than it is written and clarity aids subsequent understanding both by the original author and by others who may be called upon to maintain the program. Of course, in short mathematical or abstract subprograms, identifiers such as X and Y may be appropriate.

Identifiers are used to name all the various entities in a program. However, some identifiers are reserved for special syntactic significance and may not be reused. We encountered several of these in Chapter 2 such as **if**, **procedure** and **end**. There are 63 reserved words; they are listed in Appendix 1. For readability they are printed in boldface in this book but that is not important. In program text they could, like all identifiers, be in either case or indeed in a mixture of cases – procedure, PROCEDURE and Procedure are all acceptable. Nevertheless some discipline aids understanding and a useful convention is to use lower case for the reserved words and upper case for all others. But this is a matter of taste.

There are minor exceptions regarding the reserved words **delta**, **digits** and **range**. As will be seen later they are also used as attributes DELTA, DIGITS and RANGE. However, when so used they are always preceded by a prime or single quote character and so there is no confusion.

Some identifiers such as INTEGER and TRUE have a predefined meaning from the package STANDARD. These are not reserved and can be reused although to do so is usually unwise since the program could become very confusing.

Exercise 3.3
1   Which of the following are not legal identifiers and why?

a) Ada	d) UMO164G	g) X_
b) fish&chips	e) TIME_ _LAG	h) tax rate
c) RATE–OF–FLOW	f) 77E2	i) goto

3.4 Numbers

Numbers (or numeric literals to use the proper jargon) take two forms according to whether they denote an integer (an exact whole number) or a real (an approximate and not usually whole number). The important distinguishing feature is that real literals always contain a decimal point whereas integer literals never do. Ada is strict on mixing up types. It is illegal to use an integer literal where the context demands a real literal and vice versa. Thus

    AGE: INTEGER:=43.0;

and

    WEIGHT: REAL:=150;

are both illegal. (We are using type REAL rather than FLOAT for reasons which will become clear later.)

The simplest form of integer literal is simply a sequence of decimal digits. If the literal is very long it may be convenient to split it up into groups of digits by inserting isolated underlines thus

    123_456_789

In contrast to identifiers such underlines are, of course, of no significance other than to make the literal easier to read.

The simplest form of real literal is a sequence of decimal digits containing a decimal point. Note that there must be at least one digit on either side of the decimal point. Again, isolated underlines may be inserted to improve legibility provided they are not adjacent to the decimal point; thus

3.14159_26536

Unlike most languages both integer and real literals can have an exponent. This takes the form of the letter E (either case) followed by a signed or unsigned decimal integer. This exponent indicates the power of ten by which the preceding simple literal is to be multiplied. The exponent cannot be negative in the case of an integer literal – otherwise it might not be a whole number. (As a trivial point an exponent of -0 is not allowed for an integer literal but it is for a real literal.)

Thus the real literal 98.4 could be written with an exponent in any of the following ways.

   9.84E1   98.4e0   984.0e−1   0.984E+2

Note that 984e−1 would not be allowed.

Similarly, the integer literal 1900 could also be written as

   19E2   190e+1   1900E+0

but not as 19000e−1 nor as 1900E−0.

The exponent may itself contain underlines if it consists of two or more digits but it is unlikely that the exponent would be so large as to make this necessary. However, the exponent may not itself contain an exponent!

A final facility is the ability to express a literal in a base other than 10. This is done by enclosing the digits between # characters and preceding the result by the base. Thus

   2#111#

is an integer literal of value $4 + 2 + 1 = 7$.

Any base from 2 to 16 inclusive can be used and, of course, base 10 can always be expressed explicitly. For bases above 10 the letters A to F are used to represent the superdigits 10 to 15. Thus

   14#ABC#

equals $10 \times 14^2 + 11 \times 14 + 12 = 2126$.

A based literal can also have an exponent. But note carefully that the exponent gives the power of the base by which the simple literal is to be multiplied and not a power of ten – unless, of course, the base happens to be ten. The exponent itself, like the base, is always expressed in normal decimal notation. Thus

   16#A#E2

equals $10 \times 16^2 = 2560$ and

   2#11#E11

equals $3 \times 2^{11} = 6144$.

A based literal can be real. The distinguishing mark is again the point. (We can hardly say 'decimal point' if we are not using a decimal base! A better term is radix point.) So

2#101.11#

equals $4 + 1 + \frac{1}{2} + \frac{1}{4} = 5.75$ and

7#3.0#e–1

equals $\overset{.}{3}\!/\!7 = 0.\overset{.}{4}2857\overset{.}{1}$

The reader may have felt that the possible forms of based literal are unduly elaborate. This is not really so. Based literals are useful – especially for fixed point types since they enable the programmer to represent values in the form in which he or she thinks about them. Obviously bases 2, 8 and 16 will be the most useful. But the notation is applicable to any base and the compiler can compute to any base so why not?

Finally note that a numeric literal cannot be negative. A form such as –3 consists of a literal preceded by the unary minus operator.

Exercise 3.4

1   Which of the following are not legal literals and why? For those that are legal, state whether they are integer or real literals.

a) 38.6
b) .5
c) 32e2
d) 32e–2

e) 2#1011
f) 2.71828_18285
g) 12#ABC#
h) E+6

i) 16#FfF#
j) 1_0#1_0#E1_0
k) 27.4e_2
l) 2#11#e–1

2   What is the value of the following?

a) 16#E#E1
b) 2#11#E11

c) 16#F.FF#E+2
d) 2#1.1111_1111_111#E11

3   How many different ways can you express the following as a numeric literal?

a) the integer 41   b) the integer 150

(Forget underlines, distinction between E and e, nonsignificant leading zeros and optional + in an exponent.)

3.5   Comments

It is important to add appropriate comments to a program to aid its understanding by someone else or yourself at a later date. We met some comments in Chapter 2.

A comment in Ada is written as an arbitrary piece of text following two hyphens (or minus signs — the same thing). Thus

– – this is a comment

The comment extends to the end of the line. There is no facility in Ada to insert a comment into the middle of a line. Of course, the comment may be the only thing on the line or it may follow some other Ada text. A long comment that needs several lines is merely written as successive comments.

```
-- this comment is spread
-- over
-- several
-- lines.
```

It is important that the leading hyphens are adjacent and are not separated by spaces.

Exercise 3.5

1 How many lexical elements are there in each of the following lines of text?

```
a) X:=X+2;     -- add two to X
b) -- that was a silly comment
c) -- -- -- -- -- -- -- -- -- -- -- -- --
d) -  -  -  -  -  -  -  -  -  -  -  -
```

2 Distinguish

a) **delay** 2.0;
b) **delay**2.0;

Checklist 3

The case of a letter is immaterial in all contexts except strings and character literals.

Underlines are significant in identifiers but not in numeric literals.

Spaces are not allowed in lexical elements, except in strings, character literals and comments.

The presence or absence of a point distinguishes real and integer literals.

An integer may not have a negative exponent.

Numeric literals cannot be signed.

Nonsignificant leading zeros are allowed in all parts of a numeric literal.

Chapter 4 SCALAR TYPES

This chapter lays the foundations for the small scale aspects of Ada. We start by considering the declaration of objects, the assignment of values to them and the ideas of scope and visibility. We then introduce the important concepts of type, subtype and contraints. As examples of types, the remainder of the chapter discusses the numeric types INTEGER and REAL, enumeration types in general, the Boolean type in particular and the operations on them.

4.1 Object declarations and assignments

Values can be stored in objects which are declared to be of a specific type. Objects are either variables, in which case their value may change (or vary) as the program executes, or they may be constants, in which case they keep their same initial value throughout their life.

A variable is introduced into the program by a declaration which consists of the name (that is, the identifier) of the variable followed by a colon and then the name of the type. This can then optionally be followed by the := symbol and an initial value. The declaration terminates with a semicolon. Thus we might write

```
I: INTEGER;
P: INTEGER:=38;
```

This introduces the variable I of type INTEGER but gives it no particular initial value and then the variable P and gives it the specific initial value of 38.

We can introduce several variables at the same time in one declaration by separating them by commas thus

```
I,J,K: INTEGER;
P,Q,R: INTEGER:=38;
```

In the second case all of P,Q and R are given the initial value of 38.

If a variable is declared and not given an initial value then great care must be taken not to use the undefined value of the variable until one has been properly given to it. If a program does use the undefined value in an uninitialised variable, its behaviour will be unpredictable; the program is said to be erroneous. As mentioned in Chapter 2, this means that the program is strictly illegal but the compiler and run time system may not be able to tell us.

A common way to give a value to a variable is by using an assignment statement. In this, the identifier of the variable is followed by := and then some expression giving the new value. The statement terminates with a semicolon. Thus

    I:=36;

and

    P:=Q+R;

are both valid assignment statements and place new values in I and P thereby
overwriting their previous values.

 Note that := can be followed by any expression provided that it produces a
value of the type of the variable being assigned to. We will discuss all the rules
about expressions later but it suffices to say at this point that they can consist of
variables and constants with operations such as + and brackets and so on just like
an ordinary mathematical expression.

 There is a lot of similarity between a declaration containing an initial value
and an assignment statement. Both use := before the expression and the
expression can be of arbitrary complexity.

 An important difference, however, is that although several variables can be
declared and given the same initial value together, it is not possible for an
assignment statement to give the same value to several variables. This may seem
odd but in practice the need to give the same value to several variables usually only
arises with initial values anyway.

 Perhaps we should remark at this stage that strictly speaking a multiple
declaration such as

    A, B: INTEGER:=E;

is really a shorthand for

    A: INTEGER:=E;
    B: INTEGER:=E;

This means that in principle the expression E is evaluated for each variable. This is
a subtle point and does not usually matter but we will encounter some examples
later where the effect is important.

 A constant is declared in a similar way to a variable by inserting the reserved
word **constant** after the colon. Of course, a constant must normally be initialised
in its declaration otherwise it would be useless. Why? (An exception is mentioned
later.) An example might be

    PI: **constant** REAL :=3.14159_26536;

 In the case of numeric types, and only numeric types, it is possible to omit the
type from the declaration of a constant thus

    PI: **constant** :=3.14159_26536;

It is then technically known as a number declaration and merely provides a name
for the number. The distinction between integer and real named numbers is made
by the form of the initial value. In this case it is real because of the presence of the
decimal point. It is usually good practice to omit the type when declaring numeric

constants for reasons which will appear later. We will therefore do so in future examples. But note that the type cannot be omitted in numeric variable declarations even when an initial value is provided.

There is an important distinction between the allowed forms of initial values in constant declarations (with a type) and number declarations (without a type). In the former case the initial value may be any expression and is evaluated when the declaration is encountered at run time whereas in the latter case it must be a static expression and so is evaluated at compilation time. Full details are deferred until Chapter 12.

Exercise 4.1
1   Write a declaration of a real variable R giving it an initial value of one.

2   Write appropriate declarations of real constants ZERO and ONE.

3   What is wrong with the following declarations and statements?
   a) **var** I: INTEGER;
   b) G: **constant** :=981
   c) P,Q: **constant** INTEGER;
   d) P:=Q:=7;
   e) MN: **constant** INTEGER:=M*N;
   f) 2PI: **constant** :=2.0*PI;

4.2   Blocks and scopes

Ada carefully distinguishes between declarations which introduce new identifiers and statements which do not. It is clearly only sensible that the declarations which introduce new identifiers should precede the statements which manipulate them. Accordingly, declarations and statements occur in separate places in the program text. The simplest fragment of text which includes declarations and statements is a block.

A block commences with the reserved word **declare**, some declarations, **begin**, some statements and concludes with the reserved word **end** and the terminating semicolon. A trivial example is

```
declare
    I: INTEGER:=0;    -- declarations here
begin
    I:=I+1;           -- statements here
end;
```

A block is itself an example of a statement and so one of the statements in its body could be another block. This textual nesting of blocks can continue indefinitely.

Since a block is a statement it can be executed like any other statement. When this happens the declarations in its declarative part (the bit between **declare** and **begin**) are elaborated in order and then the statements in the body (between **begin** and **end**) are executed in the usual way. Note the terminology: we elaborate declarations and execute statements. All that the elaboration of a declaration does is make the thing being declared come into existence and then evaluate and assign any initial value to it. When we come to the **end** of the block all the things which were declared in the block automatically cease to exist.

We can now see that the above simple example of a block is rather foolish; it introduces I, adds 1 to it but then loses it before use is made of the resulting value.

Another point to note is that the objects used in an initial value must, of course, exist. They could be declared in the same declarative part but the declarations must precede their use. For example

```
declare
    I: INTEGER:=0;
    K: INTEGER:=I;
begin
```

is allowed, but

```
declare
    K: INTEGER:=I;
    I: INTEGER:=0;
begin
```

is generally not. (We will see in a moment that this could have a valid but different meaning.)

This idea of elaborating declarations in order is important; the jargon is 'linear elaboration of declarations'.

Like other block structured languages Ada also has the idea of hiding. Consider

```
declare
    I,J: INTEGER;
begin
    . . .                 − − here I is the outer one
    declare
        I: INTEGER;
    begin
        . . .             − − here I is the inner one
    end;
    . . .                 − − here I is the outer one
end;
```

In this, a variable I is declared in an outer block and then redeclared in an inner block. This redeclaration does not cause the outer I to cease to exist but merely makes it temporarily invisible. In the inner block I refers to the new I, but as soon as we leave the inner block, this new I ceases to exist and the outer one again becomes visible.

We distinguish the terms 'scope' and 'visibility'. The scope is the region of text where the entity is potentially visible and it is visible at a given point if its identifier can be used to refer to it at that point. We will now illustrate these terms but a fuller discussion has to be left until Chapter 8.

In the case of a block the scope of a variable (or constant) extends from the start of its declaration until the end of the block. However, it is not visible in its own declaration nor in any inner block after the redeclaration of the same identifier. The regions of scope and visibility are illustrated by the following

```
declare
    I: INTEGER:=0;
begin
    . . .
    declare
        K: INTEGER:=I;
        I: INTEGER:=0;
    begin
        . . .
    end;
    . . .
end;
```

scope of	visibility	scope of	visibility
outer I	of outer I	inner I	of inner I

The initial value of K refers to the outer I because it precedes the introduction of the inner I.

Thus

```
K: INTEGER:=I;
I: INTEGER:=0;
```

may or may not be legal – it depends upon its environment.

Exercise 4.2

1 How many errors can you see in the following?

```
declare
    I: INTEGER:=7;
    J,K: INTEGER
begin
    J:=I+K;
    declare
        P: INTEGER=I;
        I,J: INTEGER;
    begin
        I:=P+Q;
        J:=P−Q;
        K:=I*J;
    end;
    PUT(K);      −− output value of K
end;
```

4.3 Types

'A type is characterized by a set of values and a set of operations' (LRM 3.3).

In the case of the built in type **INTEGER**, the set of values is represented by

$$\ldots -3,-2,-1,0,1,2,3, \ldots$$

and the operations include

$+,-,$ * and so on

With two minor exceptions to be discussed later (arrays and tasks) every type has a name which is introduced in a type declaration. (The built in types such as INTEGER are considered to be declared in the package STANDARD.) Moreover, every type declaration introduces a new type quite distinct from any other type.

The set of values belonging to two distinct types are themselves quite distinct although in some cases the actual lexical form of the values may be identical – which one is meant at any point is determined by the context. The idea of one lexical form representing two or more different things is known as overloading.

Values of one type cannot be assigned to variables of another type. This is the fundamental rule of strong typing. It is an enormous aid to the rapid development of correct programs since it ensures that many errors are detected at compilation time.

A type declaration uses a somewhat different syntax to an object declaration in order to emphasise the conceptual difference. It consists of the reserved word **type**, the identifier to be associated with the type, the reserved word **is** and then the definition of the type followed by the terminating semicolon. We can imagine that the package STANDARD contains type declarations such as

type INTEGER **is** . . . ;

The type definition between **is** and ; gives in some way the set of values belonging to the type. As a concrete example consider the following

type COLOUR **is** (RED, AMBER, GREEN);

(This is an example of an enumeration type and will be dealt with in more detail in a later section in this chapter.)

This introduces a new type called COLOUR. Moreover, it states that there are only 3 values of this type and they are denoted by the identifiers RED, AMBER and GREEN.

Objects of this type can then be declared in the usual way

C: COLOUR;

An initial value can be supplied

C: COLOUR:=RED;

or a constant can be declared

DEFAULT: **constant** COLOUR:=RED;

We have stated that values of one type cannot be assigned to variables of another type. Therefore one cannot mix colours and integers and so

I: INTEGER;
C: COLOUR;
. . .
I:=C;

is illegal. In older languages it is often necessary to implement concepts such as enumeration types by more primitive types such as integers and give values such as 0,1 and 2 to variables named RED, AMBER and GREEN. Thus in Algol 60 one could write

```
integer RED, AMBER, GREEN;
RED:=0; AMBER:=1; GREEN:=2;
```

and then use RED, AMBER and GREEN as if they were literal values. Obviously the program would be easier to understand than if the code values 0,1 and 2 had been used directly. But on the other hand the compiler could not detect the accidental assignment of a notional colour to a variable which was, in the mind of the programmer, just an ordinary integer. In Ada, as we have seen, this is detected during compilation.

4.4   Subtypes

We now introduce subtypes and constraints. A subtype, as its name suggests, characterises a set of values which is just a subset of the values of some other type known as the base type. The subset is defined by means of a constraint. Constraints take various forms according to the category of the base type. As is usual with subsets, the subset may be the complete set. There is, however, no way of restricting the set of operations of the base type. The subtype takes all the operations; subsetting applies only to the values.

As an example suppose we wish to manipulate dates; we know that the day of the month must lie in the range 1 . . 31 so we declare a subtype thus

```
subtype DAY_NUMBER is INTEGER range 1 . . 31;
```

We can then declare variables and constants using the subtype identifier in exactly the same way as a type identifier.

```
D: DAY_NUMBER;
```

We are then assured that the variable D can take only integer values from 1 to 31 inclusive. The compiler will insert run time checks if necessary to ensure that this is so; if a check fails then the CONSTRAINT_ERROR exception is raised.

It is important to realise that a subtype declaration does not introduce a new distinct type. An object such as D is of type INTEGER and so the following is perfectly legal from the syntactic point of view

```
D: DAY_NUMBER;
I: INTEGER;
. . .
D:=I;
```

Of course, on execution, the value of I may or may not lie in the range 1 . . 31. If it does, then all is well; if not then CONSTRAINT_ERROR will be raised. Assignment in the other direction

I:=D;

will, of course, always work.

It is not always necessary to introduce a subtype explicitly in order to impose a constraint. We could equally have written

D: INTEGER **range** 1 . . 31;

Furthermore a subtype need not impose a constraint. It is perfectly legal to write

subtype DAY_NUMBER **is** INTEGER;

although in this instance it is not of much value.

A subtype (explicit or not) may be defined in terms of a previous subtype

subtype FEB_DAY **is** DAY_NUMBER **range** 1 . . 29;

Any additional constraint must of course satisfy existing constraints

DAY_NUMBER **range** 0 . . 10;

would be incorrect and cause CONSTRAINT_ERROR to be raised.

The above examples have shown constraints with static bounds. This is not necessarily the case; in general the bounds can be given by arbitrary expressions and so the set of values of a subtype need not be static, that is known at compilation time. However, it is an important fact that a type is always static.

In conclusion then a subtype does not introduce a new type but is merely a shorthand for an existing type with an optional constraint. However, in later chapters we will encounter several contexts in which an explicit constraint is not allowed; a subtype has to be introduced for these cases. We refer to a type or subtype name as a type mark and to the form consisting of a type mark followed by an optional constraint as a subtype indication. Thus we can restate the previous remark as saying that there are situations where a type mark has to be used whereas, as we have seen, the more general subtype indication is allowed in object declarations.

The sensible use of subtypes has two advantages. It can ensure that programming errors are detected earlier by preventing variables from being assigned inappropriate values. It can also increase the execution efficiency of a program. This particularly applies to array subscripts as we shall see later.

We have now introduced the basic concepts of types and subtypes. The remaining sections of this chapter illustrate these concepts further by considering in more detail the properties of the simple types of Ada.

4.5 Simple numeric types

Perhaps surprisingly a full description of the numeric types of Ada is deferred until much later in this book. The problems of numerical analysis (error estimates and so on) are complex and Ada is correspondingly complex in this area so that it can cope in a reasonably complete way with the needs of the numerical specialist. For our immediate purposes such complexity can be ignored. Accordingly, in this section, we merely consolidate a simple understanding of the two numeric types INTEGER and REAL which we have been using as background for elementary examples. For the everyday programmer these two numeric types will probably suffice.

First a confession. The type INTEGER is a genuine built-in Ada type. But the type REAL is not. It has to be declared somewhere in terms of one of the built-in floating point types. The reason for supposing that this has been done concerns portability and will be discussed when the truth about numeric types is revealed in more detail. For the moment, however, we will suppose that REAL is the floating point type. (The author is not deceiving you but in fact encouraging good Ada programming practice.)

As we have seen, a constraint may be imposed on the type INTEGER by using the reserved word **range**. This is then followed by two expressions separated by two dots which, of course, must produce values of integer type. These expressions need not be literal constants. One could have

        P: INTEGER **range** 1 .. I+J;

A range can be null as would happen in the above case if I+J turned out to be zero. Null ranges may seem pretty useless but they often automatically occur in limiting cases, and to exclude them would mean taking special action in such cases.

The minimum value of the type INTEGER is given by INTEGER'FIRST and the maximum value by INTEGER'LAST. These are our first examples of attributes. Ada contains various attributes denoted by a single quote followed by an identifier.

The value of INTEGER'FIRST will depend on the implementation but will always be negative. On a twos complement machine it will be −INTEGER' LAST −1 whereas on a ones complement machine it will be −INTEGER' LAST. So on a typical 16 bit twos complement implementation we will have

        INTEGER'FIRST = −32768
        INTEGER'LAST   = +32767

Of course, we should always write INTEGER'LAST rather than +32767 if that is what we logically want. Otherwise program portability could suffer.

Two useful subtypes are

        subtype NATURAL **is** INTEGER **range** 0 .. INTEGER'LAST;
        subtype POSITIVE **is** INTEGER **range** 1 .. INTEGER'LAST;

These are so useful that they are declared for us in the package STANDARD. The attributes FIRST and LAST also apply to subtypes so

        POSITIVE'FIRST = 1
        NATURAL'LAST = INTEGER'LAST

We turn now to a brief consideration of the type REAL. It is possible to apply constraints to the type REAL in order to reduce the range and precision but this takes us into the detail which has been deferred until later. There are also attributes REAL'FIRST and REAL'LAST. It is not really necessary to say any more at this point.

The other predefined operations that can be performed on the types INTEGER and REAL are much as one would expect in a modern programming language. They are summarised below.

+, −   These are either unary operators (that is, taking a single operand) or binary operators taking two operands.

   In the case of a unary operator, the operand can be either integer or real; the result will be of the same type. Unary + effectively does nothing. Unary − changes the sign.

   In the case of a binary operator, both operands must be integer or both operands must be real; the result will be of the type of the operands. Normal addition or subtraction is performed.

*   Multiplication; both operands must be integer or both operands must be real; again the result is of the same type.

/   Division; both operands must be integer or both operands must be real; again the result is of the same type. Integer division truncates towards zero.

rem   Remainder; in this case both operands must be integer and the result is an integer. It is the remainder on division.

mod   Modulo; again both operands must be integer and the result is an integer. This is the mathematical modulo operation.

abs   Absolute value; this is a unary operator and the single operand may be integer or real. The result is again of the same type and is the absolute value. That is, if the operand is positive, the result is the same but if it is negative, the result is the corresponding positive value.

**   Exponentiation; this raises the first operand to the power of the second. If the first operand is of integer type, the second must be a positive integer or zero. If the first operand is of real type, the second can be any integer. The result is of the same type as the first operand.

In addition, we can perform the operations =, / =, <, <=, >, and >= in order to return a Boolean result TRUE or FALSE. Again both operands must be of the same type. Note the form of the not equals operator / =.

Although the above operations are mostly straightforward a few points are worth noting.

It is a general rule that mixed mode arithmetic is not allowed. One cannot, for example, add an integer value to a real value; both must be of the same type. A change of type from INTEGER to REAL or vice versa can be done by using the desired type name (or indeed subtype name) followed by the expression to be converted in brackets.

So given

```
I: INTEGER:=3;
R: REAL:=5.6;
```

we cannot write

   I+R

but we must write

   REAL(I)+R

which uses real addition to give the real value 8.6, or

   I+INTEGER (R)

which uses integer addition to give the integer value 9.

Conversion from real to integer always rounds rather than truncates, thus

   1.4 becomes 1
   1.6 becomes 2

but a value midway between two integers, such as 1.5, may be rounded up or down according to the implementation.

There is a subtle distinction between **rem** and **mod**. The **rem** operation produces the remainder corresponding to the integer division operation /. Integer division truncates towards zero; this means that the absolute value of the result is always the same as that obtained by dividing the absolute values of the operands. So

$$
\begin{aligned}
7 \;/\; 3 &= 2 \\
(-7) \;/\; 3 &= -2 \\
7 \;/\; (-3) &= -2 \\
(-7) \;/\; (-3) &= 2
\end{aligned}
$$

and the corresponding remainders are

$$
\begin{aligned}
7 \text{ rem } 3 &= 1 \\
(-7) \text{ rem } 3 &= -1 \\
7 \text{ rem}(-3) &= 1 \\
(-7) \text{ rem}(-3) &= -1
\end{aligned}
$$

The remainder and quotient are always related by

   $(I/J) *J + I \text{ rem } J = I$

and it will also be noted that the sign of the remainder is always equal to the sign of the first operand I (the dividend).

However, **rem** is not always satisfactory. If we plot the values of I **rem** J for a fixed value of J (say 5) for both positive and negative values of I we get the pattern shown in Fig. 4.1.

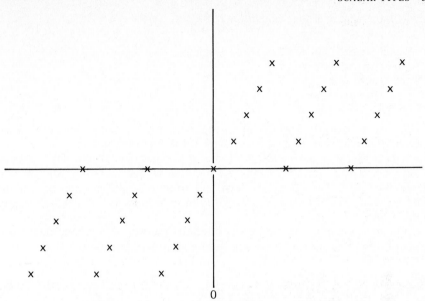

Fig 4.1 Behaviour of I **rem** 5 around zero

As we can see the pattern is symmetric about zero and consequently changes its incremental behaviour as we pass through zero.

The **mod** operation, on the other hand does have uniform incremental behaviour as shown in Fig. 4.2.

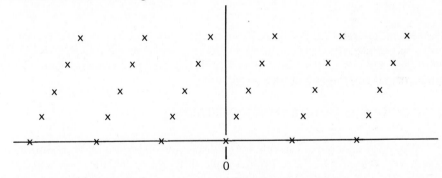

Fig. 4.2 Behaviour of I **mod** 5 around zero

The **mod** operation enables us to do normal modulo arithmetic. For example

(A+B) **mod** n = (A **mod** n + B **mod** n) **mod** n

for all values of A and B both positive and negative. For positive n, A **mod** n is always in the range 0 .ˑ. n−1; for negative n, A **mod** n is always in the range n+1. . 0. Of course, modulo arithmetic is only usually performed with a positive value for n. But the **mod** operator gives consistent and sensible behaviour for negative values of n also.

We can look upon **mod** as giving the remainder corresponding to division with truncation towards minus infinity. So

$$
\begin{array}{rl}
7 \ \textbf{mod} \ \ \ 3 = & 1 \\
(-7) \ \textbf{mod} \ \ \ 3 = & 2 \\
7 \ \textbf{mod} \ (-3) = & -2 \\
(-7) \ \textbf{mod} \ (-3) = & -1
\end{array}
$$

In the case of **mod** the sign of the result is always equal to the sign of the second operand whereas with **rem** it is the sign of the first operand.

The reader may have felt that this discussion has been somewhat protracted. In summary, it is perhaps worth saying that integer division with negative operands is rare. The operators **rem** and **mod** only differ when one or both operands is negative. It will be found that in such cases it is almost always **mod** that is wanted.

Finally some notes on the exponentiation operator **. For a positive second operand, the operation corresponds to repeated multiplication. So

$$
\begin{array}{l}
3**4 = 3*3*3*3 = 81 \\
3.0**4 = 3.0*3.0*3.0*3.0 = 81.0
\end{array}
$$

The second operand can be 0 and, of course, the result is then always the value one

$$
\begin{array}{l}
3**0 = 1 \\
3.0**0 = 1.0 \\
0**0 = 1 \\
0.0**0 = 1.0
\end{array}
$$

The second operand cannot be negative if the first operand is an integer, as the result might not be a whole number. In fact, the exception CONSTRAINT_ ERROR would be raised in such a case. But it is allowed for a real first operand and produces the corresponding reciprocal

$$
3.0**(-4) = 1.0/81.0 = 0.0123456780123. . .
$$

We conclude this section with a brief discussion on combining operators in an expression. As is usual the operators have different precedence levels and the natural precedence can be over-ruled by the use of brackets. Operators of the same precedence are applied in order from left to right. A subexpression in brackets obviously has to be evaluated before it can be used. But note that the order of evaluation of the two operands of a binary operator is not specified. The precedence levels of the operators we have met so far are shown below in increasing order of precedence

```
=  /=  <  <=  >  >=
+  −    (binary)
+  −    (unary)
*  /  mod  rem
**  abs
```

Thus

A/B*C	means	(A/B)*C
A+B*C+D	means	A+(B*C)+D
A*B+C*D	means	(A*B)+(C*D)
A*B**C	means	A*(B**C)

In general, as stated above, several operations of the same precedence can be applied from left to right and brackets are not necessary. However, the syntax rules forbid multiple instances of the exponentiating operator without brackets. Thus we cannot write

A**B**C

but must explicitly write either

(A**B)**C   or   A**(B**C)

This restriction avoids the risk of accidentally writing the wrong thing. Note however that the well established forms

A−B−C   and   A/B/C

are allowed. The syntax rules similarly prevent the mixed use of **abs** and ** without brackets.

The precedence of unary minus needs care

−A**B   means   −(A**B)   rather than   (−A)**B

as in Algol 68. Also

A**−B   and   A*−B

are illegal. Brackets are necessary.

Note finally that the precedence of **abs** is, confusingly, not the same as that of unary minus. As a consequence we can write

− **abs** X   but not   **abs** − X

Exercise 4.5

1 Evaluate the expressions below given the following

I: INTEGER:=7;
J: INTEGER:=−5;
K: INTEGER:=3;

a) I*J*K
b) I/J*K
c) I/J/K
d) J + 2 **mod** I

e) J + 2 **rem** I
f) K**K**K
g) −J **mod** 3
h) −J **rem** 3

2 Rewrite the following mathematical expressions in Ada. Use suitable identifiers of appropriate type.

a) b^2-4ac – discriminant of quadratic

b) $\frac{4}{3}\pi r^3$ – volume of sphere

c) $\dfrac{p\pi\, a^4}{8l\eta}$ – viscous flowrate through tube

4.6 Enumeration types

Here are some examples of declarations of enumeration types starting with COLOUR which we introduced when discussing types in general.

```
type COLOUR is (RED, AMBER, GREEN);
type DAY is (MON, TUE, WED, THU, FRI, SAT, SUN);
type STONE is (AMBER, BERYL, QUARTZ);
type GROOM is (TINKER, TAILOR, SOLDIER, SAILOR,
               RICH_MAN, POOR_MAN, BEGGAR_MAN, THIEF);
type SOLO is (ALONE);
```

This introduces an example of overloading. The literal AMBER can represent a COLOUR or a STONE. Both meanings of the same name are visible together and the second declaration does not hide the first whether they are declared in the same declarative part or one is in an inner declarative part. We can usually tell which is meant from the context but in those odd cases when we cannot we can always qualify the literal by placing it in brackets and preceding it by its type name (or indeed subtype name) and a single quote. Thus

```
COLOUR'(AMBER)
STONE'(AMBER)
```

Examples where this is necessary will occur later.

Although we can use AMBER as an enumeration literal in two distinct enumeration types, we cannot use it as an enumeration literal and the identifier of a variable at the same time. The declaration of one would hide the other and they could not both be declared in the same declarative part. Later we will see that an enumeration literal can be overloaded with a subprogram.

There is no upper limit on the number of values in an enumeration type but there must be at least one. An empty enumeration type is not allowed.

Constraints on enumeration types and subtypes are much as for integers. The constraint has the form

```
range lower_bound_expression . . upper_bound_expression
```

and this indicates the set of values from the lower bound to the upper bound inclusive. So we can write

```
subtype WEEKDAY is DAY range MON . . FRI;
D: WEEKDAY;
```

or

D: DAY **range** MON . . FRI;

and then we know that D cannot be SAT or SUN.

If the lower bound is above the upper bound then we get a null range, thus

subtype COLOURLESS **is** COLOUR **range** AMBER . . RED;

Note the curious anomaly that we cannot have a null subtype of a type such as SOLO.

The attributes FIRST and LAST also apply to enumeration types and subtypes, so

COLOUR'FIRST = RED
WEEKDAY'LAST = FRI

There are built in functional attributes to give the successor or predecessor of an enumeration value. These consist of SUCC or PRED following the type name and a single quote. Thus

COLOUR'SUCC(AMBER) = GREEN
STONE'SUCC(AMBER) = BERYL
DAY'PRED(FRI) = THU

Of course, the thing in brackets can be an arbitrary expression of the appropriate type. If we try to take the predecessor of the first value or the successor of the last then the exception CONSTRAINT_ERROR is raised. In the absence of this exception we have, for any type T and any value X,

T'SUCC(T'PRED(X)) = X

and vice versa.

Another functional attribute is POS. This gives the position number of the enumeration value, that is the position in the declaration with the first one having a position number of zero. So

COLOUR'POS(RED) = 0
COLOUR'POS(AMBER) = 1
COLOUR'POS(GREEN) = 2

The opposite to POS is VAL. This takes the position number and returns the corresponding enumeration value. So

COLOUR'VAL(0) = RED
DAY'VAL(6) = SUN

If we give a position value outside the range, as for example

SOLO'VAL(1)

then CONSTRAINT_ERROR is raised.

Clearly we always have

$$T'VAL(T'POS(X)) = X$$

and vice versa.

We also note that

$$T'SUCC(X) = T'VAL(T'POS(X) + 1)$$

they either both give the same value or both raise an exception.

It should be noted that these four attributes SUCC, PRED, POS and VAL may also be applied to subtypes but are then identical to the same attributes of the corresponding base type.

It is probably rather bad practice to mess about with POS and VAL when it can be avoided. To do so encourages the programmer to think in terms of numbers rather than the enumeration values and hence destroys the abstraction.

Finally the operators $=, /=, <, <=, >$ and $>=$ also apply to enumeration types. The result is defined by the order of the values in the type declaration. So

    RED < GREEN   is TRUE
    WED >= THU   is FALSE

The same result would be obtained by comparing the position values. So

$$T'POS(X) < T'POS(Y) \text{ and } X < Y$$

are always equivalent (except that $X < Y$ might be ambiguous).

Exercise 4.6
1   Evaluate

    a) DAY'SUCC(WEEKDAY'LAST)
    b) WEEKDAY'SUCC(WEEKDAY'LAST)
    c) STONE'POS(QUARTZ)

2   Write suitable declaration of enumeration types for

    a) the colours of the rainbow,
    b) typical fruits.

3   Write an expression that delivers one's predicted bridegroom after eating a portion of pie containing N stones. Use the type GROOM declared at the beginning of this section.

4   If the first of the month is in D where D is of type DAY, then write an assignment replacing D by the day of the week of the Nth day of the month.

5   Why might $X < Y$ be ambiguous?

4.7   The Boolean type

The Boolean type is a predefined enumeration type whose declaration can be considered to be

type BOOLEAN **is** (FALSE, TRUE);

Boolean values are used in constructions such as the if statement which we briefly met in Chapter 2. Boolean values are produced by the operators =, /=, <, <=, > and >= which have their expected meaning and apply to many types. So we can write constructions such as

```
if TODAY = SUN then
    TOMORROW:=MON;
else
    TOMORROW:=DAY'SUCC(TODAY);
end if;
```

The Boolean type (we capitalise the name in memory of the mathematician Boole) has all the normal properties of an enumeration type, so, for instance

```
FALSE < TRUE = TRUE!
BOOLEAN'POS(TRUE) = 1
```

We could even write

subtype ALWAYS **is** BOOLEAN **range** TRUE . . TRUE;

although it would not seem very useful.

The Boolean type also has other operators which are as follows

not   This is a unary operator and changes TRUE to FALSE and vice versa. It has the same precedence as **abs.**

and   This is a binary operator. The result is TRUE if both operands are TRUE, and FALSE otherwise.

or   This is a binary operator. The result is TRUE if one or other or both operands are TRUE, and FALSE only if they are both FALSE.

xor   This is also a binary operator. The result is TRUE if one or other operand but not both are TRUE. (Hence the name – eXclusive OR.) Another way of looking at it is to note that the result is TRUE if and only if the operands are different. (This operator is known as 'not equivalent' in some languages.)

The effects of **and**, **or** and **xor** are summarised in the usual truth tables shown in Fig. 4.3.

and	F	T		or	F	T		xor	F	T
F	F	F		F	F	T		F	F	T
T	F	T		T	T	T		T	T	F

Fig. 4.3 Truth tables for **and**, **or** and **xor**

The precedences of **and**, **or** and **xor** are equal to each other but lower than that of any other operator. In particular, they are of lower precedence than the relational operators =, /=, <, <=, > and >=. This is unlike Pascal and as a consequence brackets are not needed in expressions such as

P < Q **and** I = J

However, although the precedences are equal, **and**, **or** and **xor** cannot be mixed up in an expression without using brackets (unlike + and − for instance). So

B **and** C **or** D   is illegal

whereas

I + J − K   is legal

We have to write

B **and** (C **or** D)   or   (B **and** C) **or** D

in order to emphasise which meaning is required.
    The reader familiar with other programming languages will remember that **and** and **or** usually have a different precedence. The problem with this is that the programmer often gets confused and writes the wrong thing. It is to prevent this that Ada makes them the same precedence and insists on brackets. Of course, successive applications of the same operator are permitted so

B **and** C **and** D   is legal

and as usual evaluation goes from left to right although, of course, it does not matter in this case since the operator **and** is associative.
    Take care with **not**. Its precedence is higher than **and**, **or** and **xor** as in other languages and so

not A **or** B

means

(**not** A) **or** B

rather than

not (A **or** B)

which those familiar with logic will remember is the same as

(**not** A) **and** (**not** B)

Boolean variables and constants can be declared and manipulated in the usual way.

```
DANGER :    BOOLEAN;
SIGNAL  :    COLOUR;
. . .
DANGER : = SIGNAL = RED;
```

The variable DANGER is then TRUE if the signal is RED. We can then write

```
if DANGER then
   STOP_TRAIN;
end if;
```

Note that we do not have to write

```
if DANGER = TRUE then
```

although this is perfectly acceptable; it just misses the point that DANGER is already a Boolean and so can be used directly as the condition.

A worse sin is to write

```
if SIGNAL = RED then
   DANGER:= TRUE;
else
   DANGER:= FALSE;
end if;
```

rather than

```
DANGER:= SIGNAL = RED;
```

The literals TRUE and FALSE could be overloaded by declaring for example

```
type ANSWER is (FALSE, DONT_KNOW, TRUE);
```

but to do so might make the program rather confusing.

Exercise 4.7

1   Write declarations of constants T and F having the values TRUE and FALSE.

2   Using T and F from the previous exercise, evaluate

    a) T **and** F **and** T   d) (F = F) = (F = F)
    b) **not** T **or** T   e) T < T < T < T
    c) F = F = F = F

3   Evaluate

    (A /= B) = (A **xor** B)

for all combinations of values of Boolean variables A and B.

4.8   Type classification

At this point we pause to consolidate the material presented in this chapter so far.

The types in Ada can be classified as shown in Fig. 4.4

Fig 4.4 Classification of types

This chapter has discussed scalar types. In Chapter 6 we will deal with the composite types but access, private and task types will be dealt with much later.

The scalar types themselves can be subdivided into real types and discrete types. Our sole example of a real type has been the type REAL – the other real types are discussed in Chapter 12. The other types, INTEGER, BOOLEAN and enumeration types in general are discrete types – the only other kinds of discrete types to be introduced are other integer types, again dealt with in Chapter 12, and character types which are in fact a form of enumeration type and are dealt with in Chapter 6.

The key abstract distinction between the discrete types and the real types is that the former have a clear cut set of distinct separate (i.e. discrete) values. The type REAL, on the other hand, should be thought of as having a continuous set of values – we know in practice that a finite digital computer must implement a real type as actually a set of distinct values but this is an implementation detail, the abstract concept is of a continuous set of values.

The attributes POS, VAL, SUCC and PRED apply to all discrete types (and subtypes) because the operations reflect the discrete nature of the values. We explained their meaning with enumeration types in Section 4.6. In the case of type INTEGER the position number is simply the number itself so

```
INTEGER'POS(N) = N
INTEGER'VAL(N) = N
INTEGER'SUCC(N) = N + 1
INTEGER'PRED(N) = N - 1
```

The application of these attributes to integers does at first sight seem pretty futile but when we come to the concept of generic units in Chapter 13 we will see that it is convenient to allow them to apply to all discrete types.

The attributes FIRST and LAST however apply to all scalar types and subtypes including real types.

Again we emphasise that POS, VAL, SUCC and PRED for a subtype are identical to the corresponding operations on the base type, whereas in the case of FIRST and LAST this is not so.

Finally we note the difference between a type conversion and a type qualification.

```
REAL(I)            - - conversion
INTEGER'(I)        - - qualification
```

In the case of a conversion we are changing the type, in the second, we are just stating it (usually to overcome an ambiguity). As a mnemonic aid *qualification* uses a *quote*.

In both cases we can use a subtype name and CONSTRAINT_ERROR could consequently arise. Thus

    POSITIVE(R)

would convert the value of the real variable R to integer and then check that it was positive, whereas

    POSITIVE'(I)

would just check that the value of I was positive. In both cases, of course, the result is the checked value and is then used in an overall expression; these checks cannot just stand alone.

4.9 Expression summary

All the operators introduced so far are shown in Fig 4.5, grouped by precedence level.

Operator	Operation	Operand(s)	Result
and	conjunction	BOOLEAN	BOOLEAN
or	inclusive or	BOOLEAN	BOOLEAN
xor	exclusive or	BOOLEAN	BOOLEAN
=	equality	any	BOOLEAN
/=	inequality	any	BOOLEAN
<	less than	scalar	BOOLEAN
<=	less than or equals	scalar	BOOLEAN
>	greater than	scalar	BOOLEAN
>=	greater than or equals	scalar	BOOLEAN
+	addition	numeric	same
−	subtraction	numeric	same
+	identity	numeric	same
−	negation	numeric	same
*	multiplication	INTEGER REAL	INTEGER REAL
/	division	INTEGER REAL	INTEGER REAL
mod	modulo	INTEGER	INTEGER
rem	remainder	INTEGER	INTEGER
**	exponentiation	INTEGER: nonnegative INTEGER REAL : INTEGER	INTEGER REAL
not	negation	BOOLEAN	BOOLEAN
abs	absolute value	numeric	same

Fig.4.5 Scalar operators

In all the cases of binary operators except for **, the two operands must be of the same type.

We have actually now introduced all the operators of Ada except for one (&) although as we shall see in Chapter 6 there are further possible meanings to be added.

There are also two membership tests which apply to all scalar types. These are **in** and **not in**. They are technically not operators although their precedence is the same as that of the relational operators =,/= and so on. They enable us to test whether a value lies within a specified range (including the end values) or satisfies a constraint implied by a subtype. The first operand is therefore a scalar expression, the second is a range or type mark and the result is, of course, of type Boolean. Examples are

I **not in** 1 . . 10
I **in** POSITIVE
TODAY **in** WEEKDAY

Note that this is one of the situations where we have to use a type mark rather than a subtype indication. We could not replace the last example by

TODAY **in** DAY **range** MON . . FRI

although we could write

TODAY **in** MON . . FRI

Ada seems a bit curious here!

The test **not in** is equivalent to using **in** and then applying **not** to the result, but **not in** is usually more readable. So the first expression above could be written as

not (I **in** 1 . . 10)

where the brackets are necessary.

The reason that **in** and **not in** are not technically operators is explained in Chapter 7 when we deal with subprograms.

There are also two short circuit control forms **and then** and **or else** which like **in** and **not in** are also not technically classed as operators.

The form **and then** is closely related to the operator **and** whereas **or else** is closely related to the operator **or**. They may occur in expressions and have the same precedence as **and**, **or** and **xor**. The difference lies in the rules regarding the evaluation of their operands.

In the case of **and** and **or**, both operands are always evaluated but the order is not specified. In the case of **and then** and **or else** the left hand operand is always evaluated first and the right hand operand is only evaluated if it is necessary in order to determine the result.

So in

X **and then** Y

X is evaluated first. If X is false, the answer is false whatever the value of Y so Y is not evaluated. If X is true, Y has to be evaluated and the value of Y is the answer.

Similarly in

X or else Y

X is evaluated first. If X is true, the answer is true whatever the value of Y so Y is not evaluated. If X is false, Y has to be evaluated and the value of Y is the answer.

The forms **and then** and **or else** should be used in cases where the order of evaluation matters. A common circumstance is where the first condition protects against the evaluation of the second condition in circumstances that could raise an exception.

Suppose we need to test

I/J > K

and we wish to avoid the risk that J is zero. In such a case we could write

J /= 0 **and then** I/J > K

and we would then know that if J is zero there is no risk of an attempt to divide by zero. The observant reader will realise that this is not a very good example because one could usually write I > K*J (assuming J positive) – but even here we could get overflow. Better examples occur with arrays and access types and will be mentioned in due course.

Like **and** and **or**, the forms **and then** and **or else** cannot be mixed without using brackets.

We now summarise the primary components of an expression (that is the things upon which the operators operate) that we have met so far. They are

- identifiers   used for variables, constants, numbers and enumeration literals

- literals   such as 4.6, 2#101#

- type conversions   such as INTEGER(R)

- qualified expressions   such as COLOUR'(AMBER)

- attributes   such as INTEGER'LAST

- function calls   such as DAY'SUCC(TODAY)

A full consideration of functions and how they are declared and called has to be deferred until later. However, it is worth noting at this point that a function with one parameter is called by following its name by the parameter in brackets. The parameter can be any expression and could include further function calls. We can assume that we have available a mathematical library containing familiar functions such as

SQRT	square root
SIN	sine
COS	cosine
LOG	logarithm to base 10
LN	natural logarithm
EXP	exponential function

In each case they take a REAL argument and deliver a REAL result.

We are now in a position to write statements such as

```
ROOT:=(−B+SQRT(B**2−4.0*A*C))/(2.0*A);
SIN2X:=2.0*SIN(X)*COS(X);
```

Finally a note on errors although this is not the place to deal with them in depth. The reader will have noticed that whenever anything could go wrong we have usually stated that the exception CONSTRAINT_ERROR will be raised. This is a general exception which applies to all sorts of violations of ranges. The only other exception which needs to be mentioned at this point is NUMERIC_ ERROR. This will usually be raised if something goes wrong with the evaluation of an arithmetic expression itself before an attempt is made to store the result. An obvious example is an attempt to divide by zero. There are subtle distinctions which need not concern the normal user, for example

```
INTEGER'SUCC(INTEGER'LAST)
```

will raise CONSTRAINT_ERROR, whereas

```
INTEGER'LAST+1
```

should raise NUMERIC_ERROR. (We say should because an implementation is not obliged to raise NUMERIC_ERROR under certain conditions where optimisation is possible.)

As well as exceptions there are erroneous constructs and incorrect order dependencies as mentioned in Chapter 2. The use of a variable before a value has been assigned to it is an important example of an erroneous situation. Two cases which we have encountered so far where the order is not defined are

- The destination variable in an assignment statement may be evaluated before or after the expression to be assigned.

- The order of evaluation of the two operands of a binary operator is not defined.

Examples where these orders matter cannot be given until we deal with functions in Chapter 7.

Exercise 4.9

1 Rewrite the following mathematical expressions in Ada.

a) $2\pi\sqrt{l/g}$ – period of a pendulum

b) $\dfrac{m_0}{\sqrt{1-v^2/c^2}}$ – mass of relativistic particle

c) $\sqrt{2\pi n}\ .n^n\ .e^{-n}$ – Stirling's formula for $n!$ (integral n)

2 Rewrite 1(c) replacing n by the real value x.

Checklist 4

Declarations and statements are terminated by a semicolon.

Initialisation, like assignment uses :=.

Any initial value is evaluated for each object in a declaration.

Use number declarations rather than constants.

Elaboration of declarations is linear.

An identifier may not be used in its own declaration.

Each type definition introduces a quite distinct type.

A subtype is not a new type but merely a shorthand for a type with a possible constraint.

A type is always static, a subtype need not be.

No mixed mode arithmetic.

Distinguish **rem** and **mod** for negative operands.

Exponentiation with a negative exponent only applies to real types.

Take care with the precedence of the unary operators.

A scalar type cannot be empty, a subtype can.

POS, VAL, SUCC and PRED on subtypes are the same as on the base type.

FIRST and LAST are different for subtypes.

Qualification uses a quote.

Order of evaluation of binary operands is not defined.

Distinguish **and**, **or** and **and then**, **or else**.

Chapter 5 CONTROL STRUCTURES

This chapter describes the three bracketed sequential control structures of Ada. These are the if statement which we have briefly met before, the case statement and the loop statement. It is now recognised that these three control structures are not only necessary but also sufficient to be able to write programs with a clearly discernible flow of control without recourse to goto statements and labels. However, for pragmatic reasons, Ada does actually contain a goto statement and this is also described in this chapter.

The three control structures exhibit a similar bracketing style. There is an opening reserved word **if**, **case** or **loop** and this is matched at the end of the structure by the same reserved word preceded by **end**. The whole is, as usual terminated by a semicolon. So we have

if	**case**	**loop**
. . .	. . .	. . .
end if;	**end case;**	**end loop;**

In the case of the loop statement the word **loop** can be preceded by an iteration clause commencing with **for** or **while**.

5.1 If statements

The simplest form of if statement starts with the reserved word **if** followed by a Boolean expression and the reserved word **then**. This is then followed by a sequence of statements which will be executed if the Boolean expression turns out to be TRUE. The end of the sequence is indicated by the closing **end if**. The Boolean expression can, of course, be of arbitrary complexity and the sequence of statements can be of arbitrary length.

A simple example is

```
if HUNGRY then
     EAT;
end if;
```

In this, HUNGRY is a Boolean variable and EAT is a subprogram describing the details of the eating activity. The statement EAT; merely calls the subprogram (subprograms are dealt with in detail in Chapter 7).

The effect of this if statement is that if variable HUNGRY is TRUE then we call the subprogram EAT and otherwise we do nothing. In either case we then obey the statement following the if statement.

48

As we have said there could be a long sequence between **then** and **end if**. Thus we might break down the process into more detail

```
if HUNGRY then
    COOK;
    EAT;
    WASH_UP;
end if;
```

Note how we indent the statements to show the flow structure of the program. This is most important since it enables the program to be understood so much more easily. The **end if** should be underneath the corresponding **if** and **then** is best placed on the same line as the **if**.

Sometimes, if the whole statement is very short it can all go on one line.

```
if X < 0.0 then X:= − X; end if;
```

Note that **end if** will always be preceded by a semicolon. This is because the semicolons terminate statements rather than separate them as in Algol and Pascal. Readers familiar with those languages will probably feel initially that the Ada style is irksome. However, it is consistent and makes line by line program editing so much easier.

Often we will want to do alternative actions according to the value of the condition. In this case we add **else** followed by the alternative sequence to be obeyed if the condition is FALSE. We saw an example of this in the last chapter

```
if TODAY = SUN then
    TOMORROW:= MON;
else
    TOMORROW:= DAY'SUCC(TODAY);
end if;
```

Algol 60 and Algol 68 users should note that Ada is not an expression language and so conditional expressions are not allowed. We cannot write something like

```
TOMORROW:=
    if TODAY = SUN then MON else DAY'SUCC(TODAY) end if;
```

The statements in the sequence can be quite arbitrary and so could be further nested if statements. Suppose we have to solve the quadratic equation

$$ax^2 + bx + c = 0$$

The first thing to check is a. If $a = 0$ then the equation degenerates into a linear equation with a single root $-c/b$. (Mathematicians will understand that the other root has slipped off to infinity.) If a is not zero then we test the discriminant $b^2 - 4ac$ to see whether the roots are real or complex. We could program this as

```
if A = 0.0 then
        -- linear case
else
    if B**2 - 4.0*A*C >= 0.0 then
        -- real roots
    else
        -- complex roots
    end if;
end if;
```

Observe the repetition of **end if**. This is rather ugly and occurs sufficiently frequently to justify an additional construction. This uses the reserved word **elsif** as follows

```
if A = 0.0 then
        -- linear case
elsif B**2 - 4.0*A*C >= 0.0 then
        -- real roots
else
        -- complex roots
end if;
```

This construction emphasises the essentially equal status of the three cases and also the sequential nature of the tests.

The **elsif** part can be repeated an arbitrary number of times and the final **else** part is optional. The behaviour is simply that each condition is evaluated in turn until one that is TRUE is encountered; the corresponding sequence is then obeyed. If none of the conditions turns out to be TRUE then the else part, if any, is taken; if there is no else part then none of the sequences is obeyed.

Note the spelling of **elsif**. It is the only reserved word of Ada that is not an English word. Note also the layout – we align **elsif** and **else** with the **if** and **end if** and all the sequences are indented equally.

As a further example, suppose we are drilling soldiers and they can obey four different orders described by

```
type MOVE is (LEFT, RIGHT, BACK, ON);
```

and that their response to these orders is described by calling subprograms TURN_LEFT, TURN_RIGHT and TURN_BACK or by doing nothing at all respectively. Suppose that the variable ORDER of type MOVE contains the order to be obeyed. We could then write the following

```
if ORDER = LEFT then
    TURN_LEFT;
else
    if ORDER = RIGHT then
        TURN_RIGHT;
```

```
    else
        if ORDER = BACK then
            TURN_BACK;
        end if;
    end if;
end if;
```

But it is far clearer and neater to write

```
if ORDER = LEFT then
    TURN_LEFT;
elsif ORDER = RIGHT then
    TURN_RIGHT;
elsif ORDER = BACK then
    TURN_BACK;
end if;
```

This illustrates a situation where there is no **else** part. However, although better than using nested if statements, this is still a bad solution because it obscures the symmetry and mutual exclusion of the four cases ('mutual exclusion' means that by their very nature only one can apply). We have been forced to impose an ordering on the tests which is quite arbitrary and not the essence of the problem. The proper solution is to use the case statement as we shall see in the next section.

Contrast this with the quadratic equation. In that example, the cases were not mutually exclusive and the tests had to be performed in order. If we had tested $b^2 - 4ac$ first then we would have been forced to test a against zero in each alternative.

There is no directly corresponding contraction for **then if** as in Algol 68. Instead the short circuit control form **and then** can often be used.

So, rather than

```
if J > 0 then
    if I/J > K then
        ACTION;
    end if;
end if;
```

we can, as we have seen, write

```
if J > 0 and then I/J > K then
    ACTION;
end if;
```

Exercise 5.1
1   The variables DAY, MONTH and YEAR contain today's date.
    They are declared as

```
DAY: INTEGER range 1 .. 31;
MONTH: MONTH_NAME;
YEAR: INTEGER range 1901 .. 2099;
```

where

type MONTH_NAME **is** (JAN, FEB, MAR, APR, MAY, JUN, JUL,
AUG, SEP, OCT, NOV, DEC);

Write statements to update the variables to contain tomorrow's date. What happens if today is **31 DEC 2099**?

2   X and Y are two real variables. Write statements to swap their values, if necessary, to ensure that the larger value is in X. Use a block to declare a temporary variable T.

5.2   Case statements

A case statement allows us to choose one of several sequences of statements according to the value of an expression. For instance, the example of the drilling soldiers should be written as

```
case ORDER is
    when LEFT => TURN_LEFT;
    when RIGHT => TURN_RIGHT;
    when BACK => TURN_BACK;
    when ON => null;
end case;
```

All possible values of the expression must be provided for in order to guard against accidental omissions. If, as in this example, no action is required for one or more values then the null statement has to be used.

The null statement, written

```
null;
```

does absolutely nothing but its presence indicates that we truly want to do nothing. The sequence of statements here, as in the if statement, must contain at least one statement. (There is no empty statement as in Algol 60.)

It often happens that the same action is desired for several values of the expression. Consider the following

```
case TODAY is
    when MON|TUES|WED|THU=> WORK;
    when FRI              => WORK;
                             PARTY;
    when SAT|SUN          => null;
end case;
```

This expresses the idea that on Monday to Thursday we go to work. On Friday we also go to work but then go to a party. At the weekend we do nothing. The alternative values are separated by the vertical bar character. Note again the use of a null statement.

If several successive values have the same action then it is more convenient to use a range

when MON . . THU => WORK;

Sometimes we wish to express the idea of a default action to be taken by all values not explicitly stated; this is provided for by the reserved word **others**. The above example could be rewritten

```
case TODAY is
    when MON . . THU => WORK;
    when FRI         => WORK;
                        PARTY;
    when others      => null;
end case;
```

It is possible to have ranges as alternatives. In fact this is probably a situation where the clearest explanation of what is allowed is given by the formal syntax†.

```
case_statement ::=
    case expression is
        case_statement_alternative
        {case_statement_alternative}
    end case;
```

```
case_statement_alternative ::=
    when choice {|choice} => sequence_of_statements
```

choice ::= simple_expression I discrete_range I **others** I
    component_simple_name

discrete_range ::= discrete_subtype_indication I range

subtype_indication ::= type_mark[constraint]

type_mark ::= type_name I subtype_name

range ::= range_attribute I simple_expression . . simple_expression

We see that **when** is followed by one or more choices separated by vertical bars and that a choice may be a simple expression, a discrete range or **others**. (The syntax shows that a choice may also be a component simple name; however this only applies to choices used in a different situation which we have not yet met and so can be ignored for the moment.) A simple expression, of course, just gives a single value – FRI being a trivial example. A discrete range offers several possibilities. It can be the syntactic form range which the syntax tells us

---

† In the production for case_statement_alternative, the vertical bar stands for itself and is not a metasymbol.

can be two simple expressions separated by two dots – MON . . THU is a simple example; a range can also be given by a range attribute which we will meet in the next chapter. A discrete range can also be a subtype indication which as we know is a type mark (a type name or subtype name) followed optionally by an appropriate constraint. In this case, of course, the constraint has to be a range constraint which is merely the reserved word **range** followed by the syntactic form range. Examples of discrete ranges are

```
MON . . THU
DAY range MON . . THU
WEEKDAY
WEEKDAY range MON . . THU
```

All these possibilities may seem unnecessary but as we shall see later the form, discrete range, is used in other contexts as well as the case statement. In the case statement there is not usually much point in using the type name since this is known from the context anyway. Similarly there is not much point in using the subtype name followed by a constraint since the constraint alone will do. However, it might be useful to use a subtype name alone when that exactly corresponds to the range required. So we could rewrite the example as

```
case TODAY is
    when WEEKDAY=> WORK;
                         if TODAY = FRI then
                             PARTY;
                         end if;
    when others     => null;
end case;
```

although this solution feels untidy.

There are various other restrictions that the syntax does not tell us. One is that if we use **others** then it must appear alone and as the last alternative. As stated earlier it covers all values not explicitly covered by the previous alternatives (one is still allowed to write **others** even if there are no other cases to be considered!).

Another very important restriction is that the expressions in the choices must be static so that they can be evaluated at compilation time. In practice they will usually be literals as in our examples.

Finally we return to the point made at the beginning of this section that all possible values of the expression must be provided for. This usually means all values of the type of the expression. This is certainly the case of a variable declared as of a type without any constraints (as in the case of TODAY). However, if the expression is of a simple form and belongs to a static subtype (that is one whose constraints are static expressions and so can be determined at compilation time) then only values of that subtype need be provided for. In other words if the compiler can tell that only a subset of values is possible then only that subset need and must be covered. The simple forms allowed for the expression are the name of an object of the static subtype or a qualified or converted expression whose type mark is that of the static subtype.

In the case of our example, if TODAY had been of subtype WEEKDAY then we would know that only the values MON . . FRI are possible and so only these can and need be covered. Even if TODAY is not constrained we can still write our expression as a qualified expression WEEKDAY'(TODAY) and then again only MON . . FRI is possible. So we could write

```
case WEEKDAY'(TODAY) is
    when MON . . THU => WORK;
    when FRI         => WORK;
                        PARTY;
end case;
```

but, of course, if TODAY happens to take a value not in the subtype WEEKDAY (i.e. is SAT or SUN) then CONSTRAINT_ERROR will be raised. Mere qualification cannot prevent TODAY from being SAT or SUN. So this is not really a solution to our original problem.

As further examples, suppose we had variables

```
I:  INTEGER range 1 . . 10;
J:  INTEGER range 1 . . N;
```

where N is not static. Then we know that I belongs to a static subtype (albeit anonymous) whereas we cannot say the same about J. If I is used as an expression in a case statement then only the values 1 . . 10 have to be catered for, whereas if J is so used then the full range of values of type INTEGER (INTEGER'FIRST . . INTEGER'LAST) have to be catered for.

The above discussion on the case statement has no doubt given the reader the impression of considerable complexity. It therefore seems wise to summarise the key points which will in practice need to be remembered.

- Every possible value of the expression must be covered once and once only.

- All values and ranges must be static.

- If **others** is used it must be last and on its own.

Exercise 5.2

1   Rewrite Exercise 5.1(**1**) to use a case statement to set the correct value in END_OF_MONTH.

2   A vegetable gardener digs in winter, sows seed in spring, tends the growing plants in summer and harvests the crop in the autumn or fall. Write a case statement to call the appropriate subprogram DIG, SOW, TEND or HARVEST according to the month M. Declare appropriate subtypes if desired.

3   An improvident man is paid on the first of each month. For the first ten days he gorges himself, for the next ten he subsists and for the remainder he starves. Call subprograms GORGE, SUBSIST and STARVE according to the day D. Assume END_OF_MONTH has been set and that D is declared as

```
D: INTEGER range 1 . . END_OF_MONTH;
```

5.3   Loop statements

The simplest form of loop statement is

```
loop
    sequence_of_statements
end loop;
```

The statements of the sequence are then repeated indefinitely unless one of them terminates the loop by some means. So immortality could be represented by

```
loop
    WORK;
    EAT;
    SLEEP;
end loop;
```

As a more concrete example consider the problem of computing the base e of natural logarithms from the infinite series

$$e = 1 + \frac{1}{1!} + \frac{1}{2!} + \frac{1}{3!} + \frac{1}{4!} + \ldots$$

where

$$n! = n \times (n–1) \times (n–2) \ldots 3 \times 2 \times 1$$

A possible solution is

```
declare
    E: REAL:= 1.0;
    I: INTEGER:= 0;
    TERM: REAL:= 1.0;
begin
    loop
        I:= I + 1;
        TERM:= TERM / REAL(I);
        E:= E + TERM;
    end loop;
    ...
```

Each time around the loop a new term is computed by dividing the previous term by I. The new term is then added to the sum so far which is accumulated in E. The term number I is an integer because it is logically a counter and so we have to write REAL(I) as the divisor. The series started by setting values in E, I and TERM which correspond to the first term (that for which I = 0).

The computation then goes on for ever with E becoming a closer and closer approximation to e. In practice, because of the finite accuracy of the computer, TERM will become zero and continued computation will be pointless. But in any event we presumably want to stop at some point so that we can do something with our computed result. We can do this with the statement

exit;

If this is obeyed inside a loop then the loop terminates at once and control passes to
the point immediately after **end loop**.

Suppose we decide to stop after N terms of the series – that is when I = **N**.
We can do this by writing the loop as

```
loop
    if I = N then exit; end if;
    I:= I + 1;
    TERM:= TERM / REAL(I);
    E:= E + TERM;
end loop;
```

The construction

if condition **then exit; end if**;

is so common that a special shorthand is provided

exit when condition;

So we now have

```
loop
    exit when I = N;
    I:= I + 1;
    TERM:= TERM / REAL(I);
    E:= E + TERM;
end loop;
```

Although an exit statement can appear anywhere inside a loop – it could be in
the middle or near the end – a special form is provided for the frequent case where
we want to test a condition at the start of each iteration. This uses the reserved
word **while** and gives the condition for the loop to be continued. So we could
write

```
while I /= N loop
    I:= I + 1;
    TERM:= TERM / REAL(I);
    E:= E + TERM;
end loop;
```

The condition is naturally evaluated each time around the loop.

The final form of loop allows for a specific number of iterations with a loop
parameter taking in turn all the values of a discrete range. Our example could be
recast as

```
for I in 1 .. N loop
    TERM:= TERM / REAL(I);
    E:= E + TERM;
end loop;
```

where I takes the values 1, 2, 3 . . . N.

The parameter I is implicitly declared by its appearance in the iteration scheme and does not have to be declared outside. It takes its type from the discrete range and within the loop behaves as a constant so that it cannot be changed except by the loop mechanism itself. When we leave the loop (by whatever means) I ceases to exist (because it was implicitly declared by the loop) and so we cannot read its final value from outside.

We could leave the loop by an exit statement – if we wanted to know the final value we could copy the value of I into a variable declared outside the loop thus

```
if condition_to_exit then
    LAST_I:= I;
    exit;
end if;
```

The values of the discrete range are normally taken in ascending order. Descending order can be specified by writing

```
for I in reverse 1 .. N loop
```

but the range itself is always written in ascending order.

It is not possible to specify a numeric step size of other than 1. This should not be a problem since the vast majority of loops go up by steps of 1 and almost all the rest go down by steps of 1. The very few which do behave otherwise can be explicitly programmed using the while form of loop.

The range can be empty (as for instance if N happened to be zero or negative in our example) in which case the sequence of statements will not be obeyed at all. Of course, the range itself is evaluated only once and cannot be changed inside the loop itself.

Thus

```
N:=4;
for I in 1 .. N loop
    . . .
    N:=10;
end loop;
```

results in the loop being executed just four times despite the fact that N is changed to ten.

Our examples have all shown the lower bound of the range being 1. This, of course, need not be the case. Both bounds can be arbitrary dynamically evaluated expressions. Furthermore the loop parameter need not be of integer type. It can be of any discrete type, as determined by the discrete range.

We could, for instance, simulate a week's activity by

```
for TODAY in MON . . SUN loop
    case TODAY is
        . . .
    end case;
end loop;
```

This implicitly declares TODAY to be of type DAY and obeys the loop with the values MON, TUE, . . . SUN in turn.

The other forms of discrete range (using a type or subtype name) are of advantage here. The essence of MON . . SUN is that it embraces all the values of the type DAY. It is therefore better to write the loop using a form of discrete range that conveys the idea of completeness

```
for TODAY in DAY loop
    . . .
end loop;
```

And again since we know that we do nothing at weekends anyway we could write

```
for TODAY in DAY range MON . . FRI loop
```

or better

```
for TODAY in WEEKDAY loop
```

It is interesting to note a difference regarding the determination of types in the case statement and for statement. In the case statement, the type of the discrete range is determined from the type of the expression after **case**. In the for statement, the type of the loop parameter is determined from the type of the discrete range. The dependency is the other way round.

It is therefore necessary for the type of the discrete range to be unambiguous in the for statement. This is usually the case but if we had two enumeration types with two overloaded literals such as

```
type PLANET is (MERCURY, VENUS, EARTH, MARS, JUPITER,
                SATURN, URANUS, NEPTUNE, PLUTO);
type ROMAN_GOD is (JANUS, MARS, JUPITER, JUNO, VESTA,
                   VULCAN, SATURN, MERCURY, MINERVA);
```

then

```
for X in MARS . . SATURN loop
```

would be ambiguous and the compiler would not compile our program. We could resolve the problem by qualifying one of the expressions

```
for X in PLANET'(MARS) . . SATURN loop
```

or (probably better) by using a form of discrete range giving the type explicitly

```
for X in PLANET range MARS . . SATURN loop
```

When we have dealt with numerics in more detail we will realise that the range 1 .. 10 is not necessarily of type INTEGER. A general application of our rule that the type must not be ambiguous in a for statement would lead us to have to write

for I **in** INTEGER **range** 1 .. 10 **loop**

However, this would be so tedious in such a common case that there is a special rule which applies to discrete ranges in for statements which merely says that integer literal ranges imply type INTEGER.

Finally we reconsider the exit statement. The simple form encountered earlier always transfers control to immediately after the innermost embracing loop. But of course loops may be nested and sometimes we may wish to exit from a nested construction. As an example suppose we are searching in two dimensions

```
for I in 1 .. N loop
    for J in 1 .. M loop
        – – if values of I and J satisfy
        – – some condition then leave nested loop
    end loop;
end loop;
```

A simple exit statement in the inner loop would merely take us to the end of that loop and we would then have to recheck the condition and exit again. This can be avoided by naming the outer loop and using the name in the exit statement thus

```
SEARCH:
for I in 1 .. N loop
    for J in 1 .. M loop
        if condition_O_K then
            I_VALUE:= I;
            J_VALUE:= J;
            exit SEARCH;
        end if;
    end loop;
end loop SEARCH;
– – control passes here
```

A loop is named by preceding it with an identifier and colon. (It looks remarkably like a label in other languages but it is not and cannot be 'gone to'.) The identifier must be repeated between the corresponding **end loop** and the semicolon.

The conditional form of exit can also refer to a loop by name

exit SEARCH **when** condition;

Exercise 5.3

1 The statement GET (I); reads the next value from the input file into the integer variable I. Write statements to read and add together a series of numbers. The end of the series is indicated by a dummy negative value.

2 Write statements to determine the power of 2 in the factorisation of N. Compute the result in COUNT but do not alter N.

3 Compute

$$g = \sum_{p=1}^{n} \frac{1}{p} - \log n$$

(As $n \to \infty$, $g \to \gamma = 0.577215665 \ldots$)

5.4 Goto statements and labels

Many will be surprised that a modern programming language should contain a goto statement at all. It has become considered to be extremely bad practice to use goto statements because of the resulting difficulty in proving correctness of the program, maintenance and so on. And indeed Ada contains adequate control structures so that it should not normally be necessary to use a goto at all.

So why provide a goto statement? The main reason concerns automatically generated programs. If we try to transliterate (by hand or machine) a program from some other language into Ada then the goto will probably be useful. Another example might be where the program is generated automatically from some high level specification. Finally there may be cases where the goto is the neatest way – perhaps as a way out of some deeply nested structure – but the alternative of raising an exception (see Chapter 10) could also be considered.

In order to put us off using gotos and labels (and perhaps so that our manager can spot them if we do) the notation for a label is unusual and stands out like a sore thumb. A label is an identifier enclosed in double angled brackets thus

        <<THE_DEVIL>>

and a goto statement takes the expected form of the reserved word **goto** followed by the label identifier and semicolon

        goto THE_DEVIL;

A goto statement cannot be used to transfer control into an if, case or loop statement nor between the arms of an if or case statement.

Exercise 5.4
1 Rewrite the nested loop of Section 5.3 using a label <<SEARCH>> rather than naming the outer loop. Why is this not such a good solution?

5.5 Statement classification

The statements in Ada can be classified as shown in Fig. 5.1

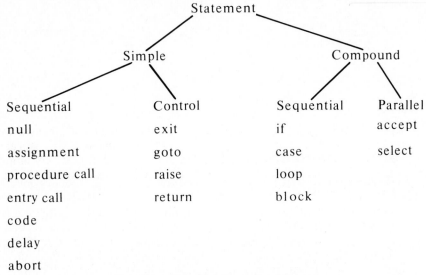

Fig. 5.1 Classification of statements

Further detail on the assignment statement is in the next chapter when we discuss composite types. Procedure calls and return statements are discussed in Chapter 7 and the raise statement which is concerned with exceptions is discussed in Chapter 10. The code statement is mentioned in Chapter 15. The remaining statements (entry call, delay, abort, accept and select) concern tasking and are dealt with in Chapter 14.

All statements can have one or more labels. The simple statements cannot be decomposed lexically into other statements whereas the compound statements can be so decomposed and can therefore be nested. Statements are obeyed sequentially unless one of them is a control statement (or an exception is implicitly raised).

Checklist 5

Statement brackets must match correctly.

Use **elsif** where appropriate.

The choices in a case statement must be static.

All possibilities in a case statement must be catered for.

If **others** is used it must be last and on its own.

The expression after **case** can be qualified in order to reduce the alternatives.

A loop parameter behaves as a constant.

A named loop must have the name at both ends.

Avoid gotos.

Use the recommended layout.

Chapter 6 COMPOSITE TYPES

In this chapter we describe the composite types which are arrays and records. We also complete our discussion of enumeration types by introducing characters and strings. At this stage we discuss arrays fairly completely but consider only simple forms of records. The more elaborate discriminated records which include variant records are deferred until Chapter 11.

6.1 Arrays

An array is a composite object consisting of a number of components all of the same type. An array can be of one, two or more dimensions. A typical array declaration might be

```
A: array (INTEGER range 1 . . 6) of REAL;
```

This declares A to be a variable object which has 6 components, each of which is of type REAL. The individual components are referred to by following the array name with an expression in brackets giving an integer value in the discrete range 1 . . 6. If this expression, known as the index value, has a value outside the range, then the exception CONSTRAINT_ERROR will be raised. We could set zero in each component of A by writing

```
for I in 1 . . 6 loop
    A(I):=0.0;
end loop;
```

An array can be of several dimensions, in which case a separate range is given for each dimension. So

```
AA: array (INTEGER range 0 . . 2, INTEGER range 0 . . 3) of REAL;
```

is an array of 12 components in total, each of which is referred to by two integer index values, the first in the range 0 . . 2 and the second in the range 0 . . 3. Each component of this two dimensional array could be set to zero by a nested loop thus

```
for I in 0 . . 2 loop
    for J in 0 . . 3 loop
        AA(I, J):=0.0;
    end loop;
end loop;
```

The discrete ranges do not have to be static: one could have

```
N: INTEGER:= ... ;
B: array (INTEGER range 1 .. N) of BOOLEAN;
```

and the value of N at the point when the declaration of B is elaborated would determine the number of components in B. Of course, the declaration of B might be elaborated many times during the course of a program – it might be inside a loop for example – and each elaboration will give rise to a new life of a new array and the value of N could be different each time. Like other declared objects, the array B ceases to exist once we pass the end of the block containing its declaration. Because of 'linear elaboration of declarations' both N and B could be declared in the same declarative part but the declaration of N would have to precede that of B.

The discrete range in an array index follows similar rules to that in a for statement. An important one is that a range such as 1 .. 6 implies type INTEGER so we could have written

```
A: array (1 .. 6) of REAL;
```

However, an array index could be of any discrete type. We could for example have

```
HOURS_WORKED: array (DAY) of REAL;
```

This array has seven components denoted by HOURS_WORKED(MON), ... HOURS_WORKED(SUN). We could set suitable values in these variables by

```
for D in WEEKDAY loop
    HOURS_WORKED(D):=8.0;
end loop;
HOURS_WORKED(SAT):=0.0;
HOURS_WORKED(SUN):=0.0;
```

If we only wanted to declare the array HOURS_WORKED to have components corresponding to MON .. FRI then we could write

```
HOURS_WORKED: array (DAY range MON .. FRI) of REAL;
```

or (better)

```
HOURS_WORKED: array (WEEKDAY) of REAL;
```

Arrays have various attributes relating to their indexes. A'FIRST and A'LAST give the lower and upper bound of the first (or only) index of A. So using our last declaration of HOURS_WORKED

```
HOURS_WORKED'FIRST = MON
HOURS_WORKED'LAST = FRI
```

A'LENGTH gives the number of values of the first (or only) index.

HOURS_WORKED'LENGTH = 5

A'RANGE is short for **A'FIRST .. A'LAST**. So

HOURS_WORKED'RANGE is MON .. FRI

The same attributes can be applied to the various dimensions of a multi-dimensional array by adding the dimension number in brackets. It has to be a static expression. So, in the case of our two dimensional array **AA** we have

```
AA'FIRST(1)   = 0
AA'FIRST(2)   = 0
AA'LAST(1)    = 2
AA'LAST(2)    = 3
AA'LENGTH(1)  = 3
AA'LENGTH(2)  = 4
```

and

```
AA'RANGE(1) is 0 .. 2
AA'RANGE(2) is 0 .. 3
```

The first dimension is assumed if (1) is omitted. It is perhaps better practice to specifically state (1) for multidimensional arrays and omit it for one dimensional arrays.

It is always best to use the attributes where possible in order to reflect relationships among entities in a program because it generally means that if the program is modified, the modifications are localised.

The **RANGE** attribute is particularly useful with loops. Our earlier examples are better written as

```
for I in A'RANGE loop
    A(I):=0.0;
end loop;

for I in AA'RANGE(1) loop
    for J in AA'RANGE(2) loop
        AA(I, J):=0.0;
    end loop;
end loop;
```

The **RANGE** attribute can also be used in a declaration. Thus

J: INTEGER **range** A'RANGE;

is equivalent to

J: INTEGER **range** 1 .. 6;

If a variable is to be used to index an array as in A(J) it is usually best if the variable has the same constraints as the discrete range in the array declaration. This will usually minimise the run time checks necessary. It has been found that in such circumstances it is usually the case that the index variable J is assigned less frequently than the array component A(J) is accessed.

The array components we have seen are just variables in the ordinary way. They can therefore be assigned to and used in expressions.

Like other variable objects, arrays can be given an initial value. This will often be denoted by an aggregate which is the literal form for an array value. The simplest form of aggregate consists of a list of expressions giving the values of the components in order, separated by commas and enclosed in brackets. So we could initialise the array A by

    A: **array** (1 .. 6) **of** REAL:=(0.0, 0.0, 0.0, 0.0, 0.0, 0.0);

In the case of a multidimensional array the aggregate is written in a nested form

    AA: **array** (0 .. 2, 0 .. 3) **of** REAL:= ((0.0, 0.0, 0.0, 0.0),
                                                  (0.0, 0.0, 0.0, 0.0),
                                                  (0.0, 0.0, 0.0, 0.0));

An aggregate must be complete. If we initialise any component of an array, we must initialise them all.

The initial values for the individual components need not be literals, they can be any expressions. These expressions are evaluated when the declaration is elaborated but the order of evaluation of the expressions in the aggregate is not specified.

An array can be declared as constant in which case an initial value is mandatory. Constant arrays are of frequent value as look-up tables. The following array can be used to determine whether a particular day is a working day or not

    WORK_DAY: **constant array** (DAY) **of** BOOLEAN
              := (TRUE, TRUE, TRUE, TRUE, TRUE, FALSE, FALSE);

An interesting example would be an array enabling tomorrow to be determined without worrying about the end of the week.

    TOMORROW: **constant array** (DAY) **of** DAY
              := (TUE, WED, THU, FRI, SAT, SUN, MON);

For any day D, TOMORROW (D) is the following day.

Finally, it should be noted that the array components can be of any type or subtype. Also the dimensions of a multidimensional array can be of different discrete types. An extreme example would be

    STRANGE: **array** (COLOUR, 2 .. 7, WEEKDAY **range** TUE .. THU)
             of PLANET **range** MARS .. SATURN;

Exercise 6.1

1 Declare an array F of integers with index running from 0 to N. Write statements to set the components of F equal to the Fibonacci numbers given by

$$F_0 = 0, \quad F_1 = 1, \quad F_i = F_{i-1} + F_{i-2}$$

2 Write statements to find the index values I, J of the maximum component of

A: **array** (1 .. N, 1 .. M) **of** REAL;

3 Declare an array DAYS_IN_MONTH giving the number of days in each month. See Exercise 5.1 (**1**). Use it to rewrite that example. See also Exercise 5.2 (**1**).

4 Declare an array YESTERDAY analogous to the example TOMORROW above.

5 Declare a constant array BOR such that

BOR(P, Q) = P **or** Q

6 Declare a constant unit matrix UNIT of order 3. A unit matrix is one for which all components are zero except those whose indexes are equal which have value one.

6.2   Array types

The arrays we introduced in the last section did not have an explicit type name. They were in fact of anonymous type. This is one of the few cases in Ada where an object can be declared without naming the type – another case is with tasks.

Reconsidering the first example in the previous section, we could write

type VECTOR_6 **is array** (1 .. 6) **of** REAL;

and then declare A using the type name in the usual way

A: VECTOR_6;

An advantage of using a type name is that it enables us to assign whole arrays that have been declared separately. If we also have

B: VECTOR_6;

then we can write

B:=A;

which has the effect of

B(1):=A(1); B(2):=A(2); ... B(6):=A(6);

although the order of assigning the components is not relevant.

On the other hand if we had written

C: **array** (1 . . 6) **of** REAL;
D: **array** (1 . . 6) **of** REAL;

then D:=C; is illegal because C and D are not of the same type. They are of different types both of which are anonymous. The underlying rule is that every type definition introduces a new type and in this case the syntax tells us that an array type definition is the piece of text from **array** up to (but not including) the semicolon.

Moreover, even if we had written

C, D: **array** (1 . . 6) **of** REAL;

then D:=C; would still have been illegal. This is because of the rule mentioned in Section 4.1 that such a multiple declaration is only a shorthand for the two declarations above. There are therefore still two distinct type definitions even though they are not explicit.

Whether we introduce a type name for particular arrays depends very much on the abstract view of each situation. If we are thinking of the array as a complete object in its own right then we should use a type name. If on the other hand we are thinking of the array as merely an indexable conglomerate not related as a whole to other arrays then it should probably be of an anonymous type.

Arrays like TOMORROW and WORK_DAY of the last section are good examples of arrays which are of the anonymous category. To be forced to introduce a type name for such arrays would introduce unnecessary clutter and a possibly false sense of abstraction.

On the other hand if we are manipulating lots of arrays of reals of length 6 then there is a common underlying abstract type and so it should be named.

The model for array types introduced so far is still not satisfactory. It does not allow us to represent an abstract view that embraces the commonality between arrays which have different bounds but are otherwise of the same type. In particular, it would not allow the writing of subprograms which could take an array of arbitrary bounds as an actual parameter. This is generally recognised as a major difficulty with Pascal. So the concept of an unconstrained array type is introduced in which the constraints for the indexes are not given. Consider

type VECTOR **is array** (INTEGER **range** <>) **of** REAL;

(The compound symbol <> is read as 'box'.)

This says that VECTOR is the name of a type which is a one dimensional array of REAL components with an INTEGER index. But the lower and upper bounds are not given; **range** <> is meant to convey the notion of information to be added later.

When we declare objects of type VECTOR we must supply the bounds. We can do this in various ways. We can introduce an intermediate subtype and then declare the objects

subtype VECTOR_5 **is** VECTOR(1 . . 5);
V: VECTOR_5;

Or we can declare the objects directly

V: VECTOR(1 . . 5);

In either case the bounds are given by an index constraint which takes the form of a discrete range in brackets. All the usual forms of discrete range can be used.

The index can also be given by a subtype name, thus

type P **is array** (POSITIVE **range** <>) **of** REAL;

in which case the actual bounds of any declared object must lie within the range implied by the index subtype POSITIVE. Note that the index subtype must be given by a type mark and not by a subtype indication.

We can now see that when we wrote

type VECTOR_6 **is array** (1 . . 6) **of** REAL;

this was really a shorthand for

subtype index **is** INTEGER **range** 1 . . 6;
type anon **is array** (index **range** <>) **of** REAL;
subtype VECTOR_6 **is** anon (1 . . 6);

Another useful array type declaration is

type MATRIX **is array** (INTEGER **range** <> , INTEGER **range** <>)
                    of REAL;

And again we could introduce subtypes thus

subtype MATRIX_3 **is** MATRIX(1 . . 3, 1 . . 3);
M: MATRIX_3;

or the objects directly

M: MATRIX(1 . . 3, 1 . . 3);

An important point to notice is that an array type or subtype must give all the bounds or none at all. It would be perfectly legal to introduce an alternative name for MATRIX by

subtype MAT **is** MATRIX;

in which no bounds are given, but we could not have a type or subtype that just gave the bounds for one dimension but not the other.

In all of the cases we have been discussing, the ranges need not have static bounds. The bounds could be any expressions and are evaluated when the index constraint is encountered. We could have

M: MATRIX(1 . . N, 1 . . N);

and then the upper bounds of M would be the value of N when M is declared. A range could even be null as would happen in the above case if N turned out to be zero. In this case the matrix M would have no components at all.

There is a further way in which the bounds of an array can be supplied but this only applies to constant arrays which like other constants have to be given an initial value. The bounds can then be taken from the initial value if they are not supplied directly. The initial value can be any expression of the appropriate type but will often be an aggregate as shown in the previous section. The form of aggregate shown there consisted of a list of expressions in brackets. Such an aggregate is known as a positional aggregate since the values are given in position order. In the case of a positional aggregate used as an initial value and supplying the bounds, the lower bound is S'FIRST where S is the subtype of the index. The upper bound is deduced from the number of components. (The bounds of positional aggregates in other contexts will be discussed in a moment.)

Suppose we had

```
type W is array (WEEKDAY range <> ) of DAY;
NEXT_WORK_DAY: constant W:= (TUE, WED, THU, FRI, MON);
```

then the lower bound of the array is WEEKDAY'FIRST = MON and the upper bound is FRI. It would not have mattered whether we had written DAY or WEEKDAY in the declaration of W because DAY'FIRST and WEEKDAY'FIRST are the same.

Using initial values to supply the bounds needs care. Consider

```
UNIT_2: constant MATRIX:= ((1.0, 0.0), (0.0, 1.0));
```

intended to declare a 2×2 unit matrix with UNIT_2(1, 1) = UNIT_2(2, 2) = 1.0 and UNIT_2(1, 2) = UNIT_2(2, 1) = 0.0.

But disaster! We have actually declared an array whose lower bounds are INTEGER'FIRST which is probably -32768 or some such number but is certainly not 1.

If we declared the type MATRIX as

```
type MATRIX is array (POSITIVE range <>, POSITIVE range <> )
                of REAL;
```

then all would have been well since POSITIVE'FIRST = 1.

So array bounds deduced from an initial value may lead to surprises.

There is another form of aggregate known as a named aggregate in which the component values are preceded by the corresponding index value and =>. A simple example would be

```
(1 => 0.0, 2=> 0.0, 3=> 0.0, 4=> 0.0, 5=> 0.0, 6 => 0.0)
```

with the expected extension to several dimensions. The bounds of such an aggregate are self evident and so our problem with the unit 2×2 matrix could be overcome by writing

```
UNIT_2: constant MATRIX:= (1=>(1 => 1.0, 2 => 0.0),
                           2 =>(1=> 0.0, 2 => 1.0));
```

The rules for named aggregates are very similar to the rules for the alternatives in a case statement.

Each choice can be given as a series of alternatives each of which can be a single value or a discrete range. We could therefore rewrite some previous examples as follows

A: **array** (1 .. 6) **of** REAL:=(1 .. 6 => 0.0);

WORK_DAY: **constant array** (DAY) **of** BOOLEAN
　　　　　:= (MON .. FRI => TRUE, SAT|SUN => FALSE);

In contrast to a positional aggregate, the index values need not appear in order. We could equally have written

(SAT|SUN => FALSE, MON .. FRI => TRUE)

We can also use **others** but then as for the case statement it must be last and on its own.

The use of **others** raises some problems since it must be clear what the totality of values is. It should also be realised that although we have been showing aggregates as initial values, they can be used quite generally in any place where an expression of an array type is required. It is therefore necessary that the context supplies the bounds if **others** is used. One way of supplying the context is by qualifying the aggregate as we did to distinguish between overloaded enumeration literals. In order to do this we must have an appropriate type or subtype name. So we introduce

type SCHEDULE **is array** (DAY) **of** BOOLEAN;

and can then write

SCHEDULE'(MON .. FRI=> TRUE, **others**=> FALSE)

(Note that when qualifying an aggregate we do not, as for an expression, need to put it in brackets because it already has brackets.)

Other acceptable contexts which supply the bounds will be met in due course when we discuss subprogram parameters and results in Chapter 7 and generic parameters in Chapter 13.

These same contexts will also supply the bounds of a positional aggregate; like a named aggregate with **others**, a positional aggregate does not have self evident bounds. However, in other contexts such as the initial value discussed above, all is not lost in the case of a positional aggregate since the lower bound is then taken to be S'FIRST where S is the index subtype and the upper bound is then deduced from the number of components. Of course a named aggregate with **others** cannot use such a rule since the number of components represented by **others** is not known and so such an aggregate would then be illegal.

Array aggregates may not mix positional and named notation except that **others** may be used at the end of a positional aggregate. Such a positional aggregate then follows the general rules for a named aggregate with **others**.

Very surprisingly the context of an assignment or an initial value with the bounds given by the type is anomalous and only considered able to supply the bounds in the case of a positional aggregate with or without **others** or a named aggregate with **others** as the only choice. It is not considered adequate for the common case of a named aggregate containing choices in addition to **others.** So we cannot write

```
WORK_DAY: constant array (DAY) of BOOLEAN
         :=(MON .. FRI => TRUE, others => FALSE);
```

but must instead write

```
WORK_DAY: constant array (DAY) of BOOLEAN
         :=(TRUE, TRUE, TRUE, TRUE, TRUE, others=> FALSE);
```

or use a type name and write

```
WORK_DAY: constant SCHEDULE
         := SCHEDULE'(MON .. FRI => TRUE, others => FALSE);
```

The rules regarding the bounds of array aggregates seem horrendously and pointlessly difficult and to be one of the most curious aspects of Ada. However, if you are very confused, do not be too worried; an aggregate can always be qualified if in doubt.

Array aggregates really are rather complicated and we still have a few points to make. The first is that in a named aggregate all the ranges and values before => must be static (as in a case statement) except for one special situation. This is where there is only one alternative consisting of a single choice – it could then be a dynamic range or (unlikely) a single dynamic value. An example might be

```
A: array (1 .. N) of INTEGER:= (1 .. N => 0);
```

This is valid even if N is zero (or negative) and then gives a null array and a null aggregate. The following example illustrates a general rule that the expression after => is evaluated once for each corresponding index value; of course it usually makes no difference but consider

```
A: array (1 .. N) of INTEGER:=(1 .. N => 1/N);
```

If N is zero then there are no values and so 1/N is not evaluated and NUMERIC_ERROR cannot occur. The reader will recall that a similar multiple evaluation also occurs when several objects are declared and initialised together.

In order to avoid awkward problems with null aggregates, a null choice is only allowed if it is the only choice. Foolish aggregates such as

```
(7 .. 6 | 1 .. 0 => 0)
```

are thus forbidden and there is no question of the lower bound of such an aggregate.

Another point is that although we cannot mix named and positional notation within an aggregate, we can, however, use different forms for the different components and levels of a multidimensional aggregate. So the initial value of our matrix UNIT_2 could also be written as

```
(1 => (1.0, 0.0),      or      ((1 => 1.0, 2 => 0.0),
 2 => (0.0, 1.0))               (1 => 0.0, 2 => 1.0))
```

or even as

```
(1 => (1 => 1.0, 2 => 0.0),
 2 => (     0.0,      1.0))
```

and so on.

Note also that the RANGE attribute stands for a range and therefore can be used as one of the choices in a named aggregate. However, we cannot use the range attribute of an object in its own initial value. Thus

```
A: array (1 .. N) of INTEGER:= (A'RANGE => 0);
```

is illegal. This is because an object is not visible until the end of its declaration. However we could write

```
A: array (1 .. N) of INTEGER:= (others => 0);
```

and this is probably better than repeating 1 .. N because it localises the dependency on N.

A final point is that a positional aggregate cannot contain just one component because otherwise it would be ambiguous. We could not distinguish an aggregate of one component from a scalar value which happened to be in brackets. An aggregate of one component must therefore use the named notation.

We continue by returning to the topic of whole array assignment. In order to perform such assignment it is necessary that the array value and the array being assigned to have the same type and that the components can be matched. This does not mean that the bounds have to be equal but merely that the number of components in corresponding dimensions is the same. So we can write

```
V: VECTOR(1 .. 5);
W: VECTOR(0 .. 4);
. . .
V:=W;
```

Both V and W are of type VECTOR and both have 5 components.

It is also valid to have

```
P: MATRIX(0 .. 1, 0 .. 1);
Q: MATRIX(6 .. 7, N .. N+1);
. . .
P:=Q;
```

Equality and inequality of arrays follow similar rules to assignment. Two arrays may only be compared if they are of the same type. They are equal if corresponding dimensions have the same number of components and the matching components are themselves equal.

Although assignment and equality can only occur if the arrays are of the same type, nevertheless an array value of one type can be converted to another type if the component types and index types are the same. The usual notation for type conversion is used. So if we have

```
type VECTOR is array (INTEGER range <>) of REAL;
type ROW    is array (INTEGER range <>) of REAL;

V: VECTOR(1 . . 5);
R: ROW(0 . . 4);
```

then

```
R: =ROW(V);
```

is valid. In fact, since ROW is an unconstrained type, the bounds of ROW(V) are those of V. The normal assignment rules then apply. However, if the conversion uses a constrained type or subtype then the bounds are those of the type or subtype and the number of components in corresponding dimensions must be the same. Array type conversion is of particular value when subprograms from different libraries are used together as we shall see later.

The reader will by now have concluded that arrays in Ada are somewhat complicated. That is a fair judgement, but in practice there should be few difficulties. There is always the safeguard that if we do something wrong, the compiler will inevitably tell us. In cases of ambiguity, qualification solves the problems provided we have an appropriate type or subtype name to use. Much of the complexity with aggregates is similar to that in the case statement.

We conclude this section by observing that the attributes FIRST, LAST, LENGTH and RANGE, as well as applying to array objects, may also be applied to array types and subtypes provided they are constrained (i.e. have their bounds given). So

```
VECTOR_6'LENGTH = 6
```

but

```
VECTOR'LENGTH      is illegal
```

Exercise 6.2

1 Rewrite the declaration of the array DAYS_IN_MONTH in Exercise 6.1(**3**) using a named aggregate for an initial value.

2 Declare a constant MATRIX whose bounds are both 1 . . N where N is dynamic and whose components are all zero.

3 Declare a constant MATRIX as in **2** but make it a unit matrix.

4 Declare an array type **BBB** corresponding to the array **BOR** of Exercise 6.1(**5**).

6.3 Characters and strings

We now complete our discussion of enumeration types by introducing character types. In the enumeration types seen so far such as

type COLOUR **is** (RED, AMBER, GREEN);

the values have been represented by identifiers. It is also possible to have an enumeration type in which some or all of the values are represented by character literals.

A character literal is a further form of lexical element. It consists of a single character within a pair of single quotes. The character must be one of the printable characters or it could be a single space. It must not be a control character such as horizontal tabulate or new line.

This is a situation where there is a distinction between upper and lower case letters. The character literals

'A',   'a'

are different.

So we could declare an enumeration type

type ROMAN_DIGIT **is** ('I', 'V', 'X', 'L', 'C', 'D', 'M');

and then

DIG: ROMAN_DIGIT:='D';

All the usual properties of enumeration types apply.

ROMAN_DIGIT'FIRST = 'I'
ROMAN_DIGIT'SUCC('X') = 'L'
ROMAN_DIGIT'POS('M') = 6

DIG < 'L' = FALSE

There is a predefined enumeration type **CHARACTER** which is (naturally) a character type. We can think of its declaration as being of the form

type CHARACTER **is** (*nul*, . . . , 'A', 'B', 'C' . . ., *del*);

but for technical reasons which cannot be explained here the literals which are not actual character literals (such as *nul*) are not really identifiers either (which is why they are represented here in italics). It is however possible to refer to them as ASCII.NUL and so on (or under suitable circumstances to be discussed later as simply NUL). This predefined type **CHARACTER** represents the standard ASCII character set and describes the set of characters normally used for input and output. It is unfortunate that the type **CHARACTER** is hedged around with subtleties but in practice these do not matter. For details the reader is referred to the LRM.

It should be noted that the introduction of both the type ROMAN_DIGIT and the predefined type CHARACTER results in overloading of some of the literals. An expression such as

'X' < 'L'

is ambiguous. We do not know whether we are comparing characters of the type ROMAN_DIGIT or CHARACTER. In order to resolve the ambiguity we must qualify one or both literals

CHARACTER'('X') < 'L' = FALSE
ROMAN_DIGIT'('X') < 'L' = TRUE

As well as the predefined type CHARACTER there is also the predefined type STRING

type STRING is array (POSITIVE range <>) of CHARACTER;

This is a perfectly normal array type and obeys all the rules of the previous section. So we can write

S: STRING (1 .. 7);

to declare an array of range 1 .. 7. In the case of a constant array the bounds can be deduced from the initial value thus

G: constant STRING:= ('P', 'I', 'G');

where the initial value takes the form of a normal positional aggregate. The lower bound of G (i.e. G'FIRST) is 1 since the index type of STRING is POSITIVE and POSITIVE'FIRST is 1.

An alternative notation is provided for a positional aggregate each of whose components is a character literal. This is the string. So we could more conveniently write

G: constant STRING:= "PIG";

The string is the last lexical element to be introduced. It consists of a sequence of printable characters and spaces enclosed in double quotes. A double quote may be represented in a string by two double quotes so that

('A', ' " ', 'B') = "A" "B"

The string may also have just one character or may be null. The equivalent aggregates using character literals have to be written in named notation.

(1 => 'A')= "A"
(1 .. 0 => 'A') = " "

Note how we have to introduce an arbitrary character in the null named form. Ada has some strange quirks!

Another rule about a lexical string is that it must fit onto a single line. Moreover it cannot contain control characters such as SOH. And, of course, as with character literals, the two cases of alphabet are distinct in strings

"PIG" /= "pig"

In the next section we will see how to overcome the limitations that a string must fit onto a single line and cannot contain control characters.

A major use for strings is, of course, for creating text to be output. A simple sequence of characters can be output by a call of the (overloaded) subprogram PUT. Thus

PUT ("The Countess of Lovelace");

will output the text

The Countess of Lovelace

onto some appropriate file.

However, the lexical string is not reserved just for use with the built-in type STRING. It can be used to represent an array of any character type. We can write

```
type ROMAN_NUMBER is array (POSITIVE range <> ) of
                       ROMAN_DIGIT;
```

and then

```
NINETEEN_EIGHTY_FOUR: constant ROMAN_NUMBER
                  :="MCMLXXXIV";
```

or indeed

```
FOUR: array (1 .. 2) of ROMAN_DIGIT:= "IV";
```

Exercise 6.3

1 Declare a constant array ROMAN_TO_INTEGER which can be used for table look-up to convert a ROMAN_DIGIT to its normal integer equivalent (e.g. converts 'C' to 100).

2 Given an object R of type ROMAN_NUMBER write statements to compute the equivalent integer value V. It may be assumed that R obeys the normal rules of construction of Roman numbers.

6.4 One dimensional array operations

Many of the operators that we met in Chapter 4 may also be applied to one dimensional arrays.

The Boolean operators **and**, **or**, **xor** and **not** may be applied to one dimensional Boolean arrays. In the case of the binary operators, the two operands must have the same number of components and be of the same type. The underlying scalar operation is applied component by component and the resulting array is again of the same type. The lower bound of the index of the result is equal to the lower bound of the subtype of the left or only operand.

Consider

```
type BIT_ROW is array (POSITIVE range <> ) of BOOLEAN;
A, B: BIT_ROW(1 . . 4);
C, D: array (1 . . 4) of BOOLEAN;
T: constant BOOLEAN:= TRUE;
F: constant BOOLEAN:= FALSE;
```

then we can write

```
A:= (T, T, F, F);
B:= (T, F, T, F);

A:= A and B;
B:= not B;
```

and A now equals (T, F, F, F), and B equals (F, T, F, T). Similarly for **or** and **xor**. But note that **C and D** would not be allowed because they are of different types. This is clearly a case where it is appropriate to give a name to the array type because we are manipulating the arrays as complete objects.

Note that these operators, like assignment as explained in Section 6.2, only demand that the types and the number of components are the same. The bounds themselves do not have to be equal.

Boolean arrays can be used to represent sets. Consider

```
type PRIMARY is (R, Y, B);
type COLOUR is array (PRIMARY) of BOOLEAN;
C: COLOUR;
```

then there are $8 = 2 \times 2 \times 2$ values that C can take. C is, of course, an array with three components and each of these has value TRUE or FALSE; the three components are

```
C(R),    C(Y)    and    C(B)
```

The 8 possible values of the type COLOUR can be represented by suitably named constants as follows

```
WHITE   : constant COLOUR:=(F, F, F);
RED     : constant COLOUR:=(T, F, F);
YELLOW  : constant COLOUR:=(F, T, F);
BLUE    : constant COLOUR:=(F, F, T);
GREEN   : constant COLOUR:=(F, T, T);
PURPLE  : constant COLOUR:=(T, F, T);
ORANGE  : constant COLOUR:=(T, T, F);
BLACK   : constant COLOUR:=(T, T, T);
```

and then we can write expressions such as

RED **or** YELLOW

which is equal to ORANGE and

not BLACK

which is WHITE.

So the values of our type COLOUR are effectively the set of colours obtained by taking all combinations of the primary colours represented by R, Y, B. The empty set is the value of WHITE and the full set is the value of BLACK.

The operations **or**, **and** and **xor** may be interpreted as set union, set intersection and symmetric difference. A test for set membership can be made by inspecting the value of the appropriate component of the set. Thus

C(R)

is TRUE if R is in the set represented by C. We cannot use the predefined operation **in** for this. A literal value can be represented using the named aggregate notation, so

(R | Y => T, **others** => F)

has the same value as ORANGE. A more elegant way of doing this will appear in the next chapter.

We now consider the equality and relational operators. The operators = and / = apply to all types anyway and we gave the rules for arrays when we discussed assignment in Section 6.2.

The relational operators <, <=, > and >= may be applied to one dimensional arrays of a discrete type. (Note discrete.) The result of the comparision is based upon the lexicographic (i.e. dictionary) order using the defined order relation for the components. This is best illustrated with strings which we assume for the moment are unambiguously values of the type STRING. The following are all TRUE

```
"CAT" < "DOG"
"CAT" < "CATERPILLAR"
"AZZ" < "B"
" "    < "A"
```

The strings are compared component by component until they differ in some position. The string with the lower component is then lower. If one string runs out of components as in CAT *versus* CATERPILLAR then the shorter one is lower. The null string is lowest of all.

If we assume that we have declared our type ROMAN_NUMBER then

"CCL" < "CCXC"

is ambiguous since we do not know whether we are comparing type STRING or type ROMAN_NUMBER. We must qualify one or both of the strings. This is done in the usual way but a string, unlike the bracketed form of aggregates, has to be placed in brackets otherwise we would get an ugly juxtaposition of a single and double quote. So

```
STRING'("CCL") < "CCXC"              is TRUE
ROMAN_NUMBER'("CCL") < "CCXC"        is FALSE
```

Note that our compiler is too stupid to know about the interpretation of Roman numbers in our minds and has said that 250 < 290 is false. The only thing that matters is the order relation of the characters 'L' and 'X' in the type definition. In the next chapter we will show how we can redefine < so that it works 'properly' for Roman numbers.

Of course, the relational operators also apply to general expressions and not just to literal strings.

```
NINETEEN_EIGHTY_FOUR < "MM"       is TRUE
```

The relational operators can be applied to arrays of any discrete types. So

```
(1, 2, 3) < (2, 3)
(JAN, JAN) < (1 => FEB)
```

The predefined operators <=, > and >= are defined by analogy with <.

We now introduce a new binary operator & which denotes catenation (or concatenation) of one dimensional arrays. It has the same precedence as binary plus and minus. The two operands must be of the same type and the result is an array of the same type whose value is obtained by juxtaposing the two operands. The lower bound of the result is, as usual, the lower bound of the left operand. So

```
"CAT" & "ERPILLAR" = "CATERPILLAR"
```

String catenation can be used to construct a string which is too long to fit on one line

```
"This string goes " &
"on and on"
```

One or both operands of & can also be a single value of the component type. If the left operand is such a single value then the lower bound of the result is the lower bound of the subtype of the array index.

```
"CAT" & 'S' = "CATS"
'S' & "CAT" = "SCAT"
'S' & 'S' = "SS"
```

This is useful for representing the control characters such as CR and LF in strings.

```
"First line" & ASCII.CR & ASCII.LF & "Next line"
```

Of course, it might be neater to declare

Wkdays
M-F 9⁰⁰ – 10⁰⁰ pm

9⁰⁰ – 5⁰⁰
12⁰⁰ – 10⁰⁰

Basement library
Pond side doors

10,828
2,166
8,662

CRLF: **constant** STRING:= (ASCII.CR, ASCII.LF);

and then write

"First line" & CRLF & "Next line"

The operation **&** can be applied to any one dimensional array type and so we can apply it to our Roman numbers. Consider

R: ROMAN_NUMBER (1 . . 5);
S: STRING (1 . . 5);

R:="CCL" & "IV";
S:="CCL" & "IV";

This is valid. The context tells us that in the first case we apply **&** to two Roman numbers whereas in the second we apply it to two values of type **STRING**. There is no ambiguity as in

B: BOOLEAN:= "CCL" < "IV";

The final special feature of one dimensional arrays is the ability to denote a slice of an array object. A slice is written as the name of the object (variable or constant) followed by a discrete range in brackets.
So given

S: STRING(1 . . 10);

then we can write S(3 . . 8) to denote the middle six characters of S. The bounds of the slice are the bounds of the range and not those of the index subtype. We could write

T: **constant** STRING:=S(3 . . 8);

and then T'FIRST = 3, T'LAST = 8.
The bounds of the slice need not be static but can be any expressions. A slice would be null if the range turned out to be null.
The use of slices emphasises the nature of array assignment. The value of the expression to be assigned is completely evaluated before any components are assigned. No problems arise with overlapping slices. So

S(1 . . 4):= "BARA";
S(4 . . 7):=S(1 . . 4);

results in S(1 . . 7) = "BARBARA". S(4) is only updated after the expression S(1 . . 4) is safely evaluated. There is no risk of setting S(4) to 'B' and then consequently making the expression "BARB" with the final result of

"BARBARB"

Exercise 6.4

1 Write the 8 possible constants WHITE . . . BLACK of the type COLOUR in ascending order as determined by the operator < applied to one dimensional arrays.

2 Evaluate

   a) RED **or** GREEN   c) **not** GREEN
   b) BLACK **xor** RED

3 Show that **not** (BLACK **xor** C) = C is true for all values of C.

4 Why did we not write

   (JAN, JAN) < (FEB)

5 Assume that R contains a Roman number. Write statements to see if the last digit of the corresponding decimal arabic value is a 4 and change it to a 6 if it is.

6 Given

   C: CHARACTER;
   S: STRING(5 . . 10);

what is the lower bound of

   a) C & S   b) S & C

6.5 Records

As stated at the beginning of this chapter we are only going to consider the simplest form of record at this point. A fuller treatment covering variant records and so on is left until Chapter 11.

A record is a composite object consisting of named components which may be of different types. In contrast to arrays, we cannot have anonymous record types − they all have to be named. Consider

```
type MONTH_NAME is (JAN, FEB, MAR, APR, MAY, JUN, JUL,
                    AUG, SEP, OCT, NOV, DEC);

type  DATE is
    record
        DAY: INTEGER range 1 .. 31;
        MONTH: MONTH_NAME;
        YEAR: INTEGER;
    end record;
```

This declares the type DATE to be a record containing three named components, DAY, MONTH and YEAR.

We can declare variables and constants of record types in the usual way.

```
D: DATE;
```

declares an object D which is a date. The individual components of D can be denoted by following D with a dot and the component name. Thus we could write

```
D.DAY:=4;
D.MONTH:=JUL;
D.YEAR:= 1776;
```

in order to assign new values to the individual components.

Records can be manipulated as whole objects. Literal values can be written as aggregates much like arrays; both positional and named forms can be used. So we could write

```
D: DATE:= (4, JUL, 1776);
E: DATE;
```

and then

```
E:= D;
```

or

```
E:= (MONTH => JUL, DAY => 4, YEAR => 1776);
```

The reader will be relieved to know that much of the complexity of array aggregates does not apply to records. This is because the number of components is always known.

In a positional aggregate the components come in order. In a named aggregate they may be in any order. In the particular example shown the use of a named aggregate avoids the necessity to know on which side of the Atlantic the record type was declared.

A named aggregate cannot use a range because the components are not considered to be closely related and the vertical bar can only be used with components which do have the same type. The choice **others** can be used but again only when the remaining components are of the same type.

There is one extra possibility for records and that is that the positional and named notations can be mixed in one aggregate. But if this is done then the positional components must come first and in order (without holes) as usual. So in other words we can change to the named notation at any point in the aggregate but must then stick to it. The above date could therefore also be expressed as

```
(4, JUL, YEAR => 1776)
(4, YEAR => 1776, MONTH => JUL)
```

and so on.

It is possible to give default expressions for some or all of the components in the type declaration. Thus

```
type COMPLEX is
    record
        RL: REAL:=0.0;
        IM: REAL:=0.0;
    end record;
```

or more succinctly

```
type COMPLEX is
    record
        RL, IM: REAL:=0.0;
    end record;
```

declares a record type containing two components of type REAL and gives a default expression of 0.0 for each. We can now declare

```
C1: COMPLEX;
C2: COMPLEX:= (1.0, 0.0);
```

The object C1 will now have the values 0.0 for its components by default. In the case of C2 we have overridden the default values. Note that, irritatingly, even if there are default expressions, an aggregate must be complete even if it supplies the same values as the default expressions for some of the components.

In this case both components are the same type and so the following named forms are possible

```
(RL | IM => 1.0)
(others => 1.0)
```

The only operations predefined on record types are = and /= as well as assignment of course. Other operations must be performed at the component level or be explicitly defined by a subprogram as we shall see in the next chapter.

A record type may have any number of components. It may pathologically have none in which case its declaration takes the form

```
type HOLE is
    record
        null;
    end record;
```

The reserved word **null** confirms that we meant to declare a null record type. Null records have their uses but they will not be apparent yet.

The components of a record type can be of any type; they can be other records or arrays. However, if a component is an array then it must be fully constrained (i.e. its index must not contain <>) and it must be of a named type and not an anonymous type. And obviously a record cannot contain an instance of itself.

The components cannot be constants but the record as a whole can be. Thus

```
I: constant COMPLEX:= (0.0, 1.0);
```

is allowed and represents the square root of -1.

A more elaborate example of a record is

```
type PERSON is
    record
        BIRTH: DATE;
        NAME: STRING (1 . . 20):= (1 . . 20 =>  ' ');
    end record;
```

The record PERSON has two components, the first is another record, a DATE, the second an array. The array which is a string of length 20 has a default value of all spaces.

We can now write

```
JOHN: PERSON;
JOHN.BIRTH:= (19, AUG, 1937);
JOHN.NAME(1 . . 4):="JOHN";
```

and we would then have

```
JOHN = ((19, AUG, 1937), "JOHN                    ")
```

The notation is as expected. The aggregates nest and for objects we proceed from left to right using the dot notation to select components of a record and indexes in brackets to select components of an array and ranges in brackets to slice arrays. There is no limit. We could have an array of persons

```
PEOPLE: array (1 . . N) of PERSON;
```

and then have

```
PEOPLE(6).BIRTH.DAY:=19;
PEOPLE(8).NAME(3):='H';
```

and so on.

A final point concerns the evaluation of expressions in a record declaration. An expression in a constraint applied to a component is evaluated when the record type is elaborated. So our type PERSON could have

```
NAME: STRING(1 . . N):= (others => ' ');
```

and the length of the component NAME will be the value of N when the type PERSON is elaborated. Of course, N need not be static and so if the type declaration is in a loop for example then each execution of the loop might give rise to a type with a different size component. However, for each elaboration of the record type declaration all objects of the type will have the same component size.

On the other hand, a default expression in a record type is only evaluated when an object of the type is declared and only then if no explicit initial value is provided. Of course, in simple cases, like our type COMPLEX, it makes no difference but it could bring surprises. For example suppose we write the component NAME as

```
NAME: STRING(1 .. N):=(1 .. N => ' ');
```

then the length of the component NAME is the value of N when the record type is declared whereas when a PERSON is subsequently declared without an initial value, the aggregate will be evaluated using the value of N which then applies. Of course, N may by then be different and so CONSTRAINT_ERROR will be raised. This is rather surprising; we do seem to have strayed into an odd backwater of Ada!

Exercise 6.5

1   Rewrite the solution to Exercise 6.1(**3**) using a variable D of type DATE rather than three individual variables.

2   Declare three variables C1, C2, and C3 of type COMPLEX. Write one or more statements to assign a) the sum, b) the product, of C1 and C2 to C3.

3   Write statements to find the index of the first person of the array PEOPLE born on or after January 1st, 1950.

Checklist 6

Array types can be anonymous, but records cannot.

Aggregates must always be complete.

Distinguish constrained array types from unconstrained array types (those with <>).

Named and positional notations cannot be mixed for array aggregates – they can for records.

An aggregate with **others** must have a context giving its bounds.

A choice in an array aggregate can only be dynamic or null if it is the only choice.

The attributes FIRST, LAST, LENGTH and RANGE apply to array objects and constrained array types and subtypes but not to unconstrained types and subtypes.

For array assignment to be valid, the number of components must be equal for each dimension – not the bounds.

The cases of alphabet are distinct in character literals and strings.

An aggregate with one component must use the named notation. This applies to records as well as to arrays.

A record component cannot be an anonymous array.

A default component expression is only evaluated when an uninitialised object is declared.

Chapter 7 SUBPROGRAMS

Subprograms are the conventional parameterised unit of programming. In Ada, subprograms fall into two categories: functions and procedures. Functions are called as components of expressions and return a result, whereas procedures are called as statements and do not return a result.

As we shall see, the actions to be performed when a subprogram is called are described by a subprogram body. Subprogram bodies are declared in the usual way in a declarative part which may for instance be in a block or indeed in another subprogram.

7.1 Functions

A function is a form of subprogram that can be called as part of an expression. In Chapter 4 we met examples of calls of functions such as DAY'SUCC, SQRT and so on.

We now consider the form of a function body which describes the statements to be executed when the function is called. For example the body of the function SQRT might have the form

```
function SQRT(X: REAL) return REAL is
    R: REAL;
begin
    -- compute value of SQRT(X) in R
    return R;
end SQRT;
```

All function bodies start with the reserved word **function** and the designator of the function being defined. If the function has parameters the designator is followed by a list of parameter specifications in brackets. If there are several specifications then they are separated by semicolons. Each specification gives the identifiers of one or more parameters followed by a colon and its type or subtype. The parameter list, if any, is then followed by the reserved word **return** and the type or subtype of the result of the function. In the case of both parameters and result the type or subtype must be given by a type mark and not by a subtype indication. This is an important example of a situation where an explicit constraint is not allowed; the reason will be mentioned later in this chapter.

The part of the body we have described so far is called the function specification. It specifies the function to the outside world in the sense of providing all the information needed to call the function.

After the specification comes **is** and then the body proper which is just like a block – it has a declarative part, **begin**, a sequence of statements, and then **end**. As for a block the declarative part can be empty but there must be at least one statement in the sequence of statements. Between **end** and the terminating semicolon we may repeat the designator of the function. This is optional but, if present, must correctly match the designator after **function**.

It is often necessary or just convenient to give the specification on its own but without the rest of the body. In such a case it is immediately followed by a semicolon and is then known as a function declaration. The uses of such declarations will be discussed later.

The formal parameters of a function act as local constants whose values are provided by the corresponding actual parameters. When the function is called the declarative part is elaborated in the usual way and then the statements are executed. A return statement is used to indicate the value of the function call and to return control back to the calling expression.

Thus considering our example suppose we had

```
S:=SQRT(T + 0.5);
```

then first T + 0.5 is evaluated and then SQRT is called. Within the body the parameter X behaves as a constant with the initial value given by T + 0.5. It is rather as if we had

```
X: constant REAL := T + 0.5;
```

The declaration of R is then elaborated. We then obey the sequence of statements and assume they compute the square root of X and assign it to R. The last statement is **return** R; this passes control back to the calling expression with the result of the function being the value of R. This value is then assigned to S.

The expression in a return statement can be of arbitrary complexity and must be of the same type as and satisfy any constraints implied by the type mark given in the function specification. If the constraints are violated then, of course, the exception CONSTRAINT_ERROR is raised.

A function body may have several return statements. The execution of any of them will terminate the function. Thus the function SIGN which takes an integer value and returns +1, 0 or −1 according to whether the parameter is positive, zero or negative could be written as

```
function SIGN(X: INTEGER) return INTEGER is
begin
    if X > 0 then
        return +1;
    elsif X < 0 then
        return −1;
    else
        return 0;
    end if;
end SIGN;
```

So we see that the last lexical statement of the body need not be a return statement since there is one in each branch of the if statement. Any attempt to 'run' into the final **end** will raise the exception PROGRAM_ERROR. This is our first example of a situation giving rise to PROGRAM_ERROR; this exception is generally used for situations which would violate the run time control structure.

It should be noted that each call of a function produces a new instance of any objects declared within it (including parameters of course) and these disappear when we leave the function. It is therefore possible for a function to be called recursively without any problems. So the factorial function could be declared as

```
function FACTORIAL(N: POSITIVE) return POSITIVE is
begin
    if N = 1 then
        return 1;
    else
        return N * FACTORIAL(N−1);
    end if;
end FACTORIAL;
```

If we write

```
F:=FACTORIAL(4);
```

then the function calls itself until, on the fourth call (with the other three calls all partly executed and waiting for the result of the call they did before doing the multiply) we find that N is 1 and the calls then all unwind and all the multiplications are performed.

Note that there is no need to check that the parameter N is positive since the parameter is of subtype POSITIVE. So calling FACTORIAL(−2) will result in CONSTRAINT_ERROR. Of course, FACTORIAL(10000) could result in the computer running out of space in which case STORAGE_ERROR would be raised. The more moderate call FACTORIAL(20) would probably raise NUMERIC_ERROR.

A formal parameter may be of any type but the type must have a name. It cannot be an anonymous type such as

```
array (1 .. 6) of REAL
```

In any event no actual parameter (other than an aggregate) could match such a formal parameter even if it were allowed since the actual and formal parameters must have the same type.

A formal parameter can, however, be an unconstrained array type such as

```
type VECTOR is array (INTEGER range <>) of REAL;
```

In such a case the bounds of the formal parameter are taken from those of the actual parameter.

Consider

```
function SUM(A: VECTOR) return REAL is
    RESULT: REAL:=0.0;
begin
```

```
        for I in A'RANGE loop
            RESULT:= RESULT + A(I);
        end loop;
        return RESULT;
    end SUM;
```

then we can write

```
    V: VECTOR(1 . . 4):=(1.0, 2.0, 3.0, 4.0);
    S: REAL;
    . . .
    S:=SUM(V);
```

The formal parameter A then takes the bounds of the actual parameter V. So for this call we have

```
    A'RANGE   is   1 . . 4
```

and the effect of the loop is to compute the sum of A(1), A(2), A(3) and A(4). The final value of RESULT which is returned and assigned to S is therefore 10.0.

The function SUM can be used to sum the components of a vector with any bounds. Ada overcomes one of the problems of Pascal which insists that array parameters have static bounds. Of course, an Ada function could have a constrained array type as a formal parameter. However, remember that we cannot apply the constraint in the parameter list using a subtype indication as in

```
    function SUM_6(A:VECTOR(1 . . 6)) return REAL
```

but must use the name of a constrained array type such as

```
    type VECTOR_6 is array (1 . . 6) of REAL;
```

as a type mark as in

```
    function SUM_6(A: VECTOR_6) return REAL
```

As another example consider

```
    function INNER(A, B: VECTOR) return REAL is
        RESULT: REAL:=0.0;
    begin
        for I in A'RANGE loop
            RESULT:=RESULT + A(I)*B(I);
        end loop;
        return RESULT;
    end INNER;
```

This computes the inner product of the two vectors A and B by adding together the sum of the products of corresponding components. This is our first example of a function with more than one parameter. Such a function is called by following the function name by a list of the expressions giving the values of the actual parameters separated by commas and in brackets. The order of evaluation of the actual parameters is not defined.

So

```
V : VECTOR(1 . . 3):=(1.0, 2.0, 3.0);
W: VECTOR(1 . . 3):=(2.0, 3.0, 4.0);
R : REAL;
. . .
R :=INNER(V, W);
```

results in R being assigned the value

$$1.0 * 2.0 + 2.0 * 3.0 + 3.0 * 4.0 = 20.0$$

Note that the function INNER is not written well since it does not check that the bounds of A and B are the same. It is not symmetric with respect to A and B since I takes (or tries to take) the values of the range A'RANGE irrespective of B'RANGE. So if the array W had bounds of 0 and 2, CONSTRAINT_ERROR would be raised on the third time round the loop. If the array W had bounds of 1 and 4 then no exception would be raised but the result might not be what we expected.

It would be nice to ensure the equality of the bounds by placing a constraint on B at the time of call but this cannot be done. The best we can do is simply check the bounds for equality inside the function body and perhaps explicitly raise CONSTRAINT_ERROR if they are not equal.

```
if A'FIRST /= B'FIRST or A'LAST /= B'LAST then
    raise CONSTRAINT_ERROR;
end if;
```

(The use of the raise statement is described in detail in Chapter 10).

We saw above that a formal parameter can be of an unconstrained array type. In a similar way the result of a function can be an array whose bounds are not known until the function is called. The result type can be an unconstrained array and the bounds are then obtained from the expression in the appropriate return statement.

As an example the following function returns a vector which has the same bounds as the parameter but whose component values are in the reverse order

```
function REV(X: VECTOR) return VECTOR is
    R: VECTOR(X'RANGE);
begin
    for I in X'RANGE loop
        R(I):= X(X'FIRST+X'LAST −I);
    end loop;
    return R;
end REV;
```

The variable R is declared to be of type VECTOR with the same bounds as X. Note how the loop reverses the value. The result takes the bounds of the expression R. Note that we have called the function REV rather than REVERSE; this is because **reverse** is a reserved word.

If a function returns a record or array value then a component can be immediately selected, indexed or sliced as appropriate without assigning the value to a variable. So we could write

REV(Y) (I)

which denotes the component indexed by I of the array returned by the call of REV.

It should be noted that a parameterless function call, like a parameterless procedure call, has no brackets. There is therefore a possible ambiguity between calling a function with one parameter and indexing the result of a parameterless call; such an ambiguity could be resolved by, for example, renaming the functions as will be described in Chapter 8.

Exercise 7.1

1 Write a function EVEN which returns TRUE or FALSE according to whether its INTEGER parameter is even or odd.

2 Rewrite the factorial function so that the parameter may be positive or zero but not negative. Remember that the value of FACTORIAL(0) is to be 1. Use the subtype NATURAL introduced in Section 4.5.

3 Write a function OUTER that forms the outer product of two vectors. The outer product C of two vectors A and B is a matrix such that $C_{ij} = A_i . B_j$.

4 Write a function MAKE_COLOUR which takes an array of values of type PRIMARY and returns the corresponding value of type COLOUR. See Section 6.4. Check that MAKE_COLOUR ((R, Y)) = ORANGE.

5 Write a function VALUE which takes a parameter of type ROMAN_NUMBER and returns the equivalent integer value. See Exercise 6.3(**2**).

6 Write a function MAKE_UNIT that takes a single parameter N and returns a unit $N \times N$ real matrix. Use the function to declare a constant unit $N \times N$ matrix. See Exercise 6.2(**3**).

7 Write a function GCD to return the greatest common divisor of two non-negative integers. Use Euclid's algorithm that

$$gcd\ (x, y) = gcd\ (y, x \bmod y) \qquad y \neq 0$$
$$gcd\ (x, 0) = x$$

Write the function using recursion and then rewrite it using a loop statement.

7.2 Operators

In the last section we carefully stated that a function body commenced with the reserved word **function** followed by the designator of the function. In all the examples of the last section the designator was in fact an identifier. However, it can also be a character string provided that the string is one of the following language operators in double quotes.

```
and   or   xor
=     <    <=      >       >=
+     −    &       abs     not
*     /    mod     rem     **
```

In such a case the function defines a new meaning of the operator concerned. As an example we can rewrite the function INNER of the last section as an operator.

```
function "*" (A, B: VECTOR) return REAL is
    RESULT: REAL:=0.0;
begin
    for I in A'RANGE loop
        RESULT:=RESULT + A(I)*B(I);
    end loop;
    return RESULT;
end "*";
```

We call this new function by the normal syntax of uses of the operator *. Thus instead of

```
R:=INNER(V, W);
```

we now write

```
R:=V*W;
```

This meaning of * is distinguished from the existing meanings of integer and real multiplication by the context provided by the types of the actual parameters V and W and the type required by R.

The giving of several meanings to an operator is another instance of overloading which we have already met with enumeration literals. The rules for the overloading of subprograms in general are discussed later in this chapter. It suffices to say at this point that any ambiguity can usually be resolved by qualification. Overloading of predefined operators is not new. It has existed in most programming languages for the past quarter century. What is new is the ability to define additional overloadings and indeed the use of the term 'overloading' is itself relatively new.

We can now see that the predefined meanings of all operators are as if there were a series of functions with declarations such as

```
function "+"(LEFT, RIGHT: INTEGER) return INTEGER;
function "<"(LEFT, RIGHT: INTEGER) return BOOLEAN;
function "<"(LEFT, RIGHT: BOOLEAN) return BOOLEAN;
```

Moreover, every time we declare a new type, new overloadings of some operators such as = and < may be created.

Although we can add new meanings to operators we cannot change the syntax of the call. Thus the number of parameters of "*" must always be two and the precedence cannot be changed and so on. The operators + and − are unusual in that a new definition can have either one parameter or two parameters according to whether it is to be called as a unary or binary operator. Thus the function SUM could be rewritten as

```
function "+"(A: VECTOR) return REAL is
    RESULT: REAL:=0.0;
begin
    for I in A'RANGE loop
        RESULT:=RESULT+A(I);
    end loop;
    return RESULT;
end "+";
```

and we would then write

```
S:=+V;
```

rather than

```
S:=SUM(V);
```

Function bodies whose designators are operators often contain interesting examples of uses of the operator being overloaded. Thus the body of "*" contains a use of * in A(I)*B(I). There is, of course, no ambiguity since the expressons A(I) and B(I) are of type REAL whereas our new overloading is for type VECTOR. Sometimes there is the risk of accidental recursion. This particularly applies if we try to replace an existing meaning rather than add a new one.

Apart from the operator "=" there are no special rules regarding the types of the operands and results of new overloadings. Thus a new overloading of "<" need not return a BOOLEAN result. The rules for "=" will be given in Chapter 9. Note that / = may not be overloaded – it always takes its meaning from =.

The membership tests **in** and **not in** and the short circuit forms **and then** and **or else** cannot be given new meanings. That is why we said in Section 4.9 that they were not technically classed as operators.

Finally note that in the case of operators represented by reserved words, the characters in the string can be in either case. Thus a new overloading of **or** can be declared as "or" or "OR" or even "Or".

Exercise 7.2

1   Write a function "<" that operates on two Roman numbers and compares them according to their corresponding numeric values. That is, so that "CCL" <"CCXC". Use the function VALUE of Exercise 7.1(**5**).

2   Write functions "+" and "*" to add and multiply two values of type COMPLEX. See Exercise 6.5(**2**).

3 Write a function "<" to test whether a value of type PRIMARY is in a set represented by a value of type COLOUR. See Section 6.4.

4 Write a function " <= " to test whether one value of type COLOUR is a subset of another.

7.3 Procedures

The other form of subprogram is a procedure; a procedure is called as a statement. We have seen many examples of procedure calls where there are no parameters such as WORK; PARTY; ACTION; and so on.

The body of a procedure is very similar to that of a function. The differences are

- a procedure starts with **procedure**,

- its name must be an identifier,

- it does not return a result,

- the parameters may be of three different modes **in**, **out** or **in out**.

The mode of a parameter is indicated by following the colon in the parameter specification by **in** or by **out** or by **in out**. If the mode is omitted then it is taken to be **in**. In the case of functions the only allowed mode is **in**; the examples earlier in this chapter omitted **in** but could have been written for instance, as

function SQRT(X: **in** REAL) **return** REAL;
function "*" (A, B: **in** VECTOR) **return** REAL;

The effect of the three modes is best summarised by quoting the LRM (section 6.2).

in   The formal parameter is a constant and permits only reading of the value of the associated actual parameter.

in out The formal parameter is a variable and permits both reading and updating of the value of the associated actual parameter.

out   The formal parameter is a variable and permits updating of the value of the associated actual parameter.

As a simple example of the modes **in** and **out** consider

procedure ADD(A, B: **in** INTEGER; C: **out** INTEGER) **is**
begin
     C:=A+B;
end ADD;

with

P, Q: INTEGER;
. . .

```
ADD(2+P, 37, Q);
```

On calling ADD, the expressions 2+P and 37 are evaluated (in any order) and assigned to the formals A and B which behave as constants. The value of A+B is then assigned to the formal variable C. On return the value of C is assigned to the variable Q. Thus it is (more or less) as if we had written

```
declare
      A: constant INTEGER:=2+P;      -- in
      B: constant INTEGER:=37;       -- in
      C: INTEGER;                    -- out
begin
      C:=A+B;                        -- body
      Q:=C;                          -- out
end;
```

As an example of the mode **in out** consider

```
procedure INCREMENT(X: in out INTEGER) is
begin
      X:=X+1;
end;
```

with

```
I: INTEGER;
. . .
```

```
INCREMENT(I);
```

On calling INCREMENT, the value of I is assigned to the formal variable X. The value of X is then incremented. On return, the final value of X is assigned to the actual parameter I. So it is rather as if we had written

```
declare
      X: INTEGER:=I;
begin
      X:=X+1;
      I:=X;
end;
```

For any scalar type (such as INTEGER) the modes correspond simply to copying the value **in** at the call or **out** upon return or both in the case of **in out**.

If the mode is **in** then the actual parameter may be any expression of the appropriate type or subtype. If the mode is **out** or **in out** then the actual parameter must be a variable. The identity of such a variable is determined when the procedure is called and cannot change during the call.

Suppose we had

```
I: INTEGER;
A: array (1 .. 10) of INTEGER;
procedure SILLY (X: in out INTEGER) is
begin
    I:=I+1;
    X:=X+1;
end;
```

then the statements

```
A(5):=1;
I:=5;
SILLY(A(I));
```

result in A(5) becoming 2, I becoming 6, but A(6) is not affected.

If a parameter is a composite type (such as an array or record) then the mechanism of copying, described above, may be used but alternatively an implementation may use a reference mechanism in which the formal parameter provides direct access to the actual parameter. A program which depends on the particular mechanism is erroneous. An example of such a program is given in the exercises at the end of this section. Note that because a formal array parameter takes its bounds from the actual parameter, the bounds are always copied in at the start even in the case of an **out** parameter. Of course, for simplicity, an implementation could always copy in the whole array anyway.

We now discuss the question of constraints on parameters.

In the case of scalar parameters the situation is as expected from the copying model. For an **in** or **in out** parameter any constraint on the formal must be satisfied by the actual at the beginning of the call. Conversely for an **in out** or **out** parameter any constraint on the variable which is the actual parameter must be satisfied by the value of the formal parameter upon return from the subprogram.

In the case of arrays the situation is somewhat different. If the formal parameter is a constrained array type, the bounds of the actual must be identical; it is not enough for the number of components in each dimension to be the same; the parameter mechanism is more rigorous than assignment. If, on the other hand, the formal parameter is an unconstrained array type, then, as we have seen, it takes its bounds from those of the actual. The foregoing applies irrespective of the mode of the array parameter. Similar rules apply to function results; if the result is a constrained array type then the expression in a return statement must have the same bounds. As an aside, one consequence of the parameter and result mechanism being more rigorous than assignment is that array aggregates with **others** are allowed as actual parameters and in return statements. On the other hand, as we saw in Section 6.2, they are not generally allowed in an assignment statement unless qualified.

In the case of the simple records we have discussed so far there are no constraints and so there is nothing to say. The parameter mechanism for other types will be discussed when they are introduced.

We stated above that an actual parameter corresponding to a formal **out** or **in out** parameter must be a variable. This includes the possibility of the actual parameter in turn being a formal parameter of some outer subprogram; but naturally an **out** parameter cannot be an actual parameter to a formal **in out** parameter because otherwise there might be an attempt to read the **out** parameter.

A further possibility is that an actual parameter can also be a type conversion of a variable provided, of course, that the conversion is allowed. As an example, since conversion is allowed between any numeric types, we can write

```
R: REAL;
...
INCREMENT(INTEGER(R));
```

If R initially had the value 2.3, it would be converted to the integer value 2 incremented to give 3 and then on return converted back to 3.0 and assigned to R.

This conversion of **in out** or **out** parameters is particularly useful with arrays. Suppose we write a library of subprograms applying to our type VECTOR and then acquire from someone else some subprograms written to apply to the type ROW of Section 6.2. The types ROW and VECTOR are essentially the same; it just so happened that the authors used different names. Array type conversion allows us to use both sets of subprograms without having to change the type names systematically.

As a final example consider the following

```
procedure QUADRATIC(A, B, C: in REAL; ROOT_1, ROOT_2:
                           out REAL; OK: out BOOLEAN) is
    D: constant REAL:=B**2–4.0*A*C;
begin
    if D<0.0 or A=0.0 then
        OK:=FALSE;
        return;
    end if;
    ROOT_1:=(–B+SQRT(D)) / (2.0*A);
    ROOT_2:=(–B–SQRT(D)) / (2.0*A);
    OK:=TRUE;
end QUADRATIC;
```

The procedure QUADRATIC attempts to solve the equation

$$ax^2 + bx + c = 0$$

If the roots are real they are returned via the parameters ROOT_1 and ROOT_2 and OK is set to TRUE. If the roots are complex (D< 0.0) or the equation degenerates (A = 0.0) then OK is set to FALSE.

Note the use of the return statement. Since this is a procedure there is no result to be returned and so the word **return** is not followed by an expression. It just updates the **out** or **in out** parameters as necessary and returns control back to where the procedure was called. Note also that unlike a function we can 'run' into the **end**; this is equivalent to obeying **return**.

The reader will note that if OK is set to FALSE then no value is assigned to the **out** parameters ROOT_1 and ROOT_2. The copy rule for scalars then implies that the corresponding actual parameters become undefined. In practice, junk values are presumably assigned to the actual parameters and this could possibly raise CONSTRAINT_ERROR if an actual parameter were constrained. This is probably bad practice and so it might be better to assign safe values such as 0.0 to the roots just in case. (In examples like this, the **out** mechanism does not seem so satisfactory as the simple reference mechanism of Algol 68 or Pascal.)

The procedure could be used in a sequence such as

```
declare
    L, M, N: REAL;
    P, Q: REAL;
    STATUS: BOOLEAN;
begin
    -- sets values into L, M and N
    QUADRATIC(L, M, N, P, Q, STATUS);
    if STATUS then
        -- roots are in P and Q
    else
        -- fails
    end if;
end;
```

We conclude this section by emphasising that an **out** parameter cannot be treated as a proper variable since it cannot be read. Thus the statements of the above example could not be recast in the form

```
begin
    OK:=D>=0.0 and A /=0.0;
    if not OK then
        return;
    end if;
    ROOT_1:= . . .;
    ROOT_2:= . . .;
end QUADRATIC;
```

because the Boolean expression **not** OK attempts to read the **out** parameter OK.

An exception to this rule is that the bounds of an **out** array can be read even though the components cannot. Remember that a formal array always takes its bounds from the actual array. A similar situation applies to discriminants of records which we will meet in Chapter 11.

Exercise 7.3
1 Write a procedure SWAP to interchange the values of the two real parameters.

2 Rewrite the function REV of Section 7.1 as a procedure with a single parameter. Use it to reverse an array R of type ROW.

3 Why is the following erroneous?

    A: VECTOR(1 . . 1);

```
procedure P(V: VECTOR) is
begin
    A(1):=V(1) + V(1);
    A(1):=V(1) + V(1);
end;

. . .
A(1):= 1.0;
P(A);
```

7.4 Named and default parameters

The forms of subprogram call we have been using so far have given the actual parameters in positional order. As with aggregates we can also use the named notation in which the formal parameter name is also supplied; the parameters do not then have to be in order.

So we could write

```
QUADRATIC(A => L, B => M, C => N, ROOT_1 => P,
          ROOT_2 => Q, OK => STATUS);
INCREMENT(X => I);
ADD(C => Q, A => 2+P, B => 37);
```

We could even write

```
INCREMENT(X => X);
```

the scopes do not interfere.

This notation can also be used with functions

```
F:=FACTORIAL(N => 4);
S:=SQRT(X => T+0.5);
R:=INNER(B => W, A => V);
```

The named notation cannot, however, be used with operators called with the infixed syntax.

As with record aggregates, the named and positional notations can be mixed and any positional parameters must come first and in their correct order. However, unlike record aggregates, each parameter must be given individually and **others** may not be used. So we could write

```
QUADRATIC(L, M, N, ROOT_1 => P, ROOT_2 => Q,
          OK => STATUS);
```

The named notation leads into the topic of default parameters. It sometimes happens that one or more **in** parameters usually take the same value on each call; we can give a default expression in the subprogram specification and then omit it from the call.

Consider the problem of ordering a dry martini in the USA. One is faced with choices described by the following enumeration types

```
type SPIRIT is (GIN, VODKA);
type STYLE is (ON_THE_ROCKS, STRAIGHT_UP);
type TRIMMING is (OLIVE, TWIST);
```

The standard default expressions can then be given in a procedure specification thus

```
procedure DRY_MARTINI(BASE: SPIRIT:=GIN;
                      HOW: STYLE:=ON_THE_ROCKS;
                      PLUS: TRIMMING:=OLIVE);
```

Typical calls might be

```
DRY_MARTINI(HOW => STRAIGHT_UP);
DRY_MARTINI(VODKA, PLUS => TWIST);
DRY_MARTINI;
DRY_MARTINI(GIN, STRAIGHT_UP);
```

The first call uses the named notation; we get gin, straight up plus olive. The second call mixes the positional and named notations; as soon as a parameter is omitted the named notation must be used. The third call illustrates that all parameters can be omitted. The final call shows that a parameter can, of course, be supplied even if it happens to take the same value as the default expression; in this case it avoids using the named form for the second parameter.

Note that default expressions can only be given for **in** parameters. They cannot be given for operators but they can be given for functions designated by identifiers. Such a default expression (like a default expression for an initial value in a record type declaration) is only evaluated when required; that is, it is evaluated each time the subprogram is called and no corresponding actual parameter is supplied. Hence the default value need not be the same on each call although it usually will be. Default expressions are widely used in the standard input output package to provide default formats.

Default expressions illustrate the subtle rule that a parameter specification of the form

```
P, Q: in INTEGER:=E
```

is strictly equivalent to

```
P: in INTEGER:=E;
Q: in INTEGER:=E
```

(The reader will recall a similar rule for object declarations; it also applies to record components.) As a consequence, the default expression is evaluated for each omitted parameter in a call. This does not usually matter but would be significant if the expression E included a function call with side effects.

Exercise 7.4

1   Write a function ADD which returns the sum of the two integer parameters and takes a default value of 1 for the second parameter. How many different ways

can it be called to return N+1 where N is the first actual parameter?

2   Rewrite the specification of DRY_MARTINI to reflect that you prefer VODKA at weekends. Hint: declare a function to return your favourite spirit according to the global variable TODAY.

7.5   Overloading

We saw in Section 7.2 how new meanings could be given to existing language operators. This overloading applies to subprograms in general.

A subprogram will overload an existing meaning rather than hide it, provided that its specification is sufficiently different. Hiding will occur if the order and base types of the parameters and result (if any) are the same. A procedure cannot hide a function and vice versa. Note that the names of the parameters, their mode and the presence or absence of default expressions do not matter. Two or more overloaded subprograms may be declared in the same declarative part.

Subprograms and enumeration literals can overload each other. In fact an enumeration literal is formally thought of as a parameterless function with a result of the enumeration type. There are two classes of uses of identifiers – the overloadable ones and the non overloadable ones. At any point an identifier either refers to a single entity of the non overloadable class or to one or many of the overloadable class. A declaration of one class hides the other class and cannot occur in the same declaration list.

As we have seen, ambiguities arising from overloading can be resolved by qualification. This was necessary when the operator "<" was used with the strings in Section 6.3. As a further example consider the British Channel Islands; the larger three are Guernsey, Jersey and Alderney. There are woollen garments named after each island

```
type GARMENT is (GUERNSEY, JERSEY, ALDERNEY);
```

and breeds of cattle named after two of them (the Alderney breed became extinct as a consequence of the Second World War)

```
type COW is (GUERNSEY, JERSEY);
```

and we can imagine (just) shops that sell both garments and cows according to

```
procedure SELL(G: GARMENT);
procedure SELL(C: COW);
```

Although

```
SELL(ALDERNEY);
```

is not ambiguous

```
SELL(JERSEY);
```

is, since we cannot tell which subprogram is being called. We must write for example

    SELL(COW'(JERSEY));

Exercise 7.5
1   How else could SELL(JERSEY); be made unambiguous?

7.6   Declarations, scopes and visibility

We said earlier that it is sometimes necessary or just convenient to give a subprogram specification on its own without the body. The specification is then followed by a semicolon and is known as a subprogram declaration. A complete subprogram, which always includes the full specification, is known as a subprogram body.

Subprogram declarations and bodies must, like other declarations, occur in a declarative part and a subprogram declaration must be followed by the corresponding body in the same declarative part.

An example of where it is necessary to use a subprogram declaration occurs with mutually recursive procedures. Suppose we wish to declare two procedures F and G which call each other. Because of the rule regarding linear elaboration of declarations we cannot write the call of F in the body of G until after F has been declared and vice versa. Clearly this is impossible if we just write the bodies because one must come second. However, we can write

```
procedure F(. . .);          -- declaration of F

procedure G(. . .) is        -- body of G
begin
    F(. . .);
end G;

procedure F(. . .) is        -- body of F repeats
begin                        -- its specification
    G(. . .);
end F;
```

and then all is well.

If the specification is repeated then it must be given in full and the two must be the same. Technically we say that the two specifications must conform. Some slight variation is allowed. A numeric literal can be replaced by another numeric literal with the same value; an identifier can be replaced by a dotted name as described later in this section; the lexical spacing can be different. It is worth noting that the key reason for not allowing subtype indications in parameter specifications is to remove any problem regarding conformance since there is then no question of evaluating constraint expressions twice and possibly having different results because of side effects. No corresponding question arises with default expressions (which are of course written out twice) since they are only evaluated when the subprogram is called.

Another important case, where we have to write a subprogram declaration as well as a body, occurs in the next chapter when we discuss packages. Even if not always necessary, it is sometimes clearer to write subprogram declarations as well as bodies. An example might be in the case where many subprogram bodies occur together. The subprogram declarations then act as a summary.

Subprogram bodies and other declarations must not be mixed up in an arbitrary way. The bodies must follow other declarations. This ensures that small declarations are not 'lost' in between large bodies.

Since subprograms occur in declarative parts and themselves contain declarative parts they may be textually nested without limit. The normal hiding rules applicable to blocks described in Section 4.2 also apply to declarations in subprograms. (The only complication concerns overloading as discussed in the previous section.) Consider

```
procedure P is
    I: INTEGER:=0;

    procedure Q is
        K: INTEGER:=I;
        I: INTEGER;
        J: INTEGER;
    begin
        . . .
    end Q;
    . . .
end P;
```

Just as for the example in Section 4.2, the inner I hides the outer one and so the outer I is not visible inside the procedure Q after the declaration of the inner I.

However, we can always refer to the outer I by the so-called dotted notation, in which it is prefixed by the name of the unit immediately containing its declaration followed by a dot. So within Q we can refer to the outer I as P.I and so, for example, we could initialise J by writing

```
J: INTEGER:=P.I;
```

If the prefix is itself hidden then it can always be written the same way. Thus the inner I could be referred to as P.Q.I.

An object declared in a block cannot usually be referred to in this way since a block does not normally have a name. However, a block can be named in a similar way to a loop as shown in the following

```
OUTER:
declare
    I: INTEGER:=0;
begin
    . . .
    declare
        K: INTEGER:=I;
        I: INTEGER;
        J: INTEGER:=OUTER.I;
    begin
        . . .
```

end;
end OUTER;

Here the outer block has the identifier OUTER. Unlike subprograms, the identifier has to be repeated after the matching **end**. Naming the block enables us to initialise the inner declaration of J with the value of the outer I.

Within a loop it is possible to refer to a hidden loop parameter in the same way. We could even rewrite the example in Section 6.1 of assigning zero to the elements of AA as

```
L:
for I in AA'RANGE(1) loop
    for I in AA'RANGE(2) loop
        AA(L.I, I):= 0.0;
    end loop;
end loop L;
```

although one would be a little crazy to do so!

It should be noted that the dotted form can always be used even if it is not necessary.

This notation can also be applied to operators and character literals. Thus the variable RESULT declared inside "*" can be referred to as "*". RESULT. And equally if "*" were declared inside a block B then it could be referred to as B."*". If it is called with this form of name then the normal function call must be used.

```
R:=B."*"(V, W);
```

Indeed, the functional form can always be used as in

```
R:="*"(V, W);
```

As we have seen, subprograms can alter global variables and therefore have side effects. (A side effect is one brought about other than via the parameter mechanism.) It is generally considered rather undesirable to write subprograms, especially functions, which have side effects. However, some side effects are beneficial. Any subprogram which performs input-output has a side effect on the file; a function delivering successive members of a sequence of random numbers only works because of its side effects; if we need to count how many times a function is called then we use a side effect; and so on. However, care must be taken when using functions with side effects that the program is correct since there are various circumstances in which the order of evaluation is not defined.

We conclude this section with a brief discussion of the hierarchy of **exit**, **return** and **goto** and the scopes of block and loop identifiers and labels.

A **return** statement terminates the execution of the immediately embracing subprogram. It can occur inside an inner block or inside a loop in the subprogram and therefore also terminate the loop. On the other hand an **exit** statement terminates the named or immediately embracing loop. It can also occur inside an inner block but cannot occur inside a subprogram declared in the loop and thereby also terminate the subprogram. A **goto** statement can transfer control out of a loop or block but not out of a subprogram.

As far as scope is concerned, identifiers of labels, blocks and loops behave as if they are declared at the end of the declarative part of the immediately embracing subprogram or block (or package or task body). Moreover distinct identifiers must be used for all blocks, loops and labels inside the same subprogram (or package or task body) even if some are in inner blocks. Thus two labels in the same subprogram cannot have the same identifier even if they are inside different inner blocks. This rule reduces the risk of goto statements going to the wrong label particularly when a program is amended.

Checklist 7

Parameter and result subtypes must be given by a type mark and not a subtype indication.

A function must return a result and so should not run into its final **end** although a procedure can.

The order of evaluation of parameters is not defined.

A default parameter expression is only evaluated when the subprogram is called and the corresponding parameter is omitted.

The actual and formal parameters of a constrained array type must have equal bounds.

Scalar parameters are copied. The mechanism for arrays and records is not defined.

Formal parameter specifications are separated by semicolons not commas.

Chapter 8 OVERALL STRUCTURE

The previous chapters have described the small scale features of Ada in considerable detail. The language presented so far corresponds to the areas addressed by languages of the sixties and early seventies, although Ada provides more functionality in those areas. However, we now come to the new areas which broadly speaking correspond to the concepts of data abstraction and programming in the large which were discussed in Chapter 1.

In this chapter we discuss packages (which is what Ada is all about) and the mechanisms for separate compilation. We also say a little more about scope and visibility.

8.1 Packages

One of the major problems with the traditional block structured languages, such as Algol and Pascal, is that they do not offer enough control of visibility. For example, suppose we have a stack represented by an array and a variable which indexes the current top element, a procedure PUSH to add an item and a function POP to remove an item. We might write

```
MAX: constant:= 100;
S: array (1 .. MAX) of INTEGER;
TOP: INTEGER range 0 .. MAX;
```

to represent the stack and then declare

```
procedure PUSH(X: INTEGER) is
begin
    TOP:=TOP+1;
    S(TOP):=X;
end PUSH;

function POP return INTEGER is
begin
    TOP:=TOP-1;
    return S(TOP+1);
end POP;
```

In a simple block structured language there is no way in which we can be given access to the subprograms PUSH and POP without also being given direct access to the variables S and TOP. As a consequence we cannot be forced to use the correct protocol and so be prevented from making use of knowledge of how the stack is implemented.

107

The Ada package overcomes this by allowing us to place a wall around a group of declarations and only permit access to those which we intend to be visible. A package actually comes in two parts: the specification which gives the interface to the outside world, and the body which gives the hidden details.

The above example should be written as

```
package STACK is                        -- specification
    procedure PUSH(X: INTEGER);
    function POP return INTEGER;
end STACK;

package body STACK is                   -- body
    MAX: constant:= 100;
    S: array (1 .. MAX) of INTEGER;
    TOP: INTEGER range 0 .. MAX;

    procedure PUSH(X: INTEGER) is
    begin
        TOP:=TOP+1;
        S(TOP):=X;
    end PUSH;

    function POP return INTEGER is
    begin
        TOP:=TOP-1;
        return S(TOP+1);
    end POP;

begin                                   -- initialisation
    TOP:=0;
end STACK;
```

The package specification starts with the reserved word **package**, the identifier of the package and **is**. This is then followed by declarations of the entities which are to be visible. It finishes with **end**, the identifier (optionally) and the terminating semicolon. In the example we just have the declarations of the two subprograms PUSH and POP.

The package body also starts with **package** but this is then followed by **body**, the identifier and **is**. We then have a normal declarative part, **begin**, sequence of statements, **end**, optional identifier and semicolon just as in a block or subprogram body.

In the example the declarative part contains the variables which represent the stack and the bodies of PUSH and POP. The sequence of statements between **begin** and **end** is executed when the package is declared and can be used for initialisation. If there is no need for an initialisation sequence, the **begin** can be omitted. Indeed in this example we could equally and perhaps more naturally have performed the initialisation by writing

```
TOP: INTEGER range 0 .. MAX:=0;
```

Note that a package is itself declared and so is just one of the items in an outer declarative part (unless it is a library unit which is the outermost layer anyway).

The package illustrates another case where we need distinct subprogram declarations and bodies. Indeed we cannot put a body into a package specification. And moreover, if a package specification contains the specification of a subprogram, then the package body must contain the corresponding subprogram body. We can think of the package specification and body as being just one large declarative part with only some items visible. But, of course, a subprogram body can be declared in a package body without its specification having to be given in the package specification. Such a subprogram would be internal to the package and could only be called from within, either from other subprograms, some of which would presumably be visible, or perhaps from the initialisation sequence.

The elaboration of a package body consists simply of the elaboration of the declarations inside it followed by the execution of the initialisation sequence if there is one. The package continues to exist until the end of the scope in which it is declared. Entities declared inside the package have the same lifetime as the package itself. Thus the variables S and TOP can be thought of as 'own' variables in the Algol 60 sense; their values are retained between successive calls of PUSH and POP.

Packages may be declared in any declarative part such as that in a block, subprogram or indeed another package. If a package specification is declared inside another package specification then, as for subprograms, the body of one must be declared in the body of the other. But again both specification and body could be in a package body.

Apart from the rule that a package specification cannot contain bodies, it can contain any of the other kinds of declarations we have met.

Now to return to the use of our package. The package itself has a name and the entities in its visible part can be thought of as components of the package in some sense. It is entirely natural therefore that, in order to call PUSH, we must also mention STACK. In fact the dotted notation is used. So we could write

```
declare
    package STACK is        -- specification
        . . .               -- and
        . . .               -- body
    end STACK;
begin
    . . .
    STACK.PUSH(M);
    . . .
    N:=STACK.POP;
    . . .
end;
```

Inside the package we would call PUSH as just PUSH, but we could still write STACK.PUSH just as in the last chapter we saw how we could refer to a local variable X of procedure P as P.X. Inside the package we can refer to S or STACK.S, but outside the package MAX, S and TOP are not accessible in any way.

It would in general be painful always to have to write STACK.PUSH to call PUSH from outside. Instead we can write

```
use STACK;
```

as a sort of declaration and we may then refer to PUSH and POP directly. The use clause could follow the declaration of STACK in the same declarative part or in another declarative part where it is visible. So we could write

```
declare
    use STACK;
begin
    . . .
    PUSH(M);
    . . .
    N:=POP;
    . . .
end;
```

The use clause is like a declaration and similarly has a scope to the end of the block. Outside we would have to revert to the dotted notation. We could have an inner use clause referring to the same package – it would do no harm.

Two or more packages could be declared in the same declarative part. Generally, we could arrange all the specifications together and then all the bodies, or alternatively the corresponding specifications and bodies, could be together. Thus we could have spec A, spec B, body A, body B, or spec A, body A, spec B, body B.

The rules governing the order are simply

● linear elaboration of declarations,

● specification must precede body for same package (or subprogram),

● small items must generally precede large ones.

More precisely this last rule means that a body can only be followed by other bodies, subprogram and package (and task) specifications or indeed use clauses.

Of course, the visible part of a package may contain things other than subprograms. Indeed an important case is where it does not contain subprograms at all but merely a group of related variables, constants and types. In such a case the package needs no body. It does not provide any hiding properties but merely gives commonality of naming. (A body could be provided; its only purpose would be for initialisation.)

As an example we could provide a package containing our type DAY and some useful related constants.

```
package DIURNAL  is
    type DAY is (MON, TUE, WED, THU, FRI, SAT, SUN);
    subtype WEEKDAY is DAY range MON . . FRI;
    TOMORROW: constant array (DAY) of DAY:=
                (TUE, WED, THU, FRI, SAT, SUN, MON);
    NEXT_WORK_DAY: constant array (WEEKDAY) of
                WEEKDAY:=(TUE, WED, THU, FRI, MON);
end DIURNAL;
```

A final point. A subprogram cannot be called during the elaboration of a declarative part if its body appears later. This does not prevent mutual recursion because in that case the call actually only occurs when we execute the sequence of statements. But it does prevent its use as an initial value. So

```
function A return INTEGER;
I: INTEGER:=A;
```

is illegal, and would result in PROGRAM_ERROR being raised.

This rule also applies to subprograms in packages. We cannot call a subprogram from outside the package until after the package body has been elaborated.

Exercise 8.1

1 The sequence defined by

$$X_{n+1} = X_n.5^5 \bmod 2^{13}$$

provides a crude source of pseudo random numbers. The initial value X_0 should be an odd integer in the range $0 \, . \, . \, 2^{13}$.
Write a package RANDOM containing a procedure INIT to initialise the sequence and a function NEXT to deliver the next value in the sequence.

2 Write a package COMPLEX_NUMBERS which makes visible

- the type COMPLEX,

- a constant I $= \sqrt{-1}$

- functions $+$, $-$, $*$, $/$ acting on values of type COMPLEX.

See Exercise 7.2 (**2**).

8.2   Library units

Many languages in the past have ignored the simple fact that programs are written in pieces, compiled separately and then joined together. Ada recognises the need for separate compilation and provides two mechanisms – one top down and one bottom up.

The top down mechanism is appropriate for the development of a large coherent program which nevertheless, for various reasons, is broken down into subunits which can be compiled separately. The subunits are compiled after the unit from which they are taken. This mechanism is described in the next section.

The bottom up mechanism is appropriate for the creation of a program library where units are written for general use and consequently are written before the programs that use them. This mechanism will now be discussed in detail.

A library unit may be a subprogram specification or a package specification; the corresponding bodies are called secondary units. These units may be compiled individually or for convenience several could be submitted to the compiler together. Thus we could compile the specification and body of a package together but as we shall see it may be more convenient to compile them individually. As usual a subprogram body alone is sufficient to define the subprogram fully; it is then classed as a library unit rather than a secondary unit.

When a unit is compiled it goes into a program library. There will obviously be several such libraries according to user and project, etc. The creation and manipulation of libraries is outside the scope of this book. Once in the library, a unit can be used by any subsequently compiled unit but the using unit must indicate the dependency by a with clause.

As a simple example suppose we compile the package STACK. This package depends on no other unit and so it needs no with clause. We will compile both specification and body together so the text submitted will be

```
package STACK is
    . . .
end STACK;
package body STACK is
    . . .
end STACK;
```

We now suppose that we write a procedure MAIN which will use the package STACK. Our procedure MAIN is going to be the main program in the usual sense. It will have no parameters and we can imagine that it is called by some magic outside the language itself. The Ada definition does not prescribe that the main program should have the identifier MAIN; it is merely a convention which we are adopting here because it has to be called something.

The text we submit to the compiler could be

```
with STACK;
procedure MAIN is
    use STACK;
    M, N: INTEGER;
begin
    . . .
    PUSH(M);
    . . .
    N:=POP;
    . . .
end MAIN;
```

The with clause goes before the unit so that the dependency of the unit on other units is clear at a glance. A with clause may not be embedded in an inner scope.

If the unit is dependent on several other units then they can go in the one with clause, or it might be a convenience to use distinct with clauses. Thus we could write

```
with STACK, DIURNAL;
procedure MAIN is
    . . .
```

or equally

```
with STACK;
with DIURNAL;
```

procedure MAIN **is**

 . . .

For convenience we can place a use clause after a with clause. Thus

with STACK; **use** STACK;
procedure MAIN **is**

 . . .

and then PUSH and POP are directly visible without more ado.

Only direct dependencies need be given in a with clause. Thus if package P uses the facilities of package Q which in turn uses the facilities of package R, then, unless P also directly uses R, the with clause for P should mention only Q. The user of P does not care about R and must not need to know since otherwise the hierarchy of development would be made more complicated.

Another point is that the with clause in front of a package or subprogram declaration will also apply to the body. It can but need not be repeated. Of course, the body may have additional dependencies which will need indicating with a with clause anyway. Dependencies which apply only to the body should not be given with the specification since otherwise the independence of the body and the specification would be reduced.

If a package specification and body are compiled separately then the body must be compiled after the specification. We say that the body is dependent on the specification. However, any unit using the package is dependent only on the specification and not the body. If the body is changed in a manner consistent with not changing the specification, any unit using the package will not need recompiling. The ability to compile specification and body separately should simplify program maintenance.

The general rule regarding the order of compilation is simply that a unit must be compiled after any units on which it depends. Consequently, if a unit is changed and recompiled then all dependent units must also be recompiled. Any order of compilation consistent with the dependency rule is acceptable.

There is one package that need not be mentioned in a with clause. This is the package STANDARD which effectively contains the declarations of all the predefined types such as INTEGER and BOOLEAN. It also contains an internal package ASCII containing constants defining the control characters such as CR and LF. We now see why the control characters were represented as ASCII.CR etc. in Chapter 6. By writing **use** ASCII; they can, of course, just be referred to as CR. The package STANDARD is described in more detail in Appendix 2.

There is a final very important rule regarding library units. They must have distinct identifiers; they cannot be overloaded. Moreover they cannot be operators.

Exercise 8.2

1 The package D and subprograms P and Q and MAIN have correct with clauses as follows

specification of D	no with clause
body of D	**with** P,Q;
subprogram P	no with clause
subprogram Q	no with clause
subprogram MAIN	**with** D;

Draw a graph showing the dependencies between the units. How many different orders of compilation are possible?

8.3 Subunits

In this section we introduce a further form of secondary unit known as a subunit. The body of a package, subprogram (or task, see Chapter 14) can be 'taken out' of an immediately embracing library unit or secondary unit and itself compiled separately. The body in the embracing unit is then replaced by a body stub. As an example suppose we remove the bodies of the subprograms PUSH and POP from the package STACK. The body of STACK would then become

```
package body STACK is
    MAX: constant:=100;
    S: array (1 .. MAX) of INTEGER;
    TOP: INTEGER range 0 .. MAX;
    procedure PUSH(X: INTEGER) is separate;      -- stub
    function POP return INTEGER is separate;     -- stub
begin
    TOP:=0;
end STACK;
```

The removed units are termed subunits; they may then be compiled separately. They have to be preceded by **separate** followed by the name of the parent unit in brackets. Thus the subunit PUSH becomes

```
separate (STACK)
procedure PUSH(X: INTEGER) is
begin
    TOP:=TOP+1;
    S(TOP):=X;
end PUSH;
```

and similarly for POP.

In the above example the parent unit is (the body of) a library unit. The parent unit could itself be a subunit; in such a case its name must be given in full using the dotted notation starting with the ancestor library unit. Thus if R is a subunit of Q which is a subunit of P which is a library unit, then the text of R must start

```
separate (P.Q)
```

As with library units, the subunits of a unit must have distinct identifiers. But, of course, this does not prevent subunits of different units having the same identifier. And again subunits cannot be operators.

A subunit is dependent on its parent (and any library units explicitly mentioned) and so must be compiled after them.

Visibility within a subunit is as at the corresponding body stub – it is exactly as if the subunit were plucked out with its environment intact. As a consequence any with clause applying to the parent need not be repeated just because the subunit is compiled separately. However, it is possible to give the subunit access to additional library units by preceding it with its own with clauses (and possible use clauses). Such clauses precede **separate**. So the text of R might commence

> **with** X; **use** X;
> **separate** (P.Q)
> . . .

A possible reason for doing this might be if we can then remove any reference to library unit X from the parent P.Q and so reduce the dependencies. This would give us greater freedom with the order of compilation; if X were recompiled for some reason then only R would need recompiling as a consequence and not also Q.

Note that a with clause only refers to library units and never to subunits. Finally observe that several subunits or a mixture of library units, library unit bodies and subunits can be compiled together.

Exercise 8.3

1 Suppose that the package STACK is written with separate subunits PUSH and POP. Draw a graph showing the dependencies between the five units: procedure MAIN, procedure PUSH, function POP, package specification STACK, package body STACK. How many different orders of compilation are possible?

8.4 Scope and visibility

We return once more to the topic of scope and visibility. In this section we summarise the major points which will be relevant to the everyday use of Ada. For some of the fine detail, the reader is referred to the LRM. It is perhaps worth mentioning that the LRM uses the term declarative region in order to explain the visibility and scope rules. Blocks and subprograms are examples of declarative regions and the scope rules associated with them were described in Sections 4.2 and 7.6. We now have to consider the effect of the introduction of packages.

A package specification and body together constitute a single declarative region. Thus if we declare a variable X in the specification then we cannot redeclare X in the body (except of course in an inner region such as a local subprogram).

In the case of a declaration in the visible part of a package, its scope extends from the declaration to the end of the scope of the package itself. Note that if the package is inside the visible part of another package then this means that, applying the rule again, the scope extends to the end of that of the outer package and so on.

In the case of a declaration in a package body (or in the private part of a package – to be described in the next chapter), its scope extends to the end of the package body.

In the case of the simple nesting of blocks and subprograms an entity is visible throughout its scope unless hidden by another declaration. We saw in Section 7.6 how even if it was hidden it could nevertheless in general be referred to by using the dotted notation where the prefixed name is that of the unit embracing the declaration. In essence, writing the name of the embracing unit makes the entity visible.

In the case of an entity declared in a package the same rules apply inside the package. But outside the package it is not visible unless we write the package name or alternatively write a use clause.

The identifiers visible at a given point are those visible before considering any use clauses plus those made visible by use clauses.

The basic rule is that an identifier in a package is made visible by a use clause provided the same identifier is not also in another package with a use clause and also provided that the identifier is not already visible anyway. If these conditions are not met then the identifier is not made visible and we have to continue to use the dotted notation.

A slightly different rule applies if all the identifiers are subprograms or enumeration literals. In this case they all overload each other unless of course their specifications clash (could hide each other) in which case they are not made visible. Thus an identifier made visible by a use clause can never hide another identifier although it may overload it.

The general purpose of these rules is to ensure that adding a use clause cannot invalidate an existing piece of text. We have only given a brief sketch here and the reader is probably confused. In practice there should be no problems since the Ada compiler will, we hope, indicate any ambiguities or other difficulties and things can always be put right by adding a qualifier or using a dotted name.

There are other rules regarding record component names, subprogram parameters and so on which are as expected. For example there is no conflict between an identifier of a record component and another use of the identifier outside the type definition itself. The reason is that although the scopes may overlap, the regions of visibility do not. Consider

```
declare
    type R is
        record
            I: INTEGER;
        end record;
    type S is
        record
            I: INTEGER;
        end record;
    AR: R;
    AS: S;
    I: INTEGER;
begin
    . . .
    I:=AR.I+AS.I;              -- legal
    . . .
end;
```

The scope of the I in the type R extends from the component declaration until the end of the block. However, its visibility is confined to within the declaration of R except that it is made visible by the use of AR in the selected component. Hence no conflict.

Similar considerations prevent conflict in named aggregates and in named parameters in subprogram calls.

Observe that a use clause can mention several packages and that it may be necessary for a package name to be given as a selected component itself. A use clause does not take effect until the semicolon. Suppose we have nested packages

```
package P1 is
    package P2 is
        . . .
    end P2;
    . . .
end P1;
```

then outside P1 we could write

```
use P1; use P2;
```

or

```
use P1, P1.P2;
```

but not

```
use P1, P2;
```

We could even write **use** P1.P2; to gain visibility of the entities in P2 but not those in P1 – however, this seems an odd thing to do.

Earlier we mentioned the existence of the package STANDARD. This contains all the predefined entities but moreover every library unit should be thought of as being declared inside and at the end of STANDARD. This explains why an explicit use clause for STANDARD is not required. Another important consequence is that, provided we do not hide the name STANDARD by redefining it, a library unit P can always be referred to as STANDARD.P. Hence, in the absence of anonymous blocks, loops and overloading every identifier in the program has a unique name commencing with STANDARD. It is probably good advice not to redefine STANDARD.

8.5 Renaming

Certain entities can be renamed. As an example we can write

```
declare
    procedure SPUSH(X: INTEGER) renames STACK.PUSH;
    function SPOP return INTEGER renames STACK.POP;
begin
    . . .
    SPUSH(M);
    . . .
    N:=SPOP;
    . . .
end;
```

A possible reason for doing this is to resolve ambiguities and yet avoid the use of the full dotted notation. Thus if we had two packages with a procedure PUSH (with an INTEGER parameter) then the use clause would be of no benefit since the full name would still be needed to resolve the ambiguity.

As another example suppose we wish to use both the function INNER and the equivalent operator "*" of Chapter 7 without declaring two distinct subprograms. We can write

function "*" (X, Y: VECTOR) **return** REAL **renames** INNER;

or

function INNER (X, Y: VECTOR) **return** REAL **renames** "*";

according to which we declare first.

Renaming is also useful in the case of library units. Thus we might wish to have two or more overloaded subprograms and yet compile them separately. This cannot be done directly since library units must have distinct names. However, differently named library units could be renamed so that the user sees the required effect. The restriction that a library unit cannot be an operator can similarly be overcome. The same tricks can be done with subunits.

If a subprogram is renamed, the number, base types and modes of the parameters (and result if a function) must be the same. This information can be used to resolve overloadings (as in the example of "*") and, of course, this matching occurs during compilation. Rather strangely, any constraints on the parameters or result in the new subprogram are ignored; those on the original still apply.

On the other hand, the presence, absence or value of default parameters do not have to match. Renaming can be used to introduce, change or delete default expressions; the default parameters associated with the new name are those shown in the renaming declaration. Hence renaming cannot be used as a trick to give an operator default values. Similarly, parameter names do not have to match but naturally the new names must be used for named parameters of calls of the new subprogram.

The unification of subprograms and enumeration literals is further illustrated by the fact that an enumeration literal can be renamed as a parameterless function with the appropriate result. For example

function TEN **return** ROMAN_DIGIT **renames** 'X';

Renaming can also be used to partially evaluate the name of an object. Suppose we have an array of records such as the array PEOPLE in Section 6.5 and that we wish to scan the array and print out the dates of birth in numerical form. We could write

```
for I in PEOPLE'RANGE loop
    PUT (PEOPLE(I).BIRTH.DAY); PUT (":");
    PUT (MONTH_NAME'POS(PEOPLE(I).BIRTH.MONTH) + 1);
    PUT (":");
    PUT (PEOPLE(I).BIRTH.YEAR);
end loop;
```

It is clearly painful to repeat PEOPLE(I) each time. We could declare a variable D of type DATE and copy PEOPLE(I).BIRTH into it, but this would be very wasteful if the record were at all large. A better technique is to use renaming thus

```
for I in PEOPLE'RANGE loop
    declare
        D: DATE renames PEOPLE(I).BIRTH;
    begin
        PUT (D.DAY); PUT (":");
        PUT (MONTH_NAME'POS (D.MONTH) + 1);
        PUT (":");
        PUT (D.YEAR);
    end;
end loop;
```

Beware that renaming does not correspond to text substitution – the identity of the object is determined when the renaming occurs. If any variable in the name subsequently changes then the identity of the object does not change. Any constraints implied by the type mark in the renaming declaration are ignored; those of the original object still apply.

Renaming can be applied to objects (variables and constants), exceptions (see Chapter 10), subprograms and packages. In the case of a package it takes the simple form

```
package P renames STACK;
```

Although renaming does not directly apply to types an identical effect can be achieved by the use of a subtype

```
subtype S is T;
```

Finally note that renaming does not hide the old name. The indiscriminate use of renaming should be avoided since the aliases introduced make program proving much more difficult.

Checklist 8

Variables inside a package exist between calls of subprograms of the package.

A library unit must be compiled after other library units mentioned in its with clause.

A subunit must be compiled after its parent.

A body must be compiled after the corresponding specification.

A package specification and body form a single declarative region.

Do not redefine STANDARD.

Renaming is not text substitution.

Chapter 9 PRIVATE TYPES

We have seen how packages enable us to hide internal objects from the user of a package. Private types enable us to hide the details of the construction of a type from a user.

9.1 Normal private types

In Exercise 8.1(**2**) we wrote a package COMPLEX_NUMBERS providing a type COMPLEX, a constant I and some operations on the type. The specification of the package was

```
package COMPLEX_NUMBERS is
    type COMPLEX is
        record
            RL, IM: REAL;
        end record;

    I: constant COMPLEX:= (0.0, 1.0);

    function "+" (X, Y: COMPLEX) return COMPLEX;
    function "−" (X, Y: COMPLEX) return COMPLEX;
    function "*" (X, Y: COMPLEX) return COMPLEX;
    function "/" (X, Y: COMPLEX) return COMPLEX;
end;
```

The trouble with this formulation is that the user can make use of the fact that the complex numbers are held in cartesian representation. Rather than always using the complex operator + , the user could also write things like

```
C.IM:= C.IM + 1.0;
```

rather than the more abstract

```
C:= C + I;
```

In fact, with the above package, the user has to make use of the representation in order to construct values of the type.

We might wish to prevent use of knowledge of the representation so that we could change the representation to perhaps polar form at a later date and know that the user's program would still be correct. We can do this with a private type. Consider

```
package COMPLEX_NUMBERS is
    type COMPLEX is private;
    I: constant COMPLEX;
    function "+" (X, Y: COMPLEX) return COMPLEX;
    function "−" (X, Y: COMPLEX) return COMPLEX;
    function "*" (X, Y: COMPLEX) return COMPLEX;
    function "/" (X, Y: COMPLEX) return COMPLEX;
    function CONS(R, I: REAL) return COMPLEX;
    function RL_PART(X: COMPLEX) return REAL;
    function IM_PART(X: COMPLEX) return REAL;
private
    type COMPLEX is
        record
            RL, IM: REAL;
        end record;
    I: constant COMPLEX:=(0.0,1.0);
end;
```

The part of the package specification before the reserved word **private** is the visible part and gives the information available externally to the package. The type COMPLEX is declared to be private. This means that outside the package nothing is known of the details of the type. The only operations available are assignment, =, and /= plus those added by the writer of the package as subprograms specified in the visible part.

We may also declare constants of a private type such as I, in the visible part. The initial value cannot be given in the visible part because the details of the type are not yet known. Hence we just state that I is a constant; we call it a deferred constant.

After **private** we have to give the details of types declared as private and give the initial values of corresponding deferred constants.

A private type can be implemented in any way consistent with the operations visible to the user. It can be a record as we have shown; equally it could be an array, an enumeration type and so on; it could even be declared in terms of another private type. In our case it is fairly obvious that the type COMPLEX is naturally implemented as a record; but we could equally have used an array of two components such as

type COMPLEX **is array** (1 .. 2) **of** REAL;

Having declared the details of the private type we can use them and so declare the constants properly and give their initial values.

It should be noted that as well as the functions +, −, * and / we have also provided CONS to create a complex number from its real and imaginary components and RL_PART and IM_PART to return the components. These functions are necessary because the user no longer has direct access to the structure of the type. Of course, the fact that CONS, RL_PART and IM_PART correspond to our thinking of the complex numbers in cartesian form does not prevent us from implementing them in polar form.

The body of the package is as shown in the answer to Exercise 8.1(**2**) plus the additional functions which are trivial. It is therefore

```
package body COMPLEX_NUMBERS is
    function "+" (X, Y: COMPLEX) return COMPLEX is
    begin
        return (X.RL + Y.RL, X.IM + Y.IM);
    end "+";

    -- - * / similarly

    function CONS(R, I: REAL) return COMPLEX is
    begin
        return (R, I);
    end CONS;

    function RL_PART(X: COMPLEX) return REAL is
    begin
        return X.RL;
    end RL_PART;

    -- IM_PART similarly

end COMPLEX_NUMBERS;
```

The package COMPLEX_NUMBERS could be used in a fragment such as

```
declare
    use COMPLEX_NUMBERS;
    C, D: COMPLEX;
    R, S: REAL;
begin
    C:= CONS(1.5, −6.0);
    D:= C+I;                  -- COMPLEX +
    R:= RL_PART (D) +6.0;     -- REAL +
    . . .
end;
```

Outside the package we can declare variables and constants of type COMPLEX in the usual way. Note the use of CONS to create a complex literal. We cannot, of course, do mixed operations between our complex and real numbers. Thus we cannot write

```
C:= 2.0*C;
```

but instead must write

```
C:= CONS(2.0, 0.0)*C;
```

If this is felt to be tedious we could add further overloadings of the operators to allow mixed operations.

Let us suppose that for some reason we now decide to represent the complex numbers in polar form. The visible part of the package will be unchanged but the private part could now become

```
private
    PI: constant:= 3.14159_26536;
    type COMPLEX is
        record
            R: REAL;
            THETA: REAL range 0.0 . . 2.0*PI;
        end record;
    I: constant COMPLEX:= (1.0, 0.5*PI);
end;
```

Note how the constant PI is for convenience declared in the private part; anything other than a body can be declared in a private part if it suits us – we are not restricted to just declaring the types and constants in full. Things declared in the private part are also available in the body.

The body of our package COMPLEX_NUMBERS will now need completely rewriting. Some functions will become simpler and others will be more intricate. In particular it will be convenient to provide a function to normalise the angle θ so that it lies in the range 0 to 2π. The details are left for the reader.

However, since the visible part has not been changed the user's program will not need changing; we are assured of this since there is no way in which the user could have written anything depending on the details of the private type. Nevertheless, the user's program will need recompiling because of the general dependency rules explained in Section 8.2. This may seem slightly contradictory but remember that the compiler needs the information in the private part in order to be able to allocate storage for objects of the private type declared in the user's program. If we change the private part the size of the objects could change.

An interesting point is that rather than declare a deferred constant we could provide a parameterless function

function I **return** COMPLEX;

This has the slight advantage that we can change the value returned without changing the package specification and so having to recompile the user's program. Of course in the case of I we are unlikely to need to change the value anyway!

Finally note that between a private type declaration and the later full type declaration, the type is in a curiously half defined state. Because of this there are severe restrictions on its use; it can only be used to declare deferred constants, other types and subtypes and subprogram specifications (also entries of tasks which we will meet in Chapter 14). It cannot be used to declare variables.

Thus we could write

type COMPLEX_ARRAY **is array** (INTEGER **range** <>) **of** COMPLEX;

and then

C: **constant** COMPLEX_ARRAY(1 . . 10);

But until the full declaration is given we cannot declare variables of the type COMPLEX or COMPLEX_ARRAY.

However, we can declare the specifications of subprograms with parameters of the types COMPLEX and COMPLEX_ARRAY and can even supply default expressions. Such default expressions can use deferred constants and functions; this is allowed because of course a default expression is only evaluated when a subprogram is called and this cannot occur until the body has been declared and this is bound to be after the full type declaration.

There are various other subtle points which need not concern the normal user but which are described in the LRM. However, the general rule is that you can only use what you know. Outside the package we know only that the type is private; inside the package and after the full type declaration we know all the properties implied by that declaration.

As an example consider the type COMPLEX_ARRAY and the operator <. (Remember that < only applies to arrays if the component type is discrete.) Outside the package we cannot use < since we do not know whether or not the type COMPLEX is discrete. Inside the package we find that it is not discrete and so still cannot use <. If it had been discrete we could have used < after the full type declaration but of course we still could not use it outside. On the other hand slicing is applicable to all one dimensional arrays and so can be used both inside and outside the package.

Exercise 9.1

1 Write additional functions ''*'' to enable mixed multiplication of real and complex numbers.

2 Complete the package RATIONAL_NUMBERS whose visible part is

```
package RATIONAL_NUMBERS is

    type RATIONAL is private;
    function "+"(X: RATIONAL) return RATIONAL;      - - unary +
    function "-"(X: RATIONAL) return RATIONAL;      - - unary -
    function "+"(X, Y: RATIONAL) return RATIONAL;
    function "-"(X, Y: RATIONAL) return RATIONAL;
    function "*"(X, Y: RATIONAL) return RATIONAL;
    function "/"(X, Y: RATIONAL) return RATIONAL;

    function "/"(X: INTEGER; Y: POSITIVE) return RATIONAL;
    function NUMERATOR(R: RATIONAL) return INTEGER;
    function DENOMINATOR(R: RATIONAL) return POSITIVE;

private
    . . .
end;
```

A rational number is a number of the form N / D where N is an integer and D is a positive integer. For predefined equality to work it is essential that rational numbers are always reduced by cancelling out common factors. This may be done using the function GCD of Exercise 7.1(**7**).

3 Why does

```
function "/"(X: INTEGER; Y: POSITIVE) return RATIONAL;
```

not hide the predefined integer division?

9.2 Limited private types

The operations available on a private type can be completely restricted to those specified in the visible part of the package. This is done by declaring the type as limited as well as private thus

type T **is limited private**;

In such a case assignment and predefined = and /= are not available outside the package. However, the package may define a function "=" if the two parameters are of the same limited type; it must return a value of type **BOOLEAN**. The operator /= always takes its meaning from = and so cannot be explicitly defined.

An important consequence of the absence of assignment for limited types is that the declaration of an object cannot include an initial value; this in turn implies that a constant cannot be declared outside the defining package. Similarly a record component of a limited type cannot have a default initial expression. However, remember that the procedure parameter mechanism is not formally assignment and in fact we can declare our own subprograms with limited types as parameters of mode **in** or **in out** outside the defining package and we can even supply default expressions for **in** parameters; parameters of mode **out** are however not allowed for a reason which will become apparent in the next section.

The advantage of making a private type limited is that the package writer has complete control over the objects of the type – the copying of resources can be monitored and so on.

As a simple example consider the following

```
package STACKS is
    type STACK is limited private;
    procedure PUSH(S: in out STACK; X: in INTEGER);
    procedure POP(S: in out STACK; X: out INTEGER);
    function "="(S, T: STACK) return BOOLEAN;
private
    MAX: constant:= 100;
    type INTEGER_VECTOR is
            array (INTEGER range <>) of INTEGER;
    type STACK is
        record
            S: INTEGER_VECTOR (1 .. MAX);
            TOP: INTEGER range 0 .. MAX:=0;
        end record;
end;
```

Each object of type **STACK** is a record containing an array **S** and integer TOP. Note that TOP has a default initial value of zero. This ensures that when we declare a stack object, it is correctly initialised to be empty. Note also the introduction of the type INTEGER_VECTOR because a record component may not be an anonymous array.

The body of the package could be

```
package body STACKS is

    procedure PUSH(S: in out STACK; X: in INTEGER) is
    begin
        S.TOP:=S.TOP+1;
        S.S(S.TOP):=X;
    end PUSH;

    procedure POP(S: in out STACK; X: out INTEGER) is
    begin
        X:=S.S(S.TOP);
        S.TOP:=S.TOP-1;
    end POP;

    function "="(S, T: STACK) return BOOLEAN is
    begin
        if S.TOP /= T.TOP then
            return FALSE;
        end if;
        for I in 1 .. S.TOP loop
            if S.S(I) /= T.S(I) then
                return FALSE;
            end if;
        end loop;
        return TRUE;
    end "=";
end STACKS;
```

This example illustrates many points. The parameter S of PUSH has mode **in out** because we need both to read from and to write to the stack. Further note that POP cannot be a function since S has to be **in out** and functions can only have **in** parameters. However, "=" can be a function because we only need to read the values of the two stacks and not to update them.

The function "=" has the interpretation that two stacks are equal only if they have the same number of items and the corresponding items have the same value. It would obviously be quite wrong to compare the whole records because the unused components of the arrays would also be compared. It is because of this that the type STACK has been made limited private rather than just private. If it were just private then we could not redefine "=" to give the correct meaning.

This is a typical example of a data structure where the value of the whole is more than just the sum of the parts; the interpretation of the array S depends on the value of TOP. Cases where there is such a relationship usually need a limited private type.

A minor point is that we are using the identifier S in two ways: as the name of the formal parameter denoting the stack and as the array inside the record. There is no conflict because, although the scopes overlap, the regions of visibility do not as was explained in Section 8.4. Of course, it is rather confusing to the reader and not good practice but it illustrates the freedom of choice of record component names.

The package could be used in a fragment such as

```
declare
    use STACKS;
    ST: STACK;
    EMPTY: STACK;
    . . .
begin
    PUSH(ST, N);

    . . .
    POP(ST, M);

    . . .
    if ST = EMPTY then
        . . .
    end if;
    . . .
end;
```

Here we have declared two stacks ST and EMPTY. Both are originally empty because their internal component TOP has an initial value of zero. Assuming that we do not manipulate EMPTY then it can be used to see whether the stack ST is empty or not by calling the function =. This seems a rather dubious way of testing for an empty stack since there is no guarantee that EMPTY has not been manipulated. It would be better if EMPTY were a constant but as mentioned earlier we cannot declare a constant of a limited private type outside the package. We could however declare a constant EMPTY in the visible part of the package. A much better technique for testing the state of a stack would, of course, be to provide a function EMPTY and a corresponding function FULL in the package.

We can write subprograms with limited private types as parameters outside the defining package despite the absence of assignment. As a simple example, the following procedure enables us to determine the top value on the stack without removing it.

```
procedure TOP_OF(S: in out STACK; X: in out INTEGER) is
begin
    POP(S, X);
    PUSH(S, X);
end;
```

The declaration of a function "=" does not have to be confined to the package containing the declaration of the limited type. The only point is that outside the package, we cannot see the structure of the type. Furthermore, a composite type containing one or more components of a limited type is itself considered to be limited and so we could define "=" for such a type. Thus outside the package STACKS we could declare

```
type STACK_ARRAY is array (INTEGER range <> ) of STACK;
function "=" (A, B: STACK_ARRAY) return BOOLEAN;
```

where the definition of an appropriate body is left to the reader.

Remember that within the private part (after the full type declaration) and within the body, any private type (limited or not) is treated in terms of how it is represented. Thus within the body of STACKS the type STACK is just a record type and so assignment and things consequential upon assignment (initialisation and constants) are allowed. So we could declare a procedure ASSIGN (intended to be used outside the package) as

```
procedure ASSIGN(S: in STACK; T: out STACK) is
begin
    T:=S;
end;
```

The parameter mechanism for a private type is simply that corresponding to how the type is represented. This applies both inside and outside the package. Of course, outside the package, we know nothing of how the type is represented and therefore should make no assumption about the mechanism used.

It is unfortunate that Ada does not separate the ability to permit assignment and user defined equality. For instance, it would be reasonable to allow assignment of stacks, but, of course, predefined equality is of no value. Equally in the case of a type such as RATIONAL of Exercise 9.1(2), it would be quite reasonable to allow manipulation – including assignment – of values which were not reduced provided that equality was suitably redefined. We are therefore forced to use a procedural form such as ASSIGN or reduce all values to a canonical form in which component by component equality is satisfactory. In the case of type STACK a suitable form would be one in which all unused elements of the stack had a standard dummy value such as zero.

Exercise 9.2

1 Rewrite the specification of STACKS to include a constant EMPTY in the visible part.

2 Write functions EMPTY and FULL for STACKS.

3 Write a suitable body for the function = applying to the type STACK_ARRAY. Make it conform to the normal rules for array equality which we mentioned towards the end of Section 6.2.

4 Rewrite ASSIGN for STACKS so that only the meaningful part of the record is copied.

5 Rewrite STACKS so that STACK is a normal private type. Ensure that predefined equality is satisfactory.

9.3 Resource management

An important example of the use of a limited private type is in providing controlled resource management. Consider the simple human model where each resource has a corresponding unique key. This key is then issued to the user when the resource is allocated and then has to be shown whenever the resource is accessed. So long as there is only one key and copying and stealing are prevented we know that the system is foolproof. A mechanism for handing in keys and reissuing them is usually necessary if resources are not to be permanently locked up. Typical human examples are the use of metal keys with post office boxes, credit cards and so on.

Now consider the following

```
package KEY_MANAGER is
    type KEY is limited private;
    procedure GET_KEY(K: in out KEY);
    procedure RETURN_KEY(K: in out KEY);
    function VALID(K: KEY) return BOOLEAN;
    . . .
    procedure ACTION(K: in KEY; . . .);
    . . .
private
    MAX: constant:=100;                    -- no. of keys
    subtype KEY_CODE is INTEGER range 0 . . MAX;
    type KEY is
        record
            CODE: KEY_CODE:=0;
        end record;
end;

package body KEY_MANAGER is
    FREE: array (KEY_CODE range 1 . . KEY_CODE'LAST) of
            BOOLEAN:=(others => TRUE);

    function VALID(K: KEY) return BOOLEAN is
    begin
        return K.CODE /=0;
    end;

    procedure GET_KEY (K: in out KEY) is
    begin
        if K.CODE =0 then
            for I in FREE'RANGE loop
                if FREE(I) then
                    FREE(I):=FALSE;
                    K.CODE:=I;
                    return;
                end if;
            end loop;
                                        -- all keys in use
        end if;
    end;

    procedure RETURN_KEY (K: in out KEY) is
    begin
        if K.CODE /=0 then
            FREE (K.CODE):=TRUE;
            K.CODE:=0;
        end if;
    end;

    . . .
```

```
        procedure ACTION(K: in KEY; . . .) is
        begin
            if VALID(K) then
               . . .
        end;
    end KEY_MANAGER;
```

The type **KEY** is represented by a record with a single component **CODE**. This has a default value of **0** which represents an illegal key. Values from **1 . . MAX** represent the allocation of the corresponding resource. When we declare a variable of type **KEY** it automatically takes an internal code value of zero. In order to use the key we must first call the procedure **GET_KEY**; this allocates the first free key number to the variable. The key may then be used with various procedures such as **ACTION** which represents a typical request for some access to the resource guarded by the key.

Finally, the key may be relinquished by calling **RETURN_KEY**. So a typical fragment of user program might be

```
    declare
        use KEY_MANAGER;
        MY_KEY: KEY;
    begin
        . . .
        GET_KEY (MY_KEY);
        . . .
        ACTION (MY_KEY, . . . );
        . . .
        RETURN_KEY (MY_KEY);
        . . .
    end;
```

A variable of type **KEY** can be thought of as a container for a key. When initially declared the default value can be thought of as representing that the container is empty; the type **KEY** has to be a record because only record components can take default initial values. Note how the various possible misuses of keys are overcome.

- If we call **GET_KEY** with a variable already containing a valid key then no new key is allocated. It is important not to overwrite an old valid key otherwise that key would be lost.

- A call of **RETURN_KEY** resets the variable to the default state so that the variable cannot be used as a key until a new one is issued by a call of **GET_KEY**. Note that the user is unable to retain a copy of the key because assignment is not valid since the type **KEY** is limited.

The function **VALID** is provided so that the user can see whether a key variable contains the default value or an allocated value. It is obviously useful to call **VALID** after **GET_KEY** to ensure that the key manager was able to provide a new key value; note that once all keys are issued, a call of **GET_KEY** does nothing.

One apparent flaw is that there is no compulsion to call **RETURN_KEY** before the scope containing the declaration of **MY_KEY** is left. The key would then be lost. This corresponds to the real life situation of losing a key (although in our model no one else can find it again – it is as if it were thrown into a black hole). To guard against this the key manager might assume (as in life) that a key not used for a certain period of time is no longer in use. Of course, the same key would not be reissued but the resource guarded might be considered reusable; this would involve keeping separate records of keys in use and resources in use and a cross reference from keys to resources.

Exercise 9.3
1   Complete the package whose visible part is

```
package BANK is
    subtype MONEY is NATURAL;
    type KEY is limited private;
    procedure OPEN_ACCOUNT (K: in out KEY; M: in MONEY);
        -- open account with initial deposit M
    procedure CLOSE_ACCOUNT (K: in out KEY; M: out MONEY);
        -- close account and return balance
    procedure DEPOSIT (K: in KEY; M: in MONEY);
        -- deposit amount M
    procedure WITHDRAW (K: in out KEY; M: in out MONEY);
        -- withdraw amount M; if account does not contain M
        -- then return what is there and close account
    function STATEMENT (K: KEY) return MONEY;
        -- returns a statement of current balance
    function VALID (K: KEY) return BOOLEAN;
        -- checks the key is valid
private
    . . .
```

2   Assuming that your solution to the previous question allowed the bank the use of the deposited money, reformulate the private type to represent a home savings box or safe deposit box where the money is in a box kept by the user.

3   A thief writes the following

```
declare
    use KEY_MANAGER;
    MY_KEY: KEY;
    procedure CHEAT (COPY: in out KEY) is
    begin
        RETURN_KEY (MY_KEY);
        ACTION (COPY, . . . );
        . . .
    end;
begin
    GET_KEY (MY_KEY);
    CHEAT (MY_KEY);
    . . .
end;
```

He attempts to return his key and then use the copy. Why is he thwarted?

4   A vandal writes the following

```
declare
    use KEY_MANAGER;
    MY_KEY: KEY;
    procedure DESTROY (K: out KEY) is
    begin
        null;
    end;
begin
    GET_KEY (MY_KEY);
    DESTROY (MY_KEY);
    . . .
end;
```

He attempts to destroy the value in his key by calling a procedure which does not update the **out** parameter; he anticipates that the copy back rule will result in a junk value being assigned to the key. Why is he thwarted?

Checklist 9

For predefined equality to be sensible, the values should be in a canonical form.

An unlimited private type can be implemented in terms of another private type provided it is also unlimited.

A limited private type can be implemented in terms of any private type limited or not.

/= can never be defined – it always follows from =.

= can be defined outside the package defining the limited private type concerned.

The rules apply transitively to composite types.

Chapter 10 EXCEPTIONS

At various times in the preceding chapters we have said that if something goes wrong when the program is executed, then an exception, usually CONSTRAINT_ ERROR, will be raised. In this chapter we describe the exception mechanism and show how remedial action can be taken when an exception occurs. We also show how we may define and use our own exceptions. Exceptions concerned with interacting tasks are dealt with when we come to Chapter 14.

10.1 Handling exceptions

We have seen that if we break various language rules then an exception may be raised when we execute the program.

There are five predefined exceptions of which we have met four so far

CONSTRAINT_ERROR   this generally corresponds to something going out of range.

NUMERIC_ERROR   this can occur when something goes wrong with arithmetic such as an attempt to divide by zero – see Section 4.9,

PROGRAM_ERROR   this will occur if we attempt to violate the control structure in some way such as running into the **end** of a function or calling a subprogram whose body has not yet been elaborated – see Sections 7.1 and 8.1,

STORAGE_ERROR   this will occur if we run out of storage space as for example if we called our recursive function FACTORIAL with a large parameter – see Section 7.1

The other predefined exception is TASKING_ERROR. This is concerned with tasking and so is dealt with in Chapter 14.

If we anticipate that an exception may occur in a part of our program then we can write an exception handler to deal with it. For example, suppose we write

```
begin
    - - sequence of statements
exception
    when CONSTRAINT_ERROR =>
    - - do something
end;
```

133

If CONSTRAINT_ERROR is raised while we are executing the sequence of statements between **begin** and **exception** then the flow of control is interrupted and immediately transferred to the sequence of statements following the =>. The clause starting **when** is known as an exception handler.

As a trivial example we could compute TOMORROW from TODAY by writing

```
begin
    TOMORROW:=DAY'SUCC(TODAY);
exception
    when CONSTRAINT_ERROR =>
        TOMORROW:=DAY'FIRST;
end;
```

If TODAY is DAY'LAST (i.e. SUN) then when we attempt to evaluate DAY'SUCC(TODAY), the exception CONSTRAINT_ERROR is raised. Control is then transferred to the handler for CONSTRAINT_ERROR and the statement TOMORROW:=DAY'FIRST; is executed. Control then passes to the end of the block.

This is really a bad example. Exceptions should be used for rarely occurring cases or those which are inconvenient to test for at their point of occurrence. By no stretch of the imagination is Sunday a rare day. Over 14% of all days are Sundays. Nor is it difficult to test for the condition at the point of occurrence. So we should really have written

```
if TODAY = DAY'LAST then
    TOMORROW:=DAY'FIRST;
else
    TOMORROW:=DAY'SUCC(TODAY);
end if;
```

However, it is a simple example with which to illustrate the mechanism involved. Several handlers can be written between **exception** and **end**. Consider

```
begin
    -- sequence of statements
exception
    when NUMERIC_ERROR|CONSTRAINT_ERROR =>
        PUT ("Numeric or Constraint error occurred");
        . . .
    when STORAGE_ERROR =>
        PUT("Ran out of space");
        . . .
    when others =>
        PUT("Something else went wrong");
        . . .
end;
```

In this example a message is output according to the exception. Note the similarity to the case statement. Each **when** is followed by one or more exception names separated by vertical bars. As usual we can write **others** but it must be last and on its own; it handles any exception not listed in the previous handlers.

Exception handlers can appear at the end of a block, subprogram body, package body (or task body) and have access to all entities declared in the unit. The examples above have shown a degenerate block in which there is no **declare** and declarative part; the block was introduced just for the purpose of providing somewhere to hang the handlers. We could rewrite our bad example to determine tomorrow as a function thus

```
function TOMORROW(TODAY: DAY) return DAY is
begin
    return DAY'SUCC(TODAY);
exception
    when CONSTRAINT_ERROR =>
        return DAY'FIRST;
end TOMORROW;
```

It is important to realise that control can never be returned to the unit where the exception was raised. The sequence of statements following => replaces the remainder of the unit containing the handler and thereby completes execution of the unit. Hence a handler for a function must generally contain a return statement in order to provide the 'emergency' result.

In particular, a goto statement cannot transfer control from a unit into one of its handlers or vice versa or from one handler to another. However, the statements of a handler can otherwise be of arbitrary complexity. They can include blocks, calls of subprograms and so on. A handler of a block could contain a goto statement which transferred control to a label outside the block and it could contain an exit statement if the block were inside a loop.

A handler at the end of a package body applies only to the initialisation sequence of the package and not to subprograms in the package. Such subprograms must have individual handlers if they are to deal with exceptions.

We now consider the question of what happens if a unit does not provide a handler for a particular exception. The answer is that the exception is propagated dynamically. This simply means that the unit is terminated and the exception is raised at the point where the unit was invoked. In the case of a block we therefore look for a handler in the unit containing the block.

In the case of a subprogram, the call is terminated and we look for a handler in the unit which called the subprogram. This unwinding process is repeated until either we reach a unit containing a handler for the particular exception or come to the top level. If we find a unit containing a relevant handler then the exception is handled at that point. Alternatively we have reached the main program and have still found no handler – the main program is then abandoned and we can expect the run time environment to provide us with a suitable diagnostic message. (Unhandled exceptions in tasks are dealt with in Chapter 14.)

It is most important to understand that exceptions are propagated dynamically and not statically. That is, an exception not handled by a subprogram is propagated to the unit calling the subprogram and not to the unit containing the declaration of the subprogram – these may or may not be the same.

If the statements in a handler themselves raise an exception then the unit is terminated and the exception propagated to the calling unit; the handler does not loop.

Exercise 10.1
Note: these are exercises to check your understanding of exceptions. They do not necessarily reflect good Ada programming techniques.

1   Assuming that calling SQRT with a negative parameter and attempting to divide by zero both raise NUMERIC_ERROR, rewrite the procedure QUADRATIC of Section 7.3 without explicitly testing D and A.

2   Rewrite the function FACTORIAL of Section 7.1 so that if it is called with a negative parameter (which would normally raise CONSTRAINT_ERROR) or a large parameter (which would normally raise STORAGE_ERROR or NUMERIC_ERROR) then a standard result of say −1 is returned. Hint: declare an inner function SLAVE which actually does the work.

10.2   Declaring and raising exceptions

Relying on the predefined exceptions to detect unusual but anticipated situations is usually bad practice because they do not provide a guarantee that the exception has in fact been raised because of the anticipated situation. Something else may have gone wrong instead.

As an illustration consider the package STACK of Section 8.1. If we call PUSH when the stack is full then the statement TOP:=TOP+1; will raise CONSTRAINT_ERROR and similarly if we call POP when the stack is empty then TOP:=TOP−1; will also raise CONSTRAINT_ERROR. Since PUSH and POP do not themselves have exception handlers, the exception will be propagated to the unit calling them. So we could write

```
declare
    use STACK;
begin
    . . .
    PUSH(M);
    . . .
    N:=POP;
    . . .
exception
    when CONSTRAINT_ERROR =>
        − − stack manipulation incorrect?
end;
```

and misuse of the stack would then result in control being transferred to the handler for CONSTRAINT_ERROR. However, there would be no guarantee that the exception had arisen because of misuse of the stack; something else in the block could have gone wrong.

A better solution is to raise an exception specifically declared to indicate misuse of the stack. Thus the package could be rewritten

```
package STACK is
    ERROR: exception;
    procedure PUSH(X: INTEGER);
    function POP return INTEGER;
end STACK;

package body STACK is
    MAX: constant:=100;
    S: array (1 .. MAX) of INTEGER;
    TOP: INTEGER range 0 .. MAX;

    procedure PUSH(X: INTEGER) is
    begin
        if TOP = MAX then
            raise ERROR;
        end if;
        TOP:=TOP+1;
        S(TOP):=X;
    end PUSH;

    function POP return INTEGER is
    begin
        if TOP = 0 then
            raise ERROR;
        end if;
        TOP:=TOP–1;
        return S(TOP+1);
    end POP;

begin
    TOP:=0;
end STACK;
```

An exception is declared in a similar way to a variable and is raised by an explicit raise statement naming the exception. The handling and propagation rules are just as for the predefined exceptions. We can now write

```
declare
    use STACK;
begin
    . . .
    PUSH (M);
    . . .
    N:=POP;
    . . .
exception
    when ERROR =>
        – – stack manipulation incorrect
    when others =>
        – – something else wrong
end;
```

We have now successfully separated the handler for misusing the stack from the handler for other exceptions.

Note that if we had not provided a use clause then we would have had to refer to the exception in the handler as STACK.ERROR; the usual dotted notation applies.

What could we expect to do in the handler in the above case? Apart from reporting that the stack manipulation has gone wrong, we might also expect to reset the stack to an acceptable state although we have not provided a convenient means of doing so. A procedure RESET in the package STACK would be useful. A further thing we might do is relinquish any resources that were acquired in the block and might otherwise be inadvertently retained. Suppose for instance that we had also been using the package KEY_MANAGER of Section 9.3. We might then call RETURN_KEY to ensure that a key declared and acquired in the block had been returned. Remember that RETURN_KEY does no harm if called unnecessarily.

We would probably also want to reset the stack and return the key in the case of any other exception as well; so it would be as well to declare a procedure CLEAN_UP to do all the actions required. So our block might look like

```
declare
    use STACK, KEY_MANAGER;
    MY_KEY: KEY;

    procedure CLEAN_UP is
    begin
        RESET;
        RETURN_KEY (MY_KEY);
    end;

begin
    GET_KEY (MY_KEY);
    . . .
    PUSH(M);
    . . .
    ACTION(MY_KEY, . . . );
    . . .
    N:=POP;
    . . .
    RETURN_KEY (MY_KEY);
exception
    when ERROR =>
        PUT("Stack used incorrectly");
        CLEAN_UP;
    when others =>
        PUT("Something else went wrong");
        CLEAN_UP;
end;
```

We have rather assumed that RESET is a further procedure declared in the package STACK but note that we could write our own procedure externally as follows

```
procedure RESET is
    JUNK: INTEGER;
    use STACK;
begin
    loop
        JUNK:=POP;
    end loop;
exception
    when ERROR =>
        null;
end RESET;
```

This works by repeatedly calling **POP** until **ERROR** is raised. We then know that the stack is empty. The handler needs to do nothing other than prevent the exception from being propagated; so we merely write **null**. This procedure seems a bit like trickery; it would be far better to have a reset procedure in the package.

Sometimes the actions that require to be taken as a consequence of an exception need to be performed on a layered basis. In the above example we returned the key and then reset the stack but it is probably the case that the block as a whole cannot be assumed to have done its job correctly. We can indicate this by raising an exception as the last action of the handler.

```
exception
    when ERROR =>
        PUT("Stack used incorrectly");
        CLEAN_UP;
        raise ANOTHER_ERROR;
    when others =>
        . . .
end;
```

The exception **ANOTHER_ERROR** will then be propagated to the unit containing the block. We could, of course, put the statement

```
raise ANOTHER_ERROR;
```

in the procedure **CLEAN_UP**.

Sometimes it is convenient to handle an exception and then propagate the same exception. This can be done by just writing

```
raise;
```

This is particularly useful when we handle several exceptions with the one handler since there is no way in which we can explicitly name the exception which occurred.

So we might have

```
    when others =>
        PUT("Something else went wrong");
        CLEAN_UP;
        raise;
end;
```

The current exception will be remembered even if the action of the handler raises and handles its own exceptions such as occurred in our trick procedure RESET. However, note that there is a rule that we can only write **raise;** directly in a handler and not for instance in a procedure called by the handler such as CLEAN_UP.

The stack example illustrates a legitimate use of exceptions. The exception ERROR should rarely, if ever, occur and it would also be inconvenient to test for the condition at each possible point of occurrence. To do that we would presumably have to provide an additional parameter to PUSH of type BOOLEAN and mode **out** to indicate that all was not well, and then test it after each call. In the case of POP we would also have to recast it as a procedure since a function cannot take a parameter of mode **out**.

The package specification would then become

```
package STACK is
    procedure PUSH(X: in INTEGER; B: out BOOLEAN);
    procedure POP(X: out INTEGER; B: out BOOLEAN);
end;
```

and we would have to write

```
declare
    use STACK;
    OK: BOOLEAN;
begin
    . . .
    PUSH(M, OK);
    if not OK then . . . .        end if;
    . . .
    POP(N, OK);
    if not OK then . . . .        end if;
    . . .
end;
```

It is clear that the use of an exception provides a better structured program.

Note finally that nothing prevents us from explicitly raising one of the predefined exceptions. We recall that in Section 7.1 when discussing the function INNER we stated that probably the best way of coping with parameters whose bounds were unequal was to explicitly raise CONSTRAINT_ERROR.

Exercise 10.2

1   Rewrite the package RANDOM of Exercise 8.1(**1**) so that it declares and raises an exception BAD if the initial value is not odd.

2   Rewrite your answer to Exercise 10.1(**2**) so that the function FACTORIAL always raises NUMERIC_ERROR if the parameter is negative or too large.

10.3   Scope of exceptions

To a large extent exceptions follow the same scope rules as other entities. An exception can hide and be hidden by another declaration; it can be made visible by the dotted notation and so on. An exception can be renamed

HELP: **exception renames** BANK.ALARM;

Exceptions are, however, different in many ways. We cannot declare arrays of exceptions, and they cannot be components of records, parameters of subprograms and so on. In short, exceptions are not objects and so cannot be manipulated. They are merely tags.

A very important characteristic of exceptions is that they are not created dynamically as a program executes but should be thought of as existing throughout the life of the program. This relates to the way in which exceptions are propagated dynamically up the chain of execution rather than statically up the chain of scope. An exception can be propagated outside its scope although of course it can then only be handled anonymously by **others**. This is illustrated by the following

```
declare
    procedure P is
        X: exception;
    begin
        raise X;
    end P;
begin
    P;
exception
    when others =>
                    -- X handled here
end;
```

The procedure P declares and raises the exception X but does not handle it. When we call P, the exception X is propagated to the block calling P where it is handled anonymously.

It is even possible to propagate an exception out of its scope, where it becomes anonymous, and then back in again where it can once more be handled by its proper name. Consider

```
declare
    package P is
        procedure F;
        procedure H;
    end P;

    procedure G is
    begin
        P.H;
    exception
        when others =>
            raise;
```

```
          end G;
          package body P is
              X: exception;
              procedure F is
              begin
                  G;
              exception
                  when X =>
                      PUT("Got it!");
              end F;

              procedure H is
              begin
                  raise X;
              end H;
          end P;
      begin
          P.F;
      end;
```

The block declares a package P containing procedures F and H and also a procedure G. The block calls F in P which calls G outside P which in turn calls H back in P. The procedure H raises the exception X whose scope is the body of P. The procedure H does not handle X, so it is propagated to G which called H. The procedure G is outside the package P, so the exception X is now outside its scope; nevertheless G handles the exception anonymously and propagates it further by reraising it. G was called by F so X is now propagated back into the package and so can be handled by F by its proper name.

A further illustration of the nature of exceptions is afforded by a recursive procedure containing an exception declaration. Unlike variables declared in a procedure we do not get a new exception for each recursive call. Each recursive activation refers to the same exception. Consider the following artificial example

```
      procedure F(N: INTEGER) is
          X: exception;
      begin
          if N = 0 then
              raise X;
          else
              F(N-1);
          end if;
      exception
          when X =>
              PUT("Got it");
              raise;
          when others =>
              null;
      end F;
```

Suppose we execute F(4); we get recursive calls F(3), F(2), F(1) and finally

F(0). When F is called with parameter zero, it raises the exception X, handles it, prints out a confirmatory message and then reraises it. The calling instance of F (which itself had N = 1) receives the exception and again handles it as X and so on. The message is therefore printed out five times in all and the exception is finally propagated anonymously. Observe that if each recursive activation had created a different exception then the message would only be printed out once.

In all the examples we have seen so far exceptions have been raised in statements. An exception can however also be raised in a declaration. Thus

```
N: POSITIVE:=0;
```

would raise CONSTRAINT_ERROR because the initial value of N does not satisfy the range constraint 1 . . INTEGER'LAST of the subtype POSITIVE. An exception raised in a declaration is not handled by a handler (if any) of the unit containing the declaration but is immediately propagated up a level. This means that in any handler we are assured that all declarations of the unit were successfully elaborated and so there is no risk of referring to something that does not exist.

Finally a warning regarding parameters of mode **out** or **in out**. If a subprogram is terminated by an exception then any actual parameter of a scalar type will not have been updated since such updating occurs on a normal return. For an array or record type the parameter mechanism is not so closely specified and the actual parameter may or may not have its original value. A program assuming a particular mechanism is of course erroneous. As an example consider the procedure WITHDRAW of the package BANK in Exercise 9.3(**1**). It would be incorrect to attempt to take the key away and raise an alarm as in

```
procedure WITHDRAW (K: in out KEY; M: in out MONEY) is
begin
    if VALID (K) then
        if M > amount remaining then
            M:= amount remaining;
            FREE (K.CODE):= TRUE;
            K.CODE:=0;
            raise ALARM;
        else
            . . .
        end if;
    end if;
end;
```

If the parameter mechanism were implemented by copy then the bank would think that the key were now free but would have left the greedy customer with a copy.

Exercise 10.3

1 Rewrite the package BANK of Exercise 9.3(**1**) to declare an exception ALARM and raise it when any illegal banking activity is attempted. Avoid problems with the parameters.

2 Consider the following pathological procedure

```ada
procedure P is
begin
    P;
exception
    when STORAGE_ERROR =>
        P;
end P;
```

What happens when P is called? To be explicit suppose that there is enough stack space for only N simultaneous recursive calls of P but that on the $N+1$th call the exception STORAGE_ERROR is raised. How many times will P be called in all and what eventually happens?

Checklist 10

Do not use exceptions unnecessarily.

Use specific user declared exceptions rather than predefined exceptions where relevant.

Ensure that handlers return resources correctly.

Out and in out parameters may not be updated correctly if a procedure is terminated by an exception.

Chapter 11 ADVANCED TYPES

In this chapter we describe most of the remaining classes of types. These are discriminated record types, access types and derived types. Numeric types, which are explained in terms of derived types, are described in the next chapter and task types are described in Chapter 14.

11.1 Discriminated record types

In the record types we have seen so far there was no formal language dependency between the components. Any dependency was purely in the mind of the programmer as for example in the case of the limited private type STACK in Section 9.2 where the interpretation of the array S depended on the value of the integer TOP.

In the case of a discriminated record type, some of the components are known as discriminants and the remaining components can depend upon these. The discriminants, which have to be of a discrete type, can be thought of as parameterising the type and the syntax reveals this analogy.

As a simple example suppose we wish to write a package providing various operations on square matrices and that in particular we wish to write a function TRACE which sums the diagonal elements of a square matrix. We could contemplate using the type MATRIX of Section 6.2.

```
type MATRIX is array (INTEGER range <>, INTEGER range <>)
                  of REAL;
```

but our function would then have to check that the matrix passed as an actual parameter was indeed square. We would have to write something like

```
function TRACE(M: MATRIX) return REAL is
    SUM: REAL:=0.0;
begin
    if M'FIRST(1) /=M'FIRST(2) or M'LAST(1) /=M'LAST(2) then
        raise NON_SQUARE;
    end if;
    for I in M'RANGE loop
        SUM:=SUM+M(I, I);
    end loop;
    return SUM;
end TRACE;
```

This is somewhat unsatisfactory; we would prefer to use a formulation which ensured that the matrix was always square. We can do this using a discriminated type. Consider

```
type SQUARE(ORDER: POSITIVE) is
    record
        MAT: MATRIX (1 . . ORDER, 1 . . ORDER);
    end record;
```

This is a record type having two components: the first, ORDER, is a discriminant of the discrete subtype POSITIVE and the second, MAT, is an array whose bounds depend upon the value of ORDER.

Variables of type SQUARE can be declared in the usual way but a value of the discriminant must be given as a constraint thus

```
M: SQUARE(3);
```

The named form can also be used

```
M: SQUARE(ORDER=> 3);
```

The value provided as the constraint could be any dynamic expression but once the variable is declared its constraint cannot be changed. An initial value for M could be provided by an aggregate, but, perhaps surprisingly, this must be complete and repeat the constraint which must match, thus

```
M: SQUARE(3):=(3, (1 . . 3 => (1 . . 3 => 0.0)));
```

However, we could not write

```
M: SQUARE(N):=(M.ORDER, (M.MAT'RANGE(1) =>
                    (M.MAT'RANGE(2) => 0.0)));
```

in order to avoid repeating N because of the rule that we cannot refer to an object in its own declaration. However

```
declare
    M: SQUARE(N);
begin
    M:= (M.ORDER, (M.MAT'RANGE(1) =>
        (M.MAT'RANGE(2) => 0.0)));
```

is perfectly valid. If we attempt to assign a value to M which does not have the correct discriminant value then CONSTRAINT_ERROR will be raised.

Constants can be declared as usual and, like array bounds, the discriminant constraint can be deduced from the initial value.

We can, of course introduce subtypes

```
subtype SQUARE_3 is SQUARE(3);
M: SQUARE_3;
```

We can now rewrite our function **TRACE** as follows

```
function TRACE(M: SQUARE) return REAL is
    SUM: REAL:=0.0;
begin
    for I in M.MAT'RANGE loop
        SUM:=SUM+M.MAT(I, I);
    end loop;
    return SUM;
end TRACE;
```

There is now no way in which a call of **TRACE** can be supplied with a non square matrix. Note that the discriminant of the formal parameter is taken from that of the actual parameter in a similar way to the bounds of an array. Discriminants of parameters have much in common with array bounds. For example, a discriminant can be read even in the case of an **out** parameter. Again like arrays, the formal parameter could be constrained as in

```
function TRACE_3(M: SQUARE_3) return REAL;
```

but then the actual parameter would have to have a discriminant value of 3; otherwise **CONSTRAINT_ERROR** would be raised.

The result of a function could be of a discriminated type and, like arrays, the result could be a value whose discriminant is not known until the function is called. Thus we could write a function to return the transpose of a square matrix

```
function TRANSPOSE(M: SQUARE) return SQUARE is
    R: SQUARE(M.ORDER);
begin
    for I in 1 .. M.ORDER loop
        for J in 1 .. M.ORDER loop
            R.MAT(I, J):=M.MAT(J, I);
        end loop;
    end loop;
    return R;
end TRANSPOSE;
```

A private type can also have discriminants and it must then be implemented in terms of a record type with corresponding discriminants. A good example is provided by considering the type **STACK** in Section 9.2. We can overcome the problem that all the stacks had the same maximum length of 100 by making **MAX** a discriminant. Thus we can write

```
package STACKS is
    type STACK(MAX:NATURAL) is limited private;
    procedure PUSH(S: in out STACK; X: in INTEGER);
    procedure POP(S: in out STACK; X out INTEGER);
    function "="(S, T: STACK) return BOOLEAN;
private
```

```
type INTEGER_VECTOR is array (INTEGER range <>) of
            INTEGER;
type STACK(MAX: NATURAL) is
    record
        S: INTEGER_VECTOR (1 .. MAX);
        TOP: INTEGER:=0;
    end record;
end;
```

Each variable of type **STACK** now includes a discriminant component giving the maximum stack size. When we declare a stack we must supply the value thus

```
ST: STACK(100);
```

and as for the type **SQUARE** the value of the discriminant cannot later be changed. Of course, the discriminant is visible and can be referred to as **ST.MAX** although the remaining components are private.

The body of the package **STACKS** remains as before (see Section 9.2). Observe in particular that the function "=" can be used to compare stacks with different values of **MAX** since it only compares those components of the internal array which are in use.

Although constants of the type **STACK** cannot be declared outside the defining package (because the type is limited private) we can declare a deferred constant in the visible part. Such a declaration need not supply a value for the discriminant since it will be given in the private part.

This is a good point to mention that discriminants bear a resemblance to subprogram parameters in several respects. The type or subtype of a discriminant must be given by a type mark and not by a subtype indication. This is so that the same simple conformance rules can be used when a discriminant specification has to be repeated in the case of a private type with discriminants, as illustrated by the type **STACK** above.

A similar conformance problem arises in the case of deferred constants with discriminants. Suppose we wish to declare a constant **STACK** with a discriminant of 3. We can omit the discriminant in the visible part and merely write

```
C: constant STACK;
```

and then give the discriminant in the private part either as a constraint or through the mandatory initial value (or both)

```
C: constant STACK(3):=(3, (1, 2, 3), 3);
```

However, if we wish to give the discriminant in the visible part then we must introduce a subtype to do so; we cannot use an explicit constraint in a subtype indication. Having introduced the subtype then the full constant declaration must also use it since the type marks must conform. Thus we can write

```
subtype STACK_3 is STACK(3);
C: constant STACK_3;
```

and then

C: **constant** STACK_3:=(3, (1, 2, 3), 3);

in the private part.

The discriminated types we have encountered so far have been such that once a variable is declared, its discriminant cannot be changed. It is possible, however, to provide a default expression for a discriminant and the situation is then different. A variable can then be declared with or without a discriminant constraint. If one is supplied then that value overrides the default and as before the discriminant cannot be changed. If, on the other hand, a variable is declared without a value for the discriminant, then the value of the default expression is taken but it can then be changed by a complete record assignment.

Suppose we wish to manipulate polynomials of the form

$$P(x) = a_0 + a_1x + a_2x^2 + \ldots a_nx^n$$

where $a_n \neq 0$ if $n \neq 0$.

Such a polynomial could be represented by

type POLY(N: INDEX) **is**
    record
        A: INTEGER_VECTOR(0 . . N);
    end record;

where

subtype INDEX **is** INTEGER **range** 0 . . MAX;

but then a variable of type **POLY** would have to be declared with a constraint and would thereafter be a polynomial of that fixed size. This would be most inconvenient because the sizes of the polynomials may be determined as the consequences of elaborate calculations. For example if we subtract two polynomials which have $n = 3$, then the result will only have $n = 3$ if the coefficients of x^3 are different.

However, if we declare

type POLYNOMIAL(N: INDEX:= 0) **is**
    record
        A: INTEGER_VECTOR (0 . . N);
    end record;

then we can declare variables

P, Q: POLYNOMIAL;

which do not have constraints. The initial value of their discriminants would be zero because the default value of N is zero but the discriminants could later be changed by assignment. Note however that a discriminant can only be changed by a complete record assignment. So

P.N:= 6;

would be illegal. This is quite natural since we cannot expect the array P.A to adjust its bounds by magic.

Variables of the type POLYNOMIAL could be declared with constraints

```
R: POLYNOMIAL(5);
```

but R would thereafter be constrained forever to be a polynomial with $n = 5$.

Initial values can be given in declarations in the usual way.

```
P: POLYNOMIAL:= (3, (5, 0, 4, 2) );
```

which represents $5 + 4x^2 + 2x^3$. Note that despite the initial value, P is not constrained.

In practice we would make the type POLYNOMIAL a private type so that we could enforce the rule that $a_n \neq 0$. Observe that predefined equality is satisfactory and so we do not have to make it a limited private type. Both the private type declaration and the full type declaration must give the default expression for N.

Note once more the similarity to subprogram parameters; the default expression is only evaluated when required and so need not produce the same value each time. Moreover, the same conformance rules apply when it has to be written out again in the case of a private type.

If we declare functions such as

```
function "−" (P, Q: POLYNOMIAL) return POLYNOMIAL;
```

then it will be necessary to ensure that the result is normalised so that a_n is not zero. This could be done by the following function.

```
function NORMAL(P: POLYNOMIAL) return POLYNOMIAL is
    SIZE: INTEGER:= P.N;
begin
    while SIZE > 0 and P.A(SIZE) = 0 loop
        SIZE:= SIZE−1;
    end loop;
    return (SIZE, P.A(0 .. SIZE));
end NORMAL;
```

This is a further illustration of a function returning a value whose discriminant is not known until it is called. Note the use of the array slice.

It is possible to declare a type with several discriminants. We may for instance wish to manipulate matrices which although not constrained to be square nevertheless have both lower bounds of 1. This could be done by

```
type RECTANGLE(ROWS, COLUMNS: POSITIVE) is
    record
        MAT: MATRIX (1 .. ROWS, 1 .. COLUMNS);
    end record;
```

and we could then declare

```
R: RECTANGLE(2, 3);
```

or

```
R: RECTANGLE(ROWS => 2, COLUMNS => 3);
```

The usual rules apply: positional values must be given in order, named ones may be in any order, mixed notation can be used but the positional ones must come first.

If default expressions are supplied then they must be supplied for all discriminants of the type. This rule is similar to that for multidimensional array types – all bounds must be constrained. And again, if default expressions are supplied then objects must be fully constrained or not at all. Similarly, a subtype must supply all the constraints or none at all. We could not declare

```
subtype ROW_3 is RECTANGLE(ROWS => 3);
```

in order to get the equivalent of

```
type ROW_3(COLUMNS: POSITIVE) is
    record
        MAT: MATRIX (1 . . 3, 1 . . COLUMNS);
    end record;
```

The attribute CONSTRAINED can be applied to an object of a discriminated type and gives a Boolean value indicating whether the object is constrained or not. For any object of types such as SQUARE and STACK which do not have default values for the discriminants this attribute will, of course, be TRUE. But in the case of objects of a type such as POLYNOMIAL which does have a default value, the attribute may be TRUE or FALSE.

```
P'CONSTRAINED = FALSE
R'CONSTRAINED = TRUE
```

We mentioned above than an unconstrained formal parameter will take the value of the discriminant of the actual parameter. In the case of an **out** or **in out** parameter, the formal parameter will be constrained if the actual parameter is constrained (an **in** parameter is constant anyway). Suppose we declare a procedure to truncate a polynomial by removing its highest order term.

```
procedure TRUNCATE (P: in out POLYNOMIAL) is
begin
    P:=(P.N−1, P.A(0 . . P.N−1));
end;
```

Then given

```
Q: POLYNOMIAL;
R: POLYNOMIAL(5);
```

the statement

    TRUNCATE(Q);

will be successful, but

    TRUNCATE(R);

will result in CONSTRAINT_ERROR being raised.

In the examples we have shown, discriminants have been used in index constraints as the upper bounds of arrays; they can also be used as the lower bounds of arrays. In the next section we describe how a discriminant can also be used to introduce a variant part. In these cases a discriminant must be used directly and not as part of a larger expression. So we could not declare

```
type SYMMETRIC_ARRAY (N: POSITIVE) is
    record
        A: VECTOR (−N . . N);
    end record;
```

or

```
type TWO_BY_ONE (N: POSITIVE) is
    record
        A: MATRIX (1 . . N, 1 . . 2*N);
    end record;
```

Exercise 11.1

1   Suppose that M is an object of the type MATRIX. Write a call of the function TRACE whose parameter is an aggregate of type SQUARE in order to determine the trace of M. What would happen if the two dimensions of M were not equal?

2   Rewrite the specification of STACKS to include a constant EMPTY in the visible part. See also Exercise 9.2(**1**).

3   Write a function FULL for STACKS. See also Exercise 9.2(**2**).

4   Declare a POLYNOMIAL representing zero (i.e. $0x^0$).

5   Write a function "**" to multiply two polynomials.

6   Write a function "−" to subtract two polynomials. Use the function NORMAL.

7   Rewrite the procedure TRUNCATE to raise TRUNCATE_ERROR if we attempt to truncate a constrained polynomial.

11.2   Variant parts

It is sometimes convenient to have a record type in which part of the structure is fixed for all objects of the type but the remainder can take one of several different forms. This can be done using a variant part and the choice between the alternatives is governed by the value of a discriminant.

Consider the following

```
type GENDER is (MALE, FEMALE);

type PERSON (SEX: GENDER) is
    record
        BIRTH: DATE;
        case SEX is
            when MALE =>
                BEARDED: BOOLEAN;
            when FEMALE =>
                CHILDREN: INTEGER;
        end case;
    end record;
```

This declares a record type **PERSON** with a discriminant **SEX**. The component **BIRTH** of type **DATE** (see Section 6.5) is common to all objects of the type. However, the remaining components depend upon **SEX** and are declared as a variant part. If the value of **SEX** is **MALE** then there is a further component **BEARDED** whereas if **SEX** is **FEMALE** then there is a component **CHILDREN**. Only men can have beards and only women (directly) have children.

Since no default expression is given for the discriminant all objects of the type must be constrained. We can therefore declare

```
JOHN: PERSON(MALE);
BARBARA: PERSON(FEMALE);
```

or we can introduce subtypes and so write

```
subtype MAN is PERSON(SEX => MALE);
subtype WOMAN is PERSON(SEX => FEMALE);
JOHN: MAN;
BARBARA: WOMAN;
```

Aggregates take the usual form but, of course, give only the components for the corresponding alternative in the variant. The value for a discriminant governing a variant must be static so that the compiler can check the consistency of the aggregate. We can therefore write

```
JOHN:= (MALE, (19, AUG, 1937), FALSE);
BARBARA:= (FEMALE, (13, MAY, 1943), 2);
```

but not

```
S: GENDER:= FEMALE;
BARBARA:= (S, (13, MAY, 1943), 2);
```

because S is not static but a variable.

The components of a variant can be accessed and changed in the usual way. We could write

```
JOHN.BEARDED:= TRUE;
BARBARA.CHILDREN:= BARBARA.CHILDREN+1;
```

but an attempt to access a component of the wrong alternative such as JOHN.CHILDREN would raise CONSTRAINT_ERROR. Note that although the sex of objects of type PERSON cannot be changed, it need not be known at compilation time. We could have

```
S: GENDER:= . . .
CHRIS: PERSON(S);
```

where the sex of CHRIS is not determined until he or she is declared. The rule that a discriminant must be static applies only to aggregates.

The variables of type PERSON are necessarily constrained because the type had no default expression for the discriminant. It is therefore not possible to assign a value which would change the sex; an attempt to do so would raise CONSTRAINT_ERROR. However, as with the type POLYNOMIAL, we could declare a default initial expression for the discriminant and consequently declare unconstrained variables. Such unconstrained variables could then be assigned values with different discriminants but only be a complete record assignment.

We could therefore have

```
type GENDER is (MALE, FEMALE, NEUTER);

type MUTANT (SEX: GENDER:= NEUTER) is
      record
            BIRTH: DATE;
            case SEX is
                  when MALE =>
                        BEARDED: BOOLEAN;
                  when FEMALE =>
                        CHILDREN: INTEGER;
                  when NEUTER =>
                        null;
            end case;
      end record;
```

Note that we have to write **null** as the alternative in the case of NEUTER where we did not want any components. In a similar way to the use of a null statement in a case statement this indicates that we really meant to have no components and did not omit them by accident.

We can now declare

```
M: MUTANT;
```

The sex of this unconstrained mutant is neuter by default but can be changed by a whole record assignment.

Note the difference between

M: MUTANT:= (NEUTER, (1, JAN, 1984));

and

N: MUTANT (NEUTER):= (NEUTER, (1, JAN, 1984));

In the first case the mutant is not constrained but just happens to be initially neuter. In the second case the mutant is permanently neuter. This example also illustrates the form of the aggregate when there are no components in the alternative; there are none so we write none – we do not write **null**.

The rules regarding the alternatives closely follow those regarding the case statement described in Section 5.2. Each **when** is followed by one or more choices separated by vertical bars and each choice is either a simple expression or a discrete range. The choice **others** can also be used but must be last and on its own. All values and ranges must be static and all possible values of the discriminant must be covered once and once only. The possible values of the discriminant are those of its static subtype (if there is one) or type. Each alternative can contain several component declarations and as we have seen could also be null.

A record can only contain one variant part and it must follow other components. However, variants can be nested; the component lists in a variant part could themselves contain one variant part but again it must follow other components.

Also observe that it is not possible to use the same identifier for components in different alternatives of a variant – all components of a record must have distinct identifiers.

It is perhaps worth emphasising the rules regarding the changing of discriminants. If an object is declared with a discriminant constraint then it cannot be changed – after all it is a constraint just like a range constraint and so the discriminant must always satisfy the constraint. Because the constraint allows only a single value this naturally means that the discriminant can only take that single value and so cannot be changed.

The other basic consideration is that, for implementation reasons, all objects must have values for discriminant components. Hence if the type does not provide a default initial expression, the object declaration must and since it is expressed as a constraint, the object is then consequently constrained.

There is a restriction on renaming components of an object of a discriminated type. If the existence of the component depends upon the value of a discriminant then it cannot be renamed if the object is unconstrained. So we cannot write

C: INTEGER **renames** M.CHILDREN;

because there is no guarantee that the component M.CHILDREN of the mutant M will continue to exist after the renaming even if it does exist at the moment of renaming. However,

```
      C: INTEGER renames BARBARA.CHILDREN;
```

is valid because **BARBARA** is a person and cannot change sex.

We have seen that a discriminant can be used as the bound of an array and also as the expression governing a variant. In a similar way it can also be used as the discriminant constraint of an inner component. We could declare a type comprising two polynomials of the same size

```
      type TWO_POLYNOMIALS(N: INDEX:=0) is
         record
            X: POLYNOMIAL(N);
            Y: POLYNOMIAL(N);
         end record;
```

Finally a discriminant can also be used as part of the expression giving a default initial value for one of the record components. Although the discriminant value may not be known until an object is declared, this is not a problem since the default initial expression is of course only evaluated when the object is declared and no other initial value is supplied.

However, we cannot use a discriminant for any other purpose. This unfortunately meant that when we declared the type **STACK** in the previous section we could not continue to apply the constraint to **TOP** by writing

```
      type STACK(MAX: NATURAL) is
         record
            S: INTEGER_VECTOR (1 .. MAX);
            TOP: INTEGER range 0 .. MAX:=0;
         end record;
```

since the use of **MAX** in the range constraint is not allowed.

Finally, a discriminant need not be used at all. It could just be treated as one component of a record. This might be particularly relevant when we wish to have a type where some components are private and others are visible. As an interesting and extreme example we can reconsider the type **KEY** of Section 9.3. We could change this to

```
      type KEY(CODE: INTEGER:=0) is limited private;
```

with

```
      type KEY(CODE: INTEGER:=0) is
         record
            null;
         end record;
```

With this formulation the user can read the code number of his key, but cannot change it.

Exercise 11.2

1   Write a procedure SHAVE which takes an object of type PERSON and removes any beard if the object is male and raises the exception SHAVING_ ERROR if the object is female.

2   Write a procedure STERILISE which takes an object of type MUTANT and ensures that its sex is NEUTER by changing it if necessary and possible and otherwise raises an appropriate exception.

3   Declare a type OBJECT which describes geometrical objects which are either a circle, a square or a rectangle. A circle is characterised by its radius, a square by its side and a rectangle by its length and breadth.

4   Write a function AREA which returns the area of an OBJECT.

5   Rewrite the declaration of the type POLYNOMIAL of Section 11.1 so that the default initial value of a polynomial of degree n represents x^n. Hint: declare an auxiliary function returning an appropriate array value.

11.3   Access types

In the case of the types we have met so far, the name of an object has been bound irretrievably to the object itself, and the lifetime of an object has been from its declaration until control leaves the unit containing the declaration. This is too restrictive for many applications where a more fluid control of the allocation of objects is desired. In Ada this can be done by access types. Objects of an access type, as the name implies, provide access to other objects and these other objects can be allocated in a manner independent of the block structure.

   For those familiar with other languages, an access object can be thought of as a reference or pointer. The term reference has been brought into disrepute because of dangling references in Algol 68 and pointer has been brought into disrepute because of anonymous pointers in PL/I. Thus the new term access can be thought of as a polite term for reference or pointer. However, Ada access objects are strongly typed and, as we shall see, there are no dangling reference problems.

   One of the simplest uses of an access type is for list processing. Consider

```
type CELL;

type LINK is access CELL;

type CELL is
    record
        VALUE: INTEGER;
        NEXT: LINK;
    end record;

L: LINK;
```

   These declarations introduce type LINK which accesses CELL. The variable L can be thought of as a reference variable which can only point at objects of type

CELL; these are records with two components, VALUE of type INTEGER and NEXT which is also a LINK and can therefore access (point to or reference) other objects of type CELL. The records can therefore be formed into a linked list. Initially there are no record objects, only the single pointer L which by default takes the value **null** which points nowhere. We could have explicitly given L this default value thus

    L: LINK:=**null**;

Note the circularity in the definitions of LINK and CELL. Because of this circularity and the rule of linear elaboration it is necessary first to give an incomplete declaration of CELL. Having done this we can declare LINK and then complete the declaration of CELL. Between the incomplete and complete declarations, the type name can only be used in the definition of an access type. Moreover, the incomplete and complete declarations must be in the same list of declarations except for one case which we will mention in the next section.

    The accessed objects are created by the execution of an allocator which can (but need not) provide an initial value. An allocator consists of the reserved word **new** followed by either just the type of the new object or a qualified expression providing also the initial value of the object. The result of an allocator is an access value which can then be assigned to a variable of the access type.

    So

    L:=**new** CELL;

creates a record of type CELL and then assigns to L a designation of (reference to or pointer to) the object. We can picture the result as in Fig. 11.1

Fig. 11.1 An access object

Note that the NEXT component of the record takes the default value **null** whereas the VALUE component is undefined.

    The components of the object referred to by L can be accessed using the normal dotted notation. So we could assign 37 to the VALUE component by

    L.VALUE:=37;

Alternatively we could have provided an initial value with the allocator

    L:=**new** CELL'(37, **null**);

The initial value here takes the form of a qualified aggregate and as usual has to provide values for all the components irrespective of whether some have default initial expressions.

    Of course, the allocator could have been used to initialise L when it was declared

L: LINK:=**new** CELL'(37, **null**);

Distinguish carefully the types **LINK** and **CELL**. L is of type **LINK** which accesses **CELL** and it is the accessed type which follows **new**.

Suppose we now want to create a further record and link it to our existing record. We can do this by declaring a further variable

N: LINK;

and then executing

N:=**new** CELL'(10, L);
L:=N;

The effect of these three steps is illustrated in Fig. 11.2.

(a) N: LINK;

(b) N:= **new** CELL' (10, L);

(c) L:= N;

Fig. 11.2 Extending a list

Note how the assignment statement

L:=N;

copies the access values (i.e. the pointers) and not the objects. If we wanted to copy the objects we could do it component by component.

L.VALUE:=N.VALUE;
L.NEXT:=N.NEXT;

or by using **all**

L.all:=N.all;

L.all refers to the whole object accessed by L. In fact we can think of **L.VALUE** as short for **L.all.VALUE**. Unlike Pascal, dereferencing is automatic.

Similarly

```
L = N
```

will be true if L and N refer to the same object, whereas

```
L.all = N.all
```

will be true if the objects referred to happen to have the same value.

We could declare a constant of an access type but, of course, being a constant we must supply an initial value.

```
C: constant LINK:=new CELL'(0, null);
```

The fact that C is constant means that it must always refer to the same object. However, the value of the object could itself be changed. So

```
C.all:=L.all;
```

is allowed but

```
C:=L;
```

is not.

We did not really need the variable N in order to extend the list since we could simply have written

```
L:=new CELL'(10, L);
```

This statement can be made into a general procedure for creating a new record and adding it to the beginning of a list.

```
procedure ADD_TO_LIST (LIST: in out LINK; V: in INTEGER) is
begin
    LIST:=new CELL'(V, LIST);
end;
```

The new record containing the value 10 can now be added to the list accessed by L by

```
ADD_TO_LIST (L, 10);
```

The parameter passing mechanism for access types is defined to be by copy like that for scalar types. However, in order to prevent an access value from becoming undefined an **out** parameter is always copied in at the start. Remember also that an uninitialised access object takes the specific default value **null**. These two facts prevent undefined access values which could cause a program to go berserk.

The value **null** is useful for determining when a list is empty. The following function returns the sum of the VALUE components of the records in a list.

```
function SUM(LIST: LINK) return INTEGER is
    L: LINK:=LIST;
    S: INTEGER:=0;
begin
    while L /= null loop
        S:=S+L.VALUE;
        L:=L.NEXT;
    end loop;
    return S;
end SUM;
```

Observe that we have to make a copy of LIST because the formal parameters of mode **in** are constants. The variable L is then used to work down the list until we reach the end. The function works even if the list is empty.

A more elaborate data structure is the binary tree. This consists of nodes each of which has a value plus two subtrees one or both of which could be null. Appropriate declarations are

```
type NODE;
type TREE is access NODE;
type NODE is
    record
        VALUE: REAL;
        LEFT, RIGHT: TREE;
    end record;
```

As an interesting example of the use of trees consider the following procedure SORT which sorts the values in an array into ascending order.

```
procedure SORT (A: in out VECTOR) is
    I: INTEGER;
    BASE: TREE:=null;

    procedure INSERT (T: in out TREE; V: REAL) is
    begin
        if T = null then
            T:=new NODE '(V, null, null);
        else
            if V < T.VALUE then
                INSERT(T.LEFT, V);
            else
                INSERT(T.RIGHT, V);
            end if;
        end if;
    end INSERT;

    procedure OUTPUT(T: TREE) is
```

```
      begin
          if T /= null then
              OUTPUT (T.LEFT);
              A(I):=T.VALUE;
              I:=I+1;
              OUTPUT (T.RIGHT);
          end if;
      end OUTPUT;

  begin - - body of SORT
      for J in A'RANGE loop
          INSERT (BASE, A(J));
      end loop;
      I:=A'FIRST;
      OUTPUT (BASE);
  end SORT;
```

The recursive procedure INSERT adds a new node containing the value V to the tree T in such a way that the values in the left subtree of a node are always less than the value at the node and the values in the right subtree are always greater than (or equal to) the value at the node.

The recursive procedure OUTPUT copies the values at all the nodes of the tree into the array A by first outputting the left subtree (which has the smaller values) and then copying the value at the node and finally outputting the right subtree.

The procedure SORT simply builds up the tree by calling INSERT with each of the components of the array in turn and then calls OUTPUT to copy the ordered values back into the array.

The access types we have met so far have referred to records. This will often be the case but an access type can refer to any type, even another access type. So we could have

```
  type REF_INT is access INTEGER;
  R: REF_INT:= new INTEGER'(46);
```

Note that the value of the integer referred to by R is, perhaps inappropriately, denoted by R.**all**. So we can write

```
  R.all:=13;
```

to change the value from 46 to 13.

It is most important to understand that all objects referred to by access types must be acquired through an allocator. We cannot write

```
  I : INTEGER;
  R: REF_INT:=I;      - - illegal
```

The accessed objects form a collection whose scope is that of the access type. The collection will cease to exist only when that scope is finally left but, of course, by then all the access variables will also have ceased to exist; so no dangling reference problems can arise.

If an object becomes inaccessible because no variables refer to it directly or indirectly then the storage it occupies may be reclaimed so that it can be reused by other objects. An implementation may (but need not) provide a garbage collector to do this.

Alternatively there is a mechanism whereby a program can indicate that an object is no longer required; if, mistakenly, there are still references to such objects then the program is erroneous. For fuller details the reader is referred to Section 15.6. In this chapter we will assume that a garbage collector tidies up for us when necessary.

A few final points of detail. Allocators illustrate the importance of the rules regarding the number of times and when an expression is evaluated in certain contexts. For example, an expression in an aggregate is evaluated for each index value concerned and so

A: **array** (1 . . 10) **of** LINK:=(1 . . 10 => **new** CELL);

creates an array of ten components and initialises each of them to access a different new cell. As a further example

A, B: LINK:=**new** CELL;

creates two new cells whereas

A: LINK:= **new** CELL;
B: LINK:= A;

naturally creates only one. Remember also that default expressions for record components, discriminants and subprogram parameters are re-evaluated each time they are required; if such an expression contains an allocator then a new object will be created each time.

If an allocator provides an initial value then this can take the form of any qualified expression. So we could have

L: LINK:=**new** CELL'(N.**all**);

in which case the object is given the same value as the object referred to by N. We could have

I: INTEGER:=46;
R: REF_INT:= **new** INTEGER'(I);

in which case the new object takes the value of I; it does not matter that I is not an access object since only its value concerns us.

The type accessed could be constrained, so we could have

type REF_POS **is access** POSITIVE;

or equivalently

type REF_POS **is access** INTEGER **range** 1 . . INTEGER'LAST;

The values of the objects referred to are all constrained to be positive. We can write

    RN: REF_POS:= **new** POSITIVE'(10);

or even

    RN: REF_POS:=**new** INTEGER'(10);

Note that if we wrote **new** POSITIVE'(0) then CONSTRAINT_ERROR would be raised because 0 is not of subtype POSITIVE. However, if we wrote **new** INTEGER'(0) then CONSTRAINT_ERROR is only raised because of the context of the allocator.

It is important to realise that each declaration of an access type introduces a new collection. Two collections can be of objects of the same type but the access objects must not refer to objects in the wrong collection. So we could have

    type REF_INT_A **is access** INTEGER;
    type REF_INT_B **is access** INTEGER;
    RA: REF_INT_A:=**new** INTEGER'(10);
    RB: REF_INT_B:=**new** INTEGER'(20);

The objects created by the two allocators are both of the same type but the access values are of different types determined by the context of the allocator and the objects are in different collections.

So, although we can write

    RA.**all**:=RB.**all**;

we cannot write

    RA:=RB;   − − illegal

Exercise 11.3
1 Write a

    procedure APPEND(FIRST: **in out** LINK; SECOND: **in** LINK);

which appends the list SECOND (without copying) to the end of the list FIRST. Take care of any special cases.

2 Write a function SIZE which returns the number of nodes in a tree.

3 Write a function COPY which makes a complete copy of a tree.

11.4 Access types and private types

A private type can be implemented as an access type. Consider once more the type STACK and suppose that we wish to impose no maximum stack size other than that imposed by the overall size of the computer. This can be done by representing the stack as a list.

```
package STACKS is
    type STACK is limited private;
    procedure PUSH(S: in out STACK; X: in INTEGER);
    procedure POP(S: in out STACK; X: out INTEGER);
private
    type CELL;
    type STACK is access CELL;
    type CELL is
        record
            VALUE: INTEGER;
            NEXT: STACK;
        end record;
end;

package body STACKS is

    procedure PUSH(S: in out STACK; X: in INTEGER) is
    begin
        S:=new CELL'(X, S);
    end;

    procedure POP(S: in out STACK; X: out INTEGER) is
    begin
        X:=S.VALUE;
        S:=S.NEXT;
    end;

end STACKS;
```

When the user declares a stack

S: STACK;

it automatically takes the default initial value **null** which denotes that the stack is empty. If we call POP when the stack is empty then this will result in attempting to evaluate

null.VALUE

and this will raise CONSTRAINT_ERROR. The only way in which PUSH can fail is by running out of storage; an attempt to evaluate

new CELL'(X, S)

could raise STORAGE_ERROR.

This formulation of stacks is one in which we have made the type limited private. Predefined equality would merely have tested two stacks to see if they were the same stack rather than if they had the same values, and assignment would, of course, copy only the pointer to the stack rather than the stack itself. The writing of an appropriate function "=" needs some care. We could attempt

function "=" (S, T: STACK) **return** BOOLEAN **is**

```
      SS: STACK:=S;
      TT: STACK:=T;
begin
   while SS /= null and TT /= null loop
      SS:=SS.NEXT;
      TT:=TT.NEXT;
      if SS.VALUE /= TT.VALUE then
         return FALSE;
      end if;
   end loop;
   return SS = TT;      -- TRUE if both null
end;
```

but this does not work because we have hidden the predefined equality (and hence inequality) which we wish to use inside the body of = by the new definition itself. So this function will recurse indefinitely. The solution is to distinguish between the type STACK and its representation in some way. One possibility would be to make the type STACK a record of one component thus

```
type CELL;
type LINK is access CELL;
type CELL is
   record
        VALUE: INTEGER;
        NEXT: LINK;
   end record;
type STACK is
   record
        LIST: LINK;
   end record;
```

so that we can then distinguish between S, the STACK, and S.LIST, its internal representation.

In the previous section we stated that if we had to write an incomplete declaration first because of circularity (as in the type CELL) then there was an exception to the general rule that the complete declaration had to occur in the same list of declarations. The exception is that a private part and the corresponding package body are treated as a single list of declarations as far as this rule is concerned.

Thus, in either of the above formulations the complete declaration of the type CELL could be moved from the private part to the body of the package STACKS. This might be an advantage since it then follows from the dependency rules that a user program would not need recompiling just because the details of the type CELL are changed. In implementation terms it is possible to do this because it is assumed that values of all access types occupy the same space – typically a single word.

Finally, an access type could conversely refer to a private type. So we could have

```
type REF_STACK is access STACK;
```

The only special point of interest is that if the accessed type is limited private then an allocator cannot provide an initial value since this would be equivalent to assignment and assignment is not allowed for limited types.

Exercise 11.4

1 Assuming that the exception ERROR is declared in the specification of STACKS, rewrite procedures PUSH and POP so that they raise ERROR rather than STORAGE_ERROR and CONSTRAINT_ERROR.

2 Rewrite PUSH, POP and "=" to use the formulation

```
type STACK is
    record
        LIST: LINK;
    end record;
```

Ignore the possibility of exceptions.

3 Complete the package whose visible part is

```
package QUEUES is
    EMPTY: exception;
    type QUEUE is limited private;
    procedure JOIN(Q: in out QUEUE; X: in ITEM);
    procedure REMOVE(Q: in out QUEUE; X: out ITEM);
    function LENGTH(Q: QUEUE) return INTEGER;
private
```

Items join a queue at one end and are removed from the other so that a normal first come first served protocol is enforced. An attempt to remove an item from an empty queue raises the exception EMPTY. Implement the queue as a singly linked list but maintain pointers to both ends of the list so that scanning of the list is avoided. The function LENGTH returns the number of items in the queue; again, avoid scanning the list.

11.5 Access types and constraints

Access types can also refer to arrays and discriminated record types. In both cases they can be constrained or not.

Consider the problem of representing a family tree. We could declare

```
type PERSON;
type PERSON_NAME is access PERSON;

type PERSON is
    record
        SEX: GENDER;
        BIRTH: DATE;
        SPOUSE: PERSON_NAME;
```

```
        FATHER: PERSON_NAME;
        FIRST_CHILD: PERSON_NAME;
        NEXT_SIBLING: PERSON_NAME;
    end record;
```

This model assumes a monogamous and legitimate system. The children are linked together through the component NEXT_SIBLING and a person's mother is identified as the spouse of the father.

It might however be more useful to use a discriminated type for a person so that different components could exist for the different sexes and more particularly so that appropriate constraints could be applied. Consider

```
    type PERSON(SEX: GENDER);
    type PERSON_NAME is access PERSON;

    type PERSON(SEX: GENDER) is
        record
            BIRTH: DATE;
            FATHER: PERSON_NAME(MALE);
            NEXT_SIBLING: PERSON_NAME;

            case SEX is
                when MALE =>
                    WIFE: PERSON_NAME(FEMALE);
                when FEMALE =>
                    HUSBAND: PERSON_NAME(MALE);
                    FIRST_CHILD: PERSON_NAME;
            end case;

        end record;
```

The incomplete declaration of PERSON also gives the discriminants (and any default initial expressions); these must, of course, conform to those in the subsequent complete declaration. The component FATHER is now constrained always to access a person whose sex is male (or **null** of course). Similarly the components WIFE and HUSBAND are constrained; note that these had to have distinct identifiers and so could not both be SPOUSE. However, the components FIRST_CHILD and NEXT_SIBLING are not constrained and so could access a person of either sex. We have also taken the opportunity to save on storage by making the children belong to the mother only.

When an object of type PERSON is created by an allocator a value must be provided for the discriminant either through an explicit initial value as in

```
    JANET:=new PERSON'(FEMALE, (22, FEB, 1967), JOHN, null,
                        null, null);
```

or by supplying a discriminant constraint thus

```
    JANET:=new PERSON(FEMALE);
```

Note the subtle distinction whereby a quote is needed in the case of the full initial value but not when we just give the constraint. This is because the first takes the form of a qualified expression whereas the second is just a subtype indication.

We could not write

```
JANET:=new PERSON;
```

because the type PERSON does not have a default discriminant. However we could declare

```
subtype WOMAN is PERSON(FEMALE);
```

and then

```
JANET:=new WOMAN;
```

Such an object cannot later have its discriminant changed. This rule applies even if the discriminant has a default initial expression; objects created by an allocator are in this respect different to objects created by a normal object declaration where, the reader will recall, a default initial expression allows unconstrained objects to be declared and later to have their discriminant changed.

On the other hand, we see that despite the absence of a default initial expression for the discriminant, we can nevertheless declare unconstrained objects of type PERSON_NAME; such objects, of course, take the default initial value **null** and so no problem arises. Thus although an allocated object cannot have its discriminant changed, nevertheless an unconstrained access object could refer from time to time to objects with different discriminants.

The reason for not allowing an allocated object to have its discriminant changed is that it could be accessed from several constrained objects such as the components FATHER and it would be difficult to ensure that such constraints were not violated.

For convenience we can define subtypes

```
subtype MANS_NAME is PERSON_NAME(MALE);
subtype WOMANS_NAME is PERSON_NAME(FEMALE);
```

We can now write a procedure to marry two people.

```
procedure MARRY(BRIDE: WOMANS_NAME; GROOM:
                    MANS_NAME) is
begin
    if BRIDE.HUSBAND /= null or GROOM.WIFE /= null then
        raise BIGAMY;
    end if;
    BRIDE.HUSBAND:= GROOM;
    GROOM.WIFE:= BRIDE;
end MARRY;
```

The constraints on the parameters are checked when the parameters are passed (remember that access parameters are always implemented by copy). An attempt to marry people of the wrong sex will raise CONSTRAINT_ERROR at the point

of call. On the other hand an attempt to marry a non-existent person will result in
CONSTRAINT_ERROR being raised inside the body of the procedure. Remember that although **in** parameters are constants we can change the components of
the accessed objects – we are not changing the values of BRIDE and GROOM to
access different objects.

A function could return an access value as for example

```
function SPOUSE(P: PERSON_NAME) return PERSON_NAME is
begin
    case P.SEX is
        when MALE =>
            return P.WIFE;
        when FEMALE =>
            return P.HUSBAND;
    end case;
end SPOUSE;
```

The result of such a function call can be directly used as part of a name so we can
write

```
SPOUSE(P).BIRTH
```

to give the birthday of the spouse of P. (See the end of Section 7.1.) We could even
write

```
SPOUSE(P).BIRTH:=NEWDATE;
```

but this is only possible because the function delivers an access value. It could not
be done if the function actually delivered a value of type PERSON rather than
PERSON_NAME. However, we cannot write

```
SPOUSE(P):=Q;
```

in an attempt to replace our spouse by someone else, whereas

```
SPOUSE(P).all:=Q.all;
```

is valid and would change all the components of our spouse to be the same as those
of Q.

The following function gives birth to a new child. We need the mother, the
sex of the child and the date as parameters.

```
function NEW_CHILD (MOTHER: WOMANS_NAME;
                    BOY_OR_GIRL: GENDER; BIRTHDAY: DATE)
                    return PERSON_NAME is
    CHILD: PERSON_NAME;
begin
    if MOTHER.HUSBAND = null then
        raise ILLEGITIMATE;
    end if;
```

```
CHILD:=new PERSON(BOY_OR_GIRL);
CHILD.BIRTH:=BIRTHDAY;
CHILD.FATHER:=MOTHER.HUSBAND;
declare
    LAST: PERSON_NAME:=MOTHER.FIRST_CHILD;
begin
    if LAST = null then
        MOTHER.FIRST_CHILD:=CHILD;
    else
        while LAST.NEXT_SIBLING /= null loop
            LAST:=LAST.NEXT_SIBLING;
        end loop;
        LAST.NEXT_SIBLING:=CHILD;
    end if;
end;
return CHILD;
end NEW_CHILD;
```

Observe that a discriminant constraint need not be static – the value of
BOY_OR_GIRL is not known until the function is called. As a consequence we
cannot give the complete initial value with the allocator because we do not know
which components to provide. Hence we allocate the child with just the value of
the discriminant and then separately assign the date of the birth and the father.
The remaining components take the default value **null**. We can now write

```
HELEN: PERSON_NAME:=NEW_CHILD(BARBARA,
                        FEMALE, (28, SEP, 1969));
```

Access types can also refer to constrained and unconstrained arrays. We
could have

```
type REF_MATRIX is access MATRIX;
R: REF_MATRIX;
```

and then obtain new matrices with an allocator thus

```
R:=new MATRIX(1 .. 10, 1 .. 10);
```

Alternatively, the matrix could be initialised

```
R:=new MATRIX'(1 .. 10 => (1 .. 10 => 0.0));
```

but as for discriminated records we could not write just

```
R:=new MATRIX;
```

because all array objects must have bounds. Moreover the bounds cannot be
changed. However, R can refer to matrices of different bounds from time to time.
    As expected we can create subtypes

```
subtype REF_MATRIX_3 is REF_MATRIX(1 .. 3, 1 .. 3);
R_3: REF_MATRIX_3;
```

and R_3 can then only reference matrices with corresponding bounds. Alternatively we could have written

```
R_3: REF_MATRIX(1 .. 3, 1 .. 3);
```

Using

```
subtype MATRIX_3 is MATRIX(1 .. 3, 1 .. 3);
```

we can then write

```
R_3:=new MATRIX_3;
```

This is allowed because the subtype supplies the array bounds just as we were allowed to write

```
JANET:=new WOMAN;
```

because the subtype WOMAN supplied the discriminant SEX.

This introduces another example of an array aggregate with **others**. Because the subtype MATRIX_3 supplies the array bounds and qualifies the aggregate, we could initialise the new object as follows

```
R_3:=new MATRIX_3'(others => (others => 0.0));
```

The components of an accessed array can be referred to by the usual mechanism, so

```
R(1, 1):=0.0;
```

would set component (1, 1) of the matrix accessed by R to zero. The whole matrix can be referred to by **all**. So

```
R_3.all:= (1 .. 3 => (1 .. 3 => 0.0));
```

would set all the components of the matrix accessed by R_3 to zero. We can therefore think of R(1, 1) as an abbreviation for R.**all**(1, 1). As with records, dereferencing is automatic. We can also write attributes R'FIRST(1) or alternatively R.**all**'FIRST(1). In the case of a one dimensional array slicing is also allowed.

Exercise 11.5
1   Write a function to return a person's heir. Follow the normal rules of primogeniture – the heir is the eldest son if there is one and otherwise is the eldest daughter. Return **null** if there is no heir.
2   Write a procedure to divorce a woman. Divorce is only permitted if there are no children.

11.6 Derived types

Sometimes it is useful to introduce a new type which is similar in most respects to an existing type but which is nevertheless a distinct type. If T is a type we can write

type S **is new** T;

and then S is said to be a derived type and T is the parent type of S.

A derived type belongs to the same class of type as its parent. If T is a record type then S will be a record type and its components will have the same names and so on.

It will be remembered that the key things that distinguish a type are its set of values and its set of operations; we now consider these.

The set of values of a derived type is a copy of the set of values of the parent. An important instance of this is that if the parent type is an access type then the derived type is also an access type and they share the same collection. Note that we say that the set of values is a copy; this reflects that they are truly different types and values of one type cannot be assigned to objects of the other type; however, as we shall see in a moment, conversion between the two types is possible. The notation for literals and aggregates (if any) is the same and any default initial expressions for the type or its components are the same.

The operations applicable to a derived type are as follows. First it has the same attributes as the parent. Second, unless the parent type, and consequently the derived type, are limited, assignment and predefined equality and inequality are also applicable. Third, a derived type will derive or inherit certain subprograms applicable to the parent type. (We say that a subprogram applies to a type if it has one or more parameters or a result of that type or one of its subtypes.) Such derived subprograms are implicitly declared at the place of the derived type definition but may be later redefined in the same declarative region.

If the parent type is a predefined type then the inherited subprograms are just the predefined subprograms. If the parent type is a user defined type then again there will be some predefined subprograms such as < and these will be inherited. If the parent type is itself a derived type then its inherited subprograms will be passed on again.

In addition, if the parent type is declared in the visible part of a package then any applicable subprograms declared in that visible part will also be inherited provided that the derived type is declared after the visible part. Thus the new subprograms only really 'belong' to the type in the sense that they can be derived with it when we reach the end of the visible part; this is quite reasonable since it is at this point that the definition of the type and its operations can be considered to be complete in an abstract sense.

We will now illustrate these rules with some examples. If we have

type INTEGER_A **is new** INTEGER;

then INTEGER_A will inherit all the predefined subprograms such as "+","−" and "abs" as well as attributes such as FIRST and LAST.

If we derive a further type from INTEGER_A then these inherited subprograms are passed on again. However, suppose that INTEGER_A is declared in a package specification and that the specification includes further subprograms, thus

```
package P is
    type INTEGER_A is new INTEGER;
    procedure INCREMENT(I: in out INTEGER_A);
    function "&"(I, J: INTEGER_A) return INTEGER_A;
end;
```

If we now have

```
type INTEGER_B is new INTEGER_A;
```

declared after the end of the specification (either outside the package or in its body) then INTEGER_B will inherit the new subprograms INCREMENT and "&" as well as the predefined ones.

If we do not like one of the inherited subprograms then it can be redefined in the same declarative region. So we could write

```
package Q is
   ·type INTEGER_X is new INTEGER;
    function "abs"(X: INTEGER_X) return INTEGER_X;
end;
```

in which for some reason we have chosen to replace the predefined operator "abs" by a new version.

If we now write

```
type INTEGER_Y is new INTEGER_X;
```

after the end of the package specification, the new version of "abs" will be inherited rather than the original one.

There are a couple of other minor rules. We cannot derive from a private type until after its full type declaration. Also, if the parent type is itself a derived type declared in the visible part of a package (such as INTEGER_A) then a type derived from it (such as INTEGER_B) cannot be declared inside that visible part. This restriction does not apply if the parent type is not a derived type; but remember that a type so derived from such a parent will inherit just the predefined subprograms and not any new or replaced ones.

Finally, it should be realised that the predefined types are not really a special case since they and the predefined subprograms are considered to be declared in the visible part of the package STANDARD.

Although derived types are distinct, the values can be converted from one to another using the same notation as was used for converting between numeric types. So given

```
type S is new T;
TX: T;
SX: S;
```

we can write

```
TX:=T(SX);
```

or

    SX:=S(TX);

but not

    TX:=SX;   – – illegal

or

    SX:=TX;   – – illegal

If multiple derivations are involved then only the overall conversion is required; the individual steps need not be given. So if we have

    type SS **is new** S;
    type TT **is new** T;
    SSX: SS;
    TTX: TT;

then we can laboriously write

    SSX:=SS(S(TX));

and

    TTX:=TT(T(SX));

or merely

    SSX:=SS(TX);

and

    TTX:=TT(SX);

The introduction of derived types extends the possibility of conversion between array types discussed in Section 6.2. In fact a value of one array type can be converted to another array type if the component types are the same and the index types are the same or convertible to each other.

Having introduced conversion we can now describe the effective specification of a derived subprogram in more detail. It is obtained from that of the parent by simply replacing all instances of the parent base type in the original specification by the new derived type. Subtypes are replaced by equivalent subtypes with corresponding constraints and default initial expressions are converted by adding a type conversion. Any parameters or result of a different type are left unchanged. As an abstract example consider

    type T **is** . . .;
    subtype S **is** T **range** L . . R;

    function F(X: T; Y: T:=E; Z: Q) **return** S;

where E is an expression of type T and the type Q is quite unrelated. If we write

```
type TT is new T;
```

then it is as if we had also written

```
subtype SS is TT range TT(L) .. TT(R);
```

and the specification of the derived function F will then be

```
function F(X: TT; Y: TT:=TT(E); Z: Q) return SS;
```

in which we have replaced T by TT, S by SS, added the conversion to the expression E but left the unrelated type Q unchanged. Note that the parameter names are naturally the same.

We can now rewrite the type STACK of Section 11.4 using a derived type as follows

```
type CELL;
type LINK is access CELL;
type CELL is
    record
        VALUE: INTEGER;
        NEXT: LINK;
    end record;
type STACK is new LINK;
```

It is now possible to write the function "=" thus

```
function "="(S, T: STACK) return BOOLEAN is
    SL: LINK:=LINK(S);
    TL: LINK:=LINK(T);
begin
    -- as the answer to Exercise 11.4(2)
end "=";
```

An advantage of using a derived type rather than making the type STACK into a record of one component is that the procedures PUSH and POP of Section 11.4 still work and do not have to be modified. This is because the type STACK is still an access type and shares its collection with the type LINK.

Derived types are often used for private types and in fact we have to use a derived type if we want to express the private type as an existing type such as INTEGER.

Another use for derived types is when we want to use the operations of existing types, but wish to avoid the accidental mixing of objects of conceptually different types. Suppose we wish to count apples and oranges. Then we could declare

```
type APPLES is new INTEGER;
type ORANGES is new INTEGER;
NO_OF_APPLES: APPLES;
NO_OF_ORANGES: ORANGES;
```

Since APPLES and ORANGES are derived from the type INTEGER they both inherit "+". So we can write

NO_OF_APPLES:=NO_OF_APPLES+1;

and

NO_OF_ORANGES:=NO_OF_ORANGES+1;

but we cannot write

NO_OF_APPLES:=NO_OF_ORANGES;

If we did want to convert the oranges to apples we would have to write

NO_OF_APPLES:=APPLES(NO_OF_ORANGES);

In the next chapter we will consider the numeric types in more detail but it is worth mentioning here that strictly speaking a type such as **INTEGER** has no literals. Literals such as 1 are of a type known as universal integer and implicit conversion to any integer type occurs if the context so demands. Thus we can use 1 with **APPLES** and **ORANGES** because of this implicit conversion and not because the literal is inherited. Enumeration literals on the other hand do properly belong to their type and are inherited; in fact, as mentioned in Section 7.5, enumeration literals behave as parameterless functions and so can be considered to be inherited in the same way as any other applicable subprogram.

Returning to our apples and oranges suppose that we have overloaded procedures to sell them

procedure SELL(N: APPLES);
procedure SELL(N: ORANGES);

Then we can write

SELL(NO_OF_APPLES);

but

SELL(6);

is ambiguous because we do not know which fruit we are selling. We can resolve the ambiguity by qualification thus

SELL(APPLES'(6));

When a subprogram is derived a new subprogram is not actually created. A call of the derived subprogram is really a call of the parent subprogram; **in** and **in out** parameters are implicitly converted just before the call; **in out** and **out** parameters or a function result are implicitly converted just after the call.

So

MY_APPLES + YOUR_APPLES

is effectively

APPLES(INTEGER(MY_APPLES) + INTEGER(YOUR_APPLES))

Derived types are in some ways an alternative to private types. Derived types have the advantage of inheriting literals but they often have the disadvantage of inheriting too much. For instance, we could derive types LENGTH and AREA from REAL.

type LENGTH **is new** REAL;
type AREA **is new** REAL;

We would then be prevented from mixing lengths and areas but we would also have inherited the ability to multiply two lengths to give a length and to multiply two areas to give an area as well as hosts of irrelevant operations such as exponentiation. Of course, it is possible to redefine these operations to be useful or to raise exceptions but it is often simpler to use private types and just define the operations we need.

As a further example of the use of derived types, reconsider the package BANK of Exercise 9.3(**1**). In that package we declared

subtype MONEY **is** NATURAL;

in order to introduce the meaningful identifier MONEY and also to ensure that monies were never negative. However, being only a subtype, we could still mix up monies and integers by mistake. It would be far better to write

type MONEY **is new** NATURAL;

so that the proper distinction is made.

In the private part shown in the solution we should perhaps similarly have written

type KEY_CODE **is new** INTEGER **range** 0 . . MAX;

The above cases illustrate that we can derive from a subtype using either a type mark or the more general subtype indication. The derived type is then actually anonymous and is derived from the underlying base type. In the case of KEY_CODE it is as if we had written

type anon **is new** INTEGER;
subtype KEY_CODE **is** anon **range** 0 . . anon(MAX);

So KEY_CODE is not really a type at all but a subtype. The set of values of the new derived type is actually the full set of values of the type INTEGER. The derived operations "+",">" and so on also work on the full set of values. So given

K: KEY_CODE;

we can legally write

K > −2

even though −2 could never be assigned to K. The Boolean expression is, of course, always true.

The reader may have felt that derived types are not very useful because in the examples we have seen there is usually an alternative mechanism open to us – usually involving record types or private types. However, one importance of derived types is that they are fundamental to the mechanism for numeric types as we shall see in the next chapter.

We finish this chapter by mentioning a curious anomaly concerning the type BOOLEAN which really does not matter so far as the normal user is concerned. If we derive a type from BOOLEAN then the predefined relational operators =, < and so on continue to deliver a result of the predefined type BOOLEAN whereas the logical operators **and**, **or**, **xor** and **not** are inherited normally and deliver a result of the derived type. We cannot go into the reason here other than to say that it is because of the fundamental nature of the type BOOLEAN. However, it does mean that the theorem of Exercise 4.7(**3**) that **xor** and /= are equivalent only applies to the type BOOLEAN and not to a type derived from it.

Exercise 11.6
1 Declare a package containing types LENGTH and AREA with appropriate redeclarations of the incorrect operations "*".

Checklist 11

If a discriminant does not have a default expression then all objects must be constrained.

The discriminant of an unconstrained object can only be changed by a complete record assignment.

Discriminants can only be used as array bounds or to govern variants or as nested discriminants or in default initial expressions for components.

A discriminant in an aggregate and governing a variant must be static.

Any variant must appear last in a component list.

An incomplete declaration can only be used in an access type.

The scope of an accessed object is that of the access type.

If an accessed object has a discriminant then it is always constrained.

Functions returning access values can be used in names.

Access objects have a default initial value of **null**.

An allocator in an aggregate is evaluated for each index value.

An allocator with a complete initial value uses a quote.

Chapter 12 NUMERIC TYPES

We now come at last to a more detailed discussion of numeric types. There are two classes of numeric types in Ada: integer types and real types. The real types are further subdivided into floating point types and fixed point types.

There are two problems concerning the representation of numeric types in a computer. First, the range may be restricted and indeed many machines have hardware operations for various ranges so that we can choose our own compromise between range of values and space occupied by values. Second, it may not be possible to represent accurately all the possible values of a type. These difficulties cause problems with program portability because the constraints vary from machine to machine. Ada recognises these difficulties and provides numeric types in such a way that a recognised minimum set of properties is provided; this enables the programmer to keep portability problems to a minimum.

We start by discussing integer types because these suffer only from range problems but not from accuracy problems.

12.1 Integer types

All implementations of Ada have the predefined type INTEGER. In addition there may be other predefined types such as LONG_INTEGER, SHORT_ INTEGER and so on. The range of values of these predefined types will be symmetric about zero except for an extra negative value in twos complement machines (which now seem to dominate over ones complement machines). All predefined types will have the same predefined operations.

Thus we might find that on machine A we have types INTEGER and LONG_INTEGER with

> range of INTEGER:
> $\qquad$ −32768 . . +32767 $\hspace{2em}$ (i.e. 16 bits)
> range of LONG_INTEGER:
> $\qquad$ −21474_83648 . . +21474_83647 $\hspace{2em}$ (i.e. 32 bits)

whereas on machine B we might have types SHORT_INTEGER, INTEGER and LONG_INTEGER with

> range of SHORT_INTEGER:
> $\qquad$ −2048 . . +2047 $\hspace{2em}$ (i.e. 12 bits)
> range of INTEGER:
> $\qquad$ −83_88608 . . +83_88607 $\hspace{2em}$ (i.e. 24 bits)
> range of LONG_INTEGER:
> $\qquad$ −14073_74883_55328 . . +14073_74883_55327 $\hspace{1em}$ (i.e. 48 bits)

For most purposes the type INTEGER will suffice on either machine and that is why we have simply used INTEGER in examples in this book so far. However, suppose we have an application where we need to manipulate signed values up to a million. The type INTEGER is inadequate on machine A and to use LONG_INTEGER on machine B would be extravagant. We can overcome our problem by using derived types and writing (for machine A)

type MY_INTEGER **is new** LONG_INTEGER;

and then using MY_INTEGER throughout the program. To move the program to machine B we just replace this one declaration by

type MY_INTEGER **is new** INTEGER;

However, Ada enables this choice to be made automatically; if we write

type MY_INTEGER **is range** −1E6 . . 1E6;

then the implementation will implicitly choose the smallest appropriate type and it will be as if we had written either

type MY_INTEGER **is new** LONG_INTEGER **range** −1E6 . . 1E6;

or

type MY_INTEGER **is new** INTEGER **range** −1E6 . . 1E6;

So in fact MY_INTEGER will be a subtype of an anonymous type derived from one of the predefined types and so objects of type MY_INTEGER will be constrained to take only the values in the range −1E6 . . 1E6 and not the full range of the anonymous type. Note that the range must have static bounds since the choice of base type is made at compilation time.

If, out of curiosity, we wanted to know the full range we could use MY_INTEGER'BASE'FIRST and MY_INTEGER'BASE'LAST.

The attribute BASE applies to any type or subtype and gives the corresponding base type. It can only be used to form other attributes as in this example. We could even go so far as to ensure that we could use the full range of the predefined type by writing

type X **is range** −1E6 . . 1E6;
type MY_INTEGER **is range** X'BASE'FIRST . . X'BASE'LAST;

This would have the dubious merit of avoiding the constraint checks when values are assigned to objects of type MY_INTEGER and would destroy the very portability we were seeking.

We can convert between one integer type and another by using the normal notation for type conversion. Given

type MY_INTEGER **is range** −1E6 . . 1E6;
type INDEX **is range** 0 . . 10000;

    M: MY_INTEGER;
    I: INDEX;

then we can write

    M:=MY_INTEGER(I);
    I:=INDEX(M);

On machine A a genuine hardware conversion is necessary but on machine B both types will be derived from INTEGER and the conversion will be null.

Note that, as mentioned in the last chapter, we can convert directly between related derived types and do not have to give each individual step. If this were not so we would have to write

    M:=MY_INTEGER(LONG_INTEGER(INTEGER(I)));

on machine A and

    M:=MY_INTEGER(INTEGER(I));

on machine B and our portability would be lost.

The integer literals are considered to belong to a type known as universal integer. The range of this type is at least as large as any of the predefined integer types and it has all the usual operations of an integer type such as $+$, $-$, $<$ and $=$. Integer numbers declared in a number declaration (see Section 4.1) such as

    TEN: constant:=10;

are also of type universal integer. However, there are no universal integer variables and as a consequence most universal integer expressions are static; such expressions are always computed exactly. The initial value in a number declaration has to be a static universal expression. So

    M: constant:=10;
    MM: constant:=M*M;

is allowed since M*M is a static universal expression. However,

    N: constant INTEGER:=10;
    NN: constant:=N*N;

is not allowed since N*N is not a static expression of type universal integer but merely a static expression of type INTEGER.

It should however be noted that certain attributes such as POS in fact deliver a universal integer value and since POS can take a dynamic argument it follows that certain universal integer expressions may actually be dynamic.

Conversion of integer literals, integer numbers and universal integer attributes to other integer types is automatic and does not require an explicit type conversion. Problems of ambiguity however demand that conversion of more general expressions has to be explicit.

The reader may recall that a range such as 1 .. 10 occurring in a for statement or in an array type definition is considered to be of type INTEGER. The full rule is in fact that the bounds must again be integer literals, integer numbers or universal integer attributes but not a more general expression. Note incidentally that specifying that the range is type INTEGER rather than any other integer type means that the predefined type INTEGER does have rather special properties.

The use of integer type declarations which reflect the need of the program rather than the arbitrary use of INTEGER and LONG_INTEGER is good practice because it not only encourages portability but also enables us to distinguish between different classes of objects as for example when we were counting apples and oranges in the last chapter.

However, complete portability is not easily obtained. For example, assume

```
type MY_INTEGER is range -1E6 .. +1E6;
I, J: MY_INTEGER;
```

and consider

```
I :=100000;
J:=I*I;
```

In order to understand the behaviour it is most important to remember that MY_INTEGER is really only a subtype of an anonymous type derived from LONG_INTEGER on machine A or INTEGER on machine B. The derived operations +, -, *, / and so on have the anonymous type as operands and results and the subtype constraint is only relevant when we attempt to assign to J. So J:=I*I; is effectively (on machine A)

```
J:=anon(LONG_INTEGER(I)*LONG_INTEGER(I));
```

and the multiplication is performed with the operation of the type LONG_ INTEGER. The result is 1E10 and this is well within the range of LONG_ INTEGER. However, when we attempt to assign the result to J we get CONSTRAINT_ERROR.

On machine B on the other hand the type is derived from INTEGER and this time the result of the multiplication is outside the range of INTEGER. So NUMERIC_ERROR is raised by the multiplication itself.

Thus, although the program fails in both cases the actual exception raised could be different.

A worse case would be

```
I :=100000;
J:=(I*I)/100000;
```

On machine A the intermediate product and final result are computed with no problem and moreover the final result lies within the range of J and so no exception is raised. But on machine B we again get NUMERIC_ERROR.

(The above analysis has ignored the possibility of optimisation. The language allows the implementation to use a wider type in order to avoid NUMERIC_ERROR provided that the correct result is obtained. However, the example is certainly valid if machine B did not have a type LONG_INTEGER.)

Finally we note that the most negative and most positive values supported by the predefined integer types are given by SYSTEM.MIN_INT and SYSTEM.MAX_INT. These are, of course, implementation dependent and are numbers declared in the package SYSTEM which is a predefined library package containing various such implementation dependent constants.

Exercise 12.1

1 What types on machines A and B are used to represent

```
type P is range 1 .. 1000;
type Q is range 0 .. +32768;
type R is range −1E14 .. +1E14;
```

2 Would it make any difference if A and B were ones complement machines with the same number of bits in the representations?

3 Given

```
N: INTEGER:=6;
P: constant:=3;
R: MY_INTEGER:=4;
```

what is the type of

a) N+P   d) N*N
b) N+R   e) P*P
c) P+R   f) R*R

4 Declare a type LONGEST_INTEGER which is the maximum supported by the implementation.

12.2 Real types

Integer types are exact types. Real types are however approximate and introduce problems of accuracy which have subtle effects. This book is not a specialised treatise on errors in numerical analysis and so we do not intend to give all the details of how the features of Ada can be used to minimise errors and maximise portability but will concentrate instead on outlining the basic principles.

Real types are subdivided into floating point types and fixed point types. Apart from the details of representation the key abstract difference is that floating point values have a relative error whereas fixed point values have an absolute error. Concepts common to both floating and fixed point types are dealt with in this section and further details of the individual types are in subsequent sections.

There is a type universal real having similar properties to the type universal integer. The real literals (see Section 3.4) are of type universal real. Real numbers declared in a number declaration such as

```
PI: constant:=3.14159_26536;
```

are also of type universal real. (The reader will recall that the difference between an integer literal and a real literal is that a real literal always has a point in it.)

As well as the usual operations on a real type, some mixing of universal real and universal integer operands is also allowed. Specifically, a universal real can be multiplied by a universal integer and vice versa and division is allowed with the first operand being universal real and the second operand being universal integer; in all cases the result is universal real.

So we can write either

```
TWO_PI: constant:=2*PI;
```

or

```
TWO_PI: constant:=2.0*PI;
```

but not

```
PI_PLUS_TWO: constant:=PI+2;
```

because mixed addition is not defined. Note that we cannot do an explicit type conversion between universal integer and universal real although we can always convert the former into the latter by multiplying by 1.0.

An important concept is the idea of a model number. When we declare a real type T we demand a certain accuracy. The implementation will, typically, use a greater accuracy just as an implementation of an integer type uses a base type which has a larger range than that requested. Corresponding to the accuracy requested will be a set of model numbers which are guaranteed to be exactly represented. Because the implemented accuracy will usually be higher, other values will also be exactly represented. Associated with each implemented value will be a model interval. If a value is a model number then the model interval is simply the model number. Otherwise the model interval is the interval consisting of the two model numbers surrounding the value. Special cases arise if a value is greater than the largest model number T'LARGE.

When an operation is performed the bounds of the result are given by the smallest model interval that can arise as a consequence of operating upon any values in the model intervals of the operands.

The relational operators =, > and so on are also defined in terms of model intervals. If the result is the same, whatever values are chosen in the intervals, then its value is clearly not in dispute. If however the result depends upon which values in the intervals are chosen then the result is undefined.

The behaviour of model numbers will be illustrated with examples in the next section.

Exercise 12.2

1 Given

```
TWO: INTEGER:=2;
E: constant:=2.71828_18285;
MAX: constant:=100;
```

what is the type of

a) TWO*E

b) TWO*MAX

c) E*MAX

d) TWO*TWO

e) E*E

f) MAX*MAX

2 Given

N: **constant**:=100;

declare a real number R having the same value as N.

12.3 Floating point types

In a similar way to integers, all implementations have a predefined type FLOAT and may also have further predefined types SHORT_FLOAT, LONG_FLOAT and so on with respectively less and more precision. These types all have the predefined operations that were described in Chapter 4 as applicable to the type REAL.

We can derive our own type directly by

type REAL **is new** FLOAT;

or perhaps

type REAL **is new** LONG_FLOAT;

according to the implemented precision but as for the integer types it is better to state the precision required and allow the implementation to choose appropriately.

If we write

type REAL **is digits** 7;

then we are asking the implementation to derive REAL from a predefined type with at least 7 decimal digits of precision.

The precise behaviour is defined in terms of our model numbers. Suppose we consider the more general case

type REAL **is digits** D;

where D is a positive static integer expression. D is the number of decimal digits required and we first convert this to B, the corresponding number of binary digits giving at least the same relative precision. B has to be one more than the least integer greater than $D.\log_2 10$ or in other words

$$B-1 < 1 + (3.3219 \ldots \times D) < B$$

The binary precision B determines the model numbers; these are defined to be zero plus all numbers of the form

$sign.mantissa.2^{exponent}$

where

> $sign$ is $+1$ or -1
> $\frac{1}{2} \leqslant mantissa < 1,$
> $-4B \leqslant exponent \leqslant +4B$

and the mantissa has exactly B digits after the binary point when expressed in base 2. The range of the exponent, which is an integer, has been chosen to be $\pm 4B$ somewhat arbitrarily after a survey of ranges provided by contemporary architectures.

When we say

type REAL is digits 7;

we are guaranteed that the model numbers of the predefined floating point type chosen will include the model numbers for decimal precision 7.

As an extreme example suppose we consider

type ROUGH is digits 1;

Then D is 1 and so B is 5. The model numbers are values where the mantissa can be one of

$^{16}\!/_{32},\ ^{17}\!/_{32},\ \ldots,\ ^{31}\!/_{32}$

and the binary exponent lies in $-20 \ldots 20$.

The model numbers around one are

$\ldots,\ ^{30}\!/_{32},\ ^{31}\!/_{32},\ 1,\ 1^{1}\!/_{16},\ 1^{2}\!/_{16},\ 1^{3}\!/_{16},\ \ldots$

and the model numbers around zero are

$\ldots,\ -^{17}\!/_{32}{\cdot}2^{-20},\ -^{16}\!/_{32}{\cdot}2^{-20},\ 0,\ +^{16}\!/_{32}{\cdot}2^{-20},\ +^{17}\!/_{32}{\cdot}2^{-20},\ \ldots$

Note the change of absolute accuracy at one and the hole around zero. By the latter we mean the gaps between zero and the smallest model numbers which in this case are 16 times the difference between them and the next model numbers. There is therefore a gross loss of accuracy at zero. These model numbers are illustrated in Fig. 12.1.

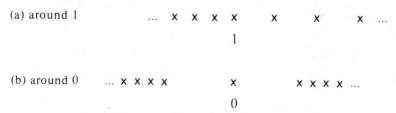

(a) around 1

1

(b) around 0

0

Fig.12.1 Model numbers of type ROUGH

The largest model numbers are

$$\ldots, {}^{29}\!/_{32}\!\cdot\!2^{20}, {}^{30}\!/_{32}\!\cdot\!2^{20}, {}^{31}\!/_{32}\!\cdot\!2^{20}$$

or

$$\ldots, 950272, 983040, 1015808$$

Suppose we write

```
R: ROUGH:=1.05;
```

then without considering the actual predefined floating point type chosen for R the literal **1.05** will be converted to a number between 1 and $1^1\!/_{16}$ inclusive which are the model numbers surrounding **1.05** but we do not know which. So all we know is that the value of R lies in the model interval $[1, 1^1\!/_{16}]$.

If we compute

```
R:=R*R;
```

then the computed mathematical result must lie between $1^2 = 1$ and $(1^1\!/_{16})^2 = {}^{289}\!/_{256} = 1^{33}\!/_{256}$. However, $1^{33}\!/_{256}$ is not a model number and so we take the next model number above as the upper bound of the result; this is $1^3\!/_{16}$. Hence all we can conclude is that R must now lie in the model interval $[1, 1^3\!/_{16}]$. And this is all we know! Type ROUGH indeed.

The result of

```
R>1.0
```

is not defined since $1>1$ is false but $1^3\!/_{16} > 1$ is true.

Similarly

```
R=1.0
```

is not defined since $1 = 1$ is true but $1^3\!/_{16} = 1$ is false.

However

```
R>=1.0
```

is well defined and is true. So, perhaps surprisingly, the operations $=, >$ and $>=$ do not always have their expected relationship when applied to floating point types.

The above example is extreme but illustrates the dangers of errors. The hole around zero is a particular danger – if a result falls in that hole then we say that underflow has occurred and all accuracy will be lost. Our value has gone down a black hole!

In practice we will do rather better because the type ROUGH will undoubtedly be derived from a predefined type with more precision. Suppose that on a particular machine we just have a predefined type FLOAT with D=7. Then writing

type ROUGH **is digits** 1;

is equivalent to

type anon **is new** FLOAT;
subtype ROUGH **is** anon **digits** 1;

The type ROUGH is therefore really a subtype of the derived type anon and operations on values will be performed with the numbers of the type FLOAT. In order to describe the mechanism more precisely we introduce the concept of safe numbers.

The safe numbers of a type are a superset of the model numbers and have similar computational properties. The safe numbers have the same number of digits B but the exponent range is $\pm E$ where E is at least equal to $4B$. Thus the safe numbers extend the reliable range and allow an implementation to take better advantage of the hardware. Another important difference between model numbers and safe numbers is that the safe numbers of a subtype are those of the base type whereas the model numbers of a subtype are those implied by the accuracy requested in its definition.

As an example, the safe numbers of the type ROUGH are the safe numbers of FLOAT whereas the model numbers of ROUGH are those defined by $D = 1$. The operations apply to the safe numbers and it is these numbers that can be stored in objects of the type ROUGH.

The point of all this is that if we wish to write a portable program then we must stick to the properties of the model numbers whereas if we wish to get the most out of an implementation then we can exploit the properties of the safe numbers. Note also that an implementation may provide additional numbers to the safe numbers; they cannot be relied upon in the sense that the language does not define their properties other than those implied by the model intervals or safe intervals.

As a minor point we could also impose a range constraint on a floating point subtype or object by for example

R: ROUGH **range** 0.0 . . 100.0;

or

subtype POSITIVE_REAL **is** REAL **range** 0.0 . . REAL'LAST;

and so on. If a range is violated then CONSTRAINT_ERROR is raised.

Various attributes are available and they can be used to help in writing more portable programs. For any type (or subtype) F (predefined or not) they are

F'DIGITS	the number of decimal digits, D,
F'MANTISSA	the corresponding number of binary digits, B,
F'EMAX	the maximum exponent, 4*F'MANTISSA,
F'SMALL	the smallest positive model number, 2.0**(−F'EMAX−1),
F'LARGE	the largest positive model number, 2.0**F'EMAX*(1.0−2.0**(−F'MANTISSA)),
F'EPSILON	the difference between 1.0 and the next model number, 2.0**(1−F'MANTISSA).

In addition there are attributes F'SAFE_EMAX, F'SAFE_SMALL and F'SAFE_LARGE which give the corresponding properties of the safe numbers of the type.

There are also the usual attributes F'FIRST and F'LAST which need not be model numbers or safe numbers but are the actual extreme values of the type or subtype.

DIGITS, MANTISSA, EMAX and SAFE_EMAX are of type universal integer; SMALL, SAFE_SMALL, LARGE, SAFE_LARGE and EPSILON are of type universal real; FIRST and LAST are of type F.

The attribute BASE can again be used to enable us to find out about the implemented type. So ROUGH'DIGITS = 1 and ROUGH'BASE'DIGITS = 7.

We do not intend to say more about floating point but hope that the reader will have understood the principles involved. In general one can simply specify the precision required and all will work. But care is sometimes needed and the advice of a professional numerical analyst should be sought when in doubt. For further details the reader should consult the LRM.

Exercise 12.3

1   What is the value of ROUGH'EPSILON?

2   Compute the model interval in which the value of R must lie after

```
type REAL is digits 5;

P: REAL:=2.0;
Q: REAL:=3.0;
R: REAL:=(P/Q)*Q;
```

3   What would be the effect of writing

```
P: constant:=2.0;
Q: constant:=3.0;
R: REAL:=(P/Q)*Q;
```

4   How many model numbers are there of type ROUGH?

5   The function

```
function HYPOTENUSE(X, Y: REAL) return REAL is
begin
    return SQRT(X**2+Y**2);
end;
```

suffers from underflow if X and Y are small. Rewrite it to avoid this by testing X and Y against a suitable value and then rescaling if necessary.

6   Explain why B is not just the least integer greater than $D.\log_2 10$ but one more. Use the type ROUGH to illustrate your answer.

7   What is the ratio between the size of the hole around zero and the gap between the next model numbers for a general value of B?

12.4 Fixed point types

Fixed point is normally used only in specialised applications or for doing approximate arithmetic on machines without floating point hardware. We give only a simple overview in this book.

The general principle of derivation from predefined types applies also to fixed point. However, unlike the integer and floating point types, the predefined fixed point types are anonymous and so cannot be used directly but have to be used via a fixed point declaration. Such a declaration specifies an absolute error and also a mandatory range. It takes the form

type F **is delta** D **range** L . . R;

In effect this is asking for values in the range L to R with an accuracy of D which must be positive. D, L and R must be real and static. The above declaration is precisely equivalent to

type anon **is new** F;
subtype F **is** anon **range** anon(L) . . anon(R);

where F is an appropriate predefined and anonymous fixed point type.

A fixed point type (or subtype) is characterised by two attributes, a positive integer B and a positive real number *small*. B indicates the number of bits required for the number (apart from the sign) and *small* is the absolute precision. The model numbers are therefore zero plus all numbers of the form

sign.mantissa.small

where

sign is $+1$ or -1
$0 < mantissa < 2^B$

The definition

delta D **range** L . . R

implies a value of *small* which is the largest power of 2 less than or equal to D and a value of B which is the smallest integer such that L and R are no more than *small* from a model number.

As an example, if we have

type T **is delta** 0.1 **range** -1.0 . . $+1.0$;

then *small* will be $\frac{1}{16}$ and B will be 4. The model numbers of T are therefore

$$-\tfrac{15}{16}, -\tfrac{14}{16}, \ldots, -\tfrac{1}{16}, 0, +\tfrac{1}{16}, \ldots, +\tfrac{14}{16}, +\tfrac{15}{16}$$

Note carefully that L and R are actually outside the range of model numbers and are both exactly *small* from a model number; the definition just allows this.

If we have a typical 16 bit implementation then there will be a wide choice of predefined types from which T can be derived. The only requirement is that the model numbers of the predefined type include those of T. Assuming therefore that the predefined type will have $B = 15$, then at one extreme *small* could be 2^{-15} which would give us a much greater accuracy but the same range whereas at the other extreme *small* could be $\frac{1}{16}$ in which case we would have a much greater range but the same accuracy.

If we assume for the sake of argument that the implementation chooses the predefined type with the greatest accuracy then its model numbers will be

$$-\frac{2^{15}-1}{2^{15}}, \ldots, -\frac{1}{2^{15}}, 0, +\frac{1}{2^{15}}, \ldots, +\frac{2^{15}-1}{2^{15}}$$

The concept of safe numbers is also defined for fixed point types. The safe numbers of a type are the model numbers of its base type and the safe numbers of a predefined type are just its model numbers. So the safe numbers of T are the model numbers of the chosen predefined type. Similar remarks apply regarding portability as with floating point types. If we just assume the properties of the model numbers then portability is assured but we can also rely upon the safe numbers if we wish to get the best out of a particular implementation.

Returning to the type T, a different implementation might use just 8 bits. Moreover using representation clauses (which will be discussed in more detail in Chapter 15) it is possible to give the compiler more precise instructions. We can say

for T'SIZE **use** 5;

which will force the implementation to use the minimum 5 bits. Of course, it might be ridiculous for a particular architecture and in fact the compiler is allowed to refuse unreasonable representation clauses.

We can also override the rule that *small* is a power of 2 by using a representation clause. Writing

for T'SIZE **use** 5;
for T'SMALL **use** 0.1;

will result in the model numbers being

$$-1.5, -1.4, \ldots, -0.1, 0, +0.1, \ldots, +1.4, +1.5$$

In this case the predefined type will have the same model numbers.

The advantage of using the default standard whereby *small* is a power of 2 is that conversion between fixed point and other numeric types can be based on shifting. The use of other values of *small* will in general mean that conversion requires implicit multiplication and division.

It should be realised that the predefined fixed point types are somewhat ephemeral; they are not so much predefined as made up anonymously on the spot as required. However, an implementation is only formally required to have one anonymous predefined type. In such a case the *small* for the one type would inevitably be a power of 2 and so any attempt to specify a value of *small* which was not a multiple of this value would fail. Hence the sophisticated use of fixed point types is very dependent upon the implementation.

A standard simple example is given by

```
DEL: constant:=2.0**(−15);
type FRAC is delta DEL range −1.0 .. 1.0;
```

which will be represented as a pure fraction on a 16 bit twos complement machine. Note that it does not really matter whether the upper bound is written as 1.0 or 1.0−DEL; the largest model number will be 1.0−DEL in either case.

Finally, a good example of the use of a specified value for *small* is given by a type representing an angle and which uses the whole of a 16 bit word

```
type ANGLE is delta 0.1 range −PI .. PI;
for ANGLE'SMALL use PI*2**(−15);
```

Note that the value given for delta is irrelevant since it is overridden by the representation clause for ANGLE'SMALL.

The arithmetic operations +, −, *, / and **abs** can be applied to fixed point values. Addition and subtraction can only be applied to values of the same type and, of course, return that type. Multiplication and division are allowed between different fixed types but always return values of an infinitely accurate type known as universal fixed. Such a value must be explicitly converted by a type conversion to a particular type before any further operation can be performed. Multiplication and division by type INTEGER are also allowed and these return a value of the fixed point type.

So given

```
F, G: FRAC;
```

we can write

```
F:=F+G;
```

but not

```
F:=F*G;
```

but must explicitly state

```
F:=FRAC(F*G);
```

The behaviour of fixed point arithmetic is, like floating point arithmetic, defined in terms of the model numbers. Literals and general expressions of type universal real are converted to à value guaranteed to be in the appropriate model interval.

The various attributes of a fixed point type or subtype F are as follows

F'DELTA	the requested delta, D,
F'MANTISSA	the number of bits, B,
F'SMALL	the smallest positive model number, small,
F'LARGE	the largest positive model number, (2**F'MANTISSA−1)*F'SMALL.

In addition there are attributes F'SAFE_SMALL and F'SAFE_LARGE which give the corresponding properties of the safe numbers. Note that F'SAFE_SMALL = F'BASE'SMALL for fixed point types.

There are also the usual attributes F'FIRST and F'LAST which give the actual upper and lower bounds of the type or subtype and of course need not be model numbers.

DELTA, SMALL, SAFE_SMALL, LARGE and SAFE_LARGE are of type universal real; MANTISSA is of type universal integer; FIRST and LAST are of type F.

For further details the reader is referred to the LRM.

Exercise 12.4

1   Given F of type FRAC compute the model interval of F after

F:=0.1;

Checklist 12

Use implicitly derived types for increased portability.

Beware of overflow in intermediate expressions.

Use numbers rather than constants.

Beware of underflow into the hole around floating point zero.

Beware of the relational operations with real types.

If in doubt consult a numerical analyst.

Chapter 13 GENERICS

In this chapter we describe the generic mechanism which allows us to parameterise subprograms and packages with parameters which can be types and subprograms as well as values and objects.

13.1 Declarations and instantiations

One of the problems with a typed language such as Ada is that all types have to be determined at compilation time. This means naturally that we cannot pass types as run time parameters. However, we often get the situation that the logic of a piece of program is independent of the types involved and it therefore seems unnecessary to repeat it for all the different types to which we might wish it to apply. A simple example is provided by the procedure **SWAP** of Exercise 7.3(**1**)

```
procedure SWAP(X, Y: in out REAL) is
    T: REAL;
begin
    T:=X; X:=Y; Y:=T;
end;
```

It is clear that the logic is independent of the type of the values being swapped. If we also wanted to swap integers or Booleans we could of course write other procedures but this would be tedious. The generic mechanism allows us to overcome this. We can declare

```
generic
    type ITEM is private;
procedure EXCHANGE(X, Y: in out ITEM);

procedure EXCHANGE(X, Y: in out ITEM) is
    T: ITEM;
begin
    T:=X; X:=Y; Y:=T;
end;
```

The subprogram **EXCHANGE** is a generic subprogram and acts as a kind of template. The subprogram specification is preceded by the generic formal part consisting of the reserved word **generic** followed by a (possibly empty) list of generic formal parameters. The subprogram body is written exactly as normal but note that, in the case of a generic subprogram, we have to give both the body and the specification separately.

The generic procedure cannot be called directly but from it we can create an actual procedure by a mechanism known as generic instantiation. For example, we may write

procedure SWAP **is new** EXCHANGE(REAL);

This is a declaration and states that SWAP is to be obtained from the template described by EXCHANGE. Actual generic parameters are provided in a parameter list in the usual way. The actual parameter in this case is the type REAL which corresponds to the formal parameter ITEM. We could also use the named notation

procedure SWAP **is new** EXCHANGE(ITEM=> REAL);

So we have now created the procedure SWAP acting on type REAL and can henceforth call it in the usual way. We can make further instantiations

procedure SWAP **is new** EXCHANGE(INTEGER);
procedure SWAP **is new** EXCHANGE(DATE);

and so on. We are here creating further overloadings of SWAP which can be distinguished by their parameter types just as if we had laboriously written them out in detail.

Superficially, it may look as if the generic mechanism is merely one of text substitution and indeed in this simple case the behaviour would be the same. However, the important difference relates to the meaning of identifiers in the generic body but which are neither parameters nor local to the body. Such non local identifiers have meanings appropriate to where the generic body is declared and not to where it is instantiated. If text substitution were used then non local identifiers would of course take their meaning at the point of instantiation and this could give very surprising results.

As well as generic subprograms we may also have generic packages. A simple example is provided by the package STACK in Section 8.1. The trouble with that package is that it only works on type INTEGER although of course the same logic applies irrespective of the type of the values manipulated. We can also take the opportunity to make MAX a parameter as well so that we are not tied to an arbitrary limit of 100. We write

```
generic
    MAX: POSITIVE;
    type ITEM is private;
package STACK is
    procedure PUSH(X: ITEM);
    function POP return ITEM;
end STACK;

package body STACK is
    S: array (1 .. MAX) of ITEM;
    TOP: INTEGER range 0 .. MAX;
    -- etc as before but with INTEGER
    -- replaced by ITEM
end STACK;
```

We can now create and use a stack of a particular size and type by instantiating the generic package as in the following

```
declare
    package MY_STACK is new STACK(100, REAL);
    use MY_STACK;

begin
    . . .
    PUSH(X);
    . . .
    Y:=POP;
    . . .
end;
```

The package MY_STACK which results from the instantiation behaves just as a normal directly written out package. The use clause allows us to refer to PUSH and POP directly. If we did a further instantiation

```
package ANOTHER_STACK is new STACK(50, INTEGER);
use ANOTHER_STACK;
```

then PUSH and POP are further overloadings and can be distinguished by the type provided by the context. Of course, if ANOTHER_STACK was also declared with the actual generic parameter being REAL, then we would have to use the dotted notation to distinguish the instances of PUSH and POP despite the use clauses.

Both generic units and generic instantiations may be library units. Thus having put the generic package STACK in the program library an instantiation could itself be separately compiled just on its own thus

```
with STACK;
package BOOLEAN_STACK is new STACK(200, BOOLEAN);
```

If we added an exception ERROR to the package as in Section 10.2 so that the generic package declaration was

```
generic
    MAX: POSITIVE;
    type ITEM is private;
package STACK is
    ERROR: exception;
    procedure PUSH(X: ITEM);
    function POP return ITEM;
end STACK;
```

then each instantiation would give rise to a distinct exception and because exceptions cannot be overloaded we would naturally have to use the dotted notation to distinguish them.

We could, of course, make the exception ERROR common to all instantiations by making it global to the generic package. It and the generic package could perhaps be declared inside a further package

```
package ALL_STACKS is
    ERROR: exception;
    generic
        MAX: POSITIVE;
        type ITEM is private;
    package STACK is
        procedure PUSH(X: ITEM);
        function POP return ITEM;
    end STACK;
end ALL_STACKS;

package body ALL_STACKS is
    package body STACK is
        . . .
    end STACK;
end ALL_STACKS;
```

This illustrates the binding of identifiers global to generic units. The meaning of **ERROR** is determined at the point of the generic declaration irrespective of the meaning at the point of instantiation.

The above examples have illustrated formal parameters which were types and also integers. In fact generic formal parameters can be any of the parameters applicable to subprograms; they can also be types and subprograms. As we shall see in the next sections, we can express the formal types and subprograms so that we can assume in the generic body that the actual parameters have the properties we require.

In the case of the familiar parameters which also apply to subprograms they can be of mode **in** or **in out** but not **out**. As with subprograms, **in** is taken by default as illustrated by **MAX** in the example above.

An **in** generic parameter acts as a constant whose value is provided by the corresponding actual parameter. A default expression is allowed as in subprogram parameters; such a default expression is evaluated at instantiation if no actual parameter is supplied in the same way that a default expression for a subprogram parameter is evaluated when the subprogram is called if no actual parameter is supplied. Observe that an **in** generic parameter cannot be of a limited type; this is because assignment is not allowed for limited types and the mechanism of giving the value to the parameter is treated as assignment. Note that this is a different mechanism to that used for **in** subprogram parameters where limited types are allowed.

An **in out** parameter, however, acts as a variable renaming the corresponding actual parameter. The actual parameter must therefore be the name of a variable and its identification occurs at the point of instantiation using the same rules as for renaming described in Section 8.5. One such rule is that any constraints on the actual parameter apply to the formal parameter and any constraints implied by the formal type mark are, perhaps surprisingly, completely ignored. Another rule is that if any identifier in the name subsequently changes then the identity of the object referred to by the generic formal parameter does not change. Because of this there is a restriction that the actual parameter cannot be a component of an unconstrained discriminated record if the very existence of the component depends on the value of the discriminant. Thus if **M** is a **MUTANT** as in Section

11.2, **M.CHILDREN** could not be an actual generic parameter because **M** could have its **SEX** changed. However, **M.BIRTH** would be valid. This restriction also applies to renaming itself.

Inside the generic body, the formal generic parameters can be used quite freely except for one restriction. There are various places where an expression has to be static such as in the alternatives in a case statement or variant, and in the range in an integer type definition, or the number of digits in a floating point type definition and so on. In all these situations a generic formal parameter cannot be used because the expression would not then be static.

Our final example in this section illustrates the nesting of generics. The following generic procedure performs a cyclic interchange of three values and for amusement is written in terms of the generic procedure **EXCHANGE**.

```
generic
    type THING is private;
procedure CAB(A, B, C: in out THING);

procedure CAB(A, B, C: in out THING) is
    procedure SWAP is new EXCHANGE(ITEM => THING);
begin
    SWAP(A, B);
    SWAP(A, C);
end CAB;
```

Although nesting is allowed, it must not be recursive.

Exercise 13.1

1 Write a generic package declaration based on the package **STACKS** in Section 11.1 so that stacks of arbitrary type may be declared. Declare a stack **S** of length 30 and type **BOOLEAN**. Use named notation.

2 Write a generic package containing both **SWAP** and **CAB**.

13.2 Type parameters

In the previous section we introduced types as generic parameters. The examples showed the formal parameter taking the form

type T **is private**;

In this case, inside the generic subprogram or package, we may assume that assignment and equality are defined for T. We can assume nothing else unless we specifically provide other parameters as we shall see in a moment. Hence T behaves in the generic unit much as a private type outside the package defining it; this analogy explains the notation for the formal parameter. The corresponding actual parameter must, of course, provide assignment and equality and so it can be any type except one that is limited.

A formal generic type parameter can take other forms. It can be

type T **is limited private**;

and in this case assignment and equality are not available automatically. The corresponding actual parameter can be any type.

Either of the above forms could have discriminants

type T(. . .) **is private;**

and the actual type must then have discriminants with the same types. The formal type must not have default expressions for the discriminants but the actual type can although they are ignored in this context.

The formal parameter could also be one of

type T **is** (<>);
type T **is range** <>;
type T **is digits** <>;
type T **is delta** <>;

In the first case the actual parameter must be a discrete type – an enumeration type or integer type. In the other cases the actual parameter must be an integer type, floating point type or fixed point type respectively. Within the generic unit the appropriate predefined operations and attributes are available.

As a simple example consider

```
generic
    type T is (<>);
function NEXT(X: T) return T;

function NEXT(X: T) return T is
begin
    if X=T'LAST then
        return T'FIRST;
    else
        return T'SUCC(X);
    end if;
end NEXT;
```

The formal parameter T requires that the actual parameter must be a discrete type. Since all discrete types have attributes **FIRST**, **LAST** and **SUCC** we can use these attributes in the body in the knowledge that the actual parameter will supply them.

We could now write

function TOMORROW **is new** NEXT(DAY);

so that TOMORROW(SUN)=MON.

An actual generic parameter can also be a subtype but an explicit constraint is not allowed; in other words the actual parameter must be just a type mark and not a subtype indication. The formal generic parameter then denotes the subtype. Thus we can have

function NEXT_WORK_DAY **is new** NEXT(WEEKDAY);

so that NEXT_WORK_DAY(FRI) = MON. Note how the behaviour depends on the fact that the LAST attribute applies to the subtype and not to the base type so that DAY'LAST is SUN and WEEKDAY'LAST is FRI.

The actual parameter could also be an integer type so we could have

```
subtype DIGIT is INTEGER range 0 . . 9;
function NEXT_DIGIT is new NEXT(DIGIT);
```

and then NEXT_DIGIT(9) = 0.

Now consider the package COMPLEX_NUMBERS of Section 9.1; this could be made generic so that the particular floating point type upon which the type COMPLEX is based can be a parameter. It would then take the form

```
generic
    type REAL is digits <>;
package COMPLEX_NUMBERS is
    type COMPLEX is private;
    - - as before
    I: constant COMPLEX:=(0.0, 1.0);
end;
```

Note that we can use the literals 0.0 and 1.0 because they are of the universal real type which can be converted to whichever type is passed as actual parameter. The package could then be instantiated by for instance

```
package MY_COMPLEX_NUMBERS is
            new COMPLEX_NUMBERS(MY_REAL);
```

A formal generic parameter can also be an array type. The actual parameter must then also be an array type with the same component type and constraints, if any, the same number of dimensions and same index subtypes. Either both must be unconstrained arrays or both must be constrained arrays. If they are constrained then the index ranges must be the same for corresponding indexes.

It is possible for one generic formal parameter to depend upon a previous formal parameter which is a type. This will often be the case with arrays. As an example consider the simple function SUM in Section 7.1. This added together the elements of a real array with integer index. We can generalise this to add together the elements of any floating point array with any index type.

```
generic
    type INDEX is (<>);
    type FLOATING is digits <>;
    type VEC is array (INDEX range <>) of FLOATING;
function SUM(A: VEC) return FLOATING;

function SUM(A: VEC) return FLOATING is
    RESULT: FLOATING:=0.0;
begin
    for I in A'RANGE loop
        RESULT:=RESULT+A(I);
    end loop;
```

```
      return RESULT;
   end SUM;
```

Note that although INDEX is a formal parameter it does not explicitly appear in the generic body; nevertheless it is implicitly used since the loop parameter I is of type INDEX.

We could instantiate this by

```
function SUM_VECTOR is new SUM(INTEGER, REAL, VECTOR);
```

and this will give the function SUM of Section 7.1.

The matching of actual and formal arrays takes place after any formal types have been replaced in the formal array by the corresponding actual types. As an example of matching index subtypes note that if we had

```
type VECTOR is array (POSITIVE range <>) of REAL;
```

then we would have to use POSITIVE (or an equivalent subtype) as the actual parameter for the INDEX.

The final possibility for formal type parameters is the case of an access type. The formal can be

```
type A is access T;
```

where T may but need not be a previous formal parameter. The actual parameter corresponding to A must then access T. Constraints on the accessed type must also be the same.

Observe that there is no concept of a formal record type. This is because the internal structure of records is somewhat arbitrary and the possibilities for matching would therefore be rare.

As a final example in this section we return to the question of sets. We saw in Section 6.4 how a Boolean array could be used to represent a set. Exercises 7.1(**4**), 7.2(**3**) and 7.2(**4**) also showed how we could write suitable functions to operate upon sets of the type COLOUR. The generic mechanism allows us to write a package to enable the manipulation of sets of an arbitrary type.

Consider

```
generic
   type BASE is (<>);
package SET_OF is
   type SET is private;
   type LIST is array (POSITIVE range <>) of BASE;

   EMPTY, FULL: constant SET;

   function MAKE_SET(X: LIST) return SET;
   function MAKE_SET(X: BASE) return SET;
   function DECOMPOSE(X: SET) return LIST;

   function "+"(X, Y: SET) return SET; -- union
   function "*"(X, Y: SET) return SET;  -- intersection
   function "-"(X, Y: SET) return SET; -- symmetric difference
```

function "<"(X: BASE; Y: SET) **return** BOOLEAN;

                                                         – – inclusion

function "<="(X, Y: SET) **return** BOOLEAN;   – – contains
function SIZE(X: SET) **return** NATURAL;   – – no of elements

  private
    type SET **is array** (BASE) **of** BOOLEAN;

    EMPTY: **constant** SET:=(SET'RANGE => FALSE);
    FULL: **constant** SET:=(SET'RANGE => TRUE);
  end;

The single generic parameter is the base type which must, of course, be discrete. The type SET is made private so that the Boolean operations cannot be inadvertently applied. Aggregates of the type LIST are used to represent literal sets. The constants EMPTY and FULL denote the empty and full set respectively. The functions MAKE_SET enable the creation of a set from a list of the base values or a single base value. DECOMPOSE turns a set back into a list.

The operators +, * and − represent union, intersection and symmetric difference; they are chosen as more natural than the underlying **or**, **and** and **xor**. The operator < tests to see whether a base value is in a set. The operator <= tests to see whether one set is a subset of another. Finally, the function SIZE returns the number of base values present in a particular set.

In the private part the type SET is of course declared as a Boolean array indexed by the base type. The constants EMPTY and FULL are declared as arrays whose elements are all FALSE and all TRUE respectively. The body of the package is left as an exercise.

Turning back to Section 6.4. we can instantiate the package to work on our type PRIMARY by

  package PRIMARY_SETS **is new** SET_OF(PRIMARY);
  use PRIMARY_SETS;

For comparison we could then write

  subtype COLOUR **is** SET;
  WHITE: COLOUR **renames** EMPTY;
  BLACK: COLOUR **renames** FULL;

and so on.

The general principle regarding the matching of types should now be clear. The formal type represents a class of types which have certain common properties and these properties can be assumed in the generic unit. The corresponding actual type must then supply these properties. The matching rules are designed so that this is assured by reference to the parameters only and without considering the details of the generic body. As a consequence the user of the generic unit need not see the body for debugging purposes. This notion of matching guaranteed by the parameters is termed the contract model.

Unfortunately there is an important violation to the contract model in the case of unconstrained types. If we have the basic formal type

type T **is private**;

then this can be matched by an unconstrained array type such as VECTOR provided that we do not use T in the generic unit in a way that would require the array to be constrained. The most obvious example is that we must not declare an object of type T. In a similar way the actual type could be an unconstrained discriminated type provided that T is not used in a way that would require constraints. Thus again we could not declare an unconstrained object of type T; this applies even if the actual type has default discriminants since such defaults are not available inside the generic body.

The attribute CONSTRAINED can be applied to the formal type T and gives a Boolean value indicating whether the actual type is a constrained type or not. Thus considering the types of Section 11.2, T'CONSTRAINED would be TRUE if the actual type were MAN but FALSE if the actual type were PERSON or MUTANT; in the last case the default constraint NEUTER is irrelevant. Remember that the actual parameter must be a type mark and not a subtype indication.

Finally note one other small restriction; the type of the expression in a case statement and similarly the type of the discriminant in a variant may not be a generic formal type.

Exercise 13.2

1 Instantiate NEXT to give a function behaving like **not**.

2 Rewrite the specification of the package RATIONAL_NUMBERS so that it is a generic package taking the integer type as a parameter. See Exercise 9.1(**2**).

3 Rewrite the function OUTER of Exercise 7.1(**3**) so that it is a generic function with appropriate parameters. Instantiate it to give the original function.

4 Write the body of the package SET_OF.

13.3 Subprogram parameters

Generic parameters can also be subprograms. In some languages, such as Algol and Pascal, parameters of subprograms can themselves be subprograms. This facility is useful for mathematical applications such as integration. In Ada, subprograms can only be parameters of generic units and so the generic mechanism is used for these applications.

We could have a generic function

```
generic
     with function F(X: REAL) return REAL;
function INTEGRATE(A, B: REAL) return REAL;
```

which evaluates $\int_a^b f(x)\mathrm{d}x$.

In order to integrate a particular function we must instantiate INTEGRATE with our function as actual generic parameter. Thus suppose we needed

$$\int_{O}^{P} e^{t} \sin t \, dt$$

We would write

```
function G(T: REAL) return REAL is
begin
    return EXP(T)*SIN(T);
end;
```

```
function INTEGRATE_G is new INTEGRATE(G);
```

and then our result is given by the expression

```
INTEGRATE_G(0.0, P)
```

Note that a formal subprogram parameter is like a subprogram declaration preceded by **with**. (The leading **with** is necessary to avoid a syntactic ambiguity and has no other subtle purpose.) The correspondence between formal and actual subprograms is such that the formal subprogram just renames the actual subprogram. Thus the matching rules regarding parameters, results and so on are as described in Section 8.5. In particular the constraints on the parameters are those of the actual subprogram and any implied by the formal subprogram are ignored. A parameterless formal function can also be matched by an enumeration literal of the result type just as for renaming.

The specification of the formal subprogram could depend on preceding formal types. Thus we could extend our integration function to apply to any floating point type by writing

```
generic
    type FLOATING is digits <>;
    with function F(X: FLOATING) return FLOATING;
function INTEGRATE(A, B: FLOATING) return FLOATING;
```

and then

```
function INTEGRATE_G is new INTEGRATE(REAL, G);
```

In practice the function **INTEGRATE** would have other parameters indicating the accuracy required and so on.

Formal subprograms can also be used to supply other properties of type parameters. Consider the generic function **SUM** of the last section. We can generalise this even further by passing the adding operator itself as a generic parameter.

```
generic
    type INDEX is (<>);
    type ITEM is private;
    type VEC is array (INDEX range <>) of ITEM;
    with function "+" (X,Y: ITEM) return ITEM;
function APPLY(A: VEC) return ITEM;
```

```
        function APPLY(A: VEC) return ITEM is
            RESULT: ITEM:=A(A'FIRST);
        begin
            for I in INDEX'SUCC(A'FIRST) .. A'LAST loop
                RESULT:=RESULT+A(I);
            end loop;
            return RESULT;
        end APPLY;
```

The operator "+" has been added as a parameter and ITEM is now just private and no longer floating. This means that we can apply the generic function to any binary operation on any type. However, we no longer have a zero value and so have to initialise RESULT with the first component of the array A and then iterate through the remainder. In doing this, note that we cannot write

for I in A'FIRST+1 .. A'LAST loop

because we have not supplied the operator "+" applying to the type INDEX. Instead we use the attribute INDEX'SUCC which we know to be available since INDEX is guaranteed to be a discrete type.

Our original function SUM of Section 7.1 is now given by

function SUM is new APPLY(INTEGER, REAL, VECTOR,"+");

We could equally have

function PROD is new APPLY(INTEGER, REAL, VECTOR,"*");

Generic subprogram parameters (like generic object parameters) can have default values. These are given in the generic formal part and take two forms. In the above example we could write

with function "+"(X, Y: ITEM) return ITEM is <>;

This means that we can omit the corresponding actual parameter if there is visible at the point of instantiation a unique subprogram with the same designator and matching specification. With this alteration to APPLY we could have omitted the last parameter in the instantiation giving SUM.

The other form of default value is where we give an explicit name for the default parameter. The usual rules for defaults apply; the default name is only evaluated if required by the instantiation but the binding of identifiers in the expression which is the name occurs at the point of declaration. In our example

with function "+"(X, Y: ITEM) return ITEM is PLUS;

could never be valid because the specification of PLUS must match that of "+" and yet the parameter ITEM is not known until instantiation. The only valid possibilities are where the formal subprogram has no parameters depending on formal types or the default subprogram is an attribute. Thus we might have

with function NEXT(X: T) **return** T **is** T'SUCC;

The same rules for mixing named and positional notation apply to generic instantiation as to subprogram calls. Hence if a parameter is omitted, subsequent parameters must be given using named notation. Of course, a generic unit need have no parameters in which case the instantiation takes the same form as for a subprogram call – the brackets are omitted.

Exercise 13.3
1   Given a function

```
generic
     with function F(X: REAL) return REAL;
function SOLVE return REAL;
```

that finds a root of the equation $f(x) = 0$, show how you would find the root of

$$e^x + x = 7$$

2   Instantiate APPLY to give a function to "and" together all the components of a Boolean array.

3   Rewrite APPLY so that a null array can be a parameter without raising an exception. Use this new version to redo the previous exercise.

4   Write a generic function EQUALS to define the equality of one dimensional arrays of a limited private type. See Exercise 9.2(**3**). Instantiate it to give the function "=" applying to the type STACK_ARRAY.

5   Describe how to make a generic sort procedure based on the procedure SORT of Section 11.3. The parameters should supply the type of item being sorted, the corresponding array type and index and the comparison rule.

Checklist 13

The generic mechanism is not text replacement – non local name binding would be different.

Object **in out** parameters are bound by renaming.

Object **in** parameters are always copied unlike parameters of subprograms.

Generic subprograms may not overload – only the instantiations can.

Formal parameters may depend upon preceding type parameters.

Chapter 14 TASKING

The final major topic to be introduced is tasking. This has been left to the end, not because it is unimportant, but because, apart from the interaction with exceptions, it is a fairly self contained part of the language.

14.1 Parallelism

So far we have only considered sequential programs in which statements are obeyed in order. In many applications it is convenient to write a program as several parallel activities which cooperate as necessary. This is particularly true of programs which interact in real time with physical processes in the real world.

In Ada, parallel activities are described by means of tasks. In simple cases a task is lexically described by a form very similar to a package. This consists of a specification describing the interface presented to other tasks and a body describing the dynamic behaviour of the task.

```
task T is          - - specification
    . . .
end T;
task body T is     - - body
    . . .
end T;
```

In some cases a task presents no interface to other tasks in which case the specification reduces to just

```
task T;
```

As a simple example of parallelism consider a family going shopping to buy ingredients for a meal. Suppose they need meat, salad and wine and that the purchase of these items can be done by calling procedures BUY_MEAT, BUY_SALAD and BUY_WINE respectively. The whole expedition could be represented by

```
procedure SHOPPING is
begin
    BUY_MEAT;
    BUY_SALAD;
    BUY_WINE;
end;
```

However, this solution corresponds to the family buying each item in sequence. It would be far more efficient for them to split up so that, for example, mother buys the meat, the children buy the salad and father buys the wine. They agree to meet again perhaps in the car park. This parallel solution can be represented by

```
procedure SHOPPING is
    task GET_SALAD;

    task body GET_SALAD is
    begin
        BUY_SALAD;
    end GET_SALAD;

    task GET_WINE;

    task body GET_WINE is
    begin
        BUY_WINE;
    end GET_WINE;

begin
    BUY_MEAT;
end SHOPPING;
```

In this formulation, mother is represented as the main processor and calls BUY_MEAT directly from the procedure SHOPPING. The children and father are considered as subservient processors and perform the locally declared tasks GET_SALAD and GET_WINE which respectively call the procedures BUY_SALAD and BUY_WINE.

The example illustrates the declaration, activation and termination of tasks. A task is a program component like a package and is declared in a similar way inside a subprogram, block, package or indeed another task body. A task specification can also be declared in a package specification in which case the task body must be declared in the corresponding package body. However, a task specification cannot be declared in the specification of another task but only in the body.

The activation of a task is automatic. In the above example the local tasks become active when the parent unit reaches the **begin** following the task declaration.

Such a task will terminate when it reaches its final **end**. Thus the task GET_SALAD calls the procedure BUY_SALAD and then promptly terminates.

A task declared in the declarative part of a subprogram, block or task body is said to depend on that unit. It is an important rule that a unit cannot be left until all dependent tasks have terminated. This termination rule ensures that objects declared in the unit and therefore potentially visible to local tasks cannot disappear while there exists a task which could access them. (Note that a task cannot depend on a package – we will return to this later.)

It is important to realise that the main program is itself considered to be called by a hypothetical main task. We can now trace the sequence of actions when this main task calls the procedure SHOPPING. First the tasks GET_SALAD and GET_WINE are declared and then when the main task reaches the **begin** these dependent tasks are set active in parallel with the main task. The dependent tasks call their respective procedures and terminate. Meanwhile the main task calls BUY_MEAT and then reaches the **end** of SHOPPING. The main task then waits until the dependent tasks have terminated if they have not already done so. This corresponds to mother waiting for father and children to return with their purchases.

In the general case termination therefore occurs in two stages. We say that a unit is completed when it reaches its final **end**. It will subsequently become terminated only when all dependent tasks, if any, are also terminated. Of course, if a unit has no dependent tasks then it becomes completed and terminated at the same time.

Exercise 14.1

1 Rewrite procedure SHOPPING to contain three local tasks so that the symmetry of the situation is revealed.

14.2   The rendezvous

In the SHOPPING example the various tasks did not interact with each other once they had been set active except that their parent unit had to wait for them to terminate. Generally, however, tasks will interact with each other during their lifetime. In Ada this is done by a mechanism known as a rendezvous. This is similar to the human situation where two people meet, perform a transaction and then go on independently.

A rendezvous between two tasks occurs as a consequence of one task calling an entry declared in another. An entry is declared in a task specification in a similar way to a procedure in a package specification.

```
task T is
    entry E( . . . );
end;
```

An entry can have **in**, **out** and **in out** parameters in the same way as a procedure. It cannot however have a result like a function. An entry is called in a similar way to a procedure

```
T.E( . . . );
```

A task name cannot appear in a use clause and so the dotted notation is necessary to call the entry from outside the task. Of course, a local task could call an entry of its parent directly – the usual scope and visibility rules apply.

The statements to be obeyed during a rendezvous are described by corresponding accept statements in the body of the task containing the declaration of the entry. An accept statement usually takes the form

```
accept E( . . . ) do
    – – sequence of statements
end E;
```

The formal parameters of the entry E are repeated in the same way that a procedure body repeats the formal parameters of a corresponding procedure declaration. The **end** is optionally followed by the name of the entry. A significant difference is that the body of the accept statement is just a sequence of statements. Any local declarations or exception handlers must be provided by writing a local block.

The most important difference between an entry call and a procedure call is that in the case of a procedure, the task that calls the procedure also immediately executes the procedure body whereas in the case of an entry, one task calls the entry but the corresponding accept statement is executed by the task owning the entry. Moreover, the accept statement cannot be executed until a task calls the entry and the task owning the entry reaches the accept statement. Naturally one of these will occur first and the task concerned will then be suspended until the other reaches its corresponding statement. When this occurs the sequence of statements of the accept statement is executed by the called task while the calling task remains suspended. This interaction is called a rendezvous. When the end of the accept statement is reached the rendezvous is completed and both tasks then proceed independently. The parameter mechanism is exactly as for a subprogram call; note that expressions in the actual parameter list are evaluated before the call is issued.

We can elaborate our shopping example by giving the task GET_SALAD two entries, one for mother to hand the children the money for the salad and one to collect the salad from them afterwards. We do the same for GET_WINE (although perhaps father has his own funds in which case he might keep the wine to himself anyway).

We can also replace the procedures BUY_SALAD, BUY_WINE and BUY_MEAT by functions which take money as a parameter and return the appropriate ingredient. Our shopping procedure might now become

```
procedure SHOPPING is
    task GET_SALAD is
        entry PAY(M: in MONEY);
        entry COLLECT(S: out SALAD);
    end GET_SALAD;

    task body GET_SALAD is
        CASH: MONEY;
        FOOD: SALAD;
    begin
        accept PAY(M: in MONEY) do
            CASH:=M;
        end PAY;

        FOOD:=BUY_SALAD(CASH);

        accept COLLECT(S: out SALAD) do
            S:=FOOD;
        end COLLECT;
    end GET_SALAD;

    -- GET_WINE similarly
```

```
begin
    GET_SALAD.PAY (50);
    GET_WINE.PAY (100);
    MM:=BUY_MEAT (200);
    GET_SALAD.COLLECT(SS);
    GET_WINE.COLLECT (WW);
end;
```

The final outcome is that the various ingredients end up in the variables MM, SS, and WW whose declarations are left to the imagination.

The logical behaviour should be noted. As soon as the tasks GET_SALAD and GET_WINE become active they encounter accept statements and wait until the main task calls the entries PAY in each of them. After calling the function BUY_MEAT, the main task calls the COLLECT entries. Curiously, mother is unable to collect the wine until after she has collected the salad from the children.

As a more abstract example consider the problem of providing a task to act as a single buffer between one or more tasks producing items and one or more tasks consuming them. Our intermediate task can hold just one item.

```
task BUFFERING is
    entry PUT(X: in ITEM);
    entry GET(X: out ITEM);
end;

task body BUFFERING is
    V: ITEM;
begin
    loop
        accept PUT(X: in ITEM) do
            V:=X;
        end PUT;
        accept GET(X: out ITEM) do
            X:=V;
        end GET;
    end loop;
end BUFFERING;
```

Other tasks may then dispose of or acquire items by calling

```
BUFFERING.PUT(. . .);
BUFFERING.GET(. . .);
```

Intermediate storage for the item is the variable V. The body of the task is an endless loop which contains an accept statement for PUT followed by one for GET. Thus the task alternately accepts calls of PUT and GET which fill and empty the variable V.

Several different tasks may call PUT and GET and consequently may have to be queued. Every entry has a queue of tasks waiting to call the entry – this queue is processed in a first in first out manner and may, of course, be empty at a particular moment. The number of tasks on the queue of entry E is given by

E'COUNT but this attribute may only be used inside the body of the task owning the entry.

An entry may have several corresponding accept statements (usually only one). Each execution of an accept statement removes one task from the queue.

Note the asymmetric naming in a rendezvous. The calling task must name the called task but not vice versa. Moreover, several tasks may call an entry and be queued but a task can only be on one queue at a time.

Entries may be overloaded both with each other and with subprograms and obey the same rules. An entry may be renamed as a procedure

procedure WRITE(X: **in** ITEM) **renames** BUFFERING.PUT;

This mechanism may be useful in avoiding excessive use of the dotted notation. An entry, renamed or not, may be an actual or default generic parameter corresponding to a formal subprogram.

An entry may have no parameters, such as

entry SIGNAL;

and it could then be called by

T.SIGNAL;

An accept statement need have no body as in

accept SIGNAL;

In such a case the purpose of the call is merely to effect a synchronisation and not to pass information. However, an entry without parameters can have an accept statement with a body and vice versa. There is nothing to prevent us writing

accept SIGNAL **do**
    FIRE;
end;

in which case the task calling SIGNAL is only allowed to continue after the call of FIRE is completed. We could also have

accept PUT(X: ITEM);

although clearly the parameter value is not used.

There are no particular constraints on the statements in an accept statement. They may include entry calls, subprogram calls, blocks and further accept statements (but not for the same entry). On the other hand an accept statement may not appear in a subprogram body but must be in the sequence of statements of the task although it could be in a block or other accept statement. The execution of a return statement in an accept statement corresponds to reaching the final end and therefore terminates the rendezvous.

A task may call one of its own entries but, of course, will promptly deadlock. This may seem foolish but programming languages allow lots of silly things such as endless loops and so on. We could expect a good compiler to warn us of obvious potential deadlocks.

Exercise 14.2

1 Write the body of a task whose specification is

```
task BUILD_COMPLEX is
    entry PUT_RL(X: REAL);
    entry PUT_IM(X: REAL);
    entry GET_COMP(X: out COMPLEX);
end;
```

and which alternately puts together a complex number from calls of PUT_RL and PUT_IM and then delivers the result on a call of GET_COMP.

2 Write the body of a task whose specification is

```
task CHAR_TO_LINE is
    entry PUT(C: in CHARACTER);
    entry GET(L: out LINE);
end;
```

where

```
type LINE is array (1 .. 80) of CHARACTER;
```

The task acts as a buffer which alternately builds up a line by accepting successive calls of PUT and then delivers a complete line on a call of GET.

14.3 Timing and scheduling

As we have seen an Ada program may contain several tasks. Conceptually it is best to think of these tasks as each having its own personal processor so that provided a task is not waiting for something to happen it will actually be executing.

In practice, of course, most implementations will not be able to allocate a unique processor to each task and indeed, in many cases, there will be only one physical processor. It will then be necessary to allocate the processor(s) to the tasks that are logically able to execute by some scheduling algorithm. This can be done in many ways.

One of the simplest mechanisms is to use time slicing. This means giving the processor to each task in turn for some fixed time interval such as 10 milliseconds. Of course, if a task cannot use its turn (perhaps because it is held up awaiting a partner in a rendezvous), then a sensible scheduler would allocate its turn to the next task. Similarly if a task cannot use all of its turn then the remaining time could be allocated to another task.

Time slicing is somewhat rudimentary since it treats all tasks equally. It is often the case that some tasks are more urgent than others and in the face of a shortage of processing power this equality is a bit wasteful. The idea of a task having a priority is therefore introduced. A simple scheduling system would be one where each task had a distinct priority and the processor would then be given to the highest priority task which could actually run. Combinations of time slicing and priority scheduling are also possible. A system might permit several tasks to have the same priority and time slice between them.

Ada allows various scheduling strategies to be used. If an implementation has the concept of priority, then the priority of a task can be indicated by a pragma appearing somewhere in the task specification as for example

```
task BUFFERING is
    pragma PRIORITY (7);
    entry PUT . . .
        . . .
    end;
```

In the case of the main program, which, as we have seen, is also considered to be a task, the pragma goes in its outermost declarative part.

The priority must be a static expression of the subtype PRIORITY of the type INTEGER but the actual range of the subtype PRIORITY depends upon the implementation. Note that the priority of a task is static and therefore cannot be changed during the course of execution of the program. A larger priority indicates a higher degree of urgency. Several tasks can have the same priority but on the other hand a task need not have an explicit priority at all.

The effect of priorities on the scheduling of Ada tasks is given by the following rule taken from the LRM.

If two tasks with different priorities are both eligible for execution and could sensibly be executed using the same physical processors and the same other processing resources, then it cannot be the case that the task with the lower priority is executing while the task with the higher priority is not.

This rule says nothing about tasks whose priorities are not defined nor does it say anything about tasks with the same priority. The implementation is therefore free to do whatever seems appropriate in these cases. Moreover, nothing prevents an implementation from having PRIORITY'FIRST = PRIORITY'LAST in which case all tasks could be time sliced equally and the concept of priority disappears. The rule also contains the phrase 'could sensibly be executed using the same . . . processing resources'; this is directed towards distributed systems where it may not be at all sensible for a processor in one part of the system to be used to execute a task in a different part of the system.

In the case of a rendezvous, a complication arises because two tasks are involved. If both tasks have explicit priorities, the rendezvous is executed with the higher priority. If only one task has an explicit priority then the rendezvous is executed with at least that priority. If neither task has a defined priority then the priority of the rendezvous is not defined. Of course, if the accept statement contains a further entry call or accept statement then the rules are applied once more.

The rendezvous rules ensure that a high priority task is not held up just because it is engaged in a rendezvous with a low priority task. On the other hand, the order of accepting the tasks in an entry queue is always first in first out and is not affected by priorities. If a high priority task wishes to guard against being held up because of lower priority tasks in the same entry queue, it can always use timed out or conditional calls as we shall see in the next section.

The use of priorities needs care. They are intended as a means of adjusting relative degrees of urgency and should not be used for synchronisation. It should not be assumed that the execution of task A precludes the execution of task B just because task A has a higher priority than task B. There might be several processors or later program maintenance might result in a change of priorities because of different real time requirements. Synchronisation should be done with the rendezvous and priorities should be avoided except for fine tuning of responsiveness.

A task may be held up for various reasons; it might be waiting for a partner in a rendezvous or for a dependent task to terminate. It can also be held up by executing a delay statement such as

delay 3.0;

This suspends the task (or main program) executing the statement for at least three seconds. (We have to say 'at least' because after the expiry of the interval there might not be a processor immediately available to execute the task.) The expression after the reserved word **delay** is of a predefined fixed point type DURATION and gives the period in seconds.

The type DURATION is a fixed point type so that the addition of durations can be done without systematic loss of accuracy. If we add together two fixed point model numbers we always get another model number; this does not apply to floating point. On the other hand we need to express fractions of a second in a convenient way and so the use of a real type rather than an integer type is much more satisfactory.

Delays can be more easily expressed by using suitable number declarations, thus

```
SECONDS: constant:=1.0;
MINUTES: constant:=60.0;
HOURS: constant:=3600.0;
```

We can then write for example

delay 2*HOURS+40*MINUTES;

A delay statement with a zero or negative argument has no effect.

Although the type DURATION is implementation defined we are guaranteed that it will allow durations (both positive and negative) of up to at least one day (86400) seconds. Delays of more than a day (which are unusual) would have to be programmed with a loop. At the other end of the scale, the smallest value of DURATION, that is DURATION'SMALL is guaranteed to be not greater than 20 milliseconds.

More sophisticated timing operations can be performed by using the predefined package CALENDAR whose specification is

```
package CALENDAR is

    type TIME is private;

    subtype YEAR_NUMBER is INTEGER range 1901 . . 2099;
    subtype MONTH_NUMBER is INTEGER range 1 . . 12;
    subtype DAY_NUMBER is INTEGER range 1 . . 31;
    subtype DAY_DURATION is DURATION range 0.0 . . 86_400.0;

    function CLOCK return TIME;

    function YEAR(DATE: TIME) return YEAR_NUMBER;
    function MONTH(DATE: TIME) return MONTH_NUMBER;
    function DAY(DATE: TIME) return DAY_NUMBER;
    function SECONDS(DATE: TIME) return DAY_DURATION;

    procedure SPLIT(DATE: in TIME;
                    YEAR: out YEAR_NUMBER;
                    MONTH: out MONTH_NUMBER;
                    DAY: out DAY_NUMBER;
                    SECONDS: out DAY_DURATION);

    function TIME_OF(YEAR: YEAR_NUMBER;
                MONTH: MONTH_NUMBER;
                DAY: DAY_NUMBER;
                SECONDS: DAY_DURATION:=0.0)
                                            return TIME;

    function "+"(LEFT: TIME; RIGHT: DURATION) return TIME;
    function "+"(LEFT: DURATION; RIGHT: TIME) return TIME;
    function "−"(LEFT: TIME; RIGHT: DURATION) return TIME;
    function "−"(LEFT: TIME; RIGHT: TIME) return DURATION;
    function "<"(LEFT, RIGHT: TIME) return BOOLEAN;
    function "<=" (LEFT, RIGHT: TIME) return BOOLEAN;
    function ">" (LEFT, RIGHT: TIME) return BOOLEAN;
    function ">=" (LEFT, RIGHT: TIME) return BOOLEAN;

    TIME_ERROR: exception;
                            − − can be raised by TIME_OF, +, and −

private
    − − implementation dependent
end CALENDAR;
```

A value of the private type TIME is a combined time and date; it can be decomposed into the year, month, day and the duration since midnight of the day concerned by the procedure SPLIT. Alternatively the functions YEAR, MONTH, DAY and SECONDS may be used to obtain the individual values. On the other hand, the function TIME_OF can be used to build a value of TIME from the four constituents; the seconds parameter has a default of zero. Note the subtypes YEAR_NUMBER, MONTH_NUMBER and DAY_NUMBER; the range of YEAR_NUMBER is such that the leap year calculation is simplified. The exception TIME_ERROR is raised if the parameters of TIME_OF satisfy the constraints but nevertheless do not form a proper date. A careful distinction must be made between TIME and DURATION. TIME is absolute but DURATION is relative.

The current TIME is returned by a call of the function CLOCK. The result is, of course, returned in an indivisible way and there is no risk of getting the time of day and the date inconsistent around midnight as there would be if there were separate functions delivering the individual components of the current time and date.

The various overloadings of "+", "−" and the relational operators allow us to add, subtract and compare times and durations as appropriate. Attempts to create a time outside the allowed range of years or to create a duration outside the implemented range will result in TIME_ERROR being raised. Note the strange formal parameter names LEFT and RIGHT; these are the normal names for the parameters of the predefined operators in the package STANDARD.

As an example of the use of the package CALENDAR suppose we wish a task to call a procedure ACTION at regular intervals, every 5 minutes perhaps. Our first attempt might be to write

```
loop
    delay 5*MINUTES;
    ACTION;
end loop;
```

However this is unsatisfactory for two reasons. Firstly we have not taken account of the time of execution of the procedure ACTION and the overhead of the loop itself, and secondly we have seen that a delay statement sets a minimum delay only. So we will inevitably get a cumulative timing drift. This can be overcome by writing for example

```
declare
    use CALENDAR;
    INTERVAL: constant DURATION:=5*MINUTES;
    NEXT_TIME: TIME:=FIRST_TIME;
begin
    loop
        delay NEXT_TIME – CLOCK;
        ACTION;
        NEXT_TIME:=NEXT_TIME + INTERVAL;
    end loop;
end;
```

In this formulation NEXT_TIME contains the time when ACTION is next to be called; its initial value is in FIRST_TIME and it is updated exactly on each iteration by adding INTERVAL. The delay statement is then used to delay by the difference between NEXT_TIME and the current time obtained by calling CLOCK. This solution will have no cumulative drift provided the mean duration of ACTION plus the overheads of the loop and updating NEXT_TIME and so on do not exceed INTERVAL. Of course, there may be a local drift if a particular call of ACTION takes a long time or other tasks temporarily use the processors. There is one other condition that must be satisfied for the required timing to be obtained: the interval has to be a model number.

Exercise 14.3

1 Write a generic procedure to call a procedure regularly. The generic parameters should be the procedure to be called, the time of the first call, the interval and the number of calls. If the time of the first call passed as parameter is in the past use the current time as the first time.

2 What is the least number of bits required to implement the type DURATION?

14.4 Select statements

The select statement allows a task to select from one of several possible rendezvous.

Consider the problem of protecting a variable V from uncontrolled access. We might consider using a package and two procedures READ and WRITE.

```
package PROTECTED_VARIABLE is
    procedure READ(X: out ITEM);
    procedure WRITE(X: in ITEM);
end;

package body PROTECTED_VARIABLE is
    V: ITEM;

    procedure READ(X: out ITEM) is
    begin
        X:=V;
    end;

    procedure WRITE(X: in ITEM) is
    begin
        V:=X;
    end;

begin
    V:=initial value;
end PROTECTED_VARIABLE;
```

However this is generally unsatisfactory. For one thing, the initial value is set in a rather arbitrary way. It would be better if somehow we could ensure that a call of WRITE had to be done first. We could, of course, have an internal state marker and raise an exception if READ is called first but this complicates the interface. The major problem, however, is that nothing prevents different tasks in our system from calling READ and WRITE simultaneously and thereby causing interference. As a more specific example suppose that the type ITEM is a record giving the coordinates of an aircraft or ship.

```
type ITEM is
    record
        X_COORD: REAL;
        Y_COORD: REAL;
    end record;
```

Suppose that a task A acquires pairs of values and uses a call of WRITE to store them into V and that another task B calls READ whenever it needs the latest position. Now assume that A is halfway through executing WRITE when it is interrupted by task B which promptly calls READ. It is clear that B could get a value consisting of the new x-coordinate and the old y-coordinate which would no doubt represent a location where the vessel had never been. The use of such inconsistent data for calculating the heading of the vessel from regularly read pairs of readings would obviously lead to inaccuracies.

The reader may wonder how the task A could be interrupted by task B anyway. In a single processor system with time slicing it may merely have been that B's turn came at an unfortunate moment. Alternatively B might have a higher priority than A; if B had been waiting for time to elapse before taking the next reading by obeying a delay statement, then A might be allowed to execute and B's delay might expire just at the wrong moment. In practical real time situations things are always happening at the wrong moment!

The proper solution is to use a task rather than a package, and entry calls rather than procedure calls. Consider now

```
task PROTECTED_VARIABLE is
    entry READ(X: out ITEM);
    entry WRITE(X: in ITEM);
end;

task body PROTECTED_VARIABLE is
    V: ITEM;
begin
    accept WRITE(X: in ITEM) do
        V:=X;
    end;
    loop
        select
            accept READ(X: out ITEM) do
                X:=V;
            end;
        or
            accept WRITE(X: in ITEM) do
                V:=X;
            end;
        end select;
    end loop;
end PROTECTED_VARIABLE;
```

The body of the task starts with an accept statement for the entry WRITE; this ensures that the first call accepted is for WRITE so that there is no risk of the variable being read before it is assigned a value. Of course, a task could call READ before any task had called WRITE but the calls of READ will be queued until a call of WRITE has been accepted.

Having accepted a call of WRITE, the task enters an endless loop containing a single select statement. A select statement starts with the reserved word **select** and finishes with **end select**; it contains two or more alternatives separated by

or. In this example each alternative consists of an accept statement – one for READ and one for WRITE.

When we encounter the select statement various possibilities have to be considered according to whether calls of READ or WRITE or both or neither have been made. We consider these in turn.

- If neither READ nor WRITE has been called then the task is suspended until one or the other is called and then the corresponding accept statement is obeyed.

- If one or more calls of READ are queued but there are no queued calls of WRITE then the first call of READ is accepted and vice versa with the roles of READ and WRITE reversed.

- If calls of both READ and WRITE are queued then an arbitrary choice is made.

Thus each execution of the select statement results in one of its branches being obeyed and one call of READ or WRITE being dealt with. We can think of the task as corresponding to a person serving two queues of customers waiting for two different services. If only one queue has customers then the server deals with it; if there are no customers then the server waits for the first irrespective of the service required; if both queues exist, the server rather capriciously serves either and makes an arbitrary choice each time.

So each time round the loop the task PROTECTED_VARIABLE will accept a call of READ or WRITE according to the demands upon it. It thus prevents multiple access to the variable V since it can only deal with one call at a time but does not impose any order upon the calls. Compare this with the task BUFFERING in Section 14.2 where an order was imposed upon the calls of PUT and GET.

Another point to notice is that this example illustrates a case where we have two accept statements for one entry. It so happens that the bodies are identical but they need not be.

The reader may wonder what the phrase 'arbitrary choice' means when deciding which alternative to choose. The intent is that there is no rule and the implementor is free to choose some efficient mechanism that nevertheless introduces an adequate degree of non-determinism so that the various queues are treated fairly and none gets starved. A random choice with equal probability would be acceptable but hard to implement efficiently. The most important point is that a program must not rely on the selection algorithm used; if it does, it is erroneous.

A more complex form of select statement is illustrated by the classic problem of the bounded buffer. This is similar to the problem in Section 14.2 except that up to N items can be buffered. A solution is

```
task BUFFERING is
    entry PUT(X: in ITEM);
    entry GET(X: out ITEM);
end;
task body BUFFERING is
    N: constant:=8;              -- for instance
    A: array (1 .. N) of ITEM;
```

```
    I, J: INTEGER range 1 .. N:=1;
    COUNT: INTEGER range 0 .. N:=0;
begin
    loop
        select
            when COUNT < N =>
            accept PUT(X: in ITEM) do
                A(I):=X;
            end;
            I:=I mod N+1; COUNT:=COUNT+1;
        or
            when COUNT > 0 =>
            accept GET(X: out ITEM) do
                X:=A(J);
            end;
            J:=J mod N+1; COUNT:=COUNT-1;
        end select;
    end loop;
end BUFFERING;
```

The buffer is the array A of length N which is a number set to 8 in this example. The variables I and J index the next free and last used locations of the buffer respectively and COUNT is the number of locations of the buffer which are full. Not only is it convenient to have COUNT but it is also necessary in order to distinguish between a completely full and completely empty buffer which both have I = J. The buffer is used cyclically so I need not be greater than J. The situation in Fig. 14.1 shows a partly filled buffer with COUNT = 5, I = 3 and J = 6. The portion of the buffer in use is shaded. The variables I and J are both initialised to 1 and COUNT is initialised to 0 so that the buffer is initially empty.

Fig. 14.1 The bounded buffer

The objective of the task is to allow items to be added to and removed from the buffer in a first in first out manner but to prevent the buffer from being overfilled or under emptied. This is done with a more general form of select statement which includes the use of guarding conditions.

Each branch of the select statement commences with

when condition =>

and is then followed by an accept statement and then some further statements. Each time the select statement is encountered all the guarding conditions are evaluated. The behaviour is then as for a select statement without guards but containing only those branches for which the conditions were true. So a branch will be taken and the corresponding rendezvous performed. After the accept statement a branch may contain further statements. These are executed by the server task as part of the select statement but outside the rendezvous.

So the guarding conditions are conditions which have to be true before a service can be offered. The accept statement represents the rendezvous with the customer and the giving of the service. The statements after the accept statement represent bookkeeping actions performed as a consequence of giving the service and which can be done after the customer has left but, of course, need to be done before the next customer is served.

In our example the condition for being able to accept a call of PUT is simply that the buffer must not be full; this is the condition COUNT < N. Similarly we can accept a call of GET provided that the buffer is not empty; this is the condition COUNT > 0. The statements in the bodies of the accept statements copy the item to or from the buffer. After the rendezvous is completed, the index I or J as appropriate and COUNT are updated to reflect the change of state. Note the use of **mod** to update I and J in a cyclic manner.

Thus we see that the first time the select statement is executed, the condition COUNT < N is true but COUNT > 0 is false. Hence only a call of PUT can be accepted. This puts the first item in the buffer. The next time both conditions will be true so either PUT or GET can be accepted, adding a further item or removing the one item. And so it goes on; allowing items to be added or removed with one of the guarding conditions becoming false in the extreme situations and thereby preventing overfilling or under emptying.

A few points need emphasis. The guards are reevaluated at the beginning of each execution of the select statement (but their order of evaluation is not defined). An absent guard is taken as true. If all guards turn out to be false then the exception PROGRAM_ERROR is raised. It should be realised that a guard need not still be true when the corresponding rendezvous is performed because it might use global variables and therefore be changed by another task. Later we will discuss an example where guards could change unexpectedly. In the example here, of course, nothing can go wrong. One guard is always true, so PROGRAM_ERROR can never be raised and they both only involve the local variable COUNT and so cannot be changed between their evaluation and the rendezvous.

For our next example consider again the task PROTECTED_VARIABLE. This allowed either read or write access but only one at a time. This is somewhat severe; the usual classical problem is to allow only one writer of course, but to allow several readers together. A simple solution is shown below. It takes the form of a package containing a local task.

```
package READER_WRITER is
    procedure READ(X: out ITEM);
    procedure WRITE(X: in ITEM);
end;

package body READER_WRITER is
    V: ITEM;

    task CONTROL is
        entry START;
        entry STOP;
        entry WRITE(X: in ITEM);
    end;
```

```
        task body CONTROL is
            READERS: INTEGER:=0;
        begin
            accept WRITE(X: in ITEM) do
                V:=X;
            end;
            loop
                select
                    accept START;
                    READERS:=READERS+1;
                or
                    accept STOP;
                    READERS:=READERS-1;
                or
                    when READERS = 0 =>
                    accept WRITE(X: in ITEM) do
                        V:=X;
                    end;
                end select;
            end loop;
        end CONTROL;

        procedure READ(X: out ITEM) is
        begin
            CONTROL.START;
            X:=V;
            CONTROL.STOP;
        end READ;

        procedure WRITE(X: in ITEM) is
        begin
            CONTROL.WRITE(X);
        end WRITE;

    end READER_WRITER;
```

The task CONTROL has three entries, WRITE to do the writing and START and STOP associated with reading. A call of START indicates a wish to start reading and a call of STOP indicates that reading has finished. The task is wrapped up in a package because we wish to provide multiple reading access. This can be done by providing a procedure READ which can then be called reentrantly; it also enforces the protocol of calling START and then STOP.

So the whole thing is a package containing the variable V, the task CONTROL and the access procedures READ and WRITE. As stated, READ enforces the desired calls of START and STOP around the statement X:=V; the procedure WRITE merely calls the entry WRITE.

The task CONTROL declares a variable READERS which indicates how many readers are present. As before it begins with an accept statement for WRITE to ensure that the variable is initialised and then enters a loop containing a select statement. This has three branches, one for each entry. On a call of START or STOP the count of number of readers is incremented or decremented. A call of

WRITE can only be accepted if the condition READERS=0 is true. Hence writing when readers are present is forbidden. Of course, since the task CONTROL actually does the writing, multiple writing is prevented and, moreover, it cannot at the same time accept calls of START and so reading is not possible when writing is in progress. However multiple reading is allowed as we have seen.

Although the above solution does fulfil the general conditions it is not really satisfactory. A steady stream of readers will completely block out a writer. Since writing is probably rather important, this is not acceptable. An obvious improvement would be to disallow further reading if one or more writers are waiting. We can do this by using the attribute WRITE'COUNT in a guard so that the select statement now becomes

```
select
    when WRITE'COUNT = 0 =>
    accept START;
    READERS:=READERS+1;
or
    accept STOP;
    READERS:=READERS-1;
or
    when READERS = 0 =>
    accept WRITE(X: in ITEM) do
        V:=X;
    end;
end select;
```

The attribute WRITE'COUNT is the number of tasks currently on the queue for the entry WRITE. The use of the count attribute in guards needs care. It gives the value when the guard is evaluated and can well change before a rendezvous is accepted. It could increase because another task joins the queue – that would not matter in this example. But, as we shall see later, it could also decrease unexpectedly and this would indeed give problems. We will return to this example in a moment.

There are also various other forms of select statement. It is possible for one or more of the branches to start with a delay statement rather than an accept statement. Consider

```
select
    accept READ(. . .)do
    . . .
    end;
or
    accept WRITE(. . .) do
    . . .
    end;
or
    delay 10*MINUTES;
    - - time out statements
end select;
```

If neither a call of **READ** nor **WRITE** is received within 10 minutes then the third branch is taken and the statements following the delay are executed. The task might decide that since its services are no longer apparently required it can do something else or maybe it can be interpreted as an emergency. In a process control system we might be awaiting an acknowledgement from the operator that some action has been taken and after a suitable interval take our own emergency action

```
OPERATOR.CALL("PUT OUT FIRE");

select
    accept ACKNOWLEDGE;
or
    delay 1*MINUTE;
    FIRE_BRIGADE.CALL;
end select;
```

A delay alternative can be guarded and indeed there could be several in a select statement although clearly only the shortest one with a true guard can be taken. It should be realised that if one of the accept statements is obeyed then any delay is cancelled – we can think of a delay alternative as waiting for a rendezvous with the clock. A delay is of course set from the start of the select statement and reset each time the select statement is encountered. Finally note that it is the start of the rendezvous that matters rather than its completion as far as the time out is concerned.

Another form of select statement is one with an else part. Consider

```
select
    accept READ(. . .) do
    . . .
    end;
or
    accept WRITE(. . .) do
    . . .
    end;
else
    – – alternative statements

end select;
```

In this case the final branch is preceded by **else** rather than **or** and consists of just a sequence of statements. The else branch is taken at once if none of the other branches can be immediately accepted. A select statement with an else part is rather like one with a branch starting **delay** 0.0; it times out at once if there are no customers to be dealt with. A select statement cannot have both an else part and delay alternatives.

There is a subtle distinction between an accept statement starting a branch of a select and an accept statement anywhere else. In the first case the accept statement is bound up with the workings of the select statement and is to some extent conditional. In the second case, once encountered, it will be obeyed come what may. The same distinction applies to a delay statement starting a branch of a select statement and one elsewhere. Thus if we change the **or** to **else** in our emergency action to give

```
select
    accept ACKNOWLEDGE;
else
    delay 1*MINUTE;
    FIRE_BRIGADE.CALL;
end select;
```

then the status of the delay is quite different. It just happens to be one of a sequence of statements and will be obeyed in the usual way. So if we cannot accept a call of ACKNOWLEDGE at once, we immediately take the else part. The fact that the first statement is a delay is fortuitous – we immediately delay for one minute and then call the fire brigade. There is no time out.

If a select statement has an else part then PROGRAM_ERROR can never be raised. The else part cannot be guarded and so will always be taken if all branches have guards and they all turn out to be false.

There are two other forms of select statement which are rather different; they concern a single entry call rather than one or more accept statements. The timed out entry call allows a sequence of statements to be taken as an alternative to an entry call if it is not accepted within the specified duration. Thus

```
select
    OPERATOR.CALL("PUT OUT FIRE");
or
    delay 1*MINUTE;
    FIRE_BRIGADE.CALL;
end select;
```

will call the fire brigade if the operator does not accept the call within one minute. Again, it is the start of the rendezvous that matters rather than its completion. Finally there is the conditional entry call. Thus

```
select
    OPERATOR.CALL("PUT OUT FIRE");
else
    FIRE_BRIGADE.CALL;
end select;
```

will call the fire brigade if the operator cannot immediately accept the call.

The timed out and conditional entry calls are quite different to the general select statement. They concern only a single unguarded call and so these select statements always have exactly two branches – one with the entry call and the other with the alternative sequence of statements. Timed out and conditional calls apply only to entries. They do not apply to procedures or even to entries renamed as procedures.

Timed out and conditional calls are useful if a task does not want to be unduly delayed when a server task is busy. They correspond to a customer in a shop giving up and leaving the queue after waiting for a time or, in the conditional case, a highly impatient customer leaving at once if not immediately served.

Timed out calls, however, need some care particularly if the COUNT attribute is used. A decision based on the value of that attribute may be invalidated because of a timed out call unexpectedly removing a task from an entry queue. Consider for example the package READER_WRITER. As it stands the entry calls cannot be timed out because they are encapsulated in the procedures READ and WRITE. However, we might decide to provide further overloadings of these procedures in order to provide timed out facilities. We might add, for example

```
procedure WRITE(X: in ITEM; T: DURATION; OK: out BOOLEAN) is
begin
    select
        CONTROL.WRITE(X);
        OK:=TRUE;
    or
        delay T;
        OK:=FALSE;
    end select;
end WRITE;
```

Unfortunately this is invalid. Suppose that one writer is waiting (so that WRITE'COUNT = 1) but the call is timed out between the evaluation of the guards and the execution of an accept statement. There are two cases to consider according to the value of READERS. If READERS = 0, then no task can call STOP since there are no current readers; a call of START cannot be accepted because its guard was false and the expected call of WRITE will not occur because it has been timed out; the result is that all new readers will be unnecessarily blocked until a new writer arrives. On the other hand, if READERS > 0, then although further calls of WRITE correctly cannot be accepted, nevertheless further calls of START are unnecessarily delayed until an existing reader calls STOP despite there being no waiting writers. We therefore seek an alternative solution.

The original reason for using WRITE'COUNT was to prevent readers from overtaking waiting writers. One possibility in cases of this sort is to make all the customers call a common entry to start with. This ensures that they are dealt with in order. This entry call can be parameterised to indicate the service required and the callers can then be placed on a secondary queue if necessary. This technique is illustrated by the solution which now follows. The package specification is as before.

```
package body READER_WRITER is
    V: ITEM;
    type SERVICE is (READ, WRITE);

    task CONTROL is
        entry START(S: SERVICE);
        entry STOP_READ;
        entry WRITE;
        entry STOP_WRITE;
    end CONTROL;
```

```
task body CONTROL is
    READERS: INTEGER:=0;
    WRITERS: INTEGER:=0;
begin
    loop
        select
            when WRITERS = 0 =>
            accept START(S: SERVICE) do
                case S is
                    when READ => READERS:=
                                        READERS+1;
                    when WRITE => WRITERS:=1;
                end case;
            end START;
        or
            accept STOP_READ;
            READERS:=READERS−1;
        or
            when READERS = 0 =>
            accept WRITE;
        or
            accept STOP_WRITE;
            WRITERS:=0;
        end select;
    end loop;
end CONTROL;

procedure READ(X: out ITEM) is
begin
    CONTROL.START(READ);
    X:=V;
    CONTROL.STOP_READ;
end READ;

procedure WRITE(X: in ITEM) is
begin
    CONTROL.START(WRITE);
    CONTROL.WRITE;
    V:=X;
    CONTROL.STOP_WRITE;
end WRITE;

end READER_WRITER;
```

We have introduced a variable **WRITERS** to indicate how many writers are in the system; it can only take values of **0** and 1. All requests initially call the common entry **START** but have to wait until there are no writers. The count of readers or writers is then updated as appropriate. In the case of a reader it can then go ahead as before and finishes by calling **STOP_READ**. A writer, on the other hand, must wait until there are no readers; it does this by calling **WRITE** and then finally calls **STOP_WRITE** in order that the control task can set **WRITERS** back to zero. Separating **STOP_WRITE** from **WRITE** enables us to cope with time outs as we shall see; we also take the opportunity to place the actual writing statement in the procedure WRITE so that it is similar to the read case.

In this solution, the variable WRITERS performs the function of WRITE' COUNT in the previous but incorrect solution. By counting for ourselves we can keep the situation under control. The calls of START and WRITE can now be timed out provided that we always call STOP_READ or STOP_WRITE once a call of START has been accepted. The details of suitable overloadings of READ and WRITE to provide timed out calls are left as an exercise.

Note that the above solution has ignored the problem of ensuring that the first call is a write. This can be catered for in various ways, by using a special initial entry, for instance, or by placing the readers on a second auxiliary queue so that they are forced to wait for the first writer.

We finish this section by showing a rather slick alternative to the above.

```
task CONTROL is
    entry START(S: SERVICE);
    entry STOP;
end CONTROL;

task body CONTROL is
    READERS: INTEGER:=0;
begin
    loop
        select
            accept START(S: SERVICE) do
                case S is
                    when READ =>
                        READERS:=READERS+1;
                    when WRITE =>
                        while READERS > 0 loop
                            accept STOP;          --from readers
                            READERS:=READERS-1;
                        end loop;
                end case;
            end START;

            if READERS = 0 then
                accept STOP;                    --from the writer
            end if;
        or
            accept STOP;                        --from a reader
            READERS:=READERS-1;
        end select;
    end loop;
end CONTROL;

procedure READ(X: out ITEM) is
begin
    CONTROL.START(READ);
    X:=V;
    CONTROL.STOP;
end READ;
```

```
procedure WRITE(X: in ITEM) is
begin
    CONTROL.START(WRITE);
    V:=X;
    CONTROL.STOP;
end WRITE;
```

The essence of this solution is that the writer waits in the rendezvous for any readers to finish and the whole of the writing process is dealt with in the one branch of the select statement. No guards are required at all and the control task only has two entries. A common STOP entry is possible because the structure is such that each accept statement deals with only one category of caller. A minor disadvantage of the solution is that less flexible timed calls are possible. Once the writer has been accepted by the call of START, he is committed to wait for all the readers to finish.

Exercise 14.4
1   Rewrite the body of the task BUILD_COMPLEX of Exercise 14.2(**1**) so that the calls of PUT_RL and PUT_IM are accepted in any order.

2   Write additional procedures READ and WRITE for the (penultimate) package READER_WRITER in order to provide timed out calls. Take care with the procedure WRITE so that the calls of the entries START and WRITE are both timed out appropriately.

14.5   Task types and activation

It is sometimes useful to have several similar but distinct tasks. Moreover, it is often not possible to predict the number of such tasks required. For example we might wish to create distinct tasks to follow each aircraft within the zone of control of an air traffic control system. Clearly such tasks need to be created and disposed of in a dynamic way not related to the static structure of the program.

A template for similar tasks is provided by a task type declaration. This is identical to the simple task declarations we have seen so far except that the reserved word **type** follows **task** in the specification. Thus we may write

```
task type T is
    entry E(. . .);
end T;

task body T is
    . . .
end T;
```

The task body follows the same rules as before.

To create an actual task we use the normal form of object declaration. So we can write

```
X: T;
```

and this declares a task X of type T. In fact the simple form of task declaration we have been using so far such as

task SIMPLE **is**
   . . .
end SIMPLE;

is exactly equivalent to writing

task type anon **is**
   . . .
end anon;

followed by

SIMPLE: anon;

Task objects can be used in structures in the usual way. Thus we can declare arrays of tasks

AT: **array** (1 . . 10) **of** T;

records containing tasks

type REC **is**
   record
        CT: T;
      . . .
   end record;
R: REC;

and so on.

The entries of such tasks are called using the task object name; thus we write

X.E(. . .);
AT(I).E(. . .);
R.CT.E(. . .);

A most important consideration is that task objects are not variables but behave as constants. A task object declaration creates a task which is permanently bound to the object. Hence assignment is not allowed for task types and nor are the comparisons for equality and inequality. A task type is therefore another form of limited type and so could be used as the actual type corresponding to a formal generic parameter specified as limited private and as the actual type in a private part corresponding to a limited private type. Although task objects behave as constants, they cannot be declared as such since a constant declaration needs an explicit initial value. Subprogram parameters may be of task types; they are always effectively passed by reference and so the formal and actual parameters always refer to the same task. As in the case of other limited types, outside their defining package, parameters of mode **out** are not allowed; of course there is no defining package in the case of task types anyway.

In Section 14.1 we briefly introduced the idea of dependency. Each task is dependent on some unit and there is a general rule that a unit cannot be left until all tasks dependent upon it have terminated.

A task declared as a task object (or using the abbreviated simple form) is dependent upon the enclosing block, subprogram or task body in which it is declared. Inner packages do not count in this rule – this is because a package is merely a passive scope wall and has no dynamic life. If a task is declared in a package (or nested packages) then the task is dependent upon the block, subprogram or task body in which the package or packages are themselves declared. For completeness, a task declared in a library package is said to depend on that package; however, since packages are passive, this has no impact on the termination of the task and indeed the language deliberately does not define whether such tasks are required to terminate at all.

We saw earlier that a task becomes active only when the declaring unit reaches the **begin** following the declaration. The execution of a task can be thought of as a two stage process. The first stage, known as activation, consists of the elaboration of the declarations of the task body whereas the second stage consists, of course, of the execution of its statements. During the activation stage the parent unit is not allowed to proceed. If several tasks are declared in a unit then their activations and the subsequent execution of their statements occur independently and in parallel. But it is only when the activation of all the tasks is complete that the parent unit can continue with the execution of the statements following the **begin** in parallel with the new tasks.

This process is depicted in Fig. 14.2 which illustrates the behaviour of a block containing the declarations of two tasks A and B

```
declare
    . . .
    A: T;
    B: T;
    . . .
begin
    . . .
end;
```

Time flows from left to right and a solid line indicates that a unit is actively doing something whereas a dashed line indicates that it exists but is suspended.

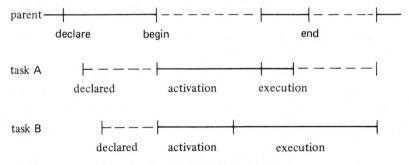

Fig.14.2 Task activation

For the sake of illustration we show task A finishing its activation after task B so that the parent resumes execution when task A enters its execution stage. We also show task A finishing its execution and therefore becoming completed and terminated before task B. The parent is shown reaching its **end** and therefore becoming completed after task A has terminated but before task B has terminated. The parent unit is therefore suspended until task B is terminated when it too is terminated and can resume execution of the statements following the block.

The reason for treating task activation in this way concerns exceptions. The reader may recall that an exception raised during the elaboration of declarations is not handled at that level but immediately propagated. So an exception raised in the declarations in a new task could not be handled by that task at all. However, since it is clearly desirable that some means be provided for detecting such an exception, it is obvious that an exception has to be raised in the parent unit. In fact the predefined exception TASKING_ERROR is raised irrespective of the original exception. It would clearly make life rather difficult if this exception were raised in the parent unit after it had moved on in parallel and so it is held up until all the new tasks have been activated. The exception TASKING_ERROR is therefore raised in the parent unit as soon as it attempts to move on from the **begin**. Note that if several of the new tasks raise exceptions during activation then TASKING_ERROR is only raised once. Such tasks become completed (not terminated) and do not affect sibling tasks being simultaneously activated.

The other thing that can go wrong is that an exception can occur in the declarations of the parent unit itself. In this case any new tasks which have been declared (but of course will not have been activated because the parent unit has not yet reached its **begin**) will automatically become terminated and are never activated at all.

Task objects can be declared in a package and although not dependent on the package are nevertheless set active at the **begin** of the package body. If the package body has no initialisation statements and therefore no **begin**, then a null initialisation statement is assumed. Worse, if a package has no body, then a body with just a null initialisation statement is assumed. So the task CONTROL in the package READER_WRITER of the previous section is set active at the end of the declaration of the package body.

Tasks can also be created through access types. We can write

type REF_T **is access** T;

and then we can create a task using an allocator in the usual way

RX: REF_T:=**new** T;

The type REF_T is a normal access type and so assignment and equality comparisons of objects of the type are allowed. The entry E of the task accessed by RX can be called as expected by

RX.E(. . .);

Tasks created through access types obey slightly different rules for activation and dependency. They commence activation immediately upon evaluation of the allocator whether it occurs in a sequence of statements or in an initial value – we do not wait until the ensuing **begin**. Furthermore, such tasks are not dependent upon the unit where they are created but are dependent upon the block, subprogram body or task body containing the declaration of the access type itself.The strong analogies between tasks declared as objects and those created through an allocator are revealed when we consider tasks which are components of a composite object.

Suppose we have the following somewhat artificial type

```
type R is
    record
        A: T;
        I: INTEGER:=E;
        B: T;
    end record;
```

where A and B are components of some task type T and E is the default initial expression for the component I.

If we declare an object X of type R thus

```
declare
    X: R;
begin
```

then it is much as if we declared the individual objects

```
declare
    XA: T;
    XI: INTEGER:=E;
    XB: T;
begin
```

using the rules explained above.

Now suppose we have an access type

```
type REF_R is access R;
```

and create an object using an allocator

```
RR: REF_R:=new R;
```

The first thing that happens is that the various components are declared and the initial expression is evaluated and assigned to RR.I. It is only when this has been done that activation of the tasks RR.A and RR.B can commence; in a sense we wait until we reach **end record** by analogy with waiting until we reach **begin** in the case of directly declared objects. The component tasks are then activated in parallel but the parent unit is suspended and the access value is not returned until all the activations are complete just as we could not move past the **begin**. Similarly, if an exception is raised by the activation of one or both component tasks, then, on return from the allocator, TASKING_ERROR is raised just once in the parent unit. Such rogue tasks will then become completed but will not interfere with any other sibling component tasks. Finally if the evaluation of E raises an exception in the parent unit then the component tasks will automatically become terminated without even being activated.

The reader will probably feel that the activation mechanism is somewhat elaborate. However, in practice, the details will rarely need to be considered. They are mentioned in order to show that the mechanism is well defined rather than because of their everyday importance.

Note that entries in a task can be called as soon as it is declared and even before activation commences – the call will just be queued. However, situations in which this is sensibly possible are rare.

A common use of task types is for the creation of agents. An agent is a task that does something on behalf of another task. As an example suppose a task SERVER provides some service that is asked for by calling an entry REQUEST. Suppose also that it may take SERVER some time to provide the service so that it is reasonable for the calling task USER to go away and do something else while waiting for the answer to be prepared. There are various ways in which the USER could expect to collect his answer. He could call another entry ENQUIRE; the SERVER task would need some means of recognising the caller – he could do this by issuing a key on the call of REQUEST and insisting that it be presented again when calling ENQUIRE. This corresponds to taking something to be repaired, being given a ticket and then having to exchange it when the repaired item is collected later. An alternative approach which avoids the issue of keys, is to create an agent. This corresponds to leaving your address and having the repaired item posted back to you. We will now illustrate this approach.

First of all we declare a task type as follows

```
task type MAILBOX is
    entry DEPOSIT(X: in ITEM);
    entry COLLECT(X: out ITEM);
end;

task body MAILBOX is
    LOCAL: ITEM;
begin
    accept DEPOSIT(X: in ITEM) do
        LOCAL:=X;
    end;
    accept COLLECT(X: out ITEM) do
        X:=LOCAL;
    end;
end MAILBOX;
```

A task of this type acts as a simple mailbox. An item can be deposited and collected later. What we are going to do is to give the identity of the mailbox to the server so that the server can deposit the item in the mailbox from which the user can collect it later. We need an access type

```
type ADDRESS is access MAILBOX;
```

The tasks SERVER and USER now take the following form

```
task SERVER is
    entry REQUEST(A: ADDRESS; X: ITEM);
end;

task body SERVER is
    REPLY: ADDRESS;
    JOB: ITEM;
begin
    loop
        accept REQUEST(A: ADDRESS; X: ITEM) do
            REPLY:=A;
            JOB:=X;
        end;

        -- work on job

        REPLY.DEPOSIT(JOB);
    end loop;
end SERVER;

task USER;

task body USER is
    MY_BOX: ADDRESS:= new MAILBOX;
    MY_ITEM: ITEM;
begin
    SERVER.REQUEST(MY_BOX, MY_ITEM);

    -- do something while waiting

    MY_BOX.COLLECT(MY_ITEM);
end USER;
```

In practice the user might poll the mailbox from time to time to see if the item is ready. This is easily done using a conditional entry call.

```
select
    MY_BOX.COLLECT(MY_ITEM);
    -- item collected successfully
else
    -- not ready yet
end select;
```

It is important to realise that the agent serves several purposes. It enables the deposit and collect to be decoupled so that the server can get on with the next job. But perhaps more important, it means that the server need know nothing about the user; to call the user directly would mean that the user would have to be of a particular task type and this would be most unreasonable. The agent enables us to factor off the only property required of the user, namely the existence of the entry DEPOSIT.

If the decoupling property were not required then the body of the agent could be written as

```
task body MAILBOX is
```

```
    begin
        accept DEPOSIT(X: in ITEM) do
            accept COLLECT(X: out ITEM) do
                COLLECT.X:=DEPOSIT.X;
            end;
        end;
    end MAILBOX;
```

The agent does not need a local variable in this case since it only exists to aid closely coupled communication. Note also the use of the dotted notation in the nested accept statements in order to distinguish the two uses of X; we could equally have written X:=DEPOSIT.X; but the use of COLLECT is more symmetric.

14.6   Termination and exceptions

A task can become completed and then terminate in various ways as well as running into its final end. It will have been noticed that in many of our earlier examples, the body of a task was an endless loop and clearly never terminated. This means that it would never be possible to leave the unit on which the task was dependent. Suppose for example that we needed to have several protected variables in our program. We could declare a task type

```
    task type PROTECTED_VARIABLE is
        entry READ(X: out ITEM);
        entry WRITE(X: in ITEM);
    end;
```

so that we can just declare variables such as

```
    PV: PROTECTED_VARIABLE;
```

and access them by

```
    PV.READ(. . .);
    PV.WRITE(. . .);
```

However, we could not leave the scope of PV without terminating the task in some way. We could, of course, add a special entry STOP and call it just before leaving the scope but this would be inconvenient. Instead it is possible to make a task automatically terminate itself when it is of no further use by a special form of select alternative.

The body of the task can be written as

```
    task body PROTECTED_VARIABLE is
        V: ITEM;
    begin
        accept WRITE(X: in ITEM) do
            V:=X;
        end;
```

```
      loop
          select
              accept READ(X: out ITEM) do
                  X:=V;
              end;
          or
              accept WRITE(X: in ITEM) do
                  V:=X;
              end;
          or
              terminate;
          end select;
      end loop;
  end PROTECTED_VARIABLE;
```

The terminate alternative is taken if the unit on which the task depends has reached its end and so is completed and all sibling tasks and dependent tasks are terminated or are similarly able to select a terminate alternative. In such circumstances all the tasks are of no use since they are the only tasks that could call their entries and they are all dormant. Thus the whole set automatically terminates.

In practice, this merely means that all service tasks should have a terminate alternative and will then quietly terminate themselves without more ado.

Strictly speaking, the initial **WRITE** should also be in a select statement with a terminate alternative otherwise we are still stuck if the task is never called at all.

A terminate alternative may be guarded. However, it cannot appear in a select statement with a delay alternative or an else part.

Selection of a terminate alternative is classified as normal termination – the task is under control of the situation and terminates voluntarily.

At the other extreme the abort statement unconditionally terminates one or more tasks. It consists of the reserved word **abort** followed by a list of task names as for example

abort X, AT(3), RX.**all**;

If a task is aborted then all tasks dependent upon it or a subprogram or block currently called by it are also aborted. If the task is suspended for some reason then it immediately becomes completed; any delay is cancelled; if the task is on an entry queue, it is removed; other possibilities are that it has not yet even commenced activation or it is at an accept or select statement awaiting a partner. If the task is not suspended then completion will occur as soon as convenient and certainly no new communication with the task will be possible. The reason for this somewhat vague statement concerns the rendezvous. If the task is engaged in a rendezvous when it is aborted, then we also have to consider the effect on the partner. This depends on the situation. If the called task is aborted, then the calling task receives the exception **TASKING_ERROR**. On the other hand, if the calling task is aborted then the called task is not affected; the rendezvous carries on to completion with the caller in a somewhat abnormal state and it is only when the rendezvous is complete that the caller becomes properly completed. The rationale is simple; if a task asks for a service and the server dies so that it cannot be provided then the customer should be told. On the other hand, if the customer dies, too bad

– but we must avoid upsetting the server who might have the database in a critical state.

Note that the above rules are formulated in terms of completing the tasks rather than terminating them. This is because a parent task cannot be terminated until its dependent tasks are terminated and if one of those is the caller in a rendezvous with a third party then its termination will be delayed. Thus completion of the tasks is the best that can be individually enforced and their termination will then automatically occur in the usual way.

The abort statement is very disruptive and should only be used in extreme situations. It might be appropriate for a command task to abort a complete subsytem in response to an operator command.

Another possible use for the abort statement might be in an exception handler. Remember that we cannot leave a unit until all dependent tasks are terminated. Hence, if an exception is raised in a unit, then we cannot tidy up that unit and propagate the exception on a layered basis while dependent tasks are still alive and so one of the actions of tidying up might be to abort all dependent tasks. Thus the procedure **CLEAN_UP** of Section 10.2 might do just this.

However, it is probably always best to attempt a controlled shutdown and only resort to the abort statement as a desperate measure. Statements in the command task might be as follows

```
select
    T.CLOSEDOWN;
or
    delay 60*SECONDS;
    abort T;
end select;
```

If the slave task does not accept the **CLOSEDOWN** call within a minute, then it is ruthlessly aborted. We are assuming, of course, that the slave task polls the **CLOSEDOWN** entry at least every minute using a conditional accept statement such as

```
select
    accept CLOSEDOWN;
    − − tidy up and die
else
    − − carry on normally
end select;
```

If we cannot trust the slave to close down properly even after accepting the entry call, then the command task can always issue an abort after a due interval just in case. Aborting a task which has already terminated has no effect. So the command task might read

```
select
    T.CLOSEDOWN;
    delay 10*SECONDS;
or
    delay 60*SECONDS;
```

```
    end select;
    abort T;
```

Of course, even this is not foolproof since the malevolent slave might continue for
ever in the rendezvous itself

```
    accept CLOSEDOWN do
        loop
            PUT("CANT CATCH ME");
        end loop;
    end;
```

Some minimal degree of cooperation is obviously needed!

The status of task T can be ascertained by the use of two attributes. Thus
T'TERMINATED is true if a task is terminated. The other attribute, **T'CALLABLE**
is true unless the task is completed or terminated or in the abnormal state pending
final abortion. The use of these attributes needs care. For example between
discovering that a task has not terminated and taking some action based on that
information, the task could become terminated. However, the reverse is not
possible since a task cannot be restarted and so it is quite safe to take an action
based on the information that a task has terminated.

As an illustration of the impact of abnormal termination and how it can be
coped with, we will reconsider the task **CONTROL** in the package
READER_WRITER in Section 14.4 in its final form

```
    task body CONTROL is
        READERS: INTEGER:=0;
    begin
        loop
            select
                accept START(S: SERVICE) do
                    case S is
                        when READ =>
                            READERS:=READERS+1;
                        when WRITE =>
                            while READERS > 0 loop
                                accept STOP;          --from readers
                                READERS:=READERS−1;
                            end loop;
                    end case;
                end START;
                if READERS = 0 then
                    accept STOP;                      --from the writer
                end if;
            or
                accept STOP;                          --from a reader
                READERS:=READERS−1;
            end select;
        end loop;
    end CONTROL;
```

Suppose that a reading task has called START and is then aborted before it can call STOP. The variable READERS will then be inconsistent and can never be zero again. The next writer will then be locked out for ever. Similarly if a writing task has called START and is then aborted before it can call STOP then all other users will be locked out for ever.

The difficulty we have run into is that our task CONTROL assumes certain behaviour on the part of the calling tasks and this behaviour is not guaranteed. (We had a similar difficulty with our elementary solution to this example in Section 14.4 regarding the COUNT attribute and timed out entry calls.) We can overcome our new difficulty by the use of intermediate agent tasks which we can guarantee cannot be aborted.

The following shows the use of agents for the readers; a similar technique can be applied to the writers. The package body now becomes

```
package body READER_WRITER is
    V: ITEM;
    type SERVICE is (READ, WRITE);

    task type READ_AGENT is
        entry READ(X: out ITEM);
    end;

    type RRA is access READ_AGENT;

    task CONTROL is
        entry START(S: SERVICE);
        entry STOP;
    end;

    task body CONTROL is
        -- as before
    end CONTROL;

    task body READ_AGENT is
    begin
        select
            accept READ(X: out ITEM) do
                CONTROL.START(READ);
                X:=V;
                CONTROL.STOP;
            end;
        or
            terminate;
        end select;
    end READ_AGENT;

    procedure READ(X: out ITEM) is
        A: RRA:=new READ_AGENT;
    begin
        A.READ(X);
    end READ;

    procedure WRITE(X: in ITEM) is
    begin
```

> . . .
>
> **end** WRITE;

end READER_WRITER;

If we now abort the task calling the procedure READ then either the rendezvous with its agent will be in progress, in which case it will be completed, or the rendezvous will not be in progress, in which case there will be no interference. The agent therefore either does its job completely or not at all. Note that if we made the agent a direct task object (rather than an access to a task object) then aborting the task calling the procedure READ would also immediately abort the agent because it would be a dependent task. Using an access type makes the agent dependent on the unit in which the READER_WRITER is declared and so it can live on.

The agent contains a select statement with a terminate alternative. This ensures that if the user task is aborted between creating the agent and calling the agent then nevertheless the agent can quietly die when the unit on which it depends is left.

It is worth summarising why the above solution works

* the agent is invisible and so cannot be aborted;

* if the calling task in a rendezvous is abnormally terminated, the called task (the agent) is not affected;

* the agent is an access task and is not dependent on the caller.

The moral is not to use abort without due care; or, as in life, if you cannot trust the calling tasks, use indestructible secret agents.

We finish this section by discussing a few remaining points on exceptions. The exception TASKING_ERROR is concerned with general communication failure. As we have seen, it is raised if a failure occurs during task activation and it is also raised in the caller of a rendezvous if the server is aborted. In addition, no matter how a task is completed, all tasks still queued on its entries receive TASKING_ERROR. Similarly calling an entry of a task that is already completed also raises TASKING_ERROR in the caller.

If an exception is raised during a rendezvous (that is as a consequence of an action by the called task) and is not handled by the accept statement, then it is propagated into both tasks as the same exception on the grounds that both need to know. Of course, if the accept statement handles the exception internally then that is the end of the matter anyway.

Finally, if an exception is not handled by a task at all, then, like the main program, the task is abandoned and the exception is lost; it is not propagated to the parent unit because it would be too disruptive to do so. However, we might expect the run time environment to provide a diagnostic message. If it does not, it might be good practice for all significant tasks to have a general handler at the outermost level in order to guard against the loss of exceptions and consequential silent death of the task.

Exercise 14.6

1   Rewrite the task BUFFERING of Section 14.4 so that it has the following specification

```
task BUFFERING is
    entry PUT(X: in ITEM);
    entry FINISH;
    entry GET(X: out ITEM);
end;
```

The writing task calls PUT as before and finally calls FINISH. The reading task calls GET as before; a call of GET when there are no further items raises the global exception DONE.

14.7   Resource scheduling

When designing tasks in Ada it is important to remember that the only queues over which we have any control are entry queues and that such queues are handled on a strictly first in first out basis. This might be thought to be a problem in situations where requests are of different prioritites or where later requests can be serviced even though earlier ones have to wait. (Note that in this section we will assume that calling tasks are not aborted.)

Requests with priorities can be handled by a family of entries. A family is rather like a one dimensional array. Suppose we have three levels of priority given by

```
type PRIORITY is (URGENT, NORMAL, LOW);
```

and that we have a task CONTROLLER providing access to some action on a type DATA but with requests for the action on three queues according to their priority. We could do this with three distinct entries but it is neater to use a family of entries. Consider

```
task CONTROLLER is
    entry REQUEST(PRIORITY) (D: DATA);
end;

task body CONTROLLER is
begin
    loop
        select
            accept REQUEST(URGENT) (D: DATA) do
                ACTION(D);
            end;
        or
            when REQUEST(URGENT)'COUNT = 0 =>
            accept REQUEST(NORMAL) (D: DATA) do
                ACTION(D);
            end;
        or
            when REQUEST(URGENT)'COUNT = 0 and
                    REQUEST(NORMAL)'COUNT = 0 =>
            accept REQUEST(LOW) (D: DATA) do
                ACTION(D);
```

```
            end;
          end select;
        end loop;
    end CONTROLLER;
```

REQUEST is a family of entries, indexed by a discrete range which in this case is the type PRIORITY. Clearly this approach is only feasible if the number of priority values is small. If it is large, a more sophisticated technique is necessary. We could try checking each queue in turn thus

```
    task body CONTROLLER is
    begin
        loop
            for P in PRIORITY loop
                select
                    accept REQUEST(P) (D: DATA) do
                        ACTION(D);
                    end;
                    exit;
                else
                    null;
                end select;
            end loop;
        end loop;
    end CONTROLLER;
```

Unfortunately this is not satisfactory since it results in the task CONTROLLER continuously polling when all the queues are empty. We need a mechanism whereby the task can wait for the first of any request. This can be done by a two stage process; the calling task must first sign in by calling a common entry and then call the appropriate entry of the family. The details are left as an exercise for the reader.

We now illustrate a quite general technique which effectively allows the requests in a single entry queue to be handled in an arbitrary order. Consider the problem of allocating a group of resources from a set. We do not wish to hold up a later request that can be satisfied just because an earlier request must wait for the release of some of the resources it wants. We suppose that the resources are represented by a discrete type RESOURCE. We can conveniently use the generic package SET_OF from Section 13.2.

```
    package RESOURCE_SETS is new SET_OF(RESOURCE);
    use RESOURCE_SETS;
```

and then

```
    package RESOURCE_ALLOCATOR is
        procedure REQUEST (S: SET);
        procedure RELEASE (S: SET);
    end;
```

```ada
package body RESOURCE_ALLOCATOR is
    task CONTROL is
        entry FIRST (S: SET; OK: out BOOLEAN);
        entry AGAIN (S: SET; OK: out BOOLEAN);
        entry RELEASE (S: SET);
    end;

    task body CONTROL is
        FREE: SET:=FULL;
        WAITERS: INTEGER:=0;
        procedure TRY (S: SET; OK: out BOOLEAN) is
        begin
            if S <= FREE then
                FREE:=FREE-S;
                OK:=TRUE;             -- allocation successful
            else
                OK:=FALSE;            -- no good, try later
            end if;
        end TRY;

    begin
        loop
            select
                accept FIRST(S: SET; OK: out BOOLEAN) do
                    TRY (S, OK);
                    if not OK then
                        WAITERS:=WAITERS+1;
                    end if;
                end;
            or
                accept RELEASE (S: SET) do
                    FREE:=FREE+S;
                end;
                for I in 1 .. WAITERS loop
                    accept AGAIN (S: SET; OK: out BOOLEAN) do
                        TRY (S, OK);
                        if OK then
                            WAITERS:=WAITERS-1;
                        end if;
                    end;
                end loop;
            end select;
        end loop;
    end CONTROL;

    procedure REQUEST (S: SET) is
        ALLOCATED: BOOLEAN;
    begin
        CONTROL.FIRST (S, ALLOCATED);
        while not ALLOCATED loop
            CONTROL.AGAIN(S, ALLOCATED);
        end loop;
    end REQUEST;
```

```
    procedure RELEASE (S: SET) is
    begin
        CONTROL.RELEASE(S);
    end RELEASE;

end RESOURCE_ALLOCATOR;
```

This is another example of a package containing a control task; the overall structure is similar to that of the package READER_WRITER introduced in Section 14.4. The package RESOURCE_ALLOCATOR contains two procedures REQUEST and RELEASE which have as parameters the set S of resources to be acquired or returned; the type SET is from the instantiation of SET_OF. These procedures call the entries of the task CONTROL as appropriate.

The task CONTROL has three entries, FIRST, AGAIN and RELEASE. The entries FIRST and AGAIN are similar; as well as the parameter S giving the set of resources required, they also have an out parameter OK which indicates whether the attempt to acquire the resources was successful or not. The accept statements for FIRST and AGAIN are identical and call a common procedure TRY. This checks the set S against the set FREE of available resources using the inclusion operator "<=" from (the instantiation of) SET_OF. If all the resources are available, FREE is altered correspondingly using the symmetric difference operator "−" from SET_OF and OK is set TRUE; if they are not all available, OK is set FALSE. The entry RELEASE returns the resources passed as the parameter S by updating FREE using the union operator "+" from SET_OF. Note that the declaration of FREE gives it the initial value FULL which is also from SET_OF.

The entries FIRST and AGAIN are called by the procedure REQUEST. It makes an immediate attempt to acquire the resources by a call of FIRST; if they are not all available, the Boolean ALLOCATED is set FALSE and the request is queued by calling AGAIN. This call is then repeated until successful. The entry RELEASE is merely called by the procedure RELEASE.

The body of CONTROL is the inevitable select statement in a loop. It has two branches one for FIRST and one for RELEASE. Thus a call of RELEASE is always acceptable and a call of FIRST is also accepted promptly except when the task is dealing with the consequences of RELEASE. After a call of RELEASE, the requests which could not be satisfied on their call of FIRST and were consequently placed on the AGAIN queue are reconsidered since the resources made available by the call of RELEASE may be able to satisfy one or more requests at arbitrary points in the queue. The queue is scanned by doing a rendezvous with each call; a user which cannot be satisfied places itself back on the queue by a further call of AGAIN in the procedure REQUEST. In order that each user should only have one retry the scan is done by a loop controlled by the variable WAITERS. This indicates how many callers have called FIRST unsuccessfully and so are waiting in the system; it is initially zero and is incremented on an unsuccessful call of FIRST and decremented on a successful call of AGAIN. Note that we cannot use AGAIN'COUNT; deadlock might arise if all the resources were released between a task unsuccessfully calling FIRST and actually calling AGAIN. The moral of the readers and writers example is thus echoed; avoid the COUNT attribute – we must count for ourselves.

The above solution is reasonably satisfactory although there is a risk of unfairness. Tasks could overtake each other in the race from the front of the queue to the back; a newcomer could also miss a turn.

It is interesting to modify the above solution so that the requests are always satisfied in order. That is, a later request is always held up for an earlier one even if the resources they require are quite different. The essence of the solution is to allow only one waiting task in the system at a time. The modification is left as an exercise for the reader.

For this modified problem the following alternative solution is perhaps better. It has the merit of avoiding the task scheduling associated with the waiting task repeatedly calling AGAIN. We show just the task CONTROL and the procedure REQUEST.

```
task CONTROL is
    entry SIGN_IN(S: SET);
    entry REQUEST;
    entry RELEASE(S: SET);
end;

task body CONTROL is
    FREE: SET:=FULL;
    WAITERS: INTEGER:=0;
    WANTED: SET;

begin
    loop
        select
            when WAITERS = 0 =>
            accept SIGN_IN(S: SET) do
                WANTED:=S;
            end;
            WAITERS:=WAITERS+1;
        or
            when WAITERS > 0 and then WANTED <= FREE =>
            accept REQUEST do
                FREE:=FREE-WANTED;
            end;
            WAITERS:=WAITERS-1;
        or
            accept RELEASE(S: SET) do
                FREE:=FREE+S;
            end;
        end select;
    end loop;
end CONTROL;

procedure REQUEST(S: SET) is
begin
    CONTROL.SIGN_IN(S);
    CONTROL.REQUEST;
end REQUEST;
```

In this solution we use a guarding condition which is true when the request can be honoured. A sign in call is required in order to hand over the parameter first because of course a guarding condition cannot depend upon the parameters of the actual entry call it is guarding. Note the short circuit condition which prevents the evaluation of WANTED when there is no waiting task. The variable WAITERS should perhaps be a Boolean; it can only be zero or one.

Exercise 14.7

1   Modify the first form of the package RESOURCE_ALLOCATOR so that requests are dealt with strictly in order.

2   Rewrite the task CONTROLLER as a package containing a task in a way which avoids continuous polling. The package specification should be

```
package CONTROLLER is
    procedure REQUEST(P: PRIORITY; D: DATA);
end;
```

14.8   Comparison with packages

Tasks and packages have a superficial lexical similarity – they both have specifications and bodies. However, there are many differences

* A task is an active construction whereas a package is passive.

* A task can only have entries in its specification. A package can have anything except entries. A task cannot have a private part.

* A package can be generic but a task cannot. The general effect of a parameterless generic task can be obtained by a task type. Alternatively the task can be encapsulated by a generic package.

* A package can appear in a use clause but a task cannot.

* A package can be a library unit but a task cannot. However, a task body can be a subunit.

The overall distinction is that the package should be considered to be the main tool for structuring purposes whereas the task is intended for synchronisation. Thus typical subsystems will consist of a (possibly generic) package containing one or more tasks. This general structure has as we have seen the merit of giving complete control over the facilities provided; internal tasks cannot be unwillingly aborted and entry calls cannot be unwillingly timed out if they are not visible.

Finally we illustrate the use of task types as private types by the following generic package which provides a general type BUFFER.

```
generic
    N: POSITIVE;
    type ITEM is private;
package BUFFERS is
    type BUFFER is limited private;
    procedure PUT(B: in out BUFFER; X: in ITEM);
    procedure GET(B: in out BUFFER; X: out ITEM);
private
```

```
task type CONTROL is
    entry PUT(X: in ITEM);
    entry GET(X: out ITEM);
end;
type BUFFER is new CONTROL;
end;

package body BUFFERS is

task body CONTROL is
    A: array (1 .. N) of ITEM;
    I, J: INTEGER range 1 .. N:=1;
    COUNT: INTEGER range 0 .. N:=0;
begin
    loop
        select
            when COUNT < N =>
            accept PUT(X: in ITEM) do
                A(I):=X;
            end;
            I:=I mod N+1; COUNT:=COUNT+1;
        or
            when COUNT > 0 =>
            accept GET(X: out ITEM) do
                X:=A(I);
            end;
            J:=J mod N+1; COUNT:=COUNT-1;
        or
            terminate;
        end select;
    end loop;
end CONTROL;

procedure PUT(B: in out BUFFER; X: in ITEM) is
begin
    B.PUT(X);
end PUT;

procedure GET(B: in out BUFFER; X: out ITEM) is
begin
    B.GET(X);
end GET;

end BUFFERS;
```

The buffer is implemented as a task object of a task type derived from CONTROL so that when we declare an object of the type BUFFER a new task is created which in turn declares the storage for the actual buffer. Calls of the procedures PUT and GET access the buffer by calling the corresponding entries of the appropriate task. Note that the select statement contains a terminate alternative so that the task object automatically disappears when we leave the scope of its declaration. Moreover, the system is robust even if the calling task is aborted.

Exercise 14.8

1   A boot repair shop has one man taking orders and three others actually repairing the boots. The shop has storage for 100 boots awaiting repair. The person taking the orders notes the address of the owner and this is attached to the boots; he then puts the boots in the store. Each repairman takes boots from the store when he is free, repairs them and then posts them.

Write a package COBBLERS whose specification is

```
package COBBLERS is
    procedure MEND(A: ADDRESS; B: BOOTS);
end;
```

The package body should contain four tasks representing the various men. Use an instantiation of the package BUFFERS to provide a store for the boots and agent tasks as mailboxes to deliver them.

Checklist 14

A task is active whereas a package is passive.

A task specification can contain only entries.

A task cannot be generic.

A task name cannot appear in a use clause.

Entries may be overloaded and renamed as procedures.

The COUNT attribute can only be used inside the task owning the entry.

An accept statement must not appear in a subprogram.

Do not attempt to use priorities for synchronisation.

A delay sets a minimum only.

The order of evaluation of guards is not defined.

A select statement can have just one of an else part, a single terminate alternative, one or more delay alternatives.

A terminate or delay alternative can be guarded.

Several alternatives can refer to the same entry.

Beware of the COUNT attribute in guards.

Task types are limited.

A task declared as an object is dependent on a block, subprogram or task body but not an inner package.

A task created by an allocator is dependent on the block, subprogram or task body containing the access type definition.

A task declared as an object is made active at the following (possibly notional) **begin**.

A task created by an allocator is made active at once.

Do not use **abort** without good reason.

Chapter 15 EXTERNAL INTERFACES

In this chapter we consider various aspects of how an Ada program interfaces to the outside world. This includes obvious areas such as input-output, interrupt handling and so on but we will also consider the mapping of our abstract Ada program onto an implementation. However, the discussion in this chapter cannot be exhaustive because many details of this area will depend upon the implementation. The intent, therefore, is to give the reader a general overview of the facilities available.

15.1 Input and output

Unlike many other languages, Ada does not have any intrinsic features for input-output. Instead, existing general features such as subprogram overloading and generic instantiation are used. This has the merit of enabling different input-output packages to be developed for different application areas without affecting the language itself. On the other hand this approach can lead to a consequential risk of anarchy in this area; the reader may recall that this was one of the reasons for the downfall of Algol 60. In order to prevent such anarchy the LRM defines standard packages for input-output. We discuss the general principles of these packages in this and the next section. For further fine detail the reader should consult the LRM.

Two categories of input-output are recognised and we can refer to these as binary and text respectively. As an example consider

    I: INTEGER:= 75;

We can output the binary image of I onto file F by

    WRITE(F, I);

and the pattern transmitted might be (on a 16 bit machine)

    0000 0000 0100 1011

In fact the file can be thought of as essentially an array of the type INTEGER. On the other hand we can output the text form of I by

    PUT(F, I);

and the pattern transmitted might then be

    0011 0111 0011 0101

252

which is the representation of the characters '7' and '5' without parity bits. In this case the file can be thought of as an array of the type CHARACTER.

Input-output of the binary category is in turn subdivided into sequential and direct access and is provided by distinct generic packages with identifiers SEQUENTIAL_IO and DIRECT_IO respectively. Text input-output (which is always sequential) is provided by the special non-generic package TEXT_IO. There is also a package IO_EXCEPTIONS which contains the declarations of the exceptions used by the three other packages. We will deal here first with SEQUENTIAL_IO and then with DIRECT_IO and consider TEXT_IO in the next section.

The specification of the package SEQUENTIAL_IO is as follows

```
with IO_EXCEPTIONS;
generic
    type ELEMENT_TYPE is private;
package SEQUENTIAL_IO is
    type FILE_TYPE is limited private;
    type FILE_MODE is (IN_FILE, OUT_FILE);

    -- File management

    procedure CREATE(FILE: in out FILE_TYPE;
                     MODE: in FILE_MODE:=OUT_FILE;
                     NAME: in STRING:="";
                     FORM: in STRING:="");
    procedure OPEN(FILE: in out FILE_TYPE;
                   MODE: in FILE_MODE;
                   NAME: in STRING;
                   FORM: in STRING:="");
    procedure CLOSE(FILE: in out FILE_TYPE);
    procedure DELETE(FILE: in out FILE_TYPE);
    procedure RESET(FILE: in out FILE_TYPE;
                                       MODE: in FILE_MODE);
    procedure RESET(FILE: in out FILE_TYPE);
    function MODE(FILE: in FILE_TYPE) return FILE_MODE;
    function NAME(FILE: in FILE_TYPE) return STRING;
    function FORM(FILE: in FILE_TYPE) return STRING;
    function IS_OPEN(FILE: in FILE_TYPE) return BOOLEAN;

    -- Input and output operations

    procedure READ(FILE: in FILE_TYPE;
                                     ITEM: out ELEMENT_TYPE);
    procedure WRITE(FILE: in FILE_TYPE;
                                     ITEM: in ELEMENT_TYPE);
    function END_OF_FILE(FILE: in FILE_TYPE) return BOOLEAN;

    -- Exceptions

    STATUS_ERROR: exception renames
                        IO_EXCEPTIONS.STATUS_ERROR;
    MODE_ERROR: exception renames
                        IO_EXCEPTIONS.MODE_ERROR;
```

```
    NAME_ERROR: exception renames
                            IO_EXCEPTIONS.NAME_ERROR;
    USE_ERROR: exception renames
                            IO_EXCEPTIONS.USE_ERROR;
    DEVICE_ERROR: exception renames
                            IO_EXCEPTIONS.DEVICE_ERROR;
    END_ERROR: exception renames
                            IO_EXCEPTIONS.END_ERROR;
    DATA_ERROR: exception renames
                            IO_EXCEPTIONS.DATA_ERROR;

private
    -- implementation dependent
end SEQUENTIAL_IO;
```

The package has a single generic parameter giving the type of element to be manipulated. Note that limited types (and that, thankfully, includes task types) cannot be handled since the generic formal parameter is private rather than limited private.

Externally a file has a name which is a string but internally we refer to a file by using objects of type FILE_TYPE. An open file also has an associated value of the enumeration type FILE_MODE; there are two possible values, IN_FILE or OUT_FILE according to whether read-only or write-only access is required. Read-write access is not allowed for sequential files. The mode of a file is originally set when the file is opened or created but can be changed later by a call of the procedure RESET. Manipulation of sequential files is done using various subprograms whose behaviour is generally as expected.

As an example suppose we have a file containing measurements of various populations and that we wish to compute the sum of these measurements. The populations are recorded as values of type INTEGER and the name of the file is "CENSUS 47". (The actual conventions for the external file name are dependent upon the implementation.) The computed sum is to be written onto a new file to be called "TOTAL 47". This could be done by the following program.

```
with SEQUENTIAL_IO
procedure COMPUTE_TOTAL_POPULATION is
    package INTEGER_IO is new SEQUENTIAL_IO(INTEGER);
    use INTEGER_IO;

    DATA_FILE: FILE_TYPE;
    RESULT_FILE: FILE_TYPE;
    VALUE: INTEGER;
    TOTAL: INTEGER:=0;
begin
    OPEN(DATA_FILE, IN_FILE, "CENSUS 47");

    while not END_OF_FILE(DATA_FILE) loop
        READ(DATA_FILE, VALUE);
        TOTAL:=TOTAL+VALUE;
    end loop;
    CLOSE(DATA_FILE);
```

– – now write the result

```
CREATE(RESULT_FILE, NAME=>"TOTAL 47");
WRITE(RESULT_FILE, TOTAL);
CLOSE(RESULT_FILE);
end COMPUTE_TOTAL_POPULATION;
```

The first thing we do is instantiate the generic package SEQUENTIAL_IO with the actual parameter INTEGER. The use clause enables us to refer to the entities in the created package directly.

The file with the data to be read is referred to via the object DATA_FILE and the output file is referred to via the object RESULT_FILE of the type FILE_TYPE. Note that this type is limited private; this enables the implementation to use techniques similar to those described in Section 9.3 where we discussed the example of the key manager.

The call of OPEN establishes the object DATA_FILE as referring to the external file "CENSUS 47" and sets its mode as read-only. The external file is then opened for reading and positioned at the beginning.

We then obey the loop statement until the function END_OF_FILE indicates that the end of the file has been reached. On each iteration the call of READ copies the item into VALUE and positions the file at the next item. TOTAL is then updated. When all the values on the file have been read, it is closed by a call of CLOSE.

The call of CREATE creates a new external file with a name "TOTAL 47" and establishes RESULT_FILE as referring to it and sets its mode by default to write-only. We then write our total onto the file and then close it.

The procedures CREATE and OPEN have a further parameter FORM; this is provided so that auxiliary implementation dependent information can be specified; the default value is a null string so its use is not mandatory. Note also that the NAME parameter of CREATE also has a default null value; such a value corresponds to a temporary file. The procedures CLOSE and DELETE both close the file and thereby sever the connection between the file variable and the external file. The variable can then be reused for another file. DELETE also destroys the external file if the implementation so allows.

The overloaded procedures RESET cause a file to be repositioned at the beginning as for OPEN. RESET can also change the access mode so that, for example, having written a file, we can now read it.

The functions MODE, NAME and FORM return the corresponding properties of the file. The function IS_OPEN indicates whether the file is open; that is indicates whether the file variable is associated with an external file or not.

The procedures READ and WRITE automatically reposition the file ready for a subsequent call so that the file is processed sequentially. The function END_OF_FILE only applies to an input file and returns true if there are no more elements to be read.

If we do something wrong then one of the exceptions in the package IO_EXCEPTIONS will be raised. This package is as follows

```
package IO_EXCEPTIONS is
    STATUS_ERROR: exception;
    MODE_ERROR:    exception;
```

```
NAME_ERROR:     exception;
USE_ERROR:      exception;
DEVICE_ERROR:   exception;
END_ERROR:      exception;
DATA_ERROR:     exception;
LAYOUT_ERROR:   exception;
```

    end IO_EXCEPTIONS;

Note that this is an example of a package that does not need a body. The various exceptions are declared in this package rather than in SEQUENTIAL_IO so that the same exceptions apply to all instantiations of SEQUENTIAL_IO. If they were inside SEQUENTIAL_IO then each instantiation would create different exceptions and this would be rather more inconvenient in the case of a program manipulating files of various types since general purpose exception handlers would need to refer to all the instances. The renaming declarations on the other hand enable the exceptions to be referred to without use of the name IO_EXCEPTIONS. For details of which exception is actually raised in various circumstances the reader is referred to the LRM.

If sequential access is too restrictive then we can alternatively use the package DIRECT_IO which is very similar to SEQUENTIAL_IO but enables us to manipulate the file position directly.

As mentioned earlier a file can be considered as a one dimensional array. The elements in the file are ordered and each has an associated positive index. This ranges from 1 to an upper value which can change since elements can be added to the end of the file. Not all elements necessarily have a defined value in the case of a direct file.

Associated with a direct file is a current index which indicates the position of the next element to be transferred. When a file is opened or created this index is set to 1 so that the program is ready to read or write the first element. The main difference between sequential and direct input-output is that in the sequential case this index is implicit and can only be altered by calls of READ, WRITE and RESET whereas in the direct case, the index is explicit and can be directly manipulated.

The extra facilities of DIRECT_IO are as follows. The enumeration type FILE_MODE has a third value INOUT_FILE so that read-write access is possible; this is also the default mode when a new file is created. The type and subtype

    type COUNT **is range** 0 . . implementation_defined;
    subtype POSITIVE_COUNT **is** COUNT **range** 1 . . COUNT'LAST;

are introduced so that the current index can be referred to and finally there are various extra subprograms whose specifications are as follows

    procedure READ(FILE: **in** FILE_TYPE; ITEM: **out** ELEMENT_TYPE;
                    FROM: POSITIVE_COUNT);
    procedure WRITE(FILE: **in** FILE_TYPE; ITEM: **in** ELEMENT_TYPE;
                    TO: POSITIVE_COUNT);
    procedure SET_INDEX(FILE: **in** FILE_TYPE; TO:
                                  in POSITIVE_COUNT);

function INDEX(FILE: **in** FILE_TYPE) **return** POSITIVE_COUNT;
function SIZE(FILE: **in** FILE_TYPE) **return** COUNT;

The extra overloadings of READ and WRITE first position the current index to the value given by the third parameter and then behave as before. A call of INDEX returns the current index value; SET_INDEX sets the current index to the given value and a call of SIZE returns the number of elements in the file. Note that a file cannot have holes in it; all elements from 1 to SIZE exist although some may not have defined values.

As an illustration of the manipulation of these positions we can alter our example to use DIRECT_IO and we can then write the total population onto the end of an existing file called "TOTALS". The last few statements then become

```
-- now write the result
OPEN(RESULT_FILE, OUT_FILE, "TOTALS");
SET_INDEX(RESULT_FILE, SIZE(RESULT_FILE)+1);
WRITE(RESULT_FILE, TOTAL);
CLOSE(RESULT_FILE);
end COMPUTE_TOTAL_POPULATION;
```

Note that if we set the current index well beyond the end of the file and then write to it, the result will be to add several undefined elements to the file and then finally the newly written element.

Note also that the language does not define whether it is possible to write a file with SEQUENTIAL_IO and then read it with DIRECT_IO or vice versa. This depends upon the implementation.

Exercise 15.1
1   Write a generic library procedure to copy a file onto another file but with the elements in reverse order. Pass the external names as parameters.

15.2   Text input-output

Text input-output, which we first met in Chapter 2, is the more familiar form and provides two overloaded procedures PUT and GET to transmit values as streams of characters as well as various other subprograms such as NEW_LINE for layout control. In addition the concept of current default files is introduced so that every call of the various subprograms need not tiresomely repeat the file name. Thus if F is the current default output file, we can write

```
PUT("MESSAGE");
```

rather than

```
PUT(F, "MESSAGE");
```

There are two current default files, one of mode OUT_FILE for output, and one of mode IN_FILE for input. There is no mode INOUT_FILE in the package TEXT_IO.

When we enter our program these two files are set to standard default files which are automatically open; we can assume that these are attached to convenient external files such as an interactive terminal or (in olden days) a card reader and line printer. If we wish to use other files and want to avoid repeating the file names in the calls of PUT and GET then we can change the default files to refer to our other files. We can also set them back to their original values. This is done with subprograms

```
function STANDARD_OUTPUT return FILE_TYPE;
function CURRENT_OUTPUT return FILE_TYPE;
procedure SET_OUTPUT(FILE: FILE_TYPE);
```

with similar subprograms for input. The function STANDARD_OUTPUT returns the initial default output file, CURRENT_OUTPUT returns the current default output file and the procedure SET_OUTPUT enables us to change the current default output file to the file passed as parameter.

Thus we could bracket a fragment of program with

```
F: FILE_TYPE;
. . .
OPEN(F, . . .);
SET_OUTPUT(F);
-- use PUT
SET_OUTPUT(STANDARD_OUTPUT);
```

so that having used the file F, we can reset the default file to its standard value.

The more general case is where we wish to reset the default file to its previous value which may, of course, not be the standard value. The reader may recall that the type FILE_TYPE is limited private and therefore values cannot be assigned; at first sight, therefore, it might not seem possible to make a copy of the original current value. However, with suitable contortion it can be done by using the parameter mechanism. We could write

```
procedure JOB(OLD_FILE, NEW_FILE: FILE_TYPE) is
begin
    SET_OUTPUT(NEW_FILE);
    ACTION;
    SET_OUTPUT(OLD_FILE);
end;
```

and then

```
JOB(CURRENT_OUTPUT, F);
```

When we call JOB, the present current value is preserved in the parameter OLD_FILE from whence it can be retrieved for the restoring call of SET_OUTPUT. However, although this works, it does feel a bit like standing on one's head!

The full specification of TEXT_IO is rather long and so only the general form is reproduced here.

```
with IO_EXCEPTIONS;
package TEXT_IO is
    type FILE_TYPE is limited private;
    type FILE_MODE is (IN_FILE, OUT_FILE);

    type COUNT is range 0 .. implementation_defined;
    subtype POSITIVE_COUNT is COUNT range 1 .. COUNT'LAST;
    UNBOUNDED: constant COUNT:=0; - - line and page length

    subtype FIELD is INTEGER range 0 .. implementation_defined;
    subtype NUMBER_BASE is INTEGER range 2 .. 16;
    type TYPE_SET is (LOWER_CASE, UPPER_CASE);

    - - File Management

    - - CREATE, OPEN, CLOSE, DELETE, RESET, MODE, NAME,
    - - FORM and IS_OPEN as for SEQUENTIAL_IO

    - - Control of default input and output files

    procedure SET_OUTPUT(FILE: in FILE_TYPE);
    function STANDARD_OUTPUT return FILE_TYPE;
    function CURRENT_OUTPUT return FILE_TYPE;

    - - Similarly for input

    - - Specification of line and page lengths

    procedure SET_LINE_LENGTH(TO: in COUNT);
    procedure SET_PAGE_LENGTH(TO: in COUNT);
    function LINE_LENGTH return COUNT;
    function PAGE_LENGTH return COUNT;

    - - also with FILE parameter

    - - Column, Line and Page Control

    procedure NEW_LINE(SPACING: in POSITIVE_COUNT:=1);
    procedure SKIP_LINE(SPACING: in POSITIVE_COUNT:=1);
    function END_OF_LINE return BOOLEAN;
    procedure NEW_PAGE;
    procedure SKIP_PAGE;
    function END_OF_PAGE return BOOLEAN;
    function END_OF_FILE return BOOLEAN;
    procedure SET_COL(TO: in POSITIVE_COUNT);
    procedure SET_LINE(TO: in POSITIVE_COUNT);
    function COL return POSITIVE_COUNT;
    function LINE return POSITIVE_COUNT;
    function PAGE return POSITIVE_COUNT;

    - - also with FILE parameter

    - - Character Input-Output

    procedure GET(FILE: in FILE_TYPE; ITEM: out CHARACTER);
    procedure GET(ITEM: out CHARACTER);
    procedure PUT(FILE: in FILE_TYPE; ITEM: in CHARACTER);
    procedure PUT(ITEM: in CHARACTER);
```

```ada
                    -- String Input-Output

          procedure GET(ITEM: out STRING);
          procedure PUT(ITEM: in STRING);
          procedure GET_LINE(ITEM: out STRING;
                                            LAST: out NATURAL);
          procedure PUT_LINE(ITEM: in STRING);


               -- Generic package for Input-Output of Integer Types

          generic
             type NUM is range <>;
          package INTEGER_IO is
             DEFAULT_WIDTH: FIELD:=NUM'WIDTH;
             DEFAULT_BASE: NUMBER_BASE:=10;

             procedure GET(ITEM: out NUM; WIDTH: in FIELD:=0);
             procedure PUT(ITEM: in NUM;
                       WIDTH: in FIELD:=DEFAULT_WIDTH;
                       BASE: in NUMBER_BASE:=DEFAULT_BASE);
                procedure GET(FROM: in STRING; ITEM: out NUM;
                          LAST: out POSITIVE);
                procedure PUT(TO: out STRING;
                       ITEM: in NUM;
                       BASE: in  NUMBER_BASE:=DEFAULT_BASE);
          end INTEGER_IO;


               -- Generic packages for Input-Output of Real Types

          generic
             type NUM is digits <>;
          package FLOAT_IO is
             DEFAULT_FORE: FIELD:=2;
             DEFAULT_AFT: FIELD:=NUM'DIGITS−1;
             DEFAULT_EXP: FIELD:=3;

             procedure GET(ITEM: out NUM; WIDTH: in FIELD:=0);
             procedure PUT(ITEM: in NUM;
                          FORE: in FIELD:=DEFAULT_FORE;
                          AFT: in FIELD:=DEFAULT_AFT;
                          EXP: in FIELD:=DEFAULT_EXP);
                procedure GET(FROM: in STRING;
                          ITEM: in NUM;
                          LAST: out POSITIVE);
                procedure PUT(TO: out STRING;
                          ITEM: in NUM;
                          AFT: in FIELD:=DEFAULT_AFT;
                          EXP: in FIELD:=DEFAULT_EXP);
          end FLOAT_IO;
```

```
generic
    type NUM is delta <>;
package FIXED_IO is
    DEFAULT_FORE: FIELD:=NUM'FORE;
    DEFAULT_AFT: FIELD:=NUM'AFT;
    DEFAULT_EXP: FIELD:=0;
    - - then as for FLOAT_IO
end FIXED_IO;
```

- - Generic package for Input-Output of Enumeration Types

```
generic
    type ENUM is (<>);
package ENUMERATION_IO is
    DEFAULT_WIDTH: FIELD:=0;
    DEFAULT_SETTING: TYPE_SET:=UPPER CASE;

    procedure GET(ITEM: out ENUM);
    procedure PUT(ITEM: in ENUM;
                    WIDTH: in FIELD:=DEFAULT_WIDTH;
                    SET: in TYPE_SET:=DEFAULT_SETTING);
    procedure GET(FROM: in STRING;
                    ITEM: out ENUM;
                    LAST: out POSITIVE);
    procedure PUT(TO: out STRING;
                    ITEM: out ENUM;
                    SET: in TYPE_SET:=DEFAULT_SETTING);
end ENUMERATION_IO;
```

- - Exceptions

```
STATUS_ERROR: exception renames
                            IO_EXCEPTION.STATUS_ERROR;
    . . .
LAYOUT_ERROR: exception renames
                            IO_EXCEPTIONS.LAYOUT_ERROR;
private

    - - implementation dependent

end TEXT_IO;
```

The types FILE_TYPE and FILE_MODE and the various file management procedures are similar to those for SEQUENTIAL_IO since text files are of course sequential in nature.

Procedures PUT and GET occur in two forms for characters and strings, one with the file and one without; both are shown only for type CHARACTER.

In the case of type CHARACTER, a call of PUT just outputs that character; for type STRING a call of PUT outputs the characters of the string.

A problem arises in the case of numeric and enumeration types since there is not a fixed number of such types. This is overcome by the use of internal generic packages for each category. Thus for integer input-output we instantiate the package INTEGER_IO with the appropriate type thus

package MY_INTEGER_IO **is new** INTEGER_IO(MY_INTEGER);
use MY_INTEGER_IO;

For integer output, PUT occurs in three forms, one with the file, one without and one with a string as the destination; only the last two are shown.

In the case of PUT to a file, there are two format parameters WIDTH and BASE which have default values provided by the variables DEFAULT_WIDTH and DEFAULT_BASE. The default width is initially NUM'WIDTH which gives the smallest field which is adequate for all values of the type expressed with base 10. Base 10 also happens to be the initial default base. These default values can be changed by the user by directly assigning new values to the variables DEFAULT_WIDTH and DEFAULT_BASE; remember that a default parameter is re-evaluated on each call requiring it and so the default obtained is always the current value of these variables. The integer is output as an integer literal without underlines and leading zeros but with a preceding minus sign if negative. It is padded with leading spaces to fill the field width specified; if the field width is too small, it is expanded as necessary. Thus a default width of 0 results in the field being the minimum to contain the literal. If base 10 is specified explicitly or by default, the value is output using the syntax of decimal literal; if the base is not 10, the syntax of based literal is used.

In the case of PUT to a string, the field width is taken as the length of the string. If this is too small, then LAYOUT_ERROR is raised.

A similar technique is used for real types. The value is output as a decimal literal without underlines and leading zeros but with a preceding minus sign if negative. If EXP is zero then there is no exponent and the format consists of FORE characters before the decimal point and AFT after the decimal point. If EXP is non-zero then a signed exponent in a field of EXP characters is output after a letter E with leading zeros if necessary; the exponent value is such that only one significant digit occurs before the decimal point. If the FORE or EXP parts of the field are inadequate then they are expanded as necessary. Base 10 is always used and the value is rounded to the size of AFT specified.

The initial default format parameters for floating point types are 2, NUM'DIGITS−1 and 3; this gives an exponent form with a space or minus sign plus single digit before the decimal point, NUM'DIGITS−1 digits after the decimal point and a two digit exponent. The corresponding parameters for fixed point types are NUM'FORE, NUM'AFT and 0; this gives a form without an exponent and the attributes give the smallest field such that all values of the type can be expressed with appropriate precision.

Enumeration types use a similar technique. A default field of zero is used. If the field has to be padded then the extra spaces go after the value and not before as with the numeric types. Upper case is normally used, but lower case may be specified. A value of a character type which is a character literal is output in single quotes.

Note the subtle distinction between PUT defined directly for the type CHARACTER and for enumeration values.

```
TEXT_IO.PUT('X');
```

outputs the single character X, whereas

```
package CHAR_IO is
    new TEXT_IO.ENUMERATION_IO(CHARACTER);
CHAR_IO.PUT('X');
```

outputs the character X between single quotes.

Input using GET works in an analogous way; a call of GET always skips line and page terminators. In the case of the type CHARACTER the next character is read. In the case of the type STRING, the procedure GET reads the exact number of characters as determined by the actual parameter. In the case of enumeration types, leading blanks (spaces or horizontal tab) are also skipped; input is terminated by a character which is not part of the value or by a line terminator. Numeric types normally have the same behaviour but they also have an additional and optional WIDTH parameter and if this has a value other than zero, then reading stops after this number of characters including skipped blanks. In the case of GET where the source is a string rather than a file, the value of LAST indexes the last character read; the end of the string behaves as the end of a file. If the data item is not of the correct form, DATA_ERROR is raised.

A text file is considered as a sequence of lines. The characters in a line have a column position starting at 1. The line length on output can be fixed or variable. A fixed line length is appropriate for the output of tables, a variable line length for dialogue. The line length can be changed within a single file. It is initially not fixed. The lines are similarly grouped into pages.

On output a call of PUT will result in all the characters going on the current line starting at the current position in the line. If, however, the line length is fixed and the characters cannot fit in the remainder of the line, a new line is started and all the characters are placed on that line starting at the beginning. If they still will not fit, LAYOUT_ERROR is raised. If the length is not fixed, the characters always go on the end of the current line.

The layout may be controlled by various subprograms. In some cases they apply to both input and output files; in these cases if the file is omitted then it is taken to apply to the output case and the default output file is assumed. In most cases, a subprogram only applies to one direction and then omitting the file naturally gives the default in that direction.

The function COL returns the current position in the line and the procedure SET_COL sets the position to the given value. A call of SET_COL never goes backwards. On output extra spaces are produced and on input characters are skipped. If the parameter of SET_COL equals the current value of COL then there is no effect; if it is less then a call of NEW_LINE or SKIP_LINE is implied.

The procedure NEW_LINE (output only) outputs the given number of newlines (default 1) and resets the current column to 1. Spare positions at the end of a line are filled with spaces. The procedure SKIP_LINE (input only) similarly moves on the given number of lines (default 1) and resets the current column. The function END_OF_LINE (input only) returns TRUE if we have reached the end of a line.

The function LINE_LENGTH (output only) returns the current line length if it is fixed and zero if it is not. The procedure SET_LINE_LENGTH (output only) sets the line length fixed to the given value; a value of zero indicates that it is not to be fixed.

There are also similar subprograms for the control of lines within pages. These are LINE, SET_LINE, NEW_PAGE, SKIP_PAGE, END_OF_PAGE, PAGE_LENGTH and SET_PAGE_LENGTH. Finally the function PAGE returns the current page number from the start of the file. There is no SET_PAGE.

The procedures PUT_LINE and GET_LINE are particularly appropriate for fixed length lines. A call of PUT_LINE outputs the string and moves to the next line; a call of GET_LINE reads successive characters into the string until the end of the string or the end of the line is encountered and then moves to the next line; LAST indexes the last character moved into the string. Successive calls of PUT_LINE and GET_LINE therefore manipulate whole lines.

The package TEXT_IO may seem somewhat elaborate but for simple output all we need is PUT and NEW_LINE and these are quite straightforward as we have seen.

Exercise 15.2
1   What do the following calls output? Assume the initial values for the default parameters.

a) PUT("FRED");   d) PUT(120, 8, 8);
b) PUT(120);   e) PUT(−38.0);
c) PUT(120, 8);   f) PUT(0.07, 6, 3, 1);

Assume that the real values are of a type with **digits** = 6 and the integer values are of a type with 16 bits.

15.3   Interrupts

An interrupt is another form of input. In Ada this is achieved through the rendezvous mechanism. From within the program, an interrupt appears as an entry call performed by an external taks whose priority is higher than that of any task in the program. The interrupt handler is then naturally represented in the program by a task with accept statements for the corresponding entry. The entry is identified as an interrupt by what is known as a representation clause giving the relevant hardware address.

As an example suppose a program wishes to act upon an interrupt arising from the closing of an electrical contact and the interrupt is associated with the address 8#72#. We could write

```
task CONTACT_HANDLER is
    entry CONTACT;
    for CONTACT use at 8#72#;
end;

task body CONTACT_HANDLER is
begin
    loop
        accept CONTACT do
            . . .
        end;
    end loop;
end CONTACT_HANDLER;
```

The body of the accept statement corresponds to the direct response to the interrupt. The rule that the external mythical task has a priority higher than that of any software task ensures that the response takes precedence over ordinary tasks.

An interrupt entry will usually have no parameters but it can have **in** parameters through which control information is passed. An accept statement for an interrupt entry can also occur in a select statement.

The detailed behaviour of interrupt entry calls is somewhat dependent upon the implementation. They could for example appear as conditional entry calls and therefore be lost if the response task is not ready to execute the corresponding accept statement. The exact interpretation of the address in the representation clause is also dependent on the implementation.

15.4 Representation clauses

In the last section we introduced the representation clause as a means of informing the compiler of additional information about the interrupt entry. Representation clauses take various forms and apply to various entities. Their general purpose is to provide the compiler with directions regarding how the entity is to be implemented.

An address clause is of the form used for the entry. It can be used to assign an explicit address to an object, to indicate the start address of the code body of a subprogram, package or task, or as we have seen, to specify an interrupt to which an entry is to be linked.

A length clause allows us to specify the amount of storage to be allocated for objects of a type, for the collection of an access type and for the working storage of a task type. This is done by indicating the value of certain attributes. Thus

```
type BYTE is range 0 .. 255;
for BYTE'SIZE use 8;
```

ensures that objects of the type BYTE occupy only 8 bits.

The space for access collections and tasks is indicated using the attribute STORAGE_SIZE. In these cases the unit is not bits but storage units. The number of bits in a storage unit is implementation dependent and is given by the constant STORAGE_UNIT in the package SYSTEM. Thus if we wanted to ensure that the access collection for

```
type LIST is access CELL;
```

will accommodate 500 cells then we write

```
for LIST'STORAGE_SIZE use
    500*(CELL'SIZE / SYSTEM.STORAGE_UNIT);
```

Similarly the data space for each task of a task type can be indicated by

```
for MAILBOX'STORAGE_SIZE use 128;
```

The value of *small* for a fixed point type can also be indicated by a length clause.

An enumeration representation clause can be used to specify, as an aggregate, the internal integer codes for the literals of an enumeration type. We might have a status value transmitted into our program as single bit settings, thus

```
type STATUS is (OFF, READY, ON);
for STATUS use (OFF => 1, READY => 2, ON => 4);
```

There is a constraint that the ordering of the values must be the same as the logical ordering of the literals. However despite the holes, the functions SUCC, PRED, POS and VAL always work in logical terms.

The final form of representation clause is used to indicate the layout of a record type. Thus if we have

```
type REGISTER is range 0 .. 15;
type OPCODE is (. . .);

type RR is
    record
        CODE: OPCODE;
        R1    : REGISTER;
        R2    : REGISTER;
    end record;
```

which represents a machine instruction of the RR format in the IBM system 370, then we can specify the exact mapping by

```
for RR use
    record at mod 2;
        CODE at 0 range 0 .. 7;
        R1    at 1 range 0 .. 3;
        R2    at 1 range 4 .. 7;
    end record;
```

The optional alignment clause

```
at mod 2;
```

indicates that the record is to be aligned on a double byte boundary; the alignment is given in terms of the number of storage units and in the case of the 370 a storage unit would naturally be one 8-bit byte.

The position and size of the individual components are given relative to the start of the record. The value after **at** gives a storage unit and the range is in terms of bits. The bit number can extend outside the storage unit; we could equally have written

```
R1 at 0 range 8 .. 11;
```

If we do not specify the location of every component, the compiler is free to juggle the rest as best it can. However, we must allow enough space for those we do specify and they must not overlap unless they are in different alternatives of a variant.

Finally it should be noted that a representation clause must occur in the same declaration list as the declaration of the entity it refers to.

15.5   Implementation considerations

It is hard to be specific in this area since so much depends upon the implementation. However, there is a package SYSTEM which includes the values of various machine constants.Its specification is as follows

```
package SYSTEM is
    type ADDRESS    is implementation_defined;
    type NAME       is implementation_defined_enumeration_type;

    SYSTEM_NAME   : constant NAME:= implementation_defined;

    STORAGE_UNIT  : constant:= implementation_defined;
    MEMORY_SIZE   : constant:= implementation_defined;

    -- system-dependent named numbers:

    MIN_INT        : constant:= implementation_defined;
    MAX_INT        : constant:= implementation_defined;
    MAX_DIGITS     : constant:= implementation_defined;
    MAX_MANTISSA : constant:= implementation_defined;
    FINE_DELTA     : constant:= implementation_defined;
    TICK           : constant:= implementation_defined;

    -- other system-dependent declarations

    subtype PRIORITY is INTEGER range implementation_defined;
    . . .
    end SYSTEM:
```

The type ADDRESS is that used in an address clause and given by the corresponding attribute. The numbers STORAGE_UNIT and MEMORY_SIZE give the size of a storage unit in bits and the memory size in storage units; both are of type universal integer. MIN_INT and MAX_INT give the most negative and most positive values of an integer type, MAX_DIGITS is the largest number of decimal digits of a floating type and MAX_MANTISSA is the largest number of binary digits of a fixed type; they are all of type universal integer.

Various pragmas enable us to set certain parameters of the implementation, and attributes enable us to read the value of certain parameters. The predefined pragmas and attributes are listed in Appendix 1 although an implementation is free to add others.

Some pragmas enable us to guide the compiler regarding the balance of the implementation between integrity and efficiency and also between space and time.

The pragma SUPPRESS can be used to indicate that the run time checks associated with detecting conditions which could give rise to exceptions can be omitted if to do so would lead to a more efficient program. However, it should be remembered that a pragma is merely a recommendation and so there is no guarantee that the exception will not be raised. Indeed it could be propagated from another unit compiled with checks.

The checks corresponding to the exception CONSTRAINT_ERROR are ACCESS_CHECK (checking that an access value is not null when attempting to access a component), DISCRIMINANT_CHECK (checking that a discriminant value is consistent with the component being accessed or a constraint), INDEX_CHECK (checking that an index is in range), LENGTH_CHECK (checking that the number of components of an array match) and RANGE_CHECK (checking that various constraints are satisfied).

The checks corresponding to NUMERIC_ERROR are DIVISION_CHECK (checking the second operand of /, **rem** and **mod**) and OVERFLOW_CHECK (checking for numeric overflow).

The check corresponding to STORAGE_ERROR is STORAGE_CHECK (checking that space for an access collection or task has not been exceeded).

The check corresponding to PROGRAM_ERROR is ELABORATION_CHECK (checking that the body of a unit has been elaborated).

The pragma takes the form

pragma SUPPRESS(RANGE_CHECK);

in which case it applies to all operations in the unit concerned or it can list the types and objects to which it is to be applied. Thus

pragma SUPPRESS(ACCESS_CHECK, LIST);

indicates that no checks are to be applied when accessing objects of the access type LIST.

The other pragmas in this category apply to the balance between speed and time. They are CONTROLLED, INLINE, OPTIMIZE and PACK; they are described in Appendix 1.

Finally there are various machine dependent attributes defined for real types. For example there is the attribute MACHINE_ROUNDS which indicates whether rounding is performed for the type concerned. Another is the attribute MACHINE_OVERFLOWS which indicates whether NUMERIC_ERROR is raised for computations which exceed the range of the type. If a program uses these attributes then care is required if portability is to be ensured.

15.6 Unchecked programming

Sometimes the strict integrity of a fully typed language is a nuisance. This particularly applies to system programs where, in different parts of a program, an object is thought of in different terms. This difficulty can be overcome by the use of a generic function called UNCHECKED_CONVERSION. Its specification is

```
generic
    type SOURCE is limited private;
    type TARGET is limited private;
function UNCHECKED_CONVERSION(S: SOURCE)
                                    return TARGET;
```

As an example, values of the type STATUS of Section 15.4 might arrive in our program as values of type BYTE. In order to perform the conversion we first instantiate the generic function thus

```
function BYTE_TO_STATUS is
    new UNCHECKED_CONVERSION (BYTE, STATUS);
```

and we can then write

```
B: BYTE:= . . .
S: STATUS;
. . .
S:= BYTE_TO_STATUS(B);
```

The effect of the unchecked conversion is nothing; the bit pattern of the source type is merely passed on unchanged and reinterpreted as the bit pattern of the target type. Clearly certain conditions must be satisfied for this to be possible; an obvious one which may be imposed by the implementation is that the number of bits in the representations of the two types must be the same. We cannot get a quart into a pint pot.

Another area where the programmer can be given extra freedom is in the deallocation of access types. As mentioned in Section 11.3 there may or may not be a garbage collector. In any event we may prefer to do our own garbage collection perhaps on the grounds that this gives us better timing control in a real time program. We can do this with a generic procedure called UNCHECKED_DEALLOCATION. Its specification is

```
generic
    type OBJECT is limited private;
    type NAME is access OBJECT;
procedure UNCHECKED_DEALLOCATION(X: in out NAME);
```

If we take our old friend

```
type LIST is access CELL;
```

then we can write

```
procedure FREE is
    new UNCHECKED_DEALLOCATION(CELL, LIST);
```

and then

```
L: LIST;
. . .
FREE(L);
```

After calling FREE, the value of L will be **null** and the cell will have been returned to free storage. Of course, if we mistakenly still had another variable referring to the cell then we would be in a mess; the program would be erroneous.

If we use unchecked deallocation then the onus is on us to get it right. We should also insert

pragma CONTROLLED(LIST);

to tell the compiler that we are looking after ourselves and that any garbage collector should not be used for this access type.

The use of both these forms of unchecked programming needs care and it would be sensible to restrict the use of these generic subprograms to privileged parts of the program.

15.7   Other languages

Another possible form of communication between an Ada program and the outside world is via other languages. These could be machine languages or other high level languages such as FORTRAN. The LRM prescribes general methods but the actual details will obviously depend so much upon the implementation that an outline description seems pointless and the reader is therefore referred to specific documentation for the implementation concerned.

Chapter 16   FINALE

This final chapter covers various overall aspects of Ada. The first three sections summarise topics which have of necessity been introduced in stages throughout the book in order to reveal their overall coherence and underlying relationships. There is then a section on the important issue of portability. Finally we discuss the general topic of program design as it relates to Ada.

16.1   Names and expressions

The idea of a name should be carefully distinguished from that of an identifier. An identifier is a syntactic form such as FRED which is used for various purposes including introducing entities when they are declared. A name, on the other hand, may be more complex and is the form used to denote entities in general. In the LRM and in particular in the syntax rules, the term simple name is used to refer to an identifier other than when it is first introduced; we have not used this term since it seems unnecessarily pedantic.

Syntactically, a name starts with an identifier such as FRED or an operator symbol such as "+" and can then be followed by one or more of the following in an arbitrary order

- one of more index expressions in brackets; this denotes a component of an array,
- a discrete range in brackets; this denotes a slice of an array,
- a dot followed by an identifier, operator or **all**; this denotes a record component, an access value or an entity in a package, task, subprogram, block or loop,
- a prime and then an identifier, possibly indexed; this denotes an attribute,
- an actual parameter list in brackets; this denotes a function call.

A function call in a name must deliver an array, record or access value and must be followed by indexing, slicing, attribution or component selection. This is not to say that a function call must always be followed by one of these things; it could deliver a value as part of an expression, but as part of a name it must be so followed. This point is clarified by considering the assignment statement. The left hand side must be a name whereas the right hand side is an expression. Hence, as we saw in Section 11.5, we can write

```
SPOUSE(P).BIRTH:=NEWDATE;
```

but not

```
SPOUSE(P):=Q;
```

although

```
Q:=SPOUSE(P);
```

is of course perfectly legal. (Ada is somewhat less consistent than Algol 68 in this respect.)

Names are just one of the primary components of an expression. The others are literals (numeric literals, enumeration literals, strings and **null**), aggregates, allocators, function calls (not considered as names), type conversions and qualified expressions as well as expressions in brackets. Expressions involving scalar operators were summarised in Section 4.9. For convenience all the operators and their predefined uses are shown in Fig. 16.1. Remember that an expression may also involve the short circuit forms **and then** and **or else** and the membership tests **in** and **not in** although these are not technically classed as operators.

Operator	Operand(s)		Result
and or xor	Boolean		same
	one dim Boolean array		same
= /=	any, not limited		BOOLEAN
< <= > >=	scalar		BOOLEAN
	one dim discrete array		BOOLEAN
+ − (binary)	numeric		same
&	one dim array		same
+ − (unary)	numeric		same
*	integer	integer	same
	fixed	INTEGER	same fixed
	INTEGER	fixed	same fixed
	fixed	fixed	univ fixed
	floating	floating	same
/	integer	integer	same
	fixed	INTEGER	same fixed
	fixed	fixed	univ fixed
	floating	floating	same
mod rem	integer	integer	same
**	integer	non neg INTEGER	same integer
	floating	INTEGER	same floating
not	Boolean		same
	one dim Boolean array		same
abs	numeric		same

Fig. 16.1 Predefined operators

The observant reader will notice that the syntax in Appendix 4 uses the syntactic form 'simple_expression' in some cases where 'expression' might have been expected. One reason for this is to avoid a potential ambiguity regarding the use of **in** as a membership test with ranges.

From time to time we have referred to the need for certain expressions to be static. As explained in Chapter 2 this means that they can be evaluated at compilation time. An expression is static if all its constituents are one of the following

- a numeric or enumeration literal,
- a named number,
- a constant initialised by a static expression,
- a predefined operator,
- a static attribute or a functional attribute with static parameters,
- a qualified static expression provided that any constraint involved is static.

The final point we wish to make about expressions concerns array bounds. If an expression delivers an array value then it will have bounds for each dimension. Such an expression can be used in various contexts which can be divided into categories according to the rules regarding the matching of the bounds.

The first category includes assignment and initialisation in an object declaration. In these cases the bounds of the expression do not have to match the bounds of the object; all that matters is that the number of components in each dimension is the same. Thus as we saw in Section 6.2 we can write

```
V: VECTOR(1 .. 5);
W: VECTOR(0 .. 4);
. . .
V:=W;
```

The same matching rules apply in the case of the predefined equality and relational operators.

The second category of contexts includes those where an array is used as an actual parameter, as a function result, as an initial value in an allocator or in a qualified expression. In all of these cases an array type or subtype is involved but it may or may not be constrained. If it is constrained then the bounds must exactly match; if it is not constrained then the 'result' takes the bounds of the expression. Thus if we had a function

```
function F return VECTOR_5 is
    V: VECTOR(1 .. 5);
    W: VECTOR(0 .. 4);
begin
    . . .
```

then we could write **return** V but not **return** W. If, however, the specification had been

function F return VECTOR

then we could write either **return** V or **return** W.

There are complications with array aggregates. In the case of a named aggregate without **others** the bounds are evident; such an aggregate can be used in any of the above contexts. In the case of a positional aggregate without **others** the bounds are not evident although the number of components is; such an aggregate can also be used in any of the above contexts – in all the cases of the first category and those of the second category with a constrained type the bounds are taken to be those required by the constraint – in cases of the second category with an unconstrained type the lower bound is given by S'FIRST where S is the index subtype. Finally, if an aggregate (positional or named) contains **others**, then neither the bounds nor the number of components is evident. Such an aggregate can be used in a situation of the second category with a constrained type; in addition a positional aggregate with **others** is also allowed in a situation of the first category.

Similar rules apply to nested aggregates; the context of the whole aggregate is applied transitively to its components.

Somewhat surprisingly, array type conversion described in Section 6.2 does not fit neatly into either of the above two categories. If the type is constrained, then the matching rules of assignment are used; if the type is unconstrained, then the result takes the bounds of the operand as for qualification.

Exercise 16.1
1 Given

    L: INTEGER:=6;
    M: **constant** INTEGER:=7;
    N: **constant**:=8;

then classify the following as static or dynamic expressions and give their type.

    a) L+1
    b) M+1
    c) N+1

16.2 Type equivalence

It is perhaps worth emphasising the rules for type equivalence. The basic rule is that every type definition introduces a new type. Remember the difference between a type definition and a type declaration. A type definition introduces a type whereas a type declaration also introduces an identifier referring to it. Thus

    type T **is** (A, B, C);

is a type declaration whereas

    (A, B, C)

is a type definition.

Most types have names but in a few cases a type may be anonymous. The obvious cases occur with the declarations of arrays and tasks. Thus

```
A: array (I range L . . R) of C;
```

is short for

```
type anon is array (I range <>) of C;
A: anon(L . . R);
```

and

```
task T is . . .
```

is short for

```
task type anon is . . .
T: anon;
```

More subtle cases occur where an apparent type declaration is actually only a subtype declaration. This occurs with array types, derived types and numeric types

```
type T is array (I range L . . R) of C;
```

is short for

```
subtype index is I range L . . R;
type anon is array (index range <>) of C;
subtype T is anon(L . . R);
```

and

```
type S is new T constraint;
```

is short for

```
type anon is new T;
subtype S is anon constraint;
```

and finally

```
type T is range L . . R;
```

is short for

```
type anon is new integer_type;
subtype T is anon range L . . R;
```

where integer_type is one of the predefined integer types.

When interpreting the rule that each type definition introduces a new type, remember that generic instantiation is equivalent to text substitution in this respect. Thus each instantiation of a package with a type definition in its specification introduces a distinct type. It will be remembered that a similar rule applies to the identification of different exceptions. Each textually distinct exception declaration introduces a new exception; an exception in a recursive procedure is the same for each incarnation but generic instantiation introduces different exceptions.

Remember also that multiple declarations are equivalent to several single declarations written out explicitly. Thus if we have

A, B: **array** (I **range** L . . R) **of** C;

then A and B are of different anonymous types.

16.3   Structure summary

Ada has four structural units in which declarations can occur; these are blocks, subprograms, packages and tasks. They can be classified in various ways. First of all packages and tasks have separate specifications and bodies; for subprograms this separation is optional; for blocks it is not possible or relevant since a block has no specification. We can also consider separate compilation: packages, tasks and subprogram bodies can all be subunits but only packages and subprograms can be library units. Note also that only packages and subprograms can be generic. Finally, tasks, subprograms and blocks can have dependent tasks but packages cannot since they are only passive scope control units. These various properties of units are summarised in Fig. 16.2.

Property	Blocks	Subprograms	Packages	Tasks
separation	no	optional	yes	yes
subunits	no	yes	yes	yes
library units	no	yes	yes	no
generic units	no	yes	yes	no
dependent tasks	yes	yes	no	yes

Fig. 16.2 Properties of units

We can also consider the scope and nesting of these four structural units. (Note that a block is a statement whereas the others are declarations.) Each unit can appear inside any of the other units and this lexical nesting can in principle go on indefinitely although in practical programs a depth of three will not often be exceeded. The only restrictions to this nesting are that a block, being a statement, cannot appear in a package specification but only in its body (and directly only in the initialisation sequence) and of course none of these units can appear in a task specification but again only in its body. In practice, however, some of the combinations will arise rarely. Blocks will usually occur inside subprograms and task bodies and occasionally other blocks. Subprograms will occur as library units and inside packages and less frequently inside tasks and other subprograms. Packages will usually be library units or inside other packages. Tasks will probably nearly always be inside packages and occasionally inside other tasks or subprograms.

The Language Reference Manual is a little vague about the concept of an Ada program. This is perhaps to be expected since Ada is about software components, and undue concern regarding what constitutes a complete program is probably out of place particularly bearing in mind the growing concern with distributed and parallel systems. However, for simple systems we can regard a program as composed out of the library units in a particular program library. The LRM does not prescribe how the program is to be started but as discussed in Sections 2.2 and 8.2 we can imagine that one of the library units which is a subprogram is called by some magic outside the language itself. Moreover, we must imagine that this originating flow of control is associated with an anonymous task. The priority of this task can be set by the pragma PRIORITY in the outermost declarative part of this main subprogram.

The main program will almost inevitably use dependent library units such as TEXT_IO. These have to be elaborated before the main program is entered and again we can imagine that this is done by our anonymous task. The order of these elaborations is not precisely specified but it must be consistent with the dependencies between the units. In addition, the pragma ELABORATE can be used to ensure that a body is elaborated before a unit that calls it; this may be necessary to prevent PROGRAM_ERROR. If no consistent order exists then the program is illegal; if there are several possible orders and the behaviour of the program depends on the particular order then it is also illegal.

A further point is that whether a main program can have parameters or not or whether there are restrictions on their types and modes or indeed whether the main program can be a function is dependent on the implementation. Again this is in line with the view that Ada is about the open world of components rather than the closed world of complete programs. It may indeed be very convenient for a main program to have parameters, and for the calling and parameter passing to be performed by the magic associated with the interpretation of a statement in some non-Ada command language.

The final point we wish to make in this section concerns the mathematical library. The LRM does not prescribe the existence of such a library in the way that it does prescribe packages for input and output. However, we have rather assumed its existence in Section 4.9 and also in Exercise 2.2(1). One of the problems that the mathematical library has to overcome concerns the derived nature of user defined floating point types. The rules for derived types are such that any library for a predefined type such as FLOAT will not automatically become inherited by a derived type such as REAL. Instead the mathematical library is best constructed as a generic package

```
generic
    type F is digits <>;
package MATHS_LIB is
    function SQRT(X: F) return F;
    function LOG(X: F) return F;
```

. . .

end MATHS_LIB;

We can then use the mathematical library with a type such as **REAL** by writing

package REAL_MATHS_LIB **is new** MATHS_LIB(REAL);
use REAL_MATHS_LIB;

16.4   Portability

An Ada program may or may not be portable. In many cases a program will be intimately concerned with the particular hardware on which it is running; this is particularly true of embedded applications. Such a program cannot be transferred to another machine without significant alteration. On the other hand it is highly desirable to write portable program libraries so that they can be reused in different applications. In some cases a library component will be totally portable; more often it will make certain demands on the implementation or be parameterised so that it can be tailored to its environment in a straightforward manner. This section contains general guidelines on the writing of portable Ada programs.

One thing to avoid is erroneous programs and those with incorrect order dependencies. They can be insidious. A program may work quite satisfactorily on one implementation and may seem superficially to be portable. However, if it happens to depend upon some undefined feature then its behaviour on another implementation cannot be guaranteed. A common example in most programming languages occurs with variables which accidentally are not initialised. It is often the case that the intended value is zero and furthermore many operating systems clear the program area before loading the program. Under such circumstances the program will behave correctly but may give surprising results when transferred to a different implementation. So the concept of erroneous programs is not confined to Ada. In the previous chapters we have mentioned various causes of such illegal programs. For convenience we summarise them here.

An important group of situations concerns the order of evaluation of expressions. Since an expression can include a function call and a function call can have side effects, it follows that different orders of evaluation can sometimes produce different results. The order of evaluation of the following is not defined

- the operands of a binary operator,
- the destination and value in an assignment,
- the components in an aggregate,
- the parameters in a subprogram or entry call,
- the index expressions in a multidimensional name,
- the expressions in a range,
- the guards in a select statement.

There is an important situation where a junk value can arise

- reading an uninitialised variable before assigning to it.

There are two situations where the language mechanism is not defined

- the passing of array, record and private parameters,
- the algorithm for choosing a branch of a select statement.

There are also situations where the programmer is given extra freedom to overcome the stringency of the type model; abuse of this freedom can lead to erroneous programs. Examples are

- suppressing exceptions,
- unchecked deallocation,
- unchecked conversion.

Finally we recall from the last section that the order of elaboration of library units is not defined.

Numeric types are another important source of portability problems. The reason is, of course, the compromise necessary between achieving absolutely uniform behaviour on all machines and maximising efficiency. Ada uses the concept of model numbers as the formalisation of this compromise. In principle, if we rely only on the properties of the model numbers then our programs will be portable. In practice this is not easy to do; the reader will recall the problems of overflow in intermediate expressions discussed in Section 12.1.

There are various attributes which, if used correctly, can make our programs more portable. Thus we can use BASE to find out what is really going on and MACHINE_OVERFLOWS to see whether NUMERIC_ERROR will occur or not. But the misuse of these attributes can lead to very non-portable programs.

There is however one simple rule that can be followed. We should always declare our own real types and not directly use the predefined types such as FLOAT. Ideally, a similar approach should be taken with integer types, but the language does encourage us to assume that the predefined type INTEGER has a sensible range.

Another area to consider is tasking. Any program that uses tasking is likely to suffer from portability problems because instruction execution times vary from machine to machine. This will affect the relative execution times of tasks as well as their individual execution times. In some cases a program may not be capable of running at all on a particular machine because it does not have adequate processing power. Hard guidelines are almost impossible to give but the following points should be kept in mind.

Take care that the type DURATION is accurate enough for the application. Remember that regular loops cannot easily be achieved if the interval required is not a model number.

Avoid the unsynchronised use of shared variables as far as possible. Sometimes, timing considerations demand quick and dirty techniques; consult your friendly real time specialist if tempted. In simple cases the pragma SHARED may be able to prevent interference between tasks.

The use of the abort statement will also give portability problems because of its asynchronous nature.

Avoid also the overuse of priorities. If you need to use priorities to obtain adequate responsiveness then the program is probably stretching the resources of the machine.

The finite speed of the machine leads to our final topic in this section – the finite space available. It is clear that different machines have different sizes and so a program that runs satisfactorily on one machine might raise STORAGE_ERROR on another. Moreover, different implementations may use different storage allocation strategies for access types and task data. We have seen how representation clauses can be used to give control of storage allocation and thereby reduce portability problems. However, the unconsidered use of recursion and access types is best avoided.

Exercise 16.4

1 The global variable I is of type INTEGER and the function F is

```
function F return INTEGER is
begin
    I:=I+1;
    return I;
end F;
```

Explain why the following fragments of program are illegal. Assume in each case that I is reset to 1.

a) I:=I+F;   c) AA(I, F):=0;
b) A(I):=F;

16.5 Program design

This final section considers the question of designing Ada programs. At the time of writing serious Ada compilers are only just coming into existence and consequently there is little accumulated experience in the actual use of Ada. Hence the guidelines in this section must be treated with some caution although there seems little reason to doubt their general validity. Note also that we are only addressing the question of designing programs in Ada. It is assumed that the reader has some knowledge of the general principles of program design.

There are various low level and stylistic issues which are perhaps obvious. Identifiers should be meaningful. The program should be laid out neatly – the style used in this book is based on that recommended from the syntax in the LRM. Useful comments should be added. The block structure should be used to localise declarations to their use. Whenever possible a piece of information should only be written once; thus number and constant declarations should be used rather than explicit literals. And so on.

Programming is really all about abstraction and the mapping of the problem onto constructions in the programming language. We recall from Section 1.2 that the development of programming languages has been concerned with the introduction of various levels of abstraction and that Ada in particular introduces a degree of data abstraction not present in other practically used languages.

An important concept in design and the use of abstractions is information hiding. Information should only be accessible to those parts of a program that need to know. The use of packages and private data types to hide unnecessary detail is the cornerstone of good Ada programming. Indeed as we have stated before Ada is a language which aims to encourage the development of reusable software components; the package is the key component.

Designing an Ada program is therefore largely concerned with designing a group of packages and the interfaces between them. Often we will hope to use one or more existing packages. For this to be possible it is clear that they must have been designed with consistent, clean and sufficiently general interfaces. The difficulties are perhaps in deciding what items are sufficiently related or fundamental to belong together in a package and also how general to make the package. If a package is too general it might be clumsy and inefficient; if not general enough it will not be as useful as it might.

The interface to a package is provided by its specification; at least that provides the syntax of how to use the interface, the semantics must also be defined and that can only be provided by a natural language commentary. Thus consider the package STACK of Section 8.1; its specification guarantees that it will provide subprograms PUSH and POP with certain parameter and result types. However the specification does not, of itself, guarantee that a call of POP will in fact remove and deliver the top item from the stack. From the point of view of the language it would be quite acceptable for the package body to be

```
package body STACK is
    procedure PUSH(X: INTEGER) is
    begin
        null;
    end;

    function POP return INTEGER is
    begin
        return 0;
    end;
end STACK;
```

However, in our imagined future world of the software components industry anyone selling such package bodies would soon go out of business.

We will now discuss some categories of related items that might make up useful packages.

A very simple form of package is one which merely consists of a group of related types and constants and has no body. The packages SYSTEM and ASCII are in this category. A further example in Section 8.1 is the package DIURNAL; this does not seem a good example – if it has an array TOMORROW then surely it should also have YESTERDAY. Better examples might be packages of related mathematical constants, conversion constants (metric to imperial say), tables of physical and chemical constants and so on. The last could be

```
package ELEMENTS is
    type ELEMENT is (H, He, Li, . . . );
        – – beware of Indium – In is reserved!
    ATOMIC_WEIGHT: array (ELEMENT) of REAL
                    :=(1.008, 4.003, 6.940, . . . );

        . . .
end ELEMENTS;
```

Another case is where the package contains functions related by application area. An obvious example is the mathematical library mentioned in Section 16.3. The individual functions in such a case are really independent although for efficiency SIN and COS for example are likely to share a common procedure. The package body enables us to hide such a procedure from the user because its existence is merely an implementation detail.

Sometimes a package is needed in order to hide a benevolent side effect – an obvious example is the package RANDOM in Exercise 8.1(1).

Packages such as SEQUENTIAL_IO encapsulate a great deal of hidden information and provide a number of related services. A problem here is deciding whether to provide additional subprograms for convenience or to stick to only those absolutely necessary. The package TEXT_IO contains many convenience subprograms.

Many packages can be classified as a means of providing controlled access to some form of database. The database may consist of just one item as in the package RANDOM or it could be the symbol tables of a compiler or a grand commercial style database and so on. The package BANK in Section 9.3 is another example.

An important use of packages is to provide new data types and asociated operations. Obvious examples are the packages COMPLEX_NUMBERS (Section 9.1), RATIONAL_NUMBERS (Exercise 9.1(2)) and QUEUES (Exercise 11.4(3)). In such cases the use of private types enables us to separate the representation of the type from the operations upon it. In a way the new types can be seen as natural extensions to the language.

Packages of this sort raise the question of whether we should use operators rather than functions. Ada is not so flexible as some other languages; new operator forms cannot be introduced and the precedence levels are fixed. This ensures that over-enthusiastic use of operators cannot lead to programs that do not even look like Ada programs as can happen with languages such as POP–2. Even so Ada provides opportunities for surprises. We could write

```
function "−"(X, Y: INTEGER) return INTEGER is
begin
    return STANDARD."+"(X, Y);
end "−";
```

but it would obviously be very foolish to do so. Hence a good general guideline is to minimise surprises.

Operators should be considered for functions with a natural mathematical flavour. As a general rule the normal algebraic properties of the operators should be preserved if this is possible. Thus "+" and "*" should be commutative. Mixed type arithmetic is best avoided but there are situations where it is necessary.

The definitions of the operators in the package COMPLEX_NUMBERS have the expected properties and do not allow mixed working. Perhaps we should also have added unary "+" and "−" for completeness as we did for the package RATIONAL_NUMBERS. It would be nice if type conversion could be done by overloading the type name so that we could write COMPLEX(2.0) rather than CONS(2.0, 0.0). However Ada does not allow this. Type conversion of this form is restricted to the predefined and derived numeric types.

On the other hand, consider the operators in the package CALENDAR in

Section 14.3. Here the very essence of the problem requires mixed type addition but commutativity is preserved by providing two overloadings of "+".

When introducing mathematical types such as **COMPLEX** and **RATIONAL** it is always best to use private types. We will then need to provide constructor and selector functions as well as the natural operations themselves. It will usually be the case that construction and selection are best done with functional notation whereas the natural operations can be done with the operators. However, in the case of rational numbers the division operator "/ " provides a natural notation for construction.

There is a general and difficult question of how much to provide in a package for a mathematical type. The bare minimum may be rather spartan and incur all users in unnecessary creation of additional subprograms. To be generous might make the package too cumbersome. For instance should we provide a relational operator and if so should we provide all four? Should input-output be included? We leave such questions for the reader to answer from his or her own experience according to the needs of the application.

Another important issue is storage allocation. This is well illustrated by a type such as **POLYNOMIAL** introduced in Section 11.1. If this is implemented using a discriminated record thus

```
type POLYNOMIAL(N: INDEX:=0) is
    record
        A: INTEGER_VECTOR(0 . . N);
    end record;
```

then in the case of unconstrained polynomials the compiler will allocate the maximum space that could be required. Hence it is important that the range of the discriminant has a sensible upper bound. If we had written

```
type POLYNOMIAL(N: INTEGER:=0) is . . .
```

then each unconstrained polynomial would have had the space for an array of length **INTEGER'LAST** and we would presumably soon run out of storage.

If all the polynomials are to be fairly small then using a discriminated record is probably satisfactory. On the other hand if they are likely to be of greatly varying size then it is probably better to use access types. Indeed a mixed strategy could be used – a fixed array for the first few terms and then the use of an access type for the remainder. In order that such alternative implementation strategies can be properly organised and hidden from the user it is clear that the polynomial should be a private type. The design of a suitable package is left as an informal exercise for the reader.

In designing packages there is the question of what to do when something goes wrong. This brings us to exceptions. Although not new to programming languages they are nevertheless not widely used except in PL/I and the experience with PL/I has not been satisfactory. However, exceptions in Ada are different to those in PL/I in one most important aspect. In Ada one cannot go back to the point where the exception was raised but is forced to consider a proper alternative to the part of the program that went wrong.

Having said that, exceptions nevertheless need care. In Chapter 10 we warned against the unnecessary use of exceptions and in particular the casual raising of the predefined exceptions since we have no guarantee, when handling such an exception, that it was raised for the reason we had in mind.

The first goal should always be to have clean and complete interfaces. As an example consider again the factorial function and the action to be taken when the parameter is illegal. We could consider

- printing a message,
- returning a default value,
- returning a status via a Boolean parameter,
- calling an error procedure,
- raising an exception.

Printing a message is highly unsatisfactory because it raises a host of detailed problems such as the identity of the file, the format of the message and so on. Moreover, it gives the calling program no control over the action it would like to take and some file is cluttered with messages. Furthermore there is still the question of what to do after having printed the message.

Another possibility is to return a default value such as − 1 as in Exercise 10.1(2). This is not satisfactory since there is no guarantee that the user will check for this default value upon return. If we could rely upon the user doing so then we could equally rely upon the user checking the parameter of the function before calling it in the first place.

If we wish to return an auxiliary status value via another parameter then, as we saw when discussing PUSH and POP in Section 10.2, we can no longer use a function anyway and would have to use a procedure instead. We also have to rely upon the caller again as in the case of the default value.

We could call a global procedure to be supplied by the user. This means agreeing on a standard name which is unsatisfactory. We cannot pass the error procedure as a parameter and to resort to the generic mechanism really is using a steam hammer to crack a nut. In any case we still have the problem, as with printing a message, of what to do afterwards and how to return finally from the function. It is highly naive to suppose that the program can just stop. The manager of the steelworks would not wish the control part of the program to stop just because of a minor error in some other part; there must be a way of carrying on.

There are only two ways out of a subprogram in Ada; back to the point of call or by a propagated exception (the global goto and label parameters of other languages are effectively replaced by the exception). We seem to have eliminated the possibility of returning to the point of call as not reliable and so have to come to the conclusion that the raising of an exception is the appropriate solution.

Another criterion we should consider when deciding whether to use exceptions is whether we expect the condition to arise in the normal course of events or not. If we do then an exception is probably wrong. As an example the end of file condition in the package SEQUENTIAL_IO is tested for by a Boolean function and not an exception. We naturally expect to come to the end of the file and so must test for it – see the answer to Exercise 15.1(1).

On the other hand if we are using the package STACK in say an interpreter for mathematical expressions, then, provided that the interpreter is written correctly, we know that the stack cannot underflow. An exception for this unexpected condition is acceptable. Note also that when using SEQUENTIAL_IO, if we accidentally attempt to read after the end of the file then an exception (END_ERROR) is raised.

The raising of exceptions is, however, not a panacea. We cannot sweep the problem under the carpet in this way. The exception must be handled somewhere otherwise the program will terminate. In fact this is one of their advantages – if the user does nothing then the program will terminate safely, whereas if we return status values and the user does nothing then the program will probably ramble on in a fruitless way.

The indiscriminate use of **others** in an exception handler should be avoided. If we write **others** we are really admitting that anything could have gone wrong and we should take appropriate action; we should not use **others** as shorthand for the exceptions we anticipate.

Another major design area concerns the use of tasks. It is usually fairly clear that a problem needs a solution involving tasks but it is not always clear how the various activities should be allocated to individual tasks.

There are perhaps two major problems to be solved regarding the inter-actions between tasks. One concerns the transmission of messages between tasks, the other the controlling of access to common data by several tasks.

The rendezvous provides a natural mechanism for the closely coupled transmission of a message; examples are provided by the interaction between mother and the other members of her family in the procedure SHOPPING in Section 14.2 and by the interaction between the server and the customer in the package COBBLERS of Exercise 14.8(**1**). If the transmission needs to be decoupled so that the sender can carry on before the message is received then some intermediary task is required. Examples are the task BUFFERING in Section 14.4 and the task type MAILBOX in Section 14.5.

Controlled access to common data is, in Ada, also done by an inter-mediary task whereas in other languages it may use passive constructions such as monitors or low level primitives such as semaphores. The Ada approach usually provides a clearer and safer solution to the problem. An example is the task PROTECTED_VARIABLE in Section 14.4. Quite often the task is encapsulated in a package in order to enforce the required protocol; examples are the package READER_WRITER of Section 14.4 and the package RESOURCE_ALLOCATOR of Section 14.7.

Sometimes the distinction between message passing and controlling data access is blurred; the task BUFFERING at the macro level is passing messages whereas at the micro level it is controlling access to the buffer.

Another categorisation of tasks is between users and servers. A pure server task is one with entries but which calls no other tasks whereas a pure user has no entries but calls other tasks. The distinction is emphasised by the asymmetry of the naming in the rendezvous. The server does not know the names of user tasks whereas the user tasks must know the names of the server tasks in order to call their entries. Sometimes a task is part server and part user; an example is the task type READ_AGENT in Section 14.6.

One problem when designing a set of interacting tasks is deciding which way round the entries are to go. Our intuitive model of servers and users should help. The entries belong in the servers. Another criterion is provided by the consideration of alternatives; if a task is to have a choice of rendezvous via a select statement then it must own the entries and therefore be a server. A select statement can be used to accept one of several entry calls but cannot be used to call one of several entries.

It cannot be emphasised too much that aborting tasks must not be done casually.The abort statement is for extreme situations only. One possible use is in a supervisory task where it may be desirable to close down a complete subsystem in response to a command from a human operator.

The reason for wishing to avoid abort is that it makes it very difficult to provide reliable services as we saw with the package READER_WRITER in Section 14.6. If we know that the users cannot be abnormally terminated then the fancy use of secret agents is not necessary; indeed that example should be considered as illustrating what can be done rather than what should be done.

A multitasking Ada program will often be seen as a set of cooperating tasks designed together. In such circumstances we can rely on the calling tasks to obey the necessary protocols and the design of the servers is then simplified.

The use of timed out entry calls also needs some care but is a very natural and common requirement in real time systems. Services should where possible be able to cope with timed out calls.

Finally there are generics and the whole question of parameterisation. Should we write specific packages or very general ones? This is a familiar problem with subprograms and generics merely add a new dimension. As stated at the beginning of this section there is as yet little experience of the use of Ada and so it seems somewhat premature to give advice in this area. Indeed, in the imagined future market for software components it is likely that packages of all sorts of generalities and performance will be available. We can conclude by imagining a future conversation in our local software shop

Customer: Could I have a look at the reader writer package you have in the window?

Server: Certainly sir. Would you be interested in this robust version – proof against abort? Or we have this slick version for trusty callers. Just arrived this week.

Customer: Well – it's for a cooperating system so the new one sounds good. How much is it?

Server: It's 250 Eurodollars but as it's new there is a special offer with it – a free copy of this random number generator and 10% off your next certification.

Customer: Great. Is it validated?

Server: All our products conform to the highest standards sir. The parameter mechanism conforms to ES98263 and it has the usual international multitasking certificate.

Customer: OK, I'll take it.

Server: Will you take it as it is or shall I instantiate it for you?

Customer: As it is please. I prefer to do my own instantiation.

                  . . .

On this fantasy note we come to the end of this book. It is hoped that the reader will have gained some general understanding of the principles of Ada as well as a lot of the detail. Further understanding will come with use and the author hopes that he has in some small way prepared the reader for the future.

Appendix 1 RESERVED WORDS, ATTRIBUTES AND PRAGMAS

This appendix lists the reserved words and predefined attributes and pragmas. An implementation may define additional attributes and pragmas but not additional reserved words.

The lists of attributes and pragmas are taken from Annexes A and B of the LRM. The references have been altered to correspond to appropriate sections of this book.

A1.1 Reserved words

The following words are reserved; their use is described in the sections indicated.

abort	14.6
abs	4.5
accept	14.2
access	11.3
all	11.3
and	4.7, 4.9
array	6.1
at	15.4
begin	4.2, 7.1, 8.1, 14.1
body	8.1, 14.1
case	5.2, 11.2
constant	4.1
declare	4.2
delay	14.3
delta	12.4, 13.2
digits	12.3, 13.2
do	14.2
else	4.9, 5.1, 14.4
elsif	5.1
end	4.2, 7.1, 8.1, 14.1, 14.2
entry	14.2
exception	10.1
exit	5.3
for	5.3, 15.4

The reserved words **delta**, **digits** and **range** are also used as attributes.

A1.2   Predefined attributes

The following attributes are predefined in the language

P′ADDRESS   For a prefix P that denotes an object, a program unit, a label, or an entry:
Yields the address of the first of the storage units allocated to P. For a subprogram, package, task unit or label, this value refers to the machine code associated with the corresponding body or statement. For an entry for which an address clause has been given, the value refers to the corresponding hardware interrupt. The value of this attribute is of the type ADDRESS defined in the package SYSTEM. (See 15.4)

P′AFT   For a prefix P that denotes a fixed point subtype:
Yields the number of decimal digits needed after the point to accommodate the precision of the subtype P, unless the delta of the subtype P is greater than 0.1, in which case the attribute yields the value one. (P′AFT is the smallest positive integer N for which (10**N)*P′DELTA is greater than or equal to one.) The value of this attribute is of the type universal integer. (See 15.2)

P′BASE   For a prefix P that denotes a type or subtype:
This attribute denotes the base type of P. It is only allowed as the prefix of the name of another attribute, for example P′BASE′FIRST. (See 12.1)

P′CALLABLE   For a prefix P that is appropriate for a task type:
Yields the value FALSE when the execution of the task P is either completed or terminated, or when the task is abnormal; yields the value TRUE otherwise. The value of this attribute is of the predefined type BOOLEAN. (See 14.6)

P′CONSTRAINED   For a prefix P that denotes an object of a type with discriminants:
Yields the value TRUE if a discriminant constraint applies to the object P, or if the object is a constant (including a formal parameter or generic formal parameter of mode **in**); yields the value FALSE otherwise. If P is a generic formal parameter of mode **in out**, or if P is a formal parameter of mode **in out** or **out** and the type mark given in the corresponding parameter specification denotes an unconstrained type with discriminants, then the value of this attribute is obtained from that of the corresponding actual parameter. The value of this attribute is of the predefined type BOOLEAN. (See 11.1)

P′CONSTRAINED   For a prefix P that denotes a private type or subtype:
Yields the value FALSE if P denotes an unconstrained nonformal private type with discriminants; also yields the value FALSE if P denotes a generic formal private type and the associated actual subtype is either an unconstrained type with discriminants or an unconstrained array type; yields the value TRUE otherwise. The value of this attribute is of the predefined type BOOLEAN. (See 13.2)

P'COUNT   For a prefix P that denotes an entry of a task unit:
Yields the number of entry calls presently queued on the entry (if the attribute is evaluated within an accept statement for the entry P, the count does not include the calling task). The value of this attribute is of the type universal integer. (See 14.4)

P'DELTA   For a prefix P that denotes a fixed point subtype:
Yields the value of the delta specified in the fixed accuracy definition for the subtype P. The value of this attribute is of the type universal real. (See 12.4)

P'DIGITS   For a prefix P that denotes a floating point subtype:
Yields the number of decimal digits in the decimal mantissa of model numbers of the subtype P. (This attribute yields the number D of section 12.3). The value of this attribute is of the type universal integer.

P'EMAX   For a prefix P that denotes a floating point subtype:
Yields the largest exponent value in the binary canonical form of model numbers of the subtype P. (This attribute yields the product 4*B of section 12.3). The value of this attribute is of the type universal integer.

P'EPSILON   For a prefix P that denotes a floating point subtype:
Yields the absolute value of the difference between the model number 1.0 and the next model number above, for the subtype P. The value of this attribute is of the type universal real. (See 12.3)

P'FIRST   For a prefix P that denotes a scalar type, or a subtype of a scalar type:
Yields the lower bound of P. The value of this attribute has the same type as P. (See 4.8)

P'FIRST   For a prefix P that is appropriate for an array type, or that denotes a constrained array subtype:
Yields the lower bound of the first index range. The value of this attribute has the same type as this lower bound. (See 6.1)

P'FIRST(N)   For a prefix P that is appropriate for an array type, or that denotes a constrained array subtype:
Yields the lower bound of the Nth index range. The value of this attribute has the same type as this lower bound. The argument N must be a static expression of type universal integer. The value of N must be positive (nonzero) and no greater than the dimensionality of the array. (See 6.1)

P'FIRST_BIT   For a prefix P that denotes a component of a record object:
Yields the offset, from the start of the first of the storage units occupied by the component, of the first bit occupied by the component. This offset is measured in bits. The value of this attribute is of the type universal integer. (See 15.4)

P'FORE   For a prefix P that denotes a fixed point subtype:
Yields the minimum number of characters needed for the integer part of the decimal representation of any value of the subtype P, assuming that the representation does not include an exponent, but includes a one character prefix that is either a minus sign or a space. (This minimum number does not include superfluous zeros or underlines; and is at least two.) The value of this attribute is of the type universal integer. (See 15.2)

P'IMAGE   For a prefix P that denotes a discrete type or subtype:

This attribute is a function with a single parameter. The actual parameter X must be a value of the base type of P. The result type is the predefined type STRING. The result is the image of the value of X, that is, a sequence of characters representing the value in display form. The image of an integer value is the corresponding decimal literal; without underlines, leading zeros, exponent, or trailing spaces; but with a one character prefix that is either a minus sign or a space.

The image of an enumeration value is either the corresponding identifier in upper case or the corresponding character literal (including the two apostrophes); neither leading nor trailing spaces are included. The image of a character other than a graphic character is implementation-defined.

P'LARGE   For a prefix P that denotes a real subtype:

The attribute yields the largest positive model number of the subtype P. The value of this attribute is of the type universal real. (See 12.3 and 12.4)

P'LAST   For a prefix P that denotes a scalar type or a subtype of a scalar type:

Yields the upper bound of P. The value of this attribute has the same type as P. (See 4.8)

P'LAST   For a prefix P that is appropriate for an array type, or that denotes a constrained array subtype:

Yields the upper bound of the first index range. The value of this attribute has the same type as this upper bound. (See 6.1)

P'LAST(N)   For a prefix P that is appropriate for an array type, or that denotes a constrained array subtype:

Yields the upper bound of the Nth index range. The value of this attribute has the same type as this upper bound. The argument N must be a static expression of type universal integer. The value of N must be positive (nonzero) and no greater than the dimensionality of the array. (See 6.1)

P'LAST_BIT   For a prefix P that denotes a component of a record object:

Yields the offset, from the start of the first of the storage units occupied by the component, of the last bit occupied by the component. This offset is measured in bits. The value of this attribute is of the type universal integer. (See 15.4)

P'LENGTH   For a prefix P that is appropriate for an array type, or that denotes a constrained array subtype:

Yields the number of values of the first index range (zero for a null range). The value of this attribute is of the type universal integer. (See 6.1)

P'LENGTH(N)   For a prefix P that is appropriate for an array type, or that denotes a constrained array subtype:

Yields the number of values of the Nth index range (zero for a null range). The value of this attribute is of the type universal integer. The argument N must be a static expression of type universal integer. The value of N must be positive (nonzero) and no greater than the dimensionality of the array. (See 6.1)

P'MACHINE_EMAX   For a prefix P that denotes a floating point type or subtype:

Yields the largest value of *exponent* for the machine representation of the base type of P. The value of this attribute is of the type universal integer. (See 15.5)

P'MACHINE_EMIN   For a prefix P that denotes a floating point type or subtype:

Yields the smallest (most negative) value of *exponent* for the machine representation of the base type of P. The value of this attribute is of the type universal integer. (See 15.5)

P'MACHINE_MANTISSA   For a prefix P that denotes a floating point type or subtype:

Yields the number of digits in the *mantissa* for the machine representation of the base type of P (the digits are extended digits in the range 0 to P'MACHINE_RADIX − 1). The value of this attribute is of the type universal integer. (See 15.5)

P'MACHINE_OVERFLOWS   For a prefix P that denotes a real type or subtype:

Yields the value TRUE if every predefined operation on values of the base type of P either provides a correct result or raises the exception NUMERIC_ERROR in overflow situations; yields the value FALSE otherwise. The value of this attribute is of the predefined type BOOLEAN. (See 15.5)

P'MACHINE_RADIX   For a prefix P that denotes a floating point type or subtype:

Yields the value of the *radix* used by the machine representation of the base type of P. The value of this attribute is of the type universal integer. (See 15.5)

P'MACHINE_ROUNDS   For a prefix P that denotes a real type or subtype:

Yields the value TRUE if every predefined arithmetic operation on values of the base type of P either returns an exact result or performs rounding; yields the value FALSE otherwise. The value of this attribute is of the predefined type BOOLEAN. (See 15.5)

P'MANTISSA   For a prefix P that denotes a real subtype:

Yields the number of binary digits in the binary mantissa of model numbers of the subtype P. (This attribute yields the number B of section 12.3 for a floating point type, or of section 12.4 for a fixed point type). The value of this attribute is of the type universal integer.

P'POS   For a prefix P that denotes a discrete type or subtype:

This attribute is a function with a single parameter. The actual parameter X must be a value of the base type of P. The result type is of the type universal integer. The result is the position number of the value of the actual parameter. (See 4.8)

P'POSITION   For a prefix P that denotes a component of a record object:

Yields the offset from the start of the first storage unit occupied by the record, of the first of the storage units occupied by the component. This offset is measured in storage units. The value of this attribute is of the type universal integer. (See 15.5)

P'PRED   For a prefix P that denotes a discrete type or subtype:

This attribute is a function with a single parameter. The actual parameter

X must be a value of the base type of P. The result is of the base type of P. The result is the value whose position number is one less than that of X. The exception CONSTRAINT_ERROR is raised if X equals P'BASE'FIRST. (See 4.8)

P'RANGE   For a prefix P that is appropriate for an array type, or that denotes a contrained array subtype:
Yields the first index range of P, that is, the range P'FIRST . . P'LAST. (See 6.1)

P'RANGE(N)   For a prefix P that is appropriate for an array type, or that denotes a constrained array subtype:
Yields the Nth index range of P, that is, the range P'FIRST(N) . . P'LAST(N). (See 6.1)

P'SAFE_EMAX   For a prefix P that denotes a floating point type or subtype:
Yields the largest exponent value in the binary canonical form of safe numbers of the base type of P. (This attribute yields the number E of section 12.3.) The value of this attribute is of the type universal integer.

P'SAFE_LARGE   For a prefix P that denotes a real type or subtype:
Yields the largest positive safe number of the base type of P. The value of this attribute is of the type universal real. (See 12.3 and 12.4)

P'SAFE_SMALL   For a prefix P that denotes a real type or subtype:
Yields the smallest positive (nonzero) safe number of the base type of P. The value of this attribute is of the type universal real. (See 12.3 and 12.4)

P'SIZE   For a prefix P that denotes an object:
Yields the number of bits allocated to hold the object. The value of this attribute is of the type universal integer. (See 15.4)

P'SIZE   For a prefix P that denotes any type or subtype:
Yields the minimum number of bits that is needed by the implementation to hold any possible object of the type or subtype P. The value of this attribute is of the type universal integer. (See 15.4)

P'SMALL   For a prefix P that denotes a real subtype:
Yields the smallest positive (nonzero) model number of the subtype P. The value of this attribute is of the type universal real. (See 12.3 and 12.4)

P'STORAGE_SIZE   For a prefix P that denotes an access type or subtype:
Yields the total number of storage units reserved for the collection associated with the base type of P. The value of this attribute is of the type universal integer. (See 15.4)

P'STORAGE_SIZE   For a prefix P that denotes a task type or a task object:
Yields the number of storage units reserved for each activation of a task of the type P or for the activation of the task object P. The value of this attribute is of the type universal integer. (See 15.4)

P'SUCC   For a prefix P that denotes a discrete type or subtype:
This attribute is a function with a single parameter. The actual parameter X must be a value of the base type of P. The result type is the base type of P. The result is the value whose position number is one greater than that of X. The exception CONSTRAINT_ERROR is raised if X equals P'BASE'LAST. (See 4.8)

P'TERMINATED   For a prefix P that is appropriate for a task type:
Yields the value TRUE if the task P is terminated; yields the value FALSE otherwise. The value of this attribute is of the predefined type BOOLEAN. (See 14.6)

P'VAL   For a prefix P that denotes a discrete type or subtype;
This attribute is a special function with a single parameter which can be of any integer type. The result type is the base type of P. The result is the value whose position number is the universal integer value corresponding to X. The exception CONSTRAINT_ERROR is raised if the universal integer value corresponding to X is not in the range P'POS(P'BASE'FIRST) .. P'POS(P'BASE'LAST). (See 4.8)

P'VALUE   For a prefix P that denotes a discrete type or subtype:
This attribute is a function with a single parameter. The actual parameter X must be a value of the predefined type STRING. The result type is the base type of P. Any leading and any trailing spaces of the sequence of characters that corresponds to X are ignored.

For an enumeration type, if the sequence of characters has the syntax of an enumeration literal and if this literal exists for the base type of P, the result is the corresponding enumeration value. For an integer type, if the sequence of characters has the syntax of an integer literal, with an optional single leading character that is a plus or minus sign, and if there is a corresponding value in the base type of P, the result is this value. In any other case, the exception CONSTRAINT_ERROR is raised.

P'WIDTH   For a prefix P that denotes a discrete subtype:
Yields the maximum image length over all values of the subtype P (the image is the sequence of characters returned by the attribute IMAGE). The value of this attribute is of the type universal integer. (See 15.2)

A1.3   Predefined pragmas

The following pragmas are predefined in the language.

CONTROLLED   Takes the simple name of an access type as the single argument. This pragma is only allowed immediately within the declarative part or package specification that contains the declaration of the access type; the declaration must occur before the pragma. This pragma is not allowed for a derived type. This pragma specifies that automatic storage reclamation must not be performed for objects designated by values of the access type, except upon leaving the innermost block statement, subprogram body, or task body that encloses the access type declaration, or after leaving the main program (see 11.3).

ELABORATE   Takes one or more simple names denoting library units as arguments. This pragma is only allowed immediately after the context clause of a compilation unit (before the subsequent library unit or secondary unit). Each argument must be the simple name of a library unit mentioned by the context clause. This pragma specifies that the corresponding library unit body must be elaborated before the given compilation unit. If the given compilation unit is a subunit, the library unit body must be elaborated before the body of the ancestor library unit of the subunit (see 16.3).

INLINE   Takes one or more names as arguments; each name is either the name of a subprogram or the name of a generic subprogram. This pragma is only allowed at the place of a declarative item in a declarative part or package specification, or after a library unit in a compilation, but before any subsequent compilation unit. This pragma specifies that the subprogram bodies should be expanded inline at each call whenever possible; in the case of a generic subprogram, the pragma applies to calls of its instantiations (see 15.5).

INTERFACE   Takes a language name and a subprogram name as arguments. This pragma is allowed at the place of a declarative item, and must apply in this case to a subprogram declared by an earlier declarative item of the same declarative part or package specification. This pragma is also allowed for a library unit; in this case the pragma must appear after the subprogram declaration, and before any subsequent compilation unit. This pragma specifies the other language (and thereby the calling conventions) and informs the compiler that an object module will be supplied for the corresponding subprogram (see 15.7).

LIST   Takes one of the identifiers ON or OFF as the single argument. This pragma is allowed anywhere a pragma is allowed. It specifies that listing of the compilation is to be continued or suspended until a LIST pragma with the opposite argument is given within the same compilation. The pragma itself is always listed if the compiler is producing a listing.

MEMORY_SIZE   Takes a numeric literal as the single argument. This pragma is only allowed at the start of a compilation, before the first compilation unit (if any) of the compilation. The effect of this pragma is to use the value of the specified numeric literal for the definition of the named number MEMORY_SIZE (see 15.5).

OPTIMIZE   Takes one of the identifiers TIME or SPACE as the single argument. This pragma is only allowed within a declarative part and it applies to the block or body enclosing the declarative part. It specifies whether time or space is the primary optimization criterion.

PACK   Takes the simple name of a record or array type as the single argument. The allowed positions for this pragma, and the restrictions on the named type, are governed by the same rules as for a representation clause. The pragma specifies that storage minimization should be the main criterion when selecting the representation of the given type (see 15.5).

PAGE   This pragma has no argument, and is allowed anywhere a pragma is allowed. It specifies that the program text which follows the pragma should start on a new page (if the compiler is currently producing a listing).

PRIORITY   Takes a static expression of the predefined integer subtype PRIORITY as the single argument. This pragma is only allowed within the specification of a task unit or immediately within the outermost declarative part of a main program. It specifies the priority of the task (or tasks of the task type) or the priority of the main program (see 14.3).

SHARED Takes the simple name of a variable as the single argument. This pragma is allowed only for a variable declared by an object declaration and whose type is a scalar or access type; the variable declaration and the pragma must both occur (in this order) immediately within the same declarative part or package specification. This pragma specifies that every read or update of the variable is a synchronisation point for that variable. An implementation must restrict the objects for which this pragma is allowed to objects for which each of direct reading and direct updating is implemented as an indivisible operation (see 16.4).

STORAGE_UNIT Takes a numeric literal as the single argument. This pragma is only allowed at the start of a compilation, before the first compilation unit (if any) of the compilation. The effect of this pragma is to use the value of the specified numeric literal for the definition of the named number **STORAGE_UNIT** (see 15.5).

SUPPRESS Takes as arguments the identifier of a check and optionally also the name of either an object, a type or subtype, a subprogram, a task unit, or a generic unit. This pragma is only allowed either immediately within a declarative part or immediately within a package specification. In the latter case, the only allowed form is with a name that denotes an entity (or several overloaded subprograms) declared immediately within the package specification. The permission to omit the given check extends from the place of the pragma to the end of the declarative region associated with the innermost enclosing block statement or program unit. For a pragma given in a package specification, the permission extends to the end of the scope of the named entity.

If the pragma includes a name, the permission to omit the given check is further restricted: it is given only for operations on the named object or on all objects of the base type of a named type or subtype; for calls of a named subprogram; for activations of tasks of the named task type; or for instantiations of the given generic unit (see 15.5).

SYSTEM_NAME Takes an enumeration literal as the single argument. This pragma is only allowed at the start of a compilation, before the first compilation unit (if any) of the compilation. The effect of this pragma is to use the enumeration literal with the specified identifier for the definition of the constant **SYSTEM_NAME**. This pragma is only allowed if the specified identifier corresponds to one of the literals of the type **NAME** declared in the package **SYSTEM** (see 15.5).

Appendix 2 PREDEFINED LANGUAGE ENVIRONMENT

As mentioned earlier, certain entities are predefined through their declaration in a special package STANDARD. It should not be thought that this package necessarily actually exists; it is just that the compiler behaves as if it does. Indeed, as we shall see, some entities notionally declared in STANDARD cannot be truly declared in Ada at all. The general effect of STANDARD is indicated by the outline specification below which is taken from Annex C of the LRM.

The operators that are predefined for the types declared in the package STANDARD are given in comments since they are implicitly declared. Italics are used for identifiers that are not available to users (such as the identifier universal real) and for undefined information (such as implementation defined).

package STANDARD **is**

    type BOOLEAN **is** (FALSE, TRUE);

    – – The predefined relational operators for this type are as follows:

    – – **function** "="   (LEFT, RIGHT: BOOLEAN) **return** BOOLEAN;
    – – **function** "/=" (LEFT, RIGHT: BOOLEAN) **return** BOOLEAN;
    – – **function** "<"   (LEFT, RIGHT: BOOLEAN) **return** BOOLEAN;
    – – **function** "<=" (LEFT, RIGHT: BOOLEAN) **return** BOOLEAN;
    – – **function** ">"   (LEFT, RIGHT: BOOLEAN) **return** BOOLEAN;
    – – **function** ">=" (LEFT, RIGHT: BOOLEAN) **return** BOOLEAN;

    – – The logical operators and the logical negation operator are as
    – – follows:

    function "and" (LEFT, RIGHT: BOOLEAN) **return** BOOLEAN;
    function "or"   (LEFT, RIGHT: BOOLEAN) **return** BOOLEAN;
    function "xor" (LEFT, RIGHT: BOOLEAN) **return** BOOLEAN;
    function "not" (RIGHT: BOOLEAN) **return** BOOLEAN;

    – – The universal type *universal_integer* is predefined

    type INTEGER **is** *implementation_defined*;

    – – The predefined operators for this type are as follows:

    – – **function** "="   (LEFT, RIGHT: INTEGER) **return** BOOLEAN;
    – – **function** "/=" (LEFT, RIGHT: INTEGER) **return** BOOLEAN;
    – – **function** "<"   (LEFT, RIGHT: INTEGER) **return** BOOLEAN;
    – – **function** "<=" (LEFT, RIGHT: INTEGER) **return** BOOLEAN;
    – – **function** ">"   (LEFT, RIGHT: INTEGER) **return** BOOLEAN;
    – – **function** ">=" (LEFT, RIGHT: INTEGER) **return** BOOLEAN;

```
-- function "+"     (RIGHT: INTEGER) return INTEGER;
-- function "-"     (RIGHT: INTEGER) return INTEGER;
-- function "abs"   (RIGHT: INTEGER) return INTEGER;

-- function "+"     (LEFT, RIGHT: INTEGER) return INTEGER;
-- function "-"     (LEFT, RIGHT: INTEGER) return INTEGER;
-- function "*"     (LEFT, RIGHT: INTEGER) return INTEGER;
-- function "/"     (LEFT, RIGHT: INTEGER) return INTEGER;
-- function "rem"   (LEFT, RIGHT: INTEGER) return INTEGER;
-- function "mod"   (LEFT, RIGHT: INTEGER) return INTEGER;
-- function "**"    (LEFT: INTEGER; RIGHT: INTEGER)
                                        return INTEGER;
```

-- An implementation may provide additional predefined integer
-- types. It is recommended that the names of such additional types
-- end with INTEGER as in SHORT_INTEGER or LONG_INTEGER.
-- The specification of each operator for the type *universal_integer*,
-- or for any additional predefined integer type, is obtained by
-- replacing INTEGER by the name of the type in the specification of
-- the corresponding operator of the type INTEGER, except for the
-- right operand of the exponentiating operator.

-- The universal type *universal_real* is predefined.

type FLOAT **is** *implementation_defined*;

-- The predefined operators for this type are as follows:

```
-- function "="     (LEFT, RIGHT: FLOAT) return BOOLEAN;
-- function "/="    (LEFT, RIGHT: FLOAT) return BOOLEAN;
-- function "<"     (LEFT, RIGHT: FLOAT) return BOOLEAN;
-- function "<="    (LEFT, RIGHT: FLOAT) return BOOLEAN;
-- function ">"     (LEFT, RIGHT: FLOAT) return BOOLEAN;
-- function ">="    (LEFT, RIGHT: FLOAT) return BOOLEAN;

-- function "+"     (RIGHT: FLOAT) return FLOAT;
-- function "-"     (RIGHT: FLOAT) return FLOAT;
-- function "abs"   (RIGHT: FLOAT) return FLOAT;

-- function "+"     (LEFT, RIGHT: FLOAT) return FLOAT;
-- function "-"     (LEFT, RIGHT: FLOAT) return FLOAT;
-- function "*"     (LEFT, RIGHT: FLOAT) return FLOAT;
-- function "/"     (LEFT, RIGHT: FLOAT) return FLOAT;
-- function "**"    (LEFT: FLOAT; RIGHT: INTEGER) return FLOAT;
```

-- An implementation may provide additional predefined floating
-- point types. It is recommended that the names of such additional
-- types end with FLOAT as in SHORT_FLOAT or LONG_FLOAT. The
-- specification of each operator for the type *universal_real*, or for
-- any additional predefined floating point type, is obtained by
-- replacing FLOAT by the name of the type in the specification of
-- the corresponding operator of the type FLOAT.

– – In addition the following operators are predefined

– – for universal types:

– – **function** *''*''*(LEFT: *universal_integer*;
          RIGHT: *universal_real*) **return** *universal_real*;

– – **function**''*''*(LEFT: *universal_real*;
          RIGHT: *universal_integer*) **return** *universal_real*;

– – **function** *''/''*(LEFT: *universal_real*;
          RIGHT: *universal_integer*) **return** *universal_real*;

– – The type *universal_fixed* is predefined. The only
– – operators declared for this type are

– – **function** *''*''*(LEFT: *any_fixed_point_type*;
          RIGHT: *any_fixed_point_type*)
          return *universal_fixed*;

– – **function** *''/''*(LEFT: *any_fixed_point_type*;
          RIGHT: *any_fixed_point_type*)
          return *universal_fixed*;

– – The following characters form the standard ASCII character set.
– – Character literals corresponding to control characters are not
– – identifiers; they are indicated in italics in this definition

type CHARACTER **is**

(*nul*,	*soh*,	*stx*,	*etx*,	*eot*,	*enq*,	*ack*,	*bel*,
bs,	*ht*,	*lf*,	*vt*,	*ff*,	*cr*,	*so*,	*si*,
dle,	*dc1*,	*dc2*,	*dc3*,	*dc4*,	*nak*,	*syn*,	*etb*,
can,	*em*,	*sub*,	*esc*,	*fs*,	*gs*,	*rs*,	*us*,
' ',	'!',	' " ',	'#',	'$',	'%',	'&',	' ' ',
'(',	')',	'*',	'+',	',',	'–',	'.',	'/',
'0',	'1',	'2',	'3',	'4',	'5',	'6',	'7',
'8',	'9',	':',	';',	'<',	'=',	'>',	'?',
'@',	'A',	'B',	'C',	'D',	'E',	'F',	'G',
'H',	'I',	'J',	'K',	'L',	'M',	'N',	'O',
'P',	'Q',	'R',	'S',	'T',	'U',	'V',	'W',
'X',	'Y',	'Z',	'[',	'\',	']',	'^',	'_',
'`',	'a',	'b',	'c',	'd',	'e',	'f',	'g',
'h',	'i',	'j',	'k',	'l',	'm',	'n',	'o',
'p',	'q',	'r',	's',	't',	'u',	'v',	'w',
'x',	'y',	'z',	'{',	'|',	'}',	'~',	*del*);

for CHARACTER **use** – – 128 ASCII character set without holes
    (0, 1, 2, 3, 4, 5, . . ., 125, 126, 127);

– – The predefined operators for the type CHARACTER are the same as
– – for any enumeration type.

package ASCII **is**

    – – Control characters:

    NUL: **constant** CHARACTER:=*nul*;
    SOH: **constant** CHARACTER:=*soh*;
    STX: **constant** CHARACTER:=*stx*;
    ETX: **constant** CHARACTER:=*etx*;
    EOT: **constant** CHARACTER:=*eot*;
    ENQ: **constant** CHARACTER:=*enq*;
    ACK: **constant** CHARACTER:=*ack*;
    BEL: **constant** CHARACTER:=*bel*;
    BS: **constant** CHARACTER:=*bs*;
    HT: **constant** CHARACTER:=*ht*;
    LF: **constant** CHARACTER:=*lf*;
    VT: **constant** CHARACTER:=*vt*;
    FF: **constant** CHARACTER:=*ff*;
    CR: **constant** CHARACTER:=*cr*;
    SO: **constant** CHARACTER:=*so*;
    SI: **constant** CHARACTER:=*si*;
    DLE: **constant** CHARACTER:=*dle*;
    DC1: **constant** CHARACTER:=*dc1*;
    DC2: **constant** CHARACTER:=*dc2*;
    DC3: **constant** CHARACTER:=*dc3*;
    DC4: **constant** CHARACTER:=*dc4*;
    NAK: **constant** CHARACTER:=*nak*;
    SYN: **constant** CHARACTER:=*syn*;
    ETB: **constant** CHARACTER:=*etb*;
    CAN: **constant** CHARACTER:=*can*;
    EM: **constant** CHARACTER:=*em*;
    SUB: **constant** CHARACTER:=*sub*;
    ESC: **constant** CHARACTER:=*esc*;
    FS: **constant** CHARACTER:=*fs*;
    GS: **constant** CHARACTER:=*gs*;
    RS: **constant** CHARACTER:=*rs*;
    US: **constant** CHARACTER:=*us*;
    DEL: **constant** CHARACTER:=*del*;

    – – Other characters

    EXCLAM   : **constant** CHARACTER:='!';
    QUOTATION   : **constant** CHARACTER:=' " ';
    SHARP   : **constant** CHARACTER:='#';
    DOLLAR   : **constant** CHARACTER:='$';
    PERCENT   : **constant** CHARACTER:='%';

```
AMPERSAND     : constant CHARACTER:='&';
COLON         : constant CHARACTER:=':';
SEMICOLON     : constant CHARACTER:=';';
QUERY         : constant CHARACTER:='?';
AT_SIGN       : constant CHARACTER:='@';
L_BRACKET     : constant CHARACTER:='[';
BACK_SLASH    : constant CHARACTER:='\';
R_BRACKET     : constant CHARACTER:=']';
CIRCUMFLEX    : constant CHARACTER:='^';
UNDERLINE     : constant CHARACTER:='_';
GRAVE         : constant CHARACTER:='`';
L_BRACE       : constant CHARACTER:='{';
BAR           : constant CHARACTER:='|';
R_BRACE       : constant CHARACTER:='}';
TILDE         : constant CHARACTER:='~';
```

-- Lower case letters
LC_A:**constant** CHARACTER:='a';

    ...

LC_Z:**constant** CHARACTERS:='z';
end ASCII;

-- Predefined subtypes:

subtype NATURAL **is** INTEGER **range** 0 .. INTEGER'LAST;
subtype POSITIVE **is** INTEGER **range** 1 .. INTEGER'LAST;

-- Predefined string type:

type STRING **is array** (POSITIVE **range** <>) **of** CHARACTER;
pragma PACK(STRING);

-- The predefined operators for this type are as follows:

```
-- function "="   (LEFT, RIGHT: STRING) return BOOLEAN;
-- function "/="  (LEFT, RIGHT: STRING) return BOOLEAN;
-- function "<"   (LEFT, RIGHT: STRING) return BOOLEAN;
-- function "<="  (LEFT, RIGHT: STRING) return BOOLEAN;
-- function ">"   (LEFT, RIGHT: STRING) return BOOLEAN;
-- function ">="  (LEFT, RIGHT: STRING) return BOOLEAN;
-- function "&"   (LEFT: STRING; RIGHT: STRING)
                                          return STRING;
-- function "&"   (LEFT: CHARACTER; RIGHT: STRING)
                                          return STRING;
-- function "&"(LEFT: STRING; RIGHT: CHARACTER)
                                          return STRING;
-- function "&"(LEFT: CHARACTER; RIGHT: CHARACTER)
                                          return STRING;
```

type DURATION **is delta** *implementation_defined* **range**
        implementation_defined;

-- The predefined operators for the type DURATION are the same as
-- for any fixed point type.

```
-- The predefined exceptions

CONSTRAINT_ERROR  : exception;
NUMERIC_ERROR     : exception;
PROGRAM_ERROR     : exception;
STORAGE_ERROR     : exception;
TASKING_ERROR     : exception;

end STANDARD;
```

The above specification is not complete. For example although the type **BOOLEAN** can be written showing the literals **FALSE** and **TRUE**, the short circuit control forms cannot be expressed explicitly. Moreover, each further type definition introduces new overloadings of some operators. All types, except limited types, introduce new overloadings of = and /=. All scalar types and discrete one dimensional array types introduce new overloadings of & and those with **BOOLEAN** components also introduce new overloadings of **and**, **or**, **xor** and **not**. Finally, all fixed point types introduce new overloadings of +, −, *, / and **abs**.

In addition there are also certain other predefined library units such as **CALENDAR** (see Section 14.3), **SEQUENTIAL_IO** and **DIRECT_IO** (see Section 15.1), **TEXT_IO** (see Section 15.2), **SYSTEM** (see Section 15.5) and **UNCHECKED_CONVERSION** and **UNCHECKED_DEALLOCATION** (see Section 15.6).

Appendix 3 GLOSSARY

The following glossary is reproduced from Appendix D of the LRM. Italicised terms in the abbreviated descriptions below either have glossary entries themselves or are described in entries for related terms.

Accept statement. See *entry*.

Access type. A value of an access type (an *access value*) is either a null value, or a value that *designates* an *object* created by an *allocator*. The designated object can be read and updated via the access value. The definition of an access type specifies the type of the objects designated by values of the access type. See also *collection*.

Actual parameter. See *parameter*.

Aggregate. The evaluation of an aggregate yields a value of a *composite type*. The value is specified by giving the value of each of the *components*. Either *positional association* or *named association* may be used to indicate which value is associated with which component.

Allocator. The evaluation of an allocator creates an *object* and returns a new *access value* which *designates* the object.

Array type. A value of an array type consists of *components* which are all of the same *subtype* (and hence, of the same type). Each component is uniquely distinguished by an *index* (for a one-dimensional array) or by a sequence of indices (for a multidimensional array). Each index must be a value of a *discrete type* and must lie in the correct index *range*.

Assignment. Assignment is the *operation* that replaces the current value of a *variable* by a new value. An *assignment statement* specifies a variable on the left, and on the right, an *expression* whose value is to be the new value of the variable.

Attribute. The evaluation of an attribute yields a predefined characteristic of a named entity; some attributes are *functions*.

Block statement. A block statement is a single statement that may contain a sequence of statements. It may also include a *declarative part*, and *exception handlers*; their effects are local to the block statement.

Body. A body defines the execution of a *subprogram, package,* or *task*. A *body stub* is a form of body that indicates that this execution is defined in a separately compiled *subunit*.

Collection. A collection is the entire set of *objects* created by evaluation of *allocators* for an *access type*.

Compilation unit. A compilation unit is the *declaration* or the *body* of a *program unit*, presented for compilation as an independent text. It is optionally preceded by a *context clause*, naming other compilation units upon which it depends by means of one or more *with clauses*.

Component. A component is a value that is a part of a larger value, or an *object* that is part of a larger object.

Composite type. A composite type is one whose values have *components*. There are two kinds of composite type: *array types* and *record types*.

Constant. See *object*.

Constraint. A constraint determines a subset of the values of a *type*. A value in that subset *satisfies* the constraint.

Context clause. See *compilation unit*.

Declaration. A declaration associates an identifier (or some other notation) with an entity. This association is in effect within a region of text called the *scope* of the declaration. Within the scope of a declaration, there are places where it is possible to use the identifier to refer to the associated declared entity. At such places the identifier is said to be a *simple name* of the entity; the *name* is said to *denote* the associated entity.

Declarative part. A declarative part is a sequence of *declarations*. It may also contain related information such as *subprogram bodies* and *representation clauses*.

Denote. See *declaration*.

Derived type. A derived type is a *type* whose operations and values are replicas of those of an existing type. The existing type is called the *parent type* of the derived type.

Designate. See *access type, task*.

Direct visibility. See *visibility*.

Discrete type. A discrete type is a *type* which has an ordered set of distinct values. The discrete types are the *enumeration* and *integer types*. Discrete types are used for indexing and iteration, and for choices in case statements and record *variants*.

Discriminant. A discriminant is a distinguished *component* of an *object* or value of a *record type*. The *subtypes* of other components, or even their presence or absence, may depend on the value of the discriminant.

Discriminant constraint. A discriminant constraint on a *record type* or *private type* specifies a value for each *discriminant* of the *type*.

Elaboration. The elaboration of a *declaration* is the process by which the declaration achieves its effect (such as creating an *object*); this process occurs during program execution.

Entry. An entry is used for communication between *tasks*. Externally, an entry is called just as a *subprogram* is called; its internal behavior is specified by one or more *accept statements* specifying the actions to be performed when the entry is called.

Enumeration type. An enumeration type is a *discrete type* whose values are represented by enumeration literals which are given explicitly in the *type declaration*. These enumeration literals are either *identifiers* or *character literals*.

Evaluation. The evaluation of an *expression* is the process by which the value of the expression is computed. This process occurs during program execution.

Exception. An exception is an error situation which may arise during program execution. To *raise* an exception is to abandon normal program execution so as to signal that the error has taken place. An *exception handler* is a portion of program text specifying a response to the exception. Execution of such a program text is called *handling* the exception.

Expanded name. An expanded name *denotes* an entity which is *declared* immediately within some construct. An expanded name has the form of a *selected component*: the *prefix* denotes the construct (a *program unit*; or a *block*, loop, or *accept statement*); the *selector* is the *simple name* of the entity.

Expression. An expression defines the computation of a value.

Fixed point type. See *real type*.

Floating point type. See *real type*.

Formal parameter. See *parameter*.

Function. See *subprogram*.

Generic unit. A generic unit is a template either for a set of *subprograms* or for a set of *packages*. A subprogram or package created using the template is called an *instance* of the generic unit. A *generic instantiation* is the kind of *declaration* that creates an instance. A generic unit is written as a subprogram or package but with the specification prefixed by a *generic formal part* which may declare *generic formal parameters*. A generic formal parameter is either a *type*, a *subprogram*, or an *object*. A generic unit is one of the kinds of *program unit*.

Handler. See *exception*.

Index. See *array type*.

Index constraint. An index constraint for an *array type* specifies the lower and upper bounds for each index *range* of the array type.

Indexed component. An indexed component *denotes* a *component* in an *array*. It is a form of *name* containing *expressions* which specify the values of the *indices* of the array component. An indexed component may also denote an *entry* in a family of entries.

Instance. See *generic unit*.

Integer type. An integer type is a *discrete type* whose values represent all integer numbers within a specific *range*.

Lexical element. A lexical element is an identifier, a *literal*, a delimiter, or a comment.

Limited type. A limited type is a *type* for which neither assignment nor the predefined comparison for equality is implicitly declared. All *task* types are limited. A *private type* can be defined to be limited. An equality operator can be explicitly declared for a limited type.

Literal. A literal represents a value literally, that is, by means of letters and other characters. A literal is either a numeric literal an enumeration literal, a character literal, or a string literal.

Mode. See *parameter*.

Model number. A model number is an exactly representable value of a *real type*. *Operations* of a real type are defined in terms of operations on the model numbers of the type. The properties of the model numbers and of their operations are the minimal properties preserved by all implementations of the real type.

Name. A name is a construct that stands for an entity: it is said that the name *denotes* the entity, and that the entity is the meaning of the name. See also *declaration, prefix*.

Named association. A named association specifies the association of an item with one or more positions in a list, by naming the positions.

Object. An object contains a value. A program creates an object either by *elaborating* an *object declaration* or by *evaluating* an *allocator*. The declaration or allocator specifies a *type* for the object: the object can only contain values of that type.

Operation. An operation is an elementary action associated with one or more *types*. It is either implicitly declared by the *declaration* of the type, or it is a *subprogram* that has a *parameter* or *result* of the type.

Operator. An operator is an operation which has one or two operands. A unary operator is written before an operand; a binary operator is written between two operands. This notation is a special kind of *function call*. An operator can be declared as a function. Many operators are implicitly declared by the *declaration* of a *type* (for example, most type declarations imply the declaration of the equality operator for values of the type).

Overloading. An identifier can have several alternative meanings at a given point in the program text: this property is called *overloading*. For example, an overloaded enumeration literal can be an identifier that appears in the definitions of two or more *enumeration types*. The effective meaning of an overloaded identifier is determined by the context. *Subprograms, aggregates, allocators*, and string *literals* can also be overloaded.

Package. A package specifies a group of logically related entities, such as *types, objects* of those types, and *subprograms* with *parameters* of those types. It is written as a *package declaration* and a *package body*. The package declaration has a *visible part*, containing the *declarations* of all entities that can be explicitly used outside the package. It may also have a *private part* containing structural details that complete the specification of the visible entities, but which are irrelevant to the user of the package. The *package body* contains implementations of *subprograms* (and possibly *tasks* and other *packages*) that have been specified in the package declaration. A package is one of the kinds of *program unit*.

Parameter. A parameter is one of the named entities associated with a *subprogram, entry,* or *generic unit*, and used to communicate with the corresponding subprogram body, *accept statement* or generic body. A *formal parameter* is an identifier used to denote the named entity within the body. An *actual parameter* is the particular entity associated with the corresponding formal parameter by a *subprogram call, entry call,* or *generic instantiation*. The *mode* of a formal parameter specifies whether the associated actual parameter supplies a value for the formal parameter, or the formal supplies a value for the actual parameter, or both. The association of actual parameters with formal parameters can be specified by *named associations,* by *positional associations,* or by a combination of these.

Parent type. See *derived type*.

Positional association. A positional association specifies the association of an item with a position in a list, by using the same position in the text to specify the item.

Pragma. A pragma conveys information to the compiler.

Prefix. A prefix is used as the first part of certain kinds of name. A prefix is either a *function call* or a *name*.

Private part. See *package*.

Private type. A private type is a *type* whose structure and set of values are clearly defined, but not directly available to the user of the type. A private type is known only by its *discriminants* (if any) and by the set of *operations* defined for it. A private type and its applicable operations are defined in the *visible part* of a *package*, or in a *generic formal part*. *Assignment*, equality, and inequality are also defined for private types, unless the private type is *limited*.

Procedure. See *subprogram*.

Program. A program is composed of a number of *compilation units*, one of which is a *subprogram* called the *main program*. Execution of the program consists of execution of the main program, which may invoke subprograms declared in the other compilation units of the program.

Program unit. A program unit is any one of a *generic unit, package, subprogram,* or *task unit*.

Qualified expression. A qualified expression is an *expression* preceded by an indication of its *type* or *subtype*. Such qualification is used when, in its absence, the expression might be ambiguous (for example as a consequence of *overloading*).

Raising an exception. See *exception*.

Range. A range is a contiguous set of values of a *scalar type*. A range is specified by giving the lower and upper bounds for the values. A value in the range is said to *belong* to the range.

Range constraint. A range constraint of a *type* specifies a *range*, and thereby determines the subset of the values of the type that *belong* to the range.

Real type. A real type is a *type* whose values represent approximations to the real numbers. There are two kinds of real type: *fixed point types* are specified by absolute error bound; *floating point types* are specified by a relative error bound expressed as a number of significant decimal digits.

Record type. A value of a record type consists of *components* which are usually of different *types* or *subtypes*. For each component of a record value or record *object*, the definition of the record type specifies an identifier that uniquely determines the component within the record.

Renaming declaration. A renaming declaration declares another *name* for an entity.

Rendezvous. A rendezvous is the interaction that occurs between two parallel *tasks* when one task has called an *entry* of the other task, and a corresponding *accept statement* is being executed by the other task on behalf of the calling task.

Representation clause. A representation clause directs the compiler in the selection of the mapping of a *type*, an *object*, or a *task* onto features of the underlying machine that executes a program. In some cases, representation clauses completely specify the mapping; in other cases, they provide criteria for choosing a mapping.

Satisfy. See *constraint, subtype*.

Scalar type. An *object* or value of a scalar *type* does not have *components*. A scalar type is either a *discrete type* or a *real type*. The values of a scalar type are ordered.

Scope. See *declaration*.

Selected component. A selected component is a *name* consisting of a *prefix* and of an identifier called the *selector*. Selected components are used to denote record components, *entries*, and *objects* designated by access values; they are also used as *expanded names*.

Selector. See *selected component*.

Simple name. See *declaration, name*.

Statement. A statement specifies one or more actions to be performed during the execution of a *program*.

Subcomponent. A subcomponent is either a *component*, or a component of another subcomponent.

Subprogram. A subprogram is either a *procedure* or a *function*. A procedure specifies a sequence of actions and is invoked by a *procedure call* statement. A function specifies a sequence of actions and also returns a value called the *result*, and so a *function call* is an *expression*. A subprogram is written as a *subprogram declaration*, which specifies its *name, formal parameters*, and (for a function) its result; and a *subprogram body* which specifies the sequence of actions. The subprogram call specifies the *actual parameters* that are to be associated with the formal parameters. A subprogram is one of the kinds of *program unit*.

Subtype. A subtype of a *type* characterises a subset of the values of the type. The subset is determined by a *constraint* on the type. Each value in the set of values of a subtype *belongs* to the subtype and *satisfies* the constraint determining the subtype.

Subunit. See *body*.

Task. A task operates in parallel with other parts of the program. It is written as a *task specification* (which specifies the *name* of the task and the names and *formal parameters* of its entries), and a *task body* which defines its execution. A *task unit* is one of the kinds of *program unit*. A *task type* is a *type* that permits the subsequent *declaration* of any number of similar tasks of the type. A value of a task type is said to *designate* a task.

Type. A type characterises both a set of values, and a set of *operations* applicable to those values. A *type definition* is a language construct that defines a type. A particular type is either an *access type*, an *array type*, a *private type*, a *record type*, a *scalar type*, or a *task type*.

Use clause. A use clause achieves *direct visibility* of *declarations* that appear in the *visible parts* of named *packages*.

Variable. See *object*.

Variant part. A variant part of a *record* specifies alternative record *components*, depending on a *discriminant* of the record. Each value of the discriminant establishes a particular alternative of the variant part.

Visibility. At a given point in a program text, the *declaration* of an entity with a certain identifier is said to be *visible* if the entity is an acceptable meaning for an occurrence at that point of the identifier. The declaration is *visible* by *selection* at the place of the *selector* in a *selected component* or at the place of the name in a *named association*. Otherwise, the declaration is *directly visible*, that is, if the identifier alone has that meaning.

Visible part. See *package*.

With clause. See *compilation unit*.

Appendix 4 SYNTAX

The following syntax rules are taken from Appendix E of the LRM. The rules have been rearranged to correspond to the order of introduction of the topics in this book but individual rules have not been changed.

It should be noted that the rules for the construction of lexical elements, which are under the subheading of Chapter 3, have a slightly different status to the other rules since spaces and newlines may be freely inserted between lexical elements but not within lexical elements.

The rules have been sequentially numbered for ease of reference; an index to them will be found in Section A4.2.

A4.1 Syntax rules

Chapter 2

  1 pragma::= **pragma** identifier [(argument_association
                                           {, argument_association})];

  2 argument_association ::= [*argument_*identifier =>] name
                        | [*argument_*identifier =>] expression

Chapter 3

  3 graphic_character ::= basic_graphic_character I lower_case_letter
                            I other_special_character

  4 basic_graphic_character ::= upper_case_letter I digit
                               I special_character I space_character

  5 basic_character ::= basic_graphic_character I format_ effector

  6 identifier ::= letter {[underline] letter_or_digit}

  7 letter_or_digit ::= letter I digit

  8 letter ::= upper_case_letter I lower_case_letter

  9 numeric_literal ::= decimal_literal I based_literal

 10 decimal_literal ::= integer [. integer] [exponent]

 11 integer ::= digit{[underline] digit}

 12 exponent ::= E [+] integer I E − integer

 13 based_literal ::= base # based_integer [. based_integer] # [exponent]

 14 base ::= integer

15   based_integer ::= extended_digit {[underline] extended_digit}

16   extended_digit ::= digit | letter

17   character_literal ::= 'graphic_character'

18   string_literal ::= "{graphic_character}"

Chapter 4

19   basic_declaration ::=
         object_declaration | number_declaration
      | type_declaration | subtype_declaration
      | subprogram_declaration | package_declaration
      | task_declaration | generic_declaration
      | exception_declaration | generic_instantiation
      | renaming_declaration | deferred_constant_declaration

20   object_declaration ::=
      identifier_list: [**constant**] subtype_indication [:= expression];
    | identifier_list: [**constant**] constrained_array_definition
                                 [:= expression];

21   number_declaration ::=
      identifier_list: **constant** := *universal_static*_expression;

22   identifier_list ::= identifier {, identifier}

23   assignment_statement ::= *variable*_name:=expression;

24   block_statement ::= [*block*_simple_name:]
                  [**declare**
                     declarative_part]
                begin
                     sequence_of_statements
                [**exception**
                     exception_handler
                     {exception_handler}
                end [*block*_simple_name];

25   type_declaration ::= full_type_declaration | incomplete_type_declaration
                      | private_type_declaration

26   full_type_declaration ::=
      type identifier [discriminant_part] **is** type_definition;

27   type_definition ::=
      enumeration_type_definition | integer_type_definition
      | real_type_definition | array_type_definition
      | record_type_definition | access_type_definition
      | derived_type_definition

28   subtype_declaration ::= **subtype** identifier **is** subtype_indication;

29   subtype_indication ::= type_mark [constraint]

30   type_ mark ::= *type*_name | *subtype*_name

31 constraint ::= range_constraint I floating_point_constraint
                   I fixed_point_constraint I index_constraint
                   I discriminant_constraint

32 range_constraint ::= **range** range

33 range ::= *range*_attribute I simple_expression . . simple_expression

34 enumeration_type_definition ::=
        (enumeration_literal_specification
                                {, enumeration_literal_specification})

35 enumeration_literal_specification ::= enumeration_literal

36 enumeration_literal ::= identifier I character_literal

37 name ::= simple_name I character_literal I operator_symbol
                 I indexed_component I slice I selected_component I attribute

38 simple_name ::= identifier

39 prefix ::= name I function_call

40 attribute ::= prefix ' attribute_designator

41 attribute_designator ::= simple_name [(*universal_static*_expression)]

42 expression ::= relation { **and** relation } I relation { **and then** relation }
                    I relation { **or** relation } I relation { **or else** relation }
                    I relation {**xor** relation }

43 relation ::= simple_expression [relational_operator simple_expression]
                  I simple_expression [**not**] **in** range
                  I simple_expression [**not**] **in** type_mark

44 simple_expression ::=
        [unary_adding_operator] term { binary_adding_operator term }

45 term ::= factor {multiplying_operator factor}

46 factor ::= primary [** primary] I **abs** primary I **not** primary

47 primary ::= numeric_literal I **null** I aggregate I string_literal I name
                 I allocator I function_call I type_conversion
                 I qualified_expression I (expression)

48 logical_operator ::= **and** I **or** I **xor**

49 relational_operator ::= = I /= I < I <= I > I >=

50 binary_adding_operator ::= + I − I &

51 unary_adding_operator ::= + I −

52 multiplying_operator ::= * I / I **mod** I **rem**

53 highest_precedence_operator ::= ** I **abs** I **not**

54 type_conversion ::= type_mark (expression)

55 qualified_expression ::= type_mark (expression) I type_mark ' aggregate

Chapter 5

56   sequence_of_statements ::= statement {statement}

57   statement ::= {label} simple_statement I {label} compound_statement

58   simple_statement ::= null_statement   I assignment_statement
                          I procedure_call_statement I exit_statement
                          I return_statement   I goto_statement
                          I entry_call_statement   I delay_statement
                          I abort_statement   I raise_statement
                          I code_statement

59   compound_statement ::= if_statement   I case_statement
                             I loop_statement   I block_statement
                             I accept_statement   I select_statement

60   label ::= <<*label*_simple_name>>

61   null_statement ::= **null;**

62   if_statement ::= **if** condition **then**
                          sequence_of_statements
                     { **elsif** condition **then**
                          sequence_of_statements}
                     [**else**
                          sequence_of_statements]
                       end if;

63   condition ::= *boolean*_expression

64   case_statement ::= **case** expression **is**
                          case_statement_alternative
                          {case_statement_alternative}
                        end case;

65   case_statement_alternative ::=
         when choice { I choice } => sequence_of_statements

66   choice ::= simple_expression I discrete_range I **others**
                I *component*_simple_name

67   discrete_range ::= *discrete*_subtype_indication I range

68   loop_statement ::= [*loop*_simple_name:]
                        [iteration_scheme] **loop**
                          sequence_of_statements
                        end loop [*loop*_simple_name];

69   iteration_scheme ::= **while** condition I **for** loop_parameter_specification

70   loop_parameter_specification ::= identifier **in** [**reverse**] discrete_range

71   exit_statement ::= **exit** [*loop*_name] [**when** condition];

72   goto_statement ::= **goto** *label*_name;

Chapter 6

73   array_type_definition ::=
            unconstrained_array_definition | constrained_array_definition

74   unconstrained_array_definition ::=
            array (index_subtype_definition {, index_subtype_definition}) **of**
            *component*_subtype_indication

75   constrained_array_definition ::=
            array index_constraint **of** *component*_subtype_indication

76   index_subtype_definition ::= type_mark **range** <>

77   index_constraint ::= (discrete_range { , discrete_range})

78   indexed_component ::= prefix (expression { , expression})

79   slice ::= prefix (discrete_range)

80   aggregate ::= (component_association {, component_association})

81   component_association ::= [choice { | choice } =>] expression

82   record_type_ definition ::= **record**
                                    component_list
                                end record

83   component_list ::= component_declaration {component_declaration}
                        | { component_declaration } variant_part
                        | **null;**

84   component_declaration ::=

            identifier_list : component_subtype_definition [:= expression];

85   component_subtype_definition ::= subtype_indication

86   selected_component ::= prefix . selector

87   selector ::= simple_name | character_literal | operator_symbol | **all**

Chapter 7

88   subprogram_declaration ::= subprogram_specification;

89   subprogram_specification ::=
            procedure identifier [formal_part]
            | **function** designator [formal_part] **return** type_mark

90   designator ::= identifier | operator_symbol

91   operator_symbol ::= string_literal

92   formal_part ::= (parameter_specification {; parameter_specification})

93   parameter_specification ::=
                        identifier_list : mode type_mark [:= expression]

94   mode ::= [**in**] | **in out** | **out**

95   subprogram_body ::= subprogram_specification **is**
                                  [declarative_part]
                                  begin
                                      sequence_of_statements
                                  [**exception**
                                      exception_handler
                                      {exception_handler}]
                                  end [designator];

96   procedure_call_statement ::= *procedure*_name [actual_parameter_part];

97   function_call ::= *function*_name [actual_parameter_part]

98   actual_parameter_part ::=
                                  (parameter_association {, parameter_association})

99   parameter_association ::= [formal_parameter =>] actual_parameter

100 formal_parameter ::= *parameter*_simple_name

101 actual_parameter ::=
                                  expression I *variable*_name I type_mark (*variable*_name)

102 return_statement ::= **return** [expression];

Chapter 8

103 package_declaration ::= package_specification;

104 package_specification ::= **package** identifier **is**
                                      { basic_declarative_item}
                                  [**private**
                                      { basic_declarative_item}]
                                  end [*package*_simple_name]

105 package_body ::= **package body** *package*_simple_name **is**
                                  [declarative_part]
                                  [**begin**
                                      sequence_of_statements
                                  [**exception**
                                      exception_handler
                                      {exception_handler}]]
                                  end [*package*_simple_name];

106 declarative_part ::=
                      {basic_declarative_item}{later_declarative_item}

107 basic_declarative_item ::= basic_declaration I representation_clause
                                  I use_clause

108 later_declarative_item ::= body
                                  I subprogram_declaration I package_declaration
                                  I task_declaration   I generic_declaration
                                  I use_clause   I generic_instantiation

109 body ::= proper_body I body_stub

110 proper_body ::= subprogram_body I package_body I task_body

111 use_clause ::= **use** *package*_name {, *package*_name};

112   compilation ::= {compilation_unit}

113   compilation_unit ::= context_clause library_unit
                            | context_clause secondary_unit

114   library_unit ::= subprogram_declaration | package_declaration
                        | generic_declaration | generic_instantiation
                        | subprogram_body

115   secondary_unit ::= library_unit_body | subunit

116   library_unit_body ::= subprogram_body | package_body

117   context_clause ::= { with_clause {use_clause}}

118   with_clause ::= **with** *unit*_simple_name {, *unit*_simple_name};

119   body_stub ::= subprogram_specification **is separate;**
                    | **package body** *package*_simple_name **is separate;**
                    | **task body** *task*_simple_name **is separate;**

120   subunit ::= **separate** (*parent_unit*_name) proper_body

121   renaming_declaration ::=
            identifier : type_mark **renames** *object*_name;
            | identifier : **exception renames** *exception*_name;
            | **package** identifier **renames** *package*_name;
            | subprogram_specification **renames** *subprogram_or_entry*_name;

Chapter 9
122   private_type_declaration ::=
            type identifier [discriminant_part] **is [limited] private;**

123   deferred_constant_declaration ::=
            identifier_list : **constant** type_mark;

Chapter 10
124   exception_handler ::=
            when exception_choice { | exception_choice } =>
                sequence_of_statements

125   exception_choice ::= *exception*_name | **others**

126   exception_declaration ::= identifier_list : **exception**;

127   raise_statement ::= **raise** [*exception*_name];

Chapter 11
128   discriminant_part ::=
            (discriminant_specification {; discriminant_specification})

129   discriminant_specification ::=
            identifier_list : type_mark [:= expression]

130   discriminant_constraint ::=
            (discriminant_association {, discriminant_association})

131   discriminant_association ::=
            [*discriminant*_simple_name { | *discriminant*_simple_name } =>]
                                                              expression

132   variant_part ::= **case** *discriminant*_simple_name **is**
                        variant
                        {variant}
                    end case;

133   variant ::= **when** choice { | choice } => component_list

134   access_type_definition ::= **access** subtype_indication

135   incomplete_type_declaration ::= **type** identifier [discriminant_part];

136   allocator ::= **new** subtype_indication I **new** qualified_expression

137   derived_type_definition ::= **new** subtype_indication

Chapter 12
138   integer_type_definition ::= range_constraint

139   real_type_definition ::=
            floating_point_constraint I fixed_point_constraint

140   floating_point_constraint ::=
            floating_accuracy_definition [range_constraint]

141   floating_accuracy_definition ::= **digits** *static*_simple_expression

142   fixed_point_constraint ::= fixed_accuracy_definition [range_constraint]

143   fixed_accuracy_definition ::= **delta** *static*_simple_expression

Chapter 13
144   generic_declaration ::= generic_specification;

145   generic_specification ::= generic_formal_part subprogram_specification
                            I generic_formal_part package_specification

146   generic_formal_part ::= **generic** {generic_parameter_declaration}

147   generic_ parameter_declaration ::=
            identifier_list : [**in** [**out**]] type_mark [:= expression];
            I **type** identifier **is** generic_type_definition;
            I private_type_declaration
            I **with** subprogram_specification [**is** name];
            I **with** subprogram_specification [**is** <>];

148   generic_type_definition ::=
            (<>) I **range** <> I **digits** <> I **delta** <>
            I array_type_definition I access_type_definition

149 generic_instantiation ::=
     package identifier **is**
        new *generic_package*_name [generic_actual_part];
     I **procedure** identifier **is**
        new *generic_procedure*_name [generic_actual_part];
     I **function** designator **is**
        new *generic_function*_name [generic_actual_part];

150 generic_actual_part ::= (generic_association {, generic_association})

151 generic_association ::=
     [generic_formal_parameter =>] generic_actual_parameter

152 generic_formal_parameter ::= *parameter*_simple_name I operator_symbol

153 generic_actual_parameter ::= expression I *variable*_name
        I *subprogram*_name I *entry*_name I type_mark

Chapter 14

154 task_declaration ::= task_specification;

155 task_specification ::= **task** [**type**] identifier [**is**
                    {entry_declaration}
                    {representation_clause}
                 end [*task*_simple_name]]

156 task_body ::= **task body** *task*_simple_name **is**
                 [declarative_part]
              begin
                 sequence_of_statements
              [**exception**
                 exception_handler
                 {exception_handler}]
              end [*task*_simple_name];

157 entry_declaration ::=
     entry identifier [(discrete_range)] [formal_part];

158 entry_call_statement ::= *entry*_name [actual_parameter_part];

159 accept_statement ::=
     accept *entry*_simple_name [(entry_index)] [formal_part] **do**
        sequence_of_statements
     end [*entry*_simple_name]];

160 entry_index ::= expression

161 delay_statement ::= **delay** simple_expression;

162 select_statement ::= selective_wait
        I conditional_entry_call I timed_entry_call

163 selective_wait ::= **select**
                    select_alternative
                 { **or**
                    select_alternative}
                 [**else**

          sequence_of_statements]
       end select;

164   select_alternative ::= [**when** condition =>]
                 selective_wait_alternative

165   selective_wait_alternative ::= accept_alternative
     | delay_alternative | terminate_alternative

166   accept_alternative ::= accept_statement [sequence_of_statements]

167   delay_alternative ::= delay_statement [sequence_of_statements]

168   terminate_alternative ::= **terminate**;

169   conditional_entry_call ::= **select**
                  entry_call_statement
                  [sequence_of_statements]
           else
                  sequence_of_statements
           end select;

170   timed_entry_call ::= **select**
                  entry_call_statement
                  [sequence_of_statements]
         or
                  delay_alternative
         end select;

171   abort_statement ::= **abort** *task*_name {, *task*_name};

Chapter 15

172   representation_clause ::= type_representation_clause | address_clause

173   type_representation_clause ::= length_clause
     | enumeration_representation_clause | record_representation_clause

174   length_clause ::= **for** attribute **use** simple_expression;

175   enumeration_representation_clause ::=
       for *type*_simple_name **use** aggregate;

176   record_representation_clause ::= **for** *type*_simple_name **use**
                       record [alignment_clause]
                         { component_clause}
                   end record;

177   alignment_clause ::= **at mod** *static*_simple_expression;

178   component_clause ::=
     *component*_name **at** *static*_simple_expression **range** *static*_range;

179   address_clause ::= **for** simple_name **use at** simple_expression;

180   code_statement ::= type_mark ' *record*_aggregate;

A4.2 Syntax index

This index lists the syntactic categories in alphabetical order and gives the number of their definition in the previous section.

Category	Definition number
decimal_literal	10
declarative_part	106
deferred_constant_declaration	123
delay_alternative	167
delay_statement	161
derived_type_definition	137
designator	90
discrete_range	67
discriminant_association	131
discriminant_constraint	130
discriminant_part	128
discriminant_specification	129
entry_call_statement	158
entry_declaration	157
entry_index	160
enumeration_literal	36
enumeration_literal_specification	35
enumeration_type_definition	34
enumeration_representation_clause	175
exception_choice	125
exception_declaration	126
exception_handler	124
exit_statement	71
exponent	12
expression	42
extended_digit	16
factor	46
fixed_accuracy_definition	143
fixed_point_constraint	142
floating_accuracy_definition	141
floating_point_constraint	140
formal_parameter	100
formal_part	92
full_type_declaration	26
function_call	97
generic_actual_parameter	153
generic_actual_part	150
generic_association	151
generic_declaration	144
generic_formal_parameter	152
generic_formal_part	146
generic_instantiation	149
generic_parameter_declaration	147
generic_specification	145
generic_type_definition	148
goto_statement	72
graphic_character	3
highest_precedence_operator	53
identifier	6
identifier_list	22

Category	Definition number
select_alternative	164
select_statement	162
selected_component	86
selective_wait	163
selective_wait_alternative	165
selector	87
sequence_of_statements	56
simple_expression	44
simple_name	38
simple_statement	58
slice	79
statement	57
string_literal	18
subprogram_body	95
subprogram_declaration	88
subprogram_specification	89
subtype_declaration	28
subtype_indication	29
subunit	120
task_body	156
task_declaration	154
task_specification	155
term	45
terminate_alternative	168
timed_entry_call	170
type_conversion	54
type_declaration	25
type_definition	27
type_mark	30
type_representation_clause	173
unary_adding_operator	51
unconstrained_array_definition	74
use_clause	111
variant	133
variant_part	132
with_clause	118

ANSWERS TO EXERCISES

Specimen answers are given to all the exercises. In some cases they do not necessarily represent the best technique for solving a problem but merely one which uses the material introduced at that point in the discussion.

Answers 2

Exercise 2.2

1
```
package SIMPLE_MATHS is
     function SQRT(F: FLOAT) return FLOAT;
     function LOG(F: FLOAT) return FLOAT;
     function EXP(F: FLOAT) return FLOAT;
     function SIN(F: FLOAT) return FLOAT;
     function COS(F: FLOAT) return FLOAT;
end SIMPLE_MATHS;
```

The first few lines of our program PRINT_ROOTS could now become

```
with SIMPLE_MATHS, SIMPLE_IO;
procedure PRINT_ROOTS is
     use SIMPLE_MATHS, SIMPLE_IO;
     . . .
```

Answers 3

Exercise 3.3

1 The following are not legal identifiers
   b) contains **&**
   c) contains hyphens not underlines
   e) adjacent underlines
   f) does not start with a letter
   g) trailing underline
   h) this is two legal identifiers
   i) this is legal – but it is a reserved word

Exercise 3.4

1 a) legal – real
   b) illegal – no digit before point
   c) legal – integer
   d) illegal – integer with negative exponent
   e) illegal – closing **#** missing
   f) legal – real
   g) illegal – **C** not a digit of base 12
   h) illegal – no number before exponent
   i) legal – integer – case of letter immaterial
   j) legal – integer
   k) illegal – underline at start of exponent
   l) illegal – integer with negative exponent

2 a) $224 = 14 \times 16$
   b) $6144 = 3 \times 2^{11}$
   c) 4095.0
   d) 4095.0

3 a) 32 ways

```
41, 2#101001#, 3#1112#, . . .
     10#41#, . . . 16#29#
41E0, 2#101001#E0, . . . 16#29#E0
```

b) **40** ways. As for example (a) plus, since 150 is not prime but $2 \times 3 \times 5^2 = 150$ also

```
2#1001011#E1
3#1212#E1
5#110#E1
5#11#E2
6#41#E1
10#15#E1
15#A#E1
```

and of course

```
15E1
```

Exercise 3.5

1 a) 7   c) 1
  b) 1   d)12

2 a) This has 3 units
    the identifier   delay
    the literal   2.0
    the single symbol   ;

  b) This has 4 units
    the identifier   delay2
    the single symbol   .
    the literal   0
    the single symbol   ;

Case (a) is a legal delay statement, (b) is just a mess.

Answers 4

Exercise 4.1

1 R: REAL:=1.0;

2 ZERO: **constant** REAL:=0.0;
  ONE: **constant** REAL:=1.0;

  but better to write number declarations

  ZERO: **constant**:=0.0;
  ONE: **constant**:=1.0;

3 a) **var** is illegal – this is Ada not Pascal
  b) terminating semicolon is missing
  c) a constant declaration must have an initial value
  d) no multiple assignment – this is Ada not Algol
  e) nothing – assuming M and N are of integer type
  f) 2PI is not a legal identifier

Exercise 4.2

1 There are four errors
  1   semicolon missing after declaration of J, K
  2   K used before a value has been assigned to it
  3   = instead of := in declaration of P
  4   Q not declared and initialised

Exercise 4.5

1 a) -105 e) -3
  b) -3 f) illegal
  c) 0   g) -1
  d) -3 h) 2

2 All variables are real.
   a) B**2 − 4.0*A*C
   b) (4.0/3.0)*PI*R**3   − − brackets not necessary
   c) (P*PI*A**4)/(8.0*L*ETA)   − − brackets are necessary

Exercise 4.6
1 a) SAT   c) 2
    b) SAT

2 a) **type** RAINBOW **is** (RED, ORANGE, YELLOW, GREEN, BLUE, INDIGO, VIOLET);
    b) **type** FRUIT **is** (APPLE, BANANA, ORANGE, PEAR);

3 GROOM'VAL ((N−1) **mod** 8)

   or perhaps better

   GROOM'VAL((N−1) **mod** (GROOM'POS(GROOM'LAST) +1))

4 D:=DAY'VAL((DAY'POS(D)+ N − 1) **mod** 7);

5 If X and Y are both overloaded literals then X < Y will be ambiguous. We would have to use qualification such as T'(X) < T'(Y).

Exercise 4.7
1 T: **constant** BOOLEAN:=TRUE;
   F: **constant** BOOLEAN:=FALSE;

2 The values are TRUE or FALSE, not T or F which are the names of constants.

   a) FALSE   d) TRUE
   b) TRUE   e) FALSE
   c) TRUE

3 The expression is always TRUE. The predefined operators **xor** and /= operating on Boolean values are the same.

Exercise 4.9
1 All variables are real except for N in example (c) which is integer.

   a) 2.0*PI*SQRT(L/G)
   b) M_0/SQRT(1.0 − (V/C)**2)
   c) SQRT(2.0*PI*REAL(N))*(REAL(N)/E)**N

2   SQRT(2.0*PI*X)*EXP(X*LN(X)−X)

Answers 5

Exercise 5.1
1 **declare**
       END_OF_MONTH: INTEGER;
   begin
       if MONTH = SEP **or** MONTH = APR **or** MONTH = JUN **or** MONTH = NOV **then**
         END_OF_MONTH:=30;
       elsif MONTH = FEB **then**
         if YEAR **mod** 4 = 0 **then**
           END_OF_MONTH:=29;
         else
           END_OF_MONTH:=28;
         end if;

```
        else
            END_OF_MONTH:=31;
        end if;
        if DAY /= END_OF_MONTH then
            DAY:=DAY+1;
        else
            DAY:=1;
            if MONTH /= DEC then
                MONTH:=MONTH_NAME'SUCC(MONTH);
            else
                MONTH:=JAN;
                YEAR:=YEAR+1;
            end if;
        end if;
    end;
```

If today is 31 DEC 2099 then CONSTRAINT_ERROR will be raised on attempting to assign 2100 to YEAR. Note that the range 1901 . . 2099 simplifies the leap year calculation.

2   if X < Y then

```
        declare
            T: REAL:=X;
        begin
            X:=Y;      Y:=T;
        end;
    end if;
```

Exercise 5.2

1   declare

```
        END_OF_MONTH: INTEGER;
    begin
        case MONTH is
            when SEP | APR | JUN | NOV =>
                END_OF_MONTH:=30;
            when FEB =>
                if YEAR mod 4 = 0 then
                    END_OF_MONTH:=29;
                else
                    END_OF_MONTH:=28;
                end if;
            when others =>
                END_OF_MONTH:=31;
        end case;
        -- then as before
        . . .
    end;
```

2   subtype WINTER is MONTH_NAME range JAN . . MAR;
    subtype SPRING is MONTH_NAME range APR . . JUN;
    subtype SUMMER is MONTH_NAME range JUL . . SEP;
    subtype AUTUMN is MONTH_NAME range OCT . . DEC;
    . . .

```
    case M is
        when WINTER => DIG;
        when SPRING => SOW;
        when SUMMER => TEND;
        when AUTUMN => HARVEST;
    end case;
```

Note that if we wished to consider winter as December to February then we could not declare a suitable subtype.

```
3  case D is
       when 1 .. 10 => GORGE;
       when 11 .. 20 => SUBSIST;
       when others => STARVE;
   end case;
```

We cannot write 21 .. END_OF_MONTH because it is not a static range. In fact **others** covers all values of type INTEGER because although D is constrained, nevertheless the constraints are not static.

Exercise 5.3

```
1  declare
       SUM: INTEGER:=0;
       I: INTEGER;
   begin
       loop
           GET(I);
           exit when I<0;
           SUM:=SUM+I;
       end loop;
   end;
```

```
2  declare
       COPY: INTEGER:=N;
       COUNT: INTEGER:=0;
   begin
       while COPY mod 2 = 0 loop
           COPY:=COPY/2;
           COUNT:=COUNT+1;
       end loop;
       ...
   end;
```

```
3  declare
       G: REAL:=−LN(REAL(N));
   begin
       for P in 1 .. N loop
           G:=G+1.0/REAL(P);
       end loop;
       ...
   end;
```

Exercise 5.4

```
1  for I in 1 .. N loop
       for J in 1 .. M loop
           if condition_O_K then
               I_VALUE:=I;
               J_VALUE:=J;
               goto SEARCH;
           end if;
       end loop;
   end loop;
```

```
   <<SEARCH>>
```

This is not such a good solution because we have no guarantee that there may not be other places in the program from where a goto statement leads to the label.

Answers 6

Exercise 6.1

1 **declare**
```
    F: array (0 .. N) of INTEGER;
begin
    F(0):=0; F(1):=1;
    for I in 2 .. F'LAST loop
        F(I):=F(I−1)+F(I−2);
    end loop;
    . . .
end;
```

2 **declare**
```
    MAXI: INTEGER:=A'FIRST(1);
    MAXJ: INTEGER:=A'FIRST(2);
    MAX : REAL:=A(MAXI, MAXJ);
begin
    for I in A'RANGE(1) loop
        for J in A'RANGE(2) loop
            if A(I, J) > MAX then
                MAX:=A(I, J);
                MAXI:=I;
                MAXJ:=J;
            end if;
        end loop;
    end loop;
    − − MAXI, MAXJ now contain the result
end;
```

3 **declare**
```
    DAYS_IN_MONTH: array (MONTH_NAME) of INTEGER
        :=(31, 28, 31, 30, 31, 30, 31, 31, 30, 31, 30, 31 );
    END_OF_MONTH: INTEGER;
begin
    if YEAR mod 4 = 0 then
        DAYS_IN_MONTH(FEB):=29;
    end if;
    END_OF_MONTH:=DAYS_IN_MONTH(MONTH);

    − − then as Exercise 5.1 (1)

end;
```

4 YESTERDAY: **constant array** (DAY) **of** DAY
```
        :=(SUN, MON, TUE, WED, THU, FRI, SAT);
```

5 BOR: **constant array** (BOOLEAN, BOOLEAN) **of** BOOLEAN
```
        :=((FALSE, TRUE), (TRUE, TRUE));
```

6 UNIT: **constant array** (1 .. 3, 1 .. 3) **of** REAL
```
        :=((1.0, 0.0, 0.0),
           (0.0, 1.0, 0.0),
           (0.0, 0.0, 1.0));
```

Exercise 6.2

1 DAYS_IN_MONTH: **array** (MONTH_NAME) **of** INTEGER
```
        :=MONTH_NAME'(SEP|APR|JUN|NOV => 30,
                      FEB => 28, others => 31);
```

2 ZERO: **constant** MATRIX:=(1 .. N => (1 .. N => 0.0));

3 This cannot be done with the material at our disposal at the moment. See Exercise 7.1(**6**).

4 **type** BBB **is array** (BOOLEAN, BOOLEAN) **of** BOOLEAN;

Exercise 6.3
1 ROMAN_TO_INTEGER: **constant array** (ROMAN_DIGIT) **of** INTEGER
                    :=(1, 5, 10, 50, 100, 500, 1000);

2 **declare**
            V: INTEGER:=0;
        begin
            for I **in** R'RANGE **loop**
                if I /= R'LAST **and then**
                    ROMAN_TO_INTEGER(R(I))<ROMAN_TO_INTEGER(R(I+1)) **then**
                    V:=V−ROMAN_TO_INTEGER(R(I));
                else
                    V:=V+ROMAN_TO_INTEGER(R(I));
                end if;
            end loop;
            . . .
        end;

Note the use of **and then** to avoid attempting to access R(I+1) when I = R'LAST.

Exercise 6.4
1 WHITE, BLUE, YELLOW, GREEN, RED, PURPLE, ORANGE, BLACK

2 a) BLACK   c) RED
       b) GREEN

3 **not** (TRUE **xor** TRUE)=TRUE
       not (TRUE **xor** FALSE)=FALSE

       the result follows

4 An aggregate of length one must be named.

5 **if** R'LAST >= 2 **and then** R(R'LAST−1 . . R'LAST) ="IV" **then**
            R(R'LAST−1 . . R'LAST):="VI";
        end if;

6 a) 1   b) 5
       We note therefore that & like **and**, **or** and **xor** is not strictly commutative.

Exercise 6.5
1 **declare**
            DAYS_IN_MONTH: **array** (MONTH_NAME) **of** INTEGER
                :=MONTH_NAME'(SEP|APR|JUN|NOV =>30, FEB => 28, **others** => 31);
            END_OF_MONTH: INTEGER;

        begin
            if D.YEAR **mod** 4 = 0 **then**
                DAYS_IN_MONTH(FEB):=29;
            end if;
            END_OF_MONTH:=DAYS_IN_MONTH(D.MONTH);
            if D.DAY /= END_OF_MONTH **then**
                D.DAY:=D.DAY+1;

```
        else
            D.DAY:=1;
            if D.MONTH /= DEC then
                D.MONTH:=MONTH_NAME'SUCC(D.MONTH);
            else
                D.MONTH:=JAN;
                D.YEAR:=D.YEAR+1;
            end if;
        end if;
    end;
```

2   C1, C2, C3: COMPLEX;

   a)   C3:=(C1.RL+C2.RL, C1.IM+C2.IM);
   b)   C3:=(C1.RL*C2.RL−C1.IM*C2.IM, C1.RL*C2.IM+C1.IM*C2.RL);

3   **declare**
```
        INDEX: INTEGER;
    begin
        for I in PEOPLE'RANGE loop
            if PEOPLE(I).BIRTH.YEAR >= 1950 then
                INDEX:=I;
                exit;
            end if;
        end loop;
        -- we assume that there is such a person
    end;
```

Answers 7

Exercise 7.1

1   **function** EVEN (X: INTEGER) **return** BOOLEAN **is**
```
    begin
        return X mod 2 = 0;
    end EVEN;
```

2   **function** FACTORIAL(N: NATURAL) **return** POSITIVE **is**
```
    begin
        if N=0 then
            return 1;
        else
            return N*FACTORIAL(N−1);
        end if;
    end FACTORIAL;
```

3   **function** OUTER(A, B: VECTOR) **return** MATRIX **is**
```
        C: MATRIX(A'RANGE, B'RANGE);
    begin
        for I in A'RANGE loop
            for J in B'RANGE loop
                C(I, J):=A(I)*B(J);
            end loop;
        end loop;
        return C;
    end OUTER;
```

```
4   type PRIMARY_ARRAY is array (INTEGER range <>) of PRIMARY;
    function MAKE_COLOUR(P: PRIMARY_ARRAY) return COLOUR is
        C: COLOUR:=(F, F, F);
    begin
        for I in P'RANGE loop
            C(P(I)):=T;
        end loop;
        return C;
    end MAKE_COLOUR;
```

Note that multiple values are allowed so that

```
MAKE_COLOUR((R, R, R)) = RED.
```

```
5   function VALUE(R: ROMAN_NUMBER) return INTEGER is
        V: INTEGER:=0;
    begin
        for I in R'RANGE loop
            if I /= R'LAST and then
                ROMAN_TO_INTEGER(R(I)) < ROMAN_TO_INTEGER(R(I+1)) then
                V:=V-ROMAN_TO_INTEGER(R(I));
            else
                V:=V+ROMAN_TO_INTEGER(R(I));
            end if;
        end loop;
        return V;
    end VALUE;
```

```
6   function MAKE_UNIT(N: NATURAL) return MATRIX is
        M: MATRIX(1 .. N, 1 .. N);
    begin
        for I in 1 .. N loop
            for J in 1 .. N loop
                if I = J then
                    M(I, J):=1.0;
                else
                    M(I, J):=0.0;
                end if;
            end loop;
        end loop;
        return M;
    end MAKE_UNIT;
```

We can then declare

```
UNIT: constant MATRIX:= MAKE_UNIT(N);
```

```
7   function GCD(X, Y: NATURAL) return NATURAL is
    begin
        if Y = 0 then
            return X;
        else
            return GCD(Y, X mod Y);
        end if;
    end GCD;
```

or

```
function GCD(X, Y: NATURAL) return NATURAL is
    XX: INTEGER:=X;
    YY: INTEGER:=Y;
    ZZ: INTEGER;
begin
    while YY /= 0 loop
        ZZ:=XX mod YY;
        XX:=YY;
        YY:=ZZ;
    end loop;
    return XX;
end GCD;
```

Note that X and Y have to be copied because formal parameters behave as constants.

Exercise 7.2

1
```
function "<" (X, Y: ROMAN_NUMBER) return BOOLEAN is
begin
    return VALUE(X) < VALUE(Y);
end "<";
```

2
```
function "+"(X, Y: COMPLEX) return COMPLEX is
begin
    return (X.RL+Y.RL, X.IM+Y.IM);
end "+";
```

```
function "*"(X, Y: COMPLEX) return COMPLEX is
begin
    return (X.RL*Y.RL−X.IM*Y.IM, X.RL*Y.IM+X.IM*Y.RL);
end "*";
```

3
```
function "<"(P: PRIMARY; C: COLOUR) return BOOLEAN is
begin
    return C(P);
end "<";
```

4
```
function "<="(X, Y: COLOUR) return BOOLEAN is
begin
    return (X and Y) = X;
end "<=";
```

Exercise 7.3

1
```
procedure SWAP(X, Y: in out REAL) is
    T: REAL;
begin
    T:=X; X:=Y; Y:=T;
end SWAP;
```

2
```
procedure REV(X: in out VECTOR) is
    R: VECTOR(X'RANGE);
begin
    for I in X'RANGE loop
        R(I):=X(X'FIRST+X'LAST−I);
    end loop;
    X:=R;
end REV;
```

or maybe

```
procedure REV(X: in out VECTOR) is
begin
    for I in X'FIRST .. X'FIRST+X'LENGTH/2−1 loop
        SWAP(X(I), X(X'FIRST+X'LAST−I));
    end loop;
end REV;
```

This procedure can be applied to an array R of type ROW by

```
REV(VECTOR(R));
```

3 The fragment is erroneous because the outcome depends upon whether the parameter is passed by copy or by reference. If it is copied then A(1) ends up as 2.0; if it is passed by reference then A(1) ends up as 4.0.

Exercise 7.4
1
```
function ADD(X: INTEGER; Y: INTEGER:=1) return INTEGER is
begin
     return X+Y;
end ADD;
```

The following 6 calls are equivalent

```
ADD(N)
ADD(N, 1)
ADD(X => N, Y => 1)
ADD(X => N)
ADD(N, Y => 1)
ADD(Y => 1, X => N)
```

2
```
function FAVOURITE_SPIRIT return SPIRIT is
begin
     case TODAY is
          when MON .. FRI => return GIN;
          when SAT|SUN => return VODKA;
     end case;
end;
```

```
procedure DRY_MARTINI( BASE: SPIRIT:=FAVOURITE_SPIRIT;
                       HOW: STYLE:=ON_THE_ROCKS;
                       PLUS: TRIMMING:=OLIVE);
```

This example illustrates that defaults are evaluated each time they are required and can therefore be changed from time to time.

Exercise 7.5
1 The named form of call

```
SELL(C => JERSEY);
```

is unambiguous since the formal parameter names are different.

Answers 8

Exercise 8.1
1
```
package RANDOM is
     MODULUS: constant:=2**13;
     subtype SMALL is INTEGER range 0 .. MODULUS;
     procedure INIT(SEED: SMALL);
     function NEXT return SMALL;
end;
```

```
package body RANDOM is
     MULTIPLIER: constant:=5**5;
     X: SMALL;

     procedure INIT(SEED: SMALL) is
     begin
          X:=SEED;
     end INIT;
```

```
    function NEXT return SMALL is
    begin
        X:=X*MULTIPLIER mod MODULUS;
        return X;
    end NEXT;

end RANDOM;
```

2   **package** COMPLEX_NUMBERS **is**

```
        type COMPLEX is
            record
                RL, IM: REAL:=0.0;
            end record;

        I: constant COMPLEX:= (0.0, 1.0);

        function "+"(X, Y: COMPLEX) return COMPLEX;
        function "-"(X, Y: COMPLEX) return COMPLEX;
        function "*"(X, Y: COMPLEX) return COMPLEX;
        function "/"(X, Y: COMPLEX) return COMPLEX;
end;

package body COMPLEX_NUMBERS is

        function "+"(X, Y: COMPLEX) return COMPLEX is
        begin
            return (X.RL+Y.RL, X.IM+Y.IM);
        end "+";

        function "-"(X, Y: COMPLEX) return COMPLEX is
        begin
            return (X.RL-Y.RL, X.IM-Y.IM);
        end "-";

        function "*"(X, Y: COMPLEX) return COMPLEX is
        begin
            return (X.RL*Y.RL-X.IM*Y.IM, X.RL*Y.IM+X.IM*Y.RL);
        end "*";

        function "/"(X, Y: COMPLEX) return COMPLEX is
            D: REAL:=Y.RL**2+Y.IM**2;
        begin
            return ((X.RL*Y.RL+X.IM*Y.IM)/D, (X.IM*Y.RL-X.RL*Y.IM) /D);

        end "/";
end COMPLEX_NUMBERS;
```

Exercise 8.2

1

There are 18 different possible orders of compilation.

Exercise 8.3

1

There are 8 different possible orders of compilation.

Answers 9

Exercise 9.1

1 Inside the package body we could write

```
function "*"(X: REAL; Y: COMPLEX) return COMPLEX is
begin
    return (X*Y.RL, X*Y.IM);
end "*";
```

but outside we could only write

```
function "*"(X: REAL; Y: COMPLEX) return COMPLEX is
    use COMPLEX_NUMBERS;
begin
    return CONS(X, 0.0)*Y;
end "*";
```

and similarly with the operands interchanged

2
```
package RATIONAL_NUMBERS is
    type RATIONAL is private;

    function "+"(X: RATIONAL) return RATIONAL;   -- unary +
    function "-"(X: RATIONAL) return RATIONAL;   -- unary -

    function "+"(X, Y: RATIONAL) return RATIONAL;
    function "-"(X, Y: RATIONAL) return RATIONAL;
    function "*"(X, Y: RATIONAL) return RATIONAL;
    function "/"(X, Y: RATIONAL) return RATIONAL;

    function "/"(X: INTEGER; Y: POSITIVE) return RATIONAL;
    function NUMERATOR(R: RATIONAL) return INTEGER;
    function DENOMINATOR(R: RATIONAL) return POSITIVE;

private
    type RATIONAL is
        record
            NUM: INTEGER;   --numerator
            DEN: POSITIVE;   --denominator
        end record;
end;

package body RATIONAL_NUMBERS is

    function NORMAL(R: RATIONAL) return RATIONAL is
        --cancel common factors

        G: POSITIVE:=GCD(abs R.NUM, R.DEN);
    begin
        return (R.NUM/G, R.DEN/G);
    end NORMAL;

    function "+"(X: RATIONAL) return RATIONAL is
    begin
        return X;
    end "+";

    function "-"(X: RATIONAL) return RATIONAL is
    begin
        return (-X.NUM, X.DEN);
    end "-";

    function "+"(X, Y: RATIONAL) return RATIONAL is
    begin
```

```
        return NORMAL((X.NUM*Y.DEN+Y.NUM*X.DEN, X.DEN*Y.DEN));
    end "+",

    function "-"(X, Y: RATIONAL) return RATIONAL is
    begin
        return NORMAL((X.NUM*Y.DEN-Y.NUM*X.DEN, X.DEN*Y.DEN));
    end "-";

    function "*"(X, Y: RATIONAL) return RATIONAL is
    begin
        return NORMAL((X.NUM*Y.NUM, X.DEN*Y.DEN));
    end "*";

    function "/"(X, Y: RATIONAL) return RATIONAL is
    begin
        return NORMAL((X.NUM*Y.DEN, X.DEN*Y.NUM));
    end "/";

    function "/"(X: INTEGER; Y: POSITIVE) return RATIONAL is
    begin
        return NORMAL((X,Y));
    end "/";

    function NUMERATOR(R: RATIONAL) return INTEGER is
    begin
        return R.NUM;
    end NUMERATOR;

    function DENOMINATOR(R: RATIONAL) return POSITIVE is
    begin
        return R.DEN;
    end DENOMINATOR;

end RATIONAL_NUMBERS;
```

3   Although the parameter base types are both INTEGER and therefore the same as for predefined integer division, nevertheless the result types are different. The result types are considered in the hiding rules for functions. See Section 7.5.

Exercise 9.2

1
```
    package STACKS is
        type STACK is limited private;
        EMPTY: constant STACK;
        . . .
    private
        . . .
        EMPTY: constant STACK:=((1 .. MAX => 0), 0);
    end;
```

Note that EMPTY has to be initialised because it is a **constant** despite the fact that TOP which is the only component whose value is of interest is automatically initialised anyway.

2
```
    function EMPTY(S: STACK) return BOOLEAN is
    begin
        return S.TOP = 0;
    end EMPTY;

    function FULL(S: STACK) return BOOLEAN is
    begin
        return S.TOP = MAX;
    end FULL;
```

```
3    function "="(A, B: STACK_ARRAY) return BOOLEAN is
     begin
         if A'LENGTH /= B'LENGTH then
             return FALSE;
         end if;
         for I in A'RANGE loop
             if A(I) /= B(I+B'FIRST−A'FIRST) then
                 return FALSE;
             end if;
         end loop;
         return TRUE;
     end "=";
```

Note that this uses the redefined $=$ (via $/=$) applying to the type STACK. This pattern of definition of array equality clearly applies to any type.

```
4    procedure ASSIGN(S: in STACK; T: out STACK) is
     begin
         T.TOP:=S.TOP;
         for I in 1 .. S.TOP loop
             T.S(I):= S.S(I);
         end loop;
     end;
```

```
5    package STACKS is
         type STACK is private;
         procedure PUSH(S: in out STACK; X: in INTEGER);
         procedure POP(S: in out STACK; X: out INTEGER);
     private
         MAX: constant:=100;
         DUMMY: constant:=0;
         type INTEGER_VECTOR is array (INTEGER range <>) of INTEGER;
         type STACK is
             record
                 S: INTEGER_VECTOR (1 .. MAX):=(1 .. MAX => DUMMY);
                 TOP: INTEGER range 0 .. MAX:=0;
             end record;
     end;

     package body STACKS is
         procedure PUSH(S: in out STACK; X: in INTEGER) is
         begin
             S.TOP:=S.TOP+1;
             S.S(S.TOP):=X;
         end;

         procedure POP(S: in out STACK; X: out INTEGER) is
         begin
             X:=S.S(S.TOP);
             S.S(S.TOP):=DUMMY;
             S.TOP:=S.TOP−1;
         end;
     end STACKS;
```

Note the use of DUMMY as default value for unused components of the stack.

Exercise 9.3
```
1    private
         MAX: constant:=1000;      − − no of accounts
         subtype KEY_CODE is INTEGER range 0 .. MAX;
```

```
        type KEY is
            record
                CODE: KEY_CODE:=0;
            end record;
end;

package body BANK is
    BALANCE: array (KEY_CODE range 1 .. KEY_CODE'LAST) of MONEY
        :=(others => 0);
    FREE: array (KEY_CODE range 1 .. KEY_CODE'LAST) of BOOLEAN
        :=(others => TRUE);

    function VALID(K: KEY) return BOOLEAN is
    begin
        return K.CODE /= 0;
    end VALID;

    procedure OPEN_ACCOUNT(K: in out KEY; M: in MONEY) is
    begin
        if K.CODE = 0 then
            for I in FREE'RANGE loop
                if FREE(I) then
                    FREE(I):=FALSE;
                    BALANCE(I):=M;
                    K.CODE:=I;
                    return;
                end if;
            end loop;
        end if;
    end OPEN_ACCOUNT;

    procedure CLOSE_ACCOUNT(K: in out KEY; M: out MONEY) is
    begin
        if VALID(K) then
            M:=BALANCE(K.CODE);
            FREE(K.CODE):=TRUE;
            K.CODE:=0;
        end if;
    end CLOSE_ACCOUNT;

    procedure DEPOSIT(K: in KEY; M: in MONEY) is
    begin
        if VALID(K) then
            BALANCE(K.CODE):=BALANCE(K.CODE)+M;
        end if;
    end DEPOSIT;

    procedure WITHDRAW(K: in out KEY; M: in out MONEY) is
    begin
        if VALID(K) then
            if M > BALANCE(K.CODE) then
                CLOSE_ACCOUNT(K, M);
            else
                BALANCE(K.CODE):=BALANCE(K.CODE)-M;
            end if;
        end if;
    end WITHDRAW;

    function STATEMENT(K:KEY) return MONEY is
    begin
        if VALID(K) then
            return BALANCE(K.CODE);
```

```
        end if;
    end STATEMENT;
```

```
end BANK;
```

Various alternative formulations are possible. It might be neater to declare a record type representing an account containing the two components FREE and BALANCE.

Note that the function STATEMENT will raise PROGRAM_ERROR if the key is not valid. Alternatively we could return a dummy value of zero but it might be better to raise our own exception as described in the next chapter.

2   An alternative formulation which represents the home savings box could be that where the limited private type is given by

```
type BOX is
    record
        CODE: BOX_CODE:=0;
        BALANCE: MONEY;
    end record;
```

In this case the money is kept in the variable declared by the user. The bank only knows which boxes have been issued but does not know how much is in a particular box. The details are left to the reader.

3   Since the parameter is of a private type, it is not defined whether the parameter is passed by copy or by reference. If it is passed by copy then the call of ACTION will succeed whereas if it is passed by reference it will not. The program is therefore erroneous. However this does not seem a very satisfactory answer and might be considered a loophole in the design of Ada.

A slight improvement would be for ACTION to check (via VALID say) whether the passed key is free or not by reference to the array FREE but this would not be any protection once the key were reissued. However, a foolproof solution can be devised using access types which will be described in Chapter 11.

4   He is thwarted because of the rule mentioned in the previous section that, outside the defining package, a procedure cannot be declared having an out parameter of a limited type. The purpose of this rule is precisely to prevent just this kind of violation of privacy. (As a minor aside note that in any case the parameter may be passed by reference.)

Answers 10

Exercise 10.1

1
```
procedure QUADRATIC(A, B, C: in REAL;
                            ROOT_1, ROOT_2: out REAL; OK: out BOOLEAN) is
    D: constant REAL:=B**2−4.0*A*C;
begin
    ROOT_1:=(−B+SQRT(D))/(2.0*A);
    ROOT_2:=(−B−SQRT(D))/(2.0*A);
    OK:=TRUE;
exception
    when NUMERIC_ERROR =>
        OK:=FALSE;
end QUADRATIC;
```

2
```
function FACTORIAL(N: INTEGER) return INTEGER is
    function SLAVE(N: NATURAL) return POSITIVE is
    begin
        if N = 0 then
            return 1;
        else
            return N*SLAVE(N−1);
        end if;
    end SLAVE;
```

```
    begin
        return SLAVE(N);
    exception
        when CONSTRAINT_ERROR | STORAGE_ERROR | NUMERIC_ERROR =>
            return −1;

    end FACTORIAL;
```

Exercise 10.2

```
1   package RANDOM is
        BAD: exception;
        MODULUS: constant:=2**13;
        subtype SMALL is INTEGER range 0 .. MODULUS;
        procedure INIT(SEED: SMALL);
        function NEXT return SMALL;
    end;

    package body RANDOM is
        MULTIPLIER: constant:=5**5;
        X: SMALL;

        procedure INIT(SEED: SMALL) is
        begin
            if SEED mod 2 = 0 then
                raise BAD;
            end if;
            X:=SEED;
        end INIT;

        function NEXT return SMALL is
        begin
            X:=X*MULTIPLIER mod MODULUS;
            return X;
        end NEXT;

    end RANDOM;

2   function FACTORIAL(N: INTEGER) return INTEGER is

        function SLAVE(N: NATURAL) return POSITIVE is
        begin
            if N = 0 then
                return 1;
            else
                return N*SLAVE(N−1);
            end if;
        end SLAVE;

    begin
        return SLAVE(N);
    exception
        when CONSTRAINT_ERROR | STORAGE_ERROR =>
            raise NUMERIC_ERROR;
    end FACTORIAL;
```

Exercise 10.3

```
1   package BANK is
        ALARM: exception;
        subtype MONEY is NATURAL;
        type KEY is limited private;
        -- as before
    private
```

```ada
        -- as before
end;

package body BANK is
    BALANCE: array (KEY_CODE range 1 .. KEY_CODE'LAST) of MONEY
        :=(others => 0);
    FREE: array (KEY_CODE range 1 .. KEY_CODE'LAST) of BOOLEAN
        :=(others => TRUE);

    function VALID(K: KEY) return BOOLEAN is
    begin
        return K.CODE /= 0;
    end VALID;

    procedure VALIDATE(K: KEY) is
    begin
        if not VALID(K) then
            raise ALARM;
        end if;
    end VALIDATE;

    procedure OPEN_ACCOUNT(K: in out KEY; M: in MONEY) is
    begin
        if K.CODE = 0 then
            for I in FREE'RANGE loop
                if FREE(I) then
                    FREE(I):=FALSE;
                    BALANCE(I):=M;
                    K.CODE:=I;
                    return;
                end if;
            end loop;
        else
            raise ALARM;
        end if;
    end OPEN_ACCOUNT;

    procedure CLOSE_ACCOUNT(K: in out KEY; M: out MONEY) is
    begin
        VALIDATE(K);
        M:=BALANCE(K.CODE);
        FREE(K.CODE):=TRUE;
        K.CODE:=0;
    end CLOSE_ACCOUNT;

    procedure DEPOSIT(K: in KEY; M: in MONEY) is
    begin
        VALIDATE(K);
        BALANCE(K.CODE):=BALANCE(K.CODE)+M;
    end DEPOSIT;

    procedure WITHDRAW(K: in out KEY; M: in out MONEY) is
    begin
        VALIDATE(K);
        if M > BALANCE(K.CODE) then
            raise ALARM;
        else
            BALANCE(K.CODE):=BALANCE(K.CODE)-M;
        end if;
    end WITHDRAW;

    function STATEMENT(K: KEY) return MONEY is
```

```
    begin
        VALIDATE(K);
        return BALANCE(K.CODE);
    end STATEMENT;
end BANK;
```

For convenience we have declared a procedure **VALIDATE** which raises the alarm in most cases. The **ALARM** is also explicitly raised if we attempt to overdraw but as remarked in the text we cannot also close the account. An attempt to open an account with a key which is in use also causes **ALARM** to be raised. We do not however raise the **ALARM** if the bank runs out of accounts but have left it to the user to check with a call of **VALID** that he was issued a genuine key; the rationale is that it is not the user's fault if the bank runs out of keys.

2   Suppose N is 2. Then on the third call, P is not entered but the exception is raised and handled at the second level. The handler again calls P without success but this time, since an exception raised in a handler is not handled there but propagated up a level, the exception is handled at the first level. The pattern then repeats but the exception is finally propagated out of the first level to the originating call. In all there are 3 successful calls and 4 unsuccessful ones. The following diagram may help.

An * indicates an unsuccessful call, H indicates a call from a handler.

More generally suppose C_n is the total number of calls for the case N = n. Then by induction

$$C_{n+1} = 2\,C_n + 1$$

with the initial condition $C_0 = 1$ since in the case N = 0 it is obvious that there is only one call which fails. It follows that the total number of calls C_N is $2^{N+1} - 1$. Of these 2^N are unsuccessful and $2^N - 1$ are successful.

I am grateful to Bob Bishop of British Telecom for this example.

Answers 11

Exercise 11.1

1   TRACE((M'LENGTH, M))

If the two dimensions of **M** were not equal then **CONSTRAINT_ERROR** would be raised. Note that the lower bounds of **M** do not have to be 1; all that matters is that the number of components in each dimension is the same.

2
```
package STACKS is
    type STACK(MAX: NATURAL) is limited private;
    EMPTY: constant STACK;
    . . .
private
    type INTEGER_VECTOR is array (INTEGER range <>) of INTEGER;
    type STACK(MAX: NATURAL) is
        record
            S: INTEGER_VECTOR (1 .. MAX);
            TOP: INTEGER:=0;
        end record;
    EMPTY: constant STACK(0):=(0, (others => 0), 0);
end;
```

We have naturally chosen to make EMPTY a stack whose value of MAX is zero. Note that the function "=" only compares the parts of the stacks which are in use. Thus we can write S = EMPTY to test whether a stack S is empty irrespective of its value of MAX.

3 **function** FULL(S: STACK) **return** BOOLEAN **is**
```
begin
    return S.TOP = S.MAX;
end FULL;
```

4 Z: POLYNOMIAL:=(0, (0 => 0));

The named notation has to be used because the array has only one component.

5 **function** "*"(P, Q: POLYNOMIAL) **return** POLYNOMIAL **is**
```
    R: POLYNOMIAL(P.N+Q.N):=(P.N+Q.N, (others => 0));
begin
    for I in P.A'RANGE loop
        for J in Q.A'RANGE loop
            R.A(I+J):=R.A(I+J)+P.A(I)*Q.A(J);
        end loop;
    end loop;
    return R;
end "*";
```

It is largely a matter of taste whether we write P.A'RANGE rather than 0 .. P.N.

6 **function** "−"(P, Q: POLYNOMIAL) **return** POLYNOMIAL **is**
```
    SIZE: INTEGER;
begin
    if P.N > Q.N then
        SIZE:=P.N;
    else
        SIZE:=Q.N;
    end if;

    declare
        R: POLYNOMIAL(SIZE);
    begin
        for I in 0 .. P.N loop
            R.A(I):=P.A(I);
        end loop;
        for I in P.N+1 .. R.N loop
            R.A(I):=0;
        end loop;
        for I in 0 .. Q.N loop
            R.A(I):=R.A(I)−Q.A(I);
        end loop;
        return NORMAL(R);
    end;
end "−";
```

There are various alternative ways of writing this function. We could initialise R.A by using slice assignments

```
R.A(0 .. P.N):=P.A;
R.A(P.N+1 .. R.N):=(P.N+1 .. R.N => 0);
```

or even more succinctly by

```
R.A:=P.A & (P.N+1 .. R.N => 0);
```

```
7    procedure TRUNCATE(P: in out POLYNOMIAL) is
     begin
         if P'CONSTRAINED then
             raise TRUNCATE_ERROR;
         else
             P:=(P.N−1, P.A(0 .. P.N−1));
         end if;
     end TRUNCATE;
```

Exercise 11.2
```
1    procedure SHAVE(P: in out PERSON) is
     begin
         if P.SEX=FEMALE then
             raise SHAVING_ERROR;
         else
             P.BEARDED:=FALSE;
         end if;
     end SHAVE;
```

```
2    procedure STERILISE(M: in out MUTANT) is
     begin
         if M'CONSTRAINED and M.SEX /= NEUTER then
             raise STERILISE_ERROR;
         else
             M:=(NEUTER, M.BIRTH);
         end if;
     end STERILISE;
```

```
3    type FIGURE is (CIRCLE, SQUARE, RECTANGLE);
     type OBJECT(SHAPE: FIGURE) is
         record
             case SHAPE is
                 when CIRCLE =>
                     RADIUS: REAL;
                 when SQUARE =>
                     SIDE: REAL;
                 when RECTANGLE =>
                     LENGTH, BREADTH: REAL;
             end case;
         end record;
```

```
4    function AREA(X: OBJECT) return REAL is
     begin
         case X.SHAPE is
             when CIRCLE =>
                 return PI*X.RADIUS**2;
             when SQUARE =>
                 return X.SIDE**2;
             when RECTANGLE =>
                 return X.LENGTH*X.BREADTH;
         end case;
     end AREA;
```

Note the similarity between the case statement in the function AREA and the variant part of the type OBJECT.

```
5    function F(N: INTEGER) return INTEGER_VECTOR;
     type POLYNOMIAL(N: INDEX:=0) is
         record
             A: INTEGER_VECTOR(0 .. N):=F(N);
         end record;
```

```
function F(N: INTEGER) return INTEGER_VECTOR is
    R: INTEGER_VECTOR(0 . .N);
begin
    for I in 0 . . N−1 loop
        R(I):=0;
    end loop;
    R(N):=1;
    return R;
end;
```

In order to declare both the function and the type in the same declarative part we have to give the
function specification on its own first. This is because a type declaration may not follow a body as
explained in Section 7.6. It does not matter that F is referred to before its body is elaborated
provided that it is not actually called. Thus if we declared a polynomial (without an initial value)
before the body of F then PROGRAM_ERROR would be raised.

Exercise 11.3

1   procedure APPEND(FIRST: in out LINK; SECOND: in LINK) is
```
        L: LINK:=FIRST;
begin
    if FIRST = null then
        FIRST:=SECOND;
    else
        while L.NEXT /= null loop
            L:=L.NEXT;
        end loop;
        L.NEXT:= SECOND;
    end if;
end APPEND;
```

2   function SIZE(T: TREE) return INTEGER is
```
begin
    if T = null then
        return 0;
    else
        return SIZE(T.LEFT)+SIZE(T.RIGHT)+1;
    end if;
end SIZE;
```

3   function COPY(T: TREE) return TREE is
```
begin
    if T = null then
        return null;
    else
        return new NODE'(T.VALUE, COPY (T.LEFT), COPY(T.RIGHT));
    end if;
end COPY;
```

Exercise 11.4

1   procedure PUSH(S: in out STACK; X: in INTEGER) is
```
begin
    S:=new CELL'(X, S);

exception
    when STORAGE_ERROR =>
        raise ERROR;
end;
procedure POP(S: in out STACK; X: out INTEGER) is
```

```
begin
    if S = null then
        raise ERROR;
    else
        X:=S.VALUE;
        S:=S.NEXT;
    end if;
end;
```

2   ```
    procedure PUSH(S: in out STACK; X: in INTEGER) is
    begin
        S.LIST:=new CELL'(X, S.LIST);
    end;

    procedure POP(S: in out STACK; X: out INTEGER) is
    begin
        X:=S.LIST.VALUE;
        S.LIST:=S.LIST.NEXT;
    end;

    function "="(S, T: STACK) return BOOLEAN is
        SL: LINK:=S.LIST;
        TL: LINK:=T.LIST;
    begin
        while SL /= null and TL /= null loop
            SL:=SL.NEXT;
            TL:=TL.NEXT;
            if SL.VALUE /= TL.VALUE then
                return FALSE;
            end if;
        end loop;
        return SL = TL;
    end "=";
    ```

3   ```
    package QUEUES is
        EMPTY: exception;
        type QUEUE is limited private;
        procedure JOIN(Q: in out QUEUE; X: in ITEM);
        procedure REMOVE(Q: in out QUEUE; X: out ITEM);
        function LENGTH(Q: QUEUE) return INTEGER;
    private
        type CELL;
        type LINK is access CELL;
        type CELL is
            record
                DATA: ITEM;
                NEXT: LINK;
            end record;
        type QUEUE is
            record
                COUNT: INTEGER:=0;
                FIRST, LAST: LINK;
            end record;
    end;

    package body QUEUES is

        procedure JOIN(Q: in out QUEUE; X: in ITEM) is
            L: LINK;
        begin
            L:=new CELL'(DATA => X, NEXT => null);
            Q.LAST.NEXT:=L;
    ```

```
            Q.LAST:=L;
            Q.COUNT:=Q.COUNT+1;
        end JOIN;

        procedure REMOVE(Q: in out QUEUE; X: out ITEM) is
        begin
            if Q.COUNT = 0 then
                raise EMPTY;
            end if;
            X:=Q.FIRST.DATA;
            Q.FIRST:=Q.FIRST.NEXT;
            Q.COUNT:=Q.COUNT-1;
        end REMOVE;

        function LENGTH(Q: QUEUE) return INTEGER is
        begin
            return Q.COUNT;
        end LENGTH;

    end QUEUES;
```

Exercise 11.5

1
```
    function HEIR(P: PERSON_NAME) return PERSON_NAME is
        MOTHER: WOMANS_NAME;
    begin
        if P.SEX = MALE then
            MOTHER:=P.WIFE;
        else
            MOTHER:=P;
        end if;
        if MOTHER = null or else MOTHER.FIRST_CHILD = null then
            return null;
        end if;
        declare
            CHILD: PERSON_NAME:=MOTHER.FIRST_CHILD;
        begin
            while CHILD.SEX = FEMALE loop
                if CHILD.NEXT_SIBLING = null then
                    return MOTHER.FIRST_CHILD;
                end if;
                CHILD:=CHILD.NEXT_SIBLING;
            end loop;
            return CHILD;
        end;
    end HEIR;
```

2
```
    procedure DIVORCE(W: WOMANS_NAME) is
    begin
        if W = null or else (W.HUSBAND = null or W.FIRST_CHILD /= null then
            return;        -- divorce not possible
        end if;
        W.HUSBAND.WIFE:=null;
        W.HUSBAND:=null;
    end DIVORCE;
```

Exercise 11.6

1
```
    package P is
        type LENGTH is new REAL;
        type AREA is new REAL;
        function "*"(X, Y: LENGTH) return LENGTH;
```

```
    function "*"(X, Y: LENGTH) return AREA;
    function "*"(X, Y: AREA) return AREA;
end;

package body P is
    function "*"(X, Y: LENGTH) return LENGTH is
    begin
        raise NUMERIC_ERROR;
    end;

    function "*"(X, Y: LENGTH) return AREA is
    begin
        return AREA(REAL(X)*REAL(Y));
    end;

    function "*"(X, Y: AREA) return AREA is
    begin
        raise NUMERIC_ERROR;
    end;

end P;
```

Answers 12

Exercise 12.1

1   P: on A: INTEGER, on B: SHORT_INTEGER
    Q: on A: LONG_INTEGER, on B: INTEGER
    R: on A: cannot be implemented, on B: LONG_INTEGER

2   No, the only critical case is type Q on machine A. Changing to ones complement changes the range of INTEGER to

$$-32767 .. +32767$$

and so only INTEGER'FIRST is altered.

3   a) INTEGER
    b) illegal – type conversion must be explicit
    c) MY_INTEGER'BASE
    d) INTEGER
    e) universal integer
    f) MY_INTEGER'BASE

4   **type** LONGEST_INTEGER **is range** SYSTEM.MIN_INT .. SYSTEM.MAX_INT;

Exercise 12.2

1   a) illegal
    b) INTEGER
    c) universal real
    d) INTEGER
    e) universal real
    f) universal integer

2   R: **constant:=N*1.0;**

Exercise 12.3

1 $\frac{1}{16}$

2 REAL has B=18.
The values of the variables P and Q are model numbers. However the result $P/Q = \frac{2}{3}$ is not. The nearest model numbers can be determined by considering $\frac{2}{3}$ as a binary recurring fraction

$$0.10101010. . .$$

The model number below (L say) is obtained by truncating after 18 digits. The difference between $\frac{2}{3}$ and L is clearly $\frac{2}{3}$ shifted down by 18 places. So L is $\frac{2}{3}(1-2^{-18})$. The model number above is obtained by adding 2^{-18} to L. Hence P/Q lies in the model interval

$$\frac{2}{3}(1- 2^{-18}), \frac{2}{3} (1+2^{-19})$$

The mathematical bounds for (P/Q)*Q are obtained by multiplying the bounds of this interval by 3. The lower bound is then $2(1-2^{-18})$ and this is a model number. The upper bound is $2(1+2^{-19})$ but this is not a model number; the next model number above is $2(1+2^{-17})$. So the final model interval in which R must lie is

$$2(1-2^{-18}), 2(1+2^{-17})$$

3 In this case P and Q are numbers of type universal real and the computation is performed exactly at compilation. The result is that R is assigned the model number 2.0.

4 $1313 = 16$ (= possible mantissae)
  $\times$ 41 (= possible exponents)
  $\times$ 2 (= possible signs)
  $+$ 1 (= zero)

5
```ada
function HYPOTENUSE(X, Y: REAL) return REAL is
    TINY: constant REAL:=2.0**(-2*REAL'MANTISSA);
begin
    if abs X < TINY and abs Y < TINY then
        return SQRT((X/TINY)**2+(Y/TINY)**2)*TINY;
    else
        return SQRT(X**2+Y**2);
    end if;
end HYPOTENUSE;
```

Note that 2.0**(−2*REAL'MANTISSA) is an expression of type universal real.

6 In the case of type ROUGH we have requested one decimal digit which implies a maximum relative precision of 1 in 10. If we took $B = 4$ then the relative precision would vary from 1 in 8 to 1 in 16. There would therefore be occassional places where the binary numbers are slightly further apart than the decimal ones. In fact, around 10000 the decimal model numbers for $D = 1$ are

8000,   9000,   10000,   20000

whereas the binary model numbers for $B = 4$ are

7680,   8192,   9216,   10240

and we see that 8192 and 9216 are more than 1000 apart. Hence we have to take $B = 5$ so that the minimum relative precision is 1 in 16. The general result follows.

7 The ratio is 2^{B-1} or 1/EPSILON. Thus the hole around zero is relatively more dangerous for higher values of B.

Exercise 12.4

1 $\frac{1}{10}(1 - 2^{-12})$, $\frac{1}{10}(1 + 2^{-14})$

Answers 13

Exercise 13.1
1   **generic**
      type ITEM **is private**;
   package STACKS **is**
      type STACK(MAX: NATURAL) **is limited private**;
      procedure PUSH(S: **in out** STACK; X: **in** ITEM);
      procedure POP(S: **in out** STACK; X: **out** ITEM);
      function "="(S, T: STACK) **return** BOOLEAN;
   private
      type ITEM_ARRAY **is array** (INTEGER **range** <>) **of** ITEM;
      type STACK(MAX: NATURAL) **is**
         record
            S: ITEM_ARRAY(1 .. MAX);
            TOP: INTEGER:=0;
         end record;
   end;

The body is much as before. To declare a stack we must first instantiate the package.

   package BOOLEAN_STACKS **is new package** STACKS (ITEM => BOOLEAN);
   use BOOLEAN_STACKS;
   S: STACK(MAX => 30);

2   **generic**
      type THING **is private**;
   package P **is**
      procedure SWAP(A, B: **in out** THING);
      procedure CAB(A, B, C: **in out** THING);
   end P;

   package body P **is**
      procedure SWAP (A, B: **in out** THING) **is**
         T: THING;
      begin
         T:=A; A:=B; B:=T;
      end;

      procedure CAB (A, B, C: **in out** THING) **is**
      begin
         SWAP(A, B);
         SWAP(A, C);
      end;
   end P;

Exercise 13.2
1   **function** "not" **is new** NEXT (BOOLEAN);

2   **generic**
      type BASE **is range** <>;
   package RATIONAL_NUMBERS **is**
      type RATIONAL **is private**;
      function "+"(X: RATIONAL) **return** RATIONAL;

```ada
        function "-"(X: RATIONAL) return RATIONAL;
        function "+"(X, Y: RATIONAL) return RATIONAL;
        function "-"(X, Y: RATIONAL) return RATIONAL;
        function "*"(X, Y: RATIONAL) return RATIONAL;
        function "/"(X, Y: RATIONAL) return RATIONAL;

        subtype POS_BASE is BASE range 1 .. BASE'LAST;
        function "/"(X: BASE; Y: POS_BASE) return RATIONAL;
        function NUMERATOR(R: RATIONAL) return BASE;
        function DENOMINATOR(R: RATIONAL) return POS_BASE;
    private
        type RATIONAL is
            record
                NUM: BASE;
                DEN: POS_BASE;
            end record;
    end;
```

3
```ada
    generic
        type INDEX is (<>);
        type FLOATING is digits <>;
        type VEC is array (INDEX range <>) of FLOATING;
        type MAT is array (INDEX range <>, INDEX range <>) of FLOATING;
    function OUTER(A, B: VEC) return MAT;

    function OUTER(A, B: VEC) return MAT is
        C: MAT(A'RANGE, B'RANGE);
    begin
        for I in A'RANGE loop
            for J in B'RANGE loop
                C(I, J):=A(I)*B(J);
            end loop;
        end loop;
        return C;
    end OUTER;

    function OUTER_VECTOR is new OUTER(INTEGER, REAL, VECTOR, MATRIX);
```

4
```ada
    package body SET_OF is

        function MAKE_SET(X: LIST) return SET is
            S: SET:=EMPTY;
        begin
            for I in X'RANGE loop
                S(X(I)):=TRUE;
            end loop;
            return S;
        end MAKE_SET;

        function MAKE_SET(X: BASE) return SET is
            S: SET:= EMPTY;
        begin
            S(X):= TRUE;
            return S;
        end MAKE_SET;

        function DECOMPOSE(X: SET) return LIST is
            L: LIST(1 .. SIZE(X));
            I: POSITIVE:=1;
        begin
            for E in SET'RANGE loop
                if X(E) then
```

```
            L(I):=E;
            I:=I+1;
        end if;
    end loop;
    return L;
end DECOMPOSE;

function "+"(X, Y: SET) return SET is
begin
    return X or Y;
end "+";

function "*"(X, Y: SET) return SET is
begin
    return X and Y;
end "*";

function "-"(X, Y: SET) return SET is
begin
    return X xor Y;
end "-";

function "<"(X: BASE; Y: SET) return BOOLEAN is
begin
    return Y(X);
end "<";

function "<="(X, Y: SET) return BOOLEAN is
begin
    return (X and Y) = X;
end "<=";

function SIZE(X: SET) return NATURAL is
    N: NATURAL:=0;
begin
    for E in SET'RANGE loop
        if X(E) then
            N:=N+1;
        end if;
    end loop;
    return N;
end SIZE;

end SET_OF;
```

Exercise 13.3

1   ```
     function G(X: REAL) return REAL is
     begin
         return EXP(X)+X-7.0;
     end;
     ...
     function SOLVE_G is new SOLVE(G);
     ...
     ANSWER: REAL:=SOLVE_G;
     ```

2    Assuming

     ```
     type BOOL_ARRAY is array (INTEGER range <>) of BOOLEAN;
     ```

     we have
     ```

```
function AND_ALL is new APPLY(INTEGER, BOOLEAN, BOOL_ARRAY, "and");
```

3   A further generic parameter is required to supply a value for zero.

```
generic
    type INDEX is (<>);
    type ITEM is private;
    ZERO: in ITEM;
    type VEC is array (INDEX range <>) of ITEM;
    with function "+"(X, Y: ITEM) return ITEM;
function APPLY(A: VEC) return ITEM;

function APPLY(A: VEC) return ITEM is
    RESULT: ITEM:=ZERO;
begin
    for I in A'RANGE loop
        RESULT:=RESULT+A(I);
    end loop;
    return RESULT;
end APPLY;
```

and then

```
function AND_ALL is new
                    APPLY(INTEGER, BOOLEAN, TRUE, BOOL_ARRAY,"and");
```

4
```
generic
    type ITEM is limited private;
    type VECTOR is array (INTEGER range <>) of ITEM;
    with function "="(X, Y: ITEM) return BOOLEAN is <>;
function EQUALS(A, B: VECTOR) return BOOLEAN;

function EQUALS(A, B: VECTOR) return BOOLEAN is
begin
    -- body exactly as for Exercise 9.2(3)
end EQUALS;
```

We can instantiate by

```
function "=" is new EQUALS(STACK, STACK_ARRAY,  "=");
```

or simply by

```
function "="is new EQUALS(STACK, STACK_ARRAY);
```

in which case the default parameter is used.

5   The generic specification could be

```
generic
    type ITEM is private;
    type INDEX is (<>);
    type VECTOR is array (INDEX range <>) of ITEM;
    with function "<"(X, Y: ITEM) return BOOLEAN;
procedure SORT(A: in out VECTOR);
```

The generic body corresponds closely to the procedure SORT in Section 11.3. The types NODE and TREE are declared inside SORT because they depend on the generic type ITEM. The incrementing of I cannot be done with "+" since the index type may not be an integer and so we have to use INDEX'SUCC. Care is needed not to cause CONSTRAINT_ERROR if the array embraces the full range of values of INDEX.

Answers 14

Exercise 14.1
1
```
procedure SHOPPING is

    task GET_SALAD;

    task body GET_SALAD is
    begin
        BUY_SALAD;
    end GET_SALAD;

    task GET_WINE;

    task body GET_WINE is
    begin
        BUY_WINE;
    end GET_WINE;

    task GET_MEAT;

    task body GET_MEAT is
    begin
        BUY_MEAT;
    end GET_MEAT;
begin
    null;
end SHOPPING;
```

Exercise 14.2
1
```
task body BUILD_COMPLEX is
    C: COMPLEX;
begin
    loop
        accept PUT_RL(X: REAL) do
            C.RL:=X;
        end;
        accept PUT_IM(X: REAL) do
            C.IM:=X;
        end;
        accept GET_COMP(X: out COMPLEX) do
            X:=C;
        end;
    end loop;
end BUILD_COMPLEX;
```

2
```
task body CHAR_TO_LINE is
    BUFFER: LINE;
begin
    loop
        for I in BUFFER'RANGE loop
            accept PUT(C: in CHARACTER) do
                BUFFER(I):=C;
            end;
        end loop;
        accept GET(L: out LINE) do
            L:=BUFFER;
        end;
    end loop;
end CHAR_TO_LINE;
```

Exercise 14.3

```
1   generic
        FIRST_TIME: CALENDAR.TIME;
        INTERVAL: DURATION;
        NUMBER: INTEGER;
        with procedure P;
    procedure CALL;

    procedure CALL is
        use CALENDAR;
        NEXT_TIME: TIME:=FIRST_TIME;
    begin
        if NEXT_TIME < CLOCK then
            NEXT_TIME:=CLOCK;
        end if;
        for I in 1 .. NUMBER loop
            delay NEXT_TIME−CLOCK;
            P;
            NEXT_TIME:=NEXT_TIME+INTERVAL;
        end loop;
    end CALL;
```

2   The **type** DURATION requires at least 24 bits.

Exercise 14.4

```
1   task body BUILD_COMPLEX is
        C: COMPLEX;
        GOT_RL, GOT_IM: BOOLEAN:=FALSE;
    begin
        loop
            select
                when not GOT_RL =>
                accept PUT_RL(X: REAL) do
                    C.RL:=X;
                end;
                GOT_RL:=TRUE;
            or
                when not GOT_IM =>
                accept PUT_IM(X: REAL) do
                    C.IM:=X;
                end;
                GOT_IM:=TRUE;
            or
                when GOT_RL and GOT_IM =>
                accept GET_COMP(X: out COMPLEX) do
                    X:=C;
                end;
                GOT_RL:=FALSE;
                GOT_IM:=FALSE;
            end select;
        end loop;
    end BUILD_COMPLEX;
```

An alternative solution is

```
    task body BUILD_COMPLEX is
        C: COMPLEX;
    begin
        loop
            select
```

```
            accept PUT_RL(X: REAL) do
                C.RL:=X;
            end;
            accept PUT_IM(X: REAL) do
                C.IM:=X;
            end;
        or
            accept PUT_IM(X: REAL) do
                C.IM:=X;
            end;
            accept PUT_RL(X: REAL) do
                C.RL:=X;
            end;
        end select;
        accept GET_COMP(X: out COMPLEX) do
            X:=C;
        end;
    end loop;
end BUILD_COMPLEX;
```

At first reading this might seem simpler but the technique does not extrapolate easily when a moderate number of components are involved because of the combinatorial explosion.

```
2   procedure READ(X: out ITEM; T: DURATION; OK: out BOOLEAN) is
    begin
        select
            CONTROL.START(READ);
        or
            delay T;
            OK:=FALSE;
            return;
        end select;
        X:=V;
        CONTROL.STOP_READ;
        OK:=TRUE;
    end READ;

    procedure WRITE(X: in ITEM; T: DURATION; OK: out BOOLEAN) is
        use CALENDAR;
        START_TIME: TIME:=CLOCK;
    begin
        select
            CONTROL.START(WRITE);
        or
            delay T;
            OK:=FALSE;
            return;
        end select;
        select
            CONTROL.WRITE;
        or
            delay T-(CLOCK-START_TIME);
            CONTROL.STOP_WRITE;
            OK:=FALSE;
            return;
        end select;
        V:=X;
        CONTROL.STOP_WRITE;
        OK:=TRUE;
    end WRITE;
```

Note how a shorter time out is imposed on the call of WRITE.

Exercise 14.6

```
1   task BUFFERING is
        entry PUT(X: in ITEM);
        entry FINISH;
        entry GET(X: out ITEM);
    end;

    task body BUFFERING is
        N: constant:=8;
        A: array (1 . . N) of ITEM;
        I, J: INTEGER range 1 . . N:=1;
        COUNT: INTEGER range 0 . . N:=0;
        FINISHED: BOOLEAN:=FALSE;
    begin
        loop
            select
                when COUNT < N =>
                accept PUT(X: in ITEM) do
                    A(I):=X;
                end;
                I:=I mod N+1; COUNT:=COUNT+1;
            or
                accept FINISH;
                FINISHED:=TRUE;
            or
                when COUNT > 0 =>
                accept GET(X: out ITEM) do
                    X:=A(J);
                end;
                J:=J mod N+1; COUNT:=COUNT-1;
            or
                when COUNT = 0 and FINISHED =>
                accept GET(X: out ITEM) do
                    raise DONE;
                end;
            end select;
        end loop;
    exception
        when DONE =>
            null;
    end BUFFERING;
```

This example illustrates that there may be several accept statements for the same entry in the one select statement. The exception **DONE** is propagated to the caller and also terminates the loop in BUFFERING before being quietly handled. Of course the exception need not be handled by BUFFERING because exceptions propagated out of tasks are lost, but it is cleaner to do so.

Exercise 14.7

1   The select statement becomes

```
select
    when WAITERS = 0 =>
    accept FIRST(S: SET; OK: out BOOLEAN) do
        TRY(S, OK);
        if not OK then
            WAITERS:=WAITERS+1;
        end if;
    end;
or
```

```
            accept RELEASE(S: SET) do
                FREE:=FREE+S;
            end;
            accept AGAIN(S: SET; OK: out BOOLEAN) do
                TRY(S, OK);
                if OK then
                    WAITERS:=WAITERS-1;
                end if;
            end;
        end select;

2   package CONTROLLER is
        procedure REQUEST(P: PRIORITY; D: DATA);
    end;

    package body CONTROLLER is

        task CONTROL is
            entry SIGN_IN(P: PRIORITY);
            entry REQUEST(PRIORITY) (D: DATA);
        end;

        task body CONTROL is
            TOTAL: INTEGER:=0;
            PENDING: array (PRIORITY) of INTEGER:=(PRIORITY => 0);
        begin
            loop
                if TOTAL = 0 then
                    accept SIGN_IN(P: PRIORITY) do
                        PENDING(P):=PENDING(P)+1;
                        TOTAL:=1;
                    end;
                end if;
                loop
                    select
                        accept SIGN_IN(P: PRIORITY) do
                            PENDING(P):=PENDING(P)+1;
                            TOTAL:=TOTAL+1;
                        end;
                    else
                        exit;
                    end select;
                end loop;

                for P in PRIORITY loop
                    if PENDING(P) > 0 then
                        accept REQUEST(P) (D: DATA) do
                            ACTION(D);
                        end;
                        PENDING(P):=PENDING(P)-1;
                        TOTAL:=TOTAL-1;
                        exit;
                    end if;
                end loop;
            end loop;
        end CONTROL;

        procedure REQUEST(P: PRIORITY; D: DATA) is
        begin
            CONTROL.SIGN_IN(P);
            CONTROL.REQUEST(P)(D);
```

```
    end REQUEST;
end CONTROLLER;
```

The variable TOTAL records the total number of requests outstanding and the array PENDING records the number at each priority. Each time round the outer loop, the task waits for a call of SIGN_IN if no requests are in the system, it then services any outstanding calls of SIGN_IN and finally deals with a request of the highest priority. We could dispense with the array PENDING and scan the queues as before but there is a slight risk of polling if a user has called SIGN_IN but not yet called REQUEST.

Finally note that the solution will not work if a calling task is aborted; this could be overcome by the use of agents.

Exercise 14.8

1   ```
    package COBBLERS is
        procedure MEND(A: ADDRESS; B: BOOTS);
    end;

    package body COBBLERS is
        type JOB is
            record
                REPLY: ADDRESS;
                ITEM: BOOTS;
            end record;

        package P is new BUFFERS(100, JOB);
        use P;
        BOOT_STORE: BUFFER;

        task SERVER is
            entry REQUEST(A: ADDRESS; B: BOOTS);
        end;

        task type REPAIRMAN;
        TOM, DICK, HARRY: REPAIRMAN;

        task body SERVER is
            NEXT_JOB: JOB;
        begin
            loop
                accept REQUEST(A: ADDRESS; B: BOOTS) do
                    NEXT_JOB:=(A, B);
                end;
                PUT(BOOT_STORE, NEXT_JOB);
            end loop;
        end SERVER;

        task body REPAIRMAN is
            MY_JOB: JOB;
        begin
            loop
                GET(BOOT_STORE, MY_JOB);
                REPAIR(MY_JOB.ITEM);
                MY_JOB.REPLY.DEPOSIT(MY_JOB.ITEM);
            end loop;
        end REPAIRMAN;

        procedure MEND(A: ADDRESS; B: BOOTS) is
        begin
            SERVER.REQUEST(A, B);
        end;
    end COBBLERS;
    ```
    ```

We have assumed that the type **ADDRESS** is an access to a mailbox for handling boots. Note one anomaly; the stupid server accepts boots from the customer before checking the store – if it turns out to be full, he is left holding them. In all, the shop can hold 104 pairs of boots – 100 in store, 1 with the server and 1 with each repairman.

Answers 15

Exercise 15.1

```
1   with DIRECT_IO;
    generic
        type ELEMENT is private;
    procedure REV(FROM, TO: STRING);

    procedure REV(FROM, TO: STRING) is
        package IO is new DIRECT_IO(ELEMENT);
        use IO;
        INPUT: FILE_TYPE;
        OUTPUT: FILE_TYPE;
        X: ELEMENT;

    begin
        OPEN(INPUT, IN_FILE, FROM);
        OPEN(OUTPUT, OUT_FILE, TO);
        SET_INDEX(OUTPUT, SIZE(INPUT));
        while not END_OF_FILE(INPUT) loop
            READ(INPUT, X);
            WRITE(OUTPUT, X);
            SET_INDEX(OUTPUT, INDEX(OUTPUT)−2);
        end loop;
        CLOSE(INPUT);
        CLOSE(OUTPUT);
    end REV;
```

Remember that **reverse** is a reserved word.

Exercise 15.2

1   The output is shown in string quotes in order to reveal the layout. Spaces are indicated by s. In reality of course, there are no quotes and spaces are spaces.

a)   "FRED"
b)   "sss120"
c)   "sssss120"
d)   "ss8#170#"
e)   "−3.80000E+01"
f)   "sssss7.00E−2"

Answers 16

Exercise 16.1

```
1   a) dynamic    INTEGER
    b) static     INTEGER
    c) static     universal integer
```

Exercise 16.4

1   a) The order of evaluation of the operands I and F of "+" is not defined.
       As a result the effect could be

```
            I:=1+2;            −− I first
      or    I:=2+2;            −− F first
```

b)   The order of evaluation of the destination A(I) and the value F is not defined. The effect could be

```
      A(1):=2;          -- I first
or A(2):=2;          -- F first
```

c)   The order of evaluation of the two indexes is not defined. The effect could be

```
      AA(1, 2):=0;      -- I first
or AA(2, 2):=0;      -- F first
```

INDEX